LAW, JUSTICE, AND SOCIETY
IN THE MEDIEVAL WORLD

FORDHAM SERIES IN MEDIEVAL STUDIES

Franklin T. Harkins and Brian Reilly, series editors

LAW, JUSTICE, AND SOCIETY IN THE MEDIEVAL WORLD

An Introduction through Film

Esther Liberman Cuenca, M. Christina Bruno,
and Anthony Perron, Editors

FORDHAM UNIVERSITY PRESS

New York   2025

Copyright © 2025 Fordham University Press

All rights reserved. No part of this publication may be reproduced, stored in a retrieval system, or transmitted in any form or by any means—electronic, mechanical, photocopy, recording, or any other—except for brief quotations in printed reviews, without the prior permission of the publisher.

Fordham University Press has no responsibility for the persistence or accuracy of URLs for external or third-party Internet websites referred to in this publication and does not guarantee that any content on such websites is, or will remain, accurate or appropriate.

Fordham University Press also publishes its books in a variety of electronic formats. Some content that appears in print may not be available in electronic books.

Visit us online at www.fordhampress.com.

For EU safety / GPSR concerns: Mare Nostrum Group B.V., Mauritskade 21D, 1091 GC Amsterdam, The Netherlands, gpsr@mare-nostrum.co.uk

Library of Congress Cataloging-in-Publication Data available online at https://catalog.loc.gov.

Printed in the United States of America

27 26 25   5 4 3 2 1

First edition

CONTENTS

Introduction
    ESTHER LIBERMAN CUENCA, M. CHRISTINA BRUNO,
    AND ANTHONY PERRON / 1

    CANON LAW AND THE WORLD OF THE MEDIEVAL
    CHURCH

1. Between Royal Law and Canon Law in *Becket* (1964)
    ANTHONY PERRON / 9

2. Relic Movement, Anathema, and Crusade in *Pilgrimage* (2017)
    SARAH C. LUGINBILL / 22

3. The Creation of the Franciscan Rule in *Francesco* (1989)
    NATHAN MELSON / 36

4. Poverty and Heresy in *The Name of the Rose* (1986)
    M. CHRISTINA BRUNO / 49

5. Joan of Arc's Inquisitorial Trial of Faith in *The Passion of Joan of Arc* (1928)
    HENRY ANSGAR KELLY / 61

    "FEUDAL" LAW AND THE CUSTOMS OF LORDSHIP

6. The Chivalric Code in *The Green Knight* (2021)
    CORAL LUMBLEY / 75

7. Crusading and Oath-Taking in *Kingdom of Heaven* (2005)
    ESTHER LIBERMAN CUENCA / 89

8. Forest Law in *The Adventures of Robin Hood* (1938)
    CASEY IRELAND / 101

9. Trial by Battle and Gendered Medievalisms in *The Last Duel* (2021)
    SARA MCDOUGALL AND DAVID M. PERRY / 114

10. Animal Trials in *The Advocate* (1993)
   JULIE K. CHAMBERLIN / 126

   WOMEN AND REPRESENTATIONS OF PREMODERN LAW

11. Religious Women's Authority and Rules for Nuns in *Vision: From the Life of Hildegard von Bingen* (2009)
    LUCY C. BARNHOUSE / 141

12. War, Family, and the Law of the Kyivan Rus in *Alexander Nevsky* (1938)
    ASIF A. SIDDIQI / 153

13. Church Law, Community Practice, and the Witch Trial That Wasn't in *Sorceress* (1987)
    RACHEL ELLEN CLARK AND LUCY C. BARNHOUSE / 166

14. The Myth of *Jus Primae Noctis*, or the "Right of the First Night," in *Braveheart* (1995)
    LORRAINE KOCHANSKE STOCK / 180

15. Medieval Satire and the Canon Law of Claustration in *The Little Hours* (2017)
    SPENCER STRUB / 195

    RELIGIOUS CONFLICT AND FORGING COMMUNITIES THROUGH LAW

16. Late Roman Law, Women's Status, and Classical Education in *Agora* (2009)
    CHRISTOPHER BONURA / 211

17. Depicting the Prophet, Social Justice, and the Pillars of Islam in *The Message* (1976)
    MARIA AMERICO / 225

18. Lawful Language and Global North Encounters in *The 13th Warrior* (1999)
    DANIEL ARMENTI AND NAHIR I. OTAÑO GRACIA / 237

19. Jewish Assimilation and the Absent "Saracens" and Africans
of *Ivanhoe* (1952)
CELIA CHAZELLE / *251*

20. Medieval Science, the Spanish Inquisition, and Religious Violence
in *1492: Conquest of Paradise* (1992)
EUGENE SMELYANSKY / *265*

Acknowledgments / *279*

Contributors / *281*

Index / *283*

LAW, JUSTICE, AND SOCIETY IN THE MEDIEVAL WORLD

INTRODUCTION

By Esther Liberman Cuenca, M. Christina Bruno, and Anthony Perron

Cinematic representations of the medieval period have been around almost as long as film itself. Medievalism—the modern recreation of medieval culture, often steeped in nostalgia—arguably reached the height of its popularity in the nineteenth century.[1] During this time, especially in Europe, interest in medieval history found expression in newly built Gothic cathedrals, in artwork that romanticized this bygone world, and in the publication of novels such as Sir Walter Scott's *Ivanhoe* (1820) and Victor Hugo's *The Hunchback of Notre Dame* (1831). Not coincidentally, it was in the late nineteenth and early twentieth centuries that filmmakers began to interpret medieval literature and historical events for the big screen. One of the earliest, *Jeanne d'Arc* (1900), was directed by famed silent film auteur Georges Méliès (1861–1938) and ran for eleven minutes.[2]

Since 1900, "medieval" cinema has often depicted literary works or figures most familiar to filmgoing audiences, such as King Arthur and his Roundtable Knights, Joan of Arc, Ivanhoe, and Robin Hood.[3] These films, moreover, have always been political in the history they portray and in their contemporary subtexts. They are artifacts of the time of their creation, confronting their audiences with a highly stylized and often distorted mirror of the medieval past. For that reason, film not only mediates the Middle Ages for the benefit of its contemporary audience, but is also itself a tool with which we can imagine this past in relation to our own present in vivid ways. Using film to represent medieval events helps us to think not only about the period being depicted, but also our own moment of encountering this history and, in many cases, the time in which the film was made.

For this reason, medieval scholars have devoted considerable attention to cinema. Historical film, in the words of Jonathan Stubbs, helps us "construct a relationship to the past."[4] And medieval cinema, as a subgenre of historical film, has its own visual language, tropes, and references to well-known source material (e.g., Arthurian romance, the life of Joan of

Arc). In the last half-century, medieval cinema has diversified, with films more broadly covering the lives of women, ethnic minorities, and people whose lives were popularized in neither medieval nor modern fiction.[5] As the subgenre has evolved, so too has its renderings of the medieval world.

WHY LAW, JUSTICE, AND SOCIETY?

Medieval cinema has consistently depicted the application of law and the conduct of justice. Planted within such scenes in narrative film are seeds that can be traced back to medieval sources. In popular culture, the Middle Ages has a reputation for being a chaotic and lawless age—violent, superstitious, and utterly alien from our own. But as legal scholars, we know that medieval society at all levels was cut through by different types of law, overlapping and at times competing with one another. From high international politics to the most intimate personal relationships, in both the religious and secular spheres, laws dictated the extent of an individual's agency, the structure of social hierarchies, the policing of personal reputation, a community's relationship to the divine, and the resolution of interpersonal disputes. Viewed in this light, medieval society, as a *collection of legal communities* and *as a society of law(s)*, draws much closer to our own. Because film is a visual and often visceral tool for communicating ideas about history, we can use it to make connections between our own experience and the medieval past, despite the popular misconception that the Middle Ages was an irrational, backward time.

Moreover, legal documents and narratives of justice represent a crucial body of evidence that we use to recreate the lives of everyday people in the Middle Ages. The unifying theme of this book— law, justice, and society—is construed broadly. It includes, for example, dramatizations of courtroom trials, codes of conduct, religious practices, and "feudal" relations. As instructors, each of us has favorite texts we teach in our courses to demonstrate the underlying logic of medieval society's laws and customs. These texts—with their particular concerns and perspectives, evident in an array of sources compiled for this book—can be a window into a set of relationships that dictated not only the rules of society, but the realities of daily life. Given that law and legal culture are fundamental to history, we urge you to think of law as a powerful lens through which insights about medieval society can be formed.

If medievalism is the persistence, influence, and reappropriation of the Middle Ages in a postmedieval era, then "legal medievalism" is the modern reimagining of the very structures that held these medieval societies together. To draw out the connective threads of this legal medievalism, we have grouped the chapters according to theme rather than chronology. The chapters fall into one of four clusters we think best exemplify legal medievalism in film: canon law and the world of the medieval church, including the lives of clergy, monks, and friars; "feudal" law and the customs of lordship, those that mainly involved nobles, knights, and aristocratic culture writ large; women and their representations in premodern law, particularly how gender and class hierarchies may have limited women's self-determination and self-fashioning; and, lastly, interreligious conflict that can reveal the processes by which the cultural and legal identities of certain communities were forged.

THE GOALS OF THIS BOOK

This book integrates the study of medieval legal cultures with cinematic medievalism and offers a considered approach to the afterlife of the Middle Ages on film, especially as it manifested in the often politically charged environment of the modern period. We offer a window into the way filmmakers have interpreted the "rules" of medieval society and reflect on the connections, disconnections, and divergences of medieval and modern culture.

Through an exploration of legal medievalism, it is not only possible to gain an appreciation of law, justice, and society as shown in cinema, but also of how filmmakers have created their own distinctive *vision* of the Middle Ages through their portrayals of legal culture. Each of the twenty chapters represents an original contribution to our understanding of cinematic medievalism and, in particular, its display of medieval society through the regulations, laws, and customs that are depicted governing peoples' lives.

The chapters reflect analyses of recent and older films, different geographic regions (Northern and Southern Europe, Eastern Europe, North Africa, and the Middle East), and avant-garde as well as popular (or "mainstream") cinema. The chapters in this book, to varying degrees, discuss the contemporary context of the film in question, the medieval literary or historical milieu that the film references, and the lessons the film can teach us about the Middle Ages, especially in relation to documentary sources.

Each chapter, with its sources, is followed by a set of reading questions to prompt critical reflection. The primary sources selected for inclusion in this book run the gamut from chronicle narratives to prescriptive regulations. But all highlight the types of rules, guidelines, and legal practices that may have at one time governed the lives of real medieval people. We invite readers to identify and respond to misappropriations of the Middle Ages in popular culture through the examination of medieval sources, but also encourage discussion of how these films raise questions about and enrich our reading of the sources.

FOR FURTHER READING

On Cinematic Medievalism

Aberth, John. *A Knight at the Movies: Medieval History on Film*. New York and London: Routledge, 2003.

Aronstein, Susan. *Hollywood Knights: Arthurian Cinema and the Politics of Nostalgia*. London: Palgrave Macmillan, 2005.

Bildhauer, Bettina. *Filming the Middle Ages*. London: Reaktion Books, 2011.

Bildhauer, Bettina, and Anke Bernau, eds. *Medieval Film*. Manchester: Manchester University Press, 2009.

Burt, Richard. *Medieval and Early Modern Film and Media*. New York: Palgrave Macmillan, 2008.

Coote, Lesley. "Survey of 21st Century 'Medieval' Film." In *Medieval Afterlives in Popular Culture*, edited by Gail Ashton and Dan Kline, 103–14. New York: Palgrave Macmillan, 2015.

D'Arcens, Louise, ed. *The Cambridge Companion to Medievalism*. Cambridge: Cambridge University Press, 2016.

Driver, Martha W., and Sid Ray, eds. *The Medieval Hero on Screen: Representations from Beowulf to Buffy*. Jefferson, N.C.: McFarland, 2004.

Elliott, Andrew B. R. *Remaking the Middle Ages: The Methods of Cinema and History in Portraying the Medieval World*. Jefferson, N.C: McFarland, 2011.

Finke, Laurie A., and Martin B. Shichtman. *Cinematic Illuminations: The Middle Ages on Film*. Baltimore: Johns Hopkins University Press, 2010.

Harty, Kevin J., ed. *Cinematic Arthuriana: Twenty Essays*. Rev. ed. Jefferson, N.C.: McFarland, 2002.

———, ed. *The Vikings on Film: Essays on Depictions of the Nordic Middle Ages*. Jefferson, N.C.: McFarland, 2014.

———. *The Reel Middle Ages: American, Western and Eastern European, Middle Eastern and Asian Films about Medieval Europe*. Jefferson, N.C.: McFarland, 2015.

———, ed. *The Holy Grail on Film: Essays on the Cinematic Quest*. Jefferson, N.C.: McFarland, 2015.

———, ed. *Medieval Women on Film: Essays on Gender, Cinema and History*. Jefferson, N.C.: McFarland, 2020.

Haydock, Nickolas. *Movie Medievalism: The Imaginary Middle Ages*. Jefferson, N.C.: McFarland, 2008.
Haydock, Nickolas, and E. L. Risden, eds. *Hollywood in the Holy Land: Essays on Film Depictions of the Crusades and Christian-Muslim Clashes*. Jefferson, N.C.: McFarland, 2008.
Johnston, Andrew James, Margitta Rouse, and Philipp Hinz, eds. *The Medieval Motion Picture: The Politics of Adaptation*. New York: Palgrave Macmillan, 2014.
Matthews, David. *Medievalism: A Critical History*. Cambridge: D. S. Brewer, 2015.
Pugh, Tison, and Kathleen Coyne Kelly, eds. *Queer Movie Medievalisms*. Farnham, UK, and Burlington, Vt.: Ashgate, 2009.
Ramey, Lynn, and Tison Pugh, eds. *Race, Class, and Gender in "Medieval" Cinema*. New York: Palgrave Macmillan, 2007.
Sturtevant, Paul B. *The Middle Ages in Popular Imagination: Memory, Film and Medievalism*. London and New York: I. B. Tauris, 2018.
Williams, David John. "Medieval Movies: A Filmography." *Film & History* 29, no. 1–2 (1999): 20–32.
Woods, William F. *The Medieval Filmscape: Reflections of Fear and Desire in a Cinematic Mirror*. Jefferson, N.C.: McFarland, 2014.

On Legal History

Abulafia, Anna Sapir. *Christian-Jewish Relations, 1000–1300: Jews in the Service of Medieval Christendom*. New York: Routledge, 2011.
Armstrong, Lawrin, and Julius Kirshner, eds. *The Politics of Law in Late Medieval and Renaissance Italy*. Toronto: University of Toronto Press, 2011.
Bartlett, Robert. *Trial by Fire and Water: The Medieval Judicial Ordeal*. Oxford: Clarendon Press; New York: Oxford University Press, 1986.
Brundage, James. *The Medieval Origins of the Legal Profession: Canonists, Civilians, and Courts*. Chicago: University of Chicago Press, 2008.
Cohen, Esther. *The Crossroads of Justice: Law and Culture in Late-Medieval France*. Leiden: Brill, 1993.
Cuenca, Esther Liberman. *The Making of Urban Customary Law in Medieval and Reformation England*. Oxford: Oxford University Press, 2025.
Hallaq, Wael. *The Origin and Evolution of Islamic Law*. Cambridge: Cambridge University Press, 2004.
Harries, Jill. *Law and Empire in Late Antiquity*. Cambridge and New York: Cambridge University Press, 2001.
Hudson, John. *The Formation of the English Common Law: Law and Society in England from the Norman Conquest to the Magna Carta*. London: Longman, 1996.
Humfress, Caroline. *Orthodoxy and the Courts*. Oxford: Oxford University Press, 2007.
Kuskowski, Ada Maria. *Vernacular Law: Writing and the Reinvention of Customary Law in Medieval France*. Cambridge: Cambridge University Press, 2023.

Liaou, Angeliki E., and Dieter Simon, eds. *Law and Society in Byzantium, Ninth to Twelfth Centuries*. Washington, D.C.: Dunbarton Oaks Research Library and Collection, 1994.
Muldoon, James. *Popes, Lawyers, and Infidels*. Philadelphia: University of Pennsylvania Press, 1979.
O'Callaghan, Joseph F. *Alfonso X, the Justinian of His Age: Law and Justice in Thirteenth-Century Castile*. Ithaca: Cornell University Press, 2019.
Oliver, Lisi. *The Body Legal in Barbarian Law*. Toronto: University of Toronto Press, 2011.
Peters, Edward. *Inquisition*. Berkeley: University of California Press, 1988.
Rennie, Kriston R. *Medieval Canon Law*. Leeds: ARC Humanities Press, 2018.

NOTES

1. For an overview on medievalism, see David Matthews, *Medievalism: A Critical History* (Cambridge: D. S. Brewer, 2015), as well as the essays in Louise D'Arcens, ed., *The Cambridge Companion to Medievalism* (Cambridge: Cambridge University Press, 2016).

2. It is likely that the first "medieval" film ever made, directed by Georges Hatot in 1898, was an even shorter film about Joan of Arc's life, which focuses solely on her execution. See David John Williams, "Medieval Movies: A Filmography," *Film & History* 29, no. 1–2 (1999): 20–32.

3. Kevin J. Harty, *The Reel Middle Ages: American, Western and Eastern European, Middle Eastern and Asian Films about Medieval Europe* (Jefferson, N.C.: McFarland, 2015).

4. Jonathan Stubbs, *Historical Film: A Critical Introduction* (New York: Bloomsbury Academic, 2013), 19. See also Robert Brent Toplin, *History by Hollywood: The Use and Abuse of the American Past* (Urbana: University of Illinois Press, 1996); Richard Francaviglia and Jerry Rodnitzky, eds., *Lights, Camera, History: Portraying the Past in Film* (College Station: Texas A & M University Press, 2007); Robert Burgoyne, *The Hollywood Historical Film* (Malden, Mass.: Blackwell, 2008); Marine Hughes-Warrington, *History Goes to the Movies: Studying History on Film* (London: Routledge, 2007); and Robert A. Rosenstone, *History on Film/Film on History*, 4th ed. (Abingdon and New York: Routledge, 2024).

5. For more on this topic, see David John Williams, "Looking at the Middle Ages in Cinema: An Overview," *Film & History* 29, no. 1–2 (1999): 8–19; Lynn Ramey and Tison Pugh, eds., *Race, Class, and Gender in "Medieval" Cinema* (New York: Palgrave Macmillan, 2007); Laurie A. Finke and Martin B. Shichtman, *Cinematic Illuminations: The Middle Ages on Film* (Baltimore: Johns Hopkins University Press, 2010); Andrew B. R. Elliott, *Remaking the Middle Ages: The Methods of Cinema and History in Portraying the Medieval World* (Jefferson, N.C: McFarland, 2011); Lesley Coote, "Survey of 21st Century 'Medieval' Film," in *Medieval Afterlives in Popular Culture*, ed. Gail Ashton and Dan Kline (New York: Palgrave Macmillan, 2015), 103–14.

CANON LAW AND THE WORLD
OF THE MEDIEVAL CHURCH

CHAPTER ONE

BETWEEN ROYAL LAW AND CANON LAW
IN *BECKET* (1964)

By Anthony Perron

Few episodes from the Middle Ages offer richer material for modern drama than the life and career of Thomas Becket (1118–70). The story of a parvenu from London who became, first, chancellor under one of the most ambitious rulers in English history, Henry II (r. 1154–89), and then archbishop of Canterbury, only to be viciously murdered as a result of his resistance to the very same king, has appealed no less to playwrights and filmmakers than to historians. Recorded in a vast dossier of sources (by twelfth-century standards, at least), the tale combines a personal narrative of ambition and betrayal with a heady framework of Big Ideas and an international cast of supporting characters that includes the pope and the king of France. Themes of justice permeate the Becket story, and a careful reading of how this tragedy has been imagined in twentieth-century culture affords valuable insights into the historical Thomas and his place in the medieval legal past. This chapter chiefly examines the 1964 film *Becket*, directed by Peter Glenville, and contends that the film deftly uses law to propel the narrative of its protagonist's troubled career. In so doing, it reminds us that the Becket affair was a watershed of change in medieval history, both for English Common Law and the evolving canon law of the church.

Becket capped a century and more of sustained interest in the archbishop. Biographies of the saint proliferated in the Victorian Age, and even some Protestants, who had long reviled Becket as a traitor, eventually regarded him as a patriot.[1] The nineteenth-century preoccupation with Thomas's cult manifested perhaps most clearly in the production of competing plays about the martyr by Aubrey de Vere and Alfred Lord Tennyson in 1876. The archbishop's appeal by no means declined in the twentieth century. Readers may already be familiar with T. S. Eliot's 1935 verse drama *Murder in the Cathedral*, a brooding meditation on the ineluctable and violent logic of the state transposed into the reign of Henry II. In 1951, and with the collaboration of Eliot himself, G. M. Hoellering oversaw a cinematic version of the play that starred the Anglican priest and social activist John Groser as Becket and featured a haunting tableau of statues, tapestries, and austere peasants, culminating in a chilling scene of the archbishop's murder. In 1959, the French playwright Jean Anouilh made still another attempt to bring Thomas to the stage with his *Becket, ou l'honneur de Dieu*.[2] In contrast to the bleak solemnity of Eliot's work, Anouilh injected moments of levity into the story while nonetheless crafting a complex psychological portrait of a man incapable of loving or being loved, without a fixed sense of self until he becomes archbishop. If Eliot stressed the bond that joined Becket with the oppressed poor, Anouilh reached for a tie more immediately relatable to audiences, the intimate friendship between Thomas and Henry II.

Anouilh's play, the English-language version of which debuted in New York on October 5, 1960, won the Tony Award for Best Play in 1961. Capitalizing on this success, Peter Glenville, who had directed the Broadway production, ushered the story to movie theaters four years later. Though filmed in England and generally classed as a "British" film, *Becket* was spearheaded by Hollywood legend Hal Wallis and distributed by Paramount Pictures. An American writer, Edward Anhalt, was tasked with adapting Anouilh's play for the screen, for which he won an Oscar. Peter O'Toole, in his first role since *Lawrence of Arabia* (1962), was cast as Henry II opposite Richard Burton's Becket. Unlike Hoellering's *Murder in the Cathedral*, *Becket* enjoyed popular acclaim, garnering twelve Oscar nominations, including one for Best Picture.

Needless to say, the project has been assailed by some for its "errors," and, to be sure, *Becket* is no documentary. The point, of course, is not to assess how precisely Broadway and Hollywood convey historical facts, but to appreciate how these works of art might focus our gaze on specific aspects of medieval society and especially medieval legal culture. Accordingly, this chapter analyzes essential and deliberate plot elements of the film that foreground issues of law and justice. First, however, it is necessary to establish some background on Becket's controversial life and rise to prominence.[3]

BECKET FROM MERCHANT TO MARTYR

Thomas grew up in a prosperous, though financially vulnerable, merchant family in London. Solidly educated, his real talents lay in finance and management more than scholarship. It was probably these skills that drew the attention of Henry II, who came to power in 1154 at the close of a long and troubled period in English history often called simply "the Anarchy" (1135–53). The new king's reign was thus defined by efforts to restore fiscal and legal order. To help facilitate these goals, Henry asked Thomas to serve as his chancellor, the highest-ranking official in royal service, with responsibility for issuing mandates, keeping records, and supervising the crown's finances. In 1162, Henry orchestrated Becket's election as archbishop of Canterbury, the most eminent position in the English church, with the understanding that Thomas would continue to serve as chancellor.

If Henry expected Thomas to be pliant in his new role, the king was soon disappointed. Within just a few months, Becket distanced himself from his former boss by surrendering the post of chancellor. The following year (1163), Henry insisted that the English bishops recognize what he considered to be ancient "customs of the realm," codified as a set of statutes known as the "Constitutions of Clarendon." Among them were several provisions that the church saw as infringing on its freedoms, on account of which Becket opposed the customs. Henry retaliated by putting Becket on trial at the Council of Northampton (1164) for largely fallacious charges. Fleeing out of concern for his safety, the archbishop sought refuge in France, where he remained in exile from late 1164 until December 1170. In the meantime, Henry seized incomes and properties from Becket and drove the archbishop's friends and relatives out of the country. Thomas, for his part, further aggravated the king by excommunicating many of Henry's closest supporters.

The bishops of England, led by Archbishop Roger of York (r. 1154–81) and Gilbert Foliot, bishop of London (r. 1163–87), largely backed the king, or at least attempted to steer a pragmatic course that would avoid damaging relations with the crown to the point that the church might suffer grave harm. Outside the country, Pope Alexander III (r. 1159–81) and the French king Louis VII (r. 1137–80), strove to broker a peace; on several occasions, legates were dispatched from the papal court to decide the issues in dispute, and numerous conferences were hosted in France to help the parties negotiate a compromise.

Thwarting these efforts, Henry refused to concede his "customary" rights over the church, while the archbishop would only acknowledge such prerogatives "saving his order" (meaning, so long as they did not require him to violate canon law). Other issues also intruded to worsen relations between Thomas and the king; notably, Henry II's push to have his son, Henry the Young King (d. 1183), crowned as co-regent and successor. Coronations were an established prerogative of the archbishop of Canterbury, but with Becket in exile, the ceremony was in this case performed instead by Thomas's bitter rivals, the archbishop of York alongside the bishops of London and Salisbury.

After a tenuous reconciliation with Henry in July 1170, Becket finally arranged to return. The king granted the archbishop safe conduct, but denied him the "kiss of peace," a more solemn pledge of security. While Thomas was greeted with reverent enthusiasm by the common people and simple clergy of Canterbury, his critics soon gained the king's ear. Reacting above all to Becket's excommunication of the bishops who had participated in the coronation of Henry's son as well as several barons who continued to oppose the archbishop, the king exploded with rage. Taking this as a call to arms, four of Henry's barons, aided by others, broke into the enclosure of Canterbury Cathedral on December 29, 1170, and brutally murdered Becket. Although papal canonization was still a new process within the church, barely more than two years following his assassination, Thomas was declared a saint by Pope Alexander III in February 1173.

LAW AS NARRATIVE IN *BECKET*

Becket's tragic career as archbishop of Canterbury sank deeply into the loam of medieval jurisprudence. Despite this, law plays a surprisingly marginal and inconsistent role in twentieth-century drama about the saint. T. S. Eliot, for instance, referred but sparingly to the topic in *Murder in the Cathedral*: only in part two of the poem do we hear Thomas proclaim that he, as an avatar of "the Law of Christ's Church," is willing to submit his cause to Rome but ready to surrender his life "to the Law of God above the Law of Man."[4] Tellingly, when his work was brought to the screen in 1951, Eliot was asked to write a new opening scene in which appear the main opponents of the archbishop, including Henry (Alexander Gauge) and Bishop Foliot (Alban Blakelock), as well as the specific juridical setting resulting in the ensuing murder—namely, the Constitutions of Clarendon and Becket's trial at Northampton. In his stage drama, Anouilh wove in occasional references to law. Scutage (taxes paid by a vassal to a lord in lieu of military service) makes a cameo appearance in the first act, and, toward the end of act two, the king refers offhandedly to the custom of allowing the crown a say in episcopal elections.[5] After the split between Becket and Henry, moreover, other legal issues crop up: the murder of a priest by William of Aynsford (a real figure, though the crime alleged in the play is fictitious) and an incidental nod to the summoning of a cleric before secular courts by a baron, Gilbert of Clare, all justified by Henry's conviction that "the King is Might and he is the law."[6]

Although such references give color to the story in Anouilh's hands, law cannot really be said to drive the action of his play. A curious failing of *Becket, or the Honor of God*, is that we do not clearly understand the reasons for Thomas's breach with Henry. When he is made archbishop, Becket simply tells the king that they can no longer be friends, and, as act three opens, the erstwhile boon companions are suddenly at odds. Remedying this lacuna, the film *Becket* suggests that *law* is behind the otherwise inexplicable enmity between the two men. Less than fifteen minutes after the opening credits, the movie introduces the disagreement behind the notorious third chapter of the Constitutions of Clarendon (see the appendix; in the action of the film, however, it is still some nine years in the future and so not named). This third chapter of the Constitutions of Clarendon dealt with the question of where clerical defendants should be tried. Storming into the Privy Council, Henry proclaims to the bishops in *Becket*:

> There are many troublesome issues between us which call for a reckoning. Amongst other abuses is the claim you make of judging your clerics accused of civil crimes in your own ecclesiastical courts. I warn you: there can be only one justice in this country, and that is the king's.

The prominence of this statement early on becomes clear in the second half of the film with the insertion of a subplot absent from the play. Foliot here Donald Wolfit) visits Becket and informs him that a priest accused of "debauching a young girl" has been arrested by "Lord Gilbert" (the baron mentioned in passing by Anouilh) and hauled before a secular court. The bishop insists that Thomas stand up for ecclesiastical jurisdiction and convince the king to remand the priest to a church court. Yet, before Becket can act, we learn that the priest in question was killed while trying to escape Lord Gilbert's men, acting as royal agents. These events drive the split between the king and the archbishop, as Becket returns the chancellor's seal to Henry and, in one of the film's most elaborately choreographed scenes, thunderously excommunicates Lord Gilbert. In response to this impudence, Henry has Thomas tried for embezzlement (a reference to the Council of Northampton), thus leading to the archbishop's exile.

BECKET'S CAUSE: CLERICAL IMMUNITY

Although much of the storyline in Glenville's work is invented, it nonetheless faithfully channels key aspects of the historical record. As William Fitzstephen, one of Thomas's contemporary biographers, wrote, King Henry was deeply angered by what he saw as the church's protection of criminous priests, including a shocking case, loosely adapted by the movie into the William of Aynsford/Gilbert of Clare episode described previously, in which Thomas refused to hand over to royal justice a cleric in Worcester who had killed "a certain distinguished man" who was in the process of seducing his daughter. These concerns fed into the Constitutions of Clarendon and their insistence that the king exercise jurisdiction over clerical offenders.[7] Henry's plan to define and set in writing the "customs" of his realm fit into a mold of princely power found elsewhere in the twelfth century, but some historians have argued that the substance of his reforms went too far, and it was here that Becket's opposition gained purchase.[8]

Canon law of the period staunchly asserted the right of clerics to be tried only in ecclesiastical courts (a benefit known as the *privilegium fori*).[9] This immunity shielded the ordained from many of the more severe penalties that might be imposed by secular trials—namely, corporal and capital punishment. Generally, the worst that clerics might be sentenced to was removal from office and rank. Once they had been demoted to lay status, of course, such criminals could be liable to discipline under royal law, but only for newly committed offenses. Naturally, there were exceptions to this, and the church might well want some malefactors to face harsher justice under civil jurisdiction. Thus, in the main collection of canon law current in Becket's time, the *Decretum Gratiani*, a copy of which the archbishop himself likely owned, several authoritative texts allow "incorrigible" clerics to be surrendered to "the secular arm" for discipline.[10] Where these exceptional cases differ from the Constitutions of Clarendon is in the fact that bishops, and not the king or his officials, were to take the initiative.

BECKET'S SWORD: THE POWER OF EXCOMMUNICATION

To return to the film, if Becket's defense of the *privilegium fori* placed him in the vanguard of legal thought, his next step, abruptly excommunicating the baron, instead harked back to an older juridical order.[11] At a basic level, excommunication meant depriving someone of access to the sacraments, potentially imperiling that person's soul. It also might entail certain social disadvantages. Perhaps because of its spiritual power and potential for disruption, excommunication was typically not imposed as a first-line punishment; it was rather a means of forcing those who were convicted by church courts, but later proved recalcitrant, to fulfill the terms of sentences already imposed. Yet, some wrongs were considered so grave that they warranted automatic excommunication. Among them was the assault of a cleric. In the film, Becket sentences Lord Gilbert for his complicity in such a crime—the "sacrilegious murder" of a parish priest, no less. While this particular case is a fabrication of the screenplay, if such an act had taken place, there would have been no need for the archbishop to declare the nobleman excommunicate; he would already have been considered thus in the eyes of the church. Nor would Thomas have had the ability to release Lord Gilbert from such a sanction, as Henry asks the archbishop to do toward the end of the movie in their final meeting on the beach. This power under canon law rested with the pope alone.

It should be noted that the film's novel excommunication scene spotlights a very important and highly problematic aspect of Thomas's conduct as archbishop in the legal context of his day. In the earlier Middle Ages, bishops might summarily declare someone excommunicate as a form of penitential admonishment, but without hewing to any legal procedure. By the later 1100s, however, this "primitive" form of sanction was giving way to a more "judicialized" ritual.[12] Those subject to excommunication had to be warned before a sentence was delivered. They also had the right to defend themselves and to appeal their verdict. All the same, the older idea of excommunication as a sort of spiritual denunciation of the wicked, delivered without any judicial finding, persisted. Thomas Becket was among those accused of circumventing legal standards in pronouncing excommunication in breach of due process.

The archbishop's most trenchant critic in this regard was none other than Bishop Foliot. Indeed, Foliot was excommunicated by Thomas not once, but twice, for failing to heed the archbishop's commands and favoring Henry's agenda. As Foliot memorably charged, Becket's order of proceeding was "hitherto unknown in canon and civil law: first to condemn and only later to make a determination of guilt."[13] In order to protect himself against such attacks, Foliot wrote to Pope Alexander III with a bold claim: one might legitimately preempt a sentence of excommunication by appealing *before* the sanction had even been delivered.[14] (The bishop's letter is translated in the appendix.) This notion, which remained murky in canon law well after the Becket affair, was largely untested, if not entirely without precedent, and must have seemed specious to many of Foliot's contemporaries. But it demonstrates the degree to which the quarrels between the king and the archbishop at every step went beyond the personal to force innovations in legal thinking.

CONCLUSION

Historians have long associated the Becket story with law, and with good reason. Both of the principal characters in the drama represented seminal developments in twelfth-century legal culture: Henry II as a foundational figure in English Common Law and Thomas as a champion of the emerging canon law centered on the "papal monarchy."[15] Twentieth-century depictions of Becket have sought to look past law to emphasize the archbishop's inner struggles and his fraught intimacy with the king. The genius of Glenville's *Becket* is that it returns to the clash of law(s) to render the personal tension between Thomas and Henry intelligible to audiences.

APPENDIX

Becket (1964)

CONSTITUTIONS OF CLARENDON, C. 3 (1164)

This decree was one of sixteen "customs" issued by Henry II, based on practices he claimed had been in place during the reign of his grandfather, Henry I. Though Pope Alexander III tolerated six of them, the remaining ten were condemned. Above all, Becket set himself against c. 3.
Source: Albert Beebe White and Wallace Notestein, eds., trans., *Source Problems in English History* (New York: Harper, 1915), 370–72. Original in Latin.

[Clerics] charged and accused of any matter, summoned by the king's justice, shall come into his court to answer there to whatever it shall seem to the king's court should be answered there, and in the church court to what it seems should be answered there. However, the king's justice shall send [someone] into the court of holy Church for the purpose of seeing how the matter shall be treated there. And if the [cleric] be convicted or confess, the Church ought not to protect him further.

GILBERT FOLIOT, LETTER TO POPE ALEXANDER III AGAINST THOMAS BECKET (C. 1169–1170)

Bishop Gilbert Foliot of London calls upon the help of Pope Alexander III and lays out his grievances against Thomas Becket, specifically how the archbishop conducted Foliot's excommunication.
Source: Z. N. Brooke, Adrian Morey, and C. N. L. Brooke, eds., *The Letters and Charters of Gilbert Foliot* (Cambridge: Cambridge University Press, 1967), 282–85 (no. 212). Original in Latin. Translated by Anthony Perron.

To his father and lord, Pope Alexander, Brother Gilbert [Foliot], minister of the church of London, [sends] everything that the devotion in him, humble and ready to obey, is able.

... Everyone who is hastening to you from the borders of England so that they might please (doubtfully!) certain people—they all wrongly denounce me as a seedbed of discord, an overthrower of the church, a spark of evils, as fuel for strife and for all hatreds, and they do not cease to whisper into your holy ears against me, with the promises and pleas of certain people, things that neither are true nor could ever be proven with the Lord's help. And behold, father, I am perishing, though I have done none of those things, nor am I complicit in any of them. Verdicts are given against me when I have neither confessed nor been convicted; I have not even been summoned. An indictment is fashioned and fabricated, and so that no form of hatred might be lacking for the one oppressing me, they boldly assert that what is known to none is clearly obvious. Blood is demanded from my hands which I did not spill, and most unjustly I am forced to pay back things I did not plunder (Genesis 9:5–6). Fearing of course that all of these things would fall back upon me, in an effort to head off any sentence, I immediately launched an appeal to the papal court, wishing, concerning all these things, to stand before him who, it is certain, does not err in law.

To be sure, if I did not follow through on this appeal, it is because you dispatched from your court legates to our lord the king and entrusted them with the task of hearing and deciding all the issues that were at stake between the archbishop of Canterbury and us, with letters sent to us stating that we should present ourselves to them and steadfastly observe whatever they might decide against us after listening to both sides.[16] As the legates were in no way carrying out the task, I, along with our brethren, appealed once again in their presence, owing to fear of the peril looming. At that point, we were also released from carrying out this appeal by your grace upon the intervention of the lord king. The letters in our possession, fortified by the papal seal, attest to this. And yet, although it is unbecoming for a judge to be upset if an appeal is directed to his superior when he is suspected of unfairness, nonetheless the archbishop of Canterbury, offended that I petitioned your court, is determined to seek my head, to smother me through excommunication, with no respect for order. Knowing of this matter ahead of time and anticipating the sentence, I appealed to your mercy, seeking out the scrutiny of the one who, correctly weighing the merits of cases, with fair reason upholds for each and every person what is their right. For where it is read that in one and the same case there ought not be a third appeal, this should not be taken to mean that a bishop should not freely appeal however many times he believes himself to be treated unfairly by his archbishop, but rather that one who has been defeated ought not to appeal from a sentence approved successively by three judges following an appeal.[17] We say this indeed not to help the sun with torches, but so that we might answer those (even though they are few) who criticize us for frequent appeals.[18]

To the apostolic summit therefore I have appealed, hoping this will aid me, so that before the deadline set for my appeal, my position could not to any degree be weakened by him against whom I have petitioned. For it is in reference to the bulwark of the papacy that it was said to the sea, "You will come all the way to this point, and here you will break your swelling waves" (Job 38:11). Dashed against this by virtue of an appeal, the verdict of any judge is stayed, even if it is already delivered; if the appeal was sent beforehand, then a verdict delivered afterwards is altogether without force, such that both in fact and in name it is forthwith considered void, to be held more worthless than a verdict that has to be nullified outwardly by some ceremony. Nonetheless, because the people do not understand the details of the law and the hidden meanings of church statutes, now that a sentence has been delivered against me following an appeal, I choose to be blamed by the learned for humility rather than rebuked by the masses for impious daring, so to speak, by conducting divine services, and I live and behave in all things as if a verdict bound me, a verdict that, from the very start of its declaration, the apostolic highness dashed to bits; the appeal sent to the papacy beforehand most powerfully suppressed the sentence such that it had no power whatsoever.

Reading questions

- Apply c. 3 of the Constitutions of Clarendon to the story of the transgressing cleric referred to in *Becket*. Given the portrayal of Henry and Thomas in the film, how do you imagine the case might have played out had Lord Gilbert's men not killed the accused priest?
- *Becket* portrays Bishop Foliot as a collaborator with Henry, jealous of Becket's success. In this letter, how does Foliot instead present himself as a victim of the archbishop?
- As a defender of conscience and freedom from royal tyranny, the Thomas of our modern imagination is an undeniably sympathetic character. How might it challenge our views of the saint if we take seriously Foliot's argument that the archbishop was in fact violating the rights of others in the church?

- *Becket* focuses chiefly on the relationship between Thomas and King Henry II, but the ramifications of the Becket controversy impacted many other people's lives and careers. In what ways does this letter reveal the difficult position of someone like Bishop Foliot?

NOTES

1. For a concise discussion of nineteenth-century British views on Becket, see Nicholas Vincent, "Thomas Becket," in *Making and Remaking Saints in Nineteenth-Century Britain*, ed. Gareth Atkins (Manchester: Manchester University Press, 2016), 92–111. A more detailed treatment of Becket's legacy, spanning the Reformation and going through the eighteenth and nineteenth centuries, can be found in Kay Brainerd Slocum's *The Cult of Thomas Becket: History and Historiography through Eight Centuries* (Abingdon: Oxon; New York: Routledge, 2018).

2. Jean Anouilh, *Becket, or the Honor of God*, trans. Lucienne Hill (1960; repr. New York: Riverhead, 1995), xvii.

3. A useful summary of this enormously complicated history can be found in the introduction to Michael Staunton, trans., *The Lives of Thomas Becket* (Manchester: Manchester University Press, 2001), 1–39. For more exhaustive studies, see Frank Barlow, *Thomas Becket* (Berkeley: University of California Press, 1986), and Anne Duggan, *Thomas Becket* (Aldershot and Burlington, Vt.: Ashgate, 2007).

4. T. S. Eliot, *Murder in the Cathedral* (1935: repr. New York, 1988), 65–66, 74.

5. The full text of the Constitutions of Clarendon can be found online through the Yale Law School's Avalon Project: https://avalon.law.yale.edu/medieval/constcla.asp.

6. Anouilh, *Becket*, 9, 59, 78–79. The historical William of Eynsford crossed Becket not by murdering a cleric, but simply by expelling a priest named by the archbishop in a church on William's lands, for which transgression the lord was excommunicated. See Barlow, *Thomas Becket*, 93–94.

7. A careful dissection of this law's background can be found in John Hudson, "Constitutions of Clarendon, Clause 3, and Henry II's Reforms of Law and Administration," in *Laws, Lawyers, and Texts: Studies in Medieval Legal History in Honour of Paul Brand*, ed. Susanne Jenks, Jonathan Rose, and Christopher Whittick (Leiden: Brill, 2012), 1–19 (see appendix). The relevant passage from William Fitzstephen is translated in Staunton, *Lives of Thomas Becket*, 78–79.

8. A superb analysis of this is contained in Duggan, *Thomas Becket*, 48–58. See also Duggan's "Clerical Exemption in Canon Law from Gratian to the *Decretals*," *Medieval Worlds* 6 (2017): 70–100.

9. For a reflection on Becket's defense of clerical immunity and its contemporary legacy, see Rowan Williams, "'Saving Our Order: Becket and the Law," *Ecclesiastical Law Journal* 23 (2021): 127–39.

10. On Thomas's link to the *Decretum*, a magnificent twelfth-century copy of the work, likely from the archbishop's circle, is now housed at the J. Paul Getty

Museum (MS. Ludwig XIV 2), a few miles from the actual Hollywood. See Leena Löfstedt, "Traces of Saint Thomas Becket in the Getty Gratian," *Getty Research Journal* 7 (2015): 151–56.

11. For an accessible survey on the law of excommunication, see R. H. Helmholz, *The Spirit of Classical Canon Law* (Athens: University of Georgia Press, 1996), 366–93, upon whose work I am especially dependent in what follows. See also Richard Helmholz, "Excommunication in Twelfth Century England," *Journal of Law and Religion* 11 (1994): 235–53.

12. Helmholz, *Spirit of Classical Canon Law*, 370–73.

13. Anne J. Duggan, ed., *The Correspondence of Thomas Becket, Archbishop of Canterbury* (Oxford: Clarendon Press, 2000), 1:380 (the translation is my own and differs slightly from Duggan's).

14. For a discussion of Foliot's argument and its context, see Adrian Morey and C. N. L. Brooke, *Gilbert Foliot and His Letters* (Cambridge: Cambridge University Press, 1965), 162–66.

15. On Henry II's place in English legal history, see Paul Brand, "Henry II and the Creation of the English Common Law," in *Henry II: New Interpretations*, ed. Christopher Harper-Bill and Nicholas Vincent (Woodbridge: Boydell Press, 2007), 215–41.

16. The papal representatives in question were Cardinals William of Pavia and Otto of Brescia, whose negotiations took place in the autumn of 1167.

17. Roman law forbade a third appeal in a single case. Canon law, meanwhile, allowed a bishop to appeal against his archbishop whenever he felt aggrieved.

18. The proverb "to aid the sun with torches" meant to do or say something superfluous or unnecessary.

CHAPTER TWO

RELIC MOVEMENT, ANATHEMA, AND CRUSADE IN *PILGRIMAGE* (2017)

By Sarah C. Luginbill

The 2017 Irish film *Pilgrimage*, directed by Brendan Muldowney, combines breathtaking cinematography, an ethereal score, and a compelling narrative to explore the relationship between faith, religion, and violence in medieval Europe. It touches on the ongoing tension between Christianity and paganism, the English invasion of Ireland, multilingualism, papal authority, and the cult of relics. The story is carried by a talented cast: Tom Holland as a young Irish novice who has been raised by the monks of a remote monastery; Jon Bernthal as a mute laborer who arrived in Ireland five years before, presumably after participating in the disastrous Fourth Crusade (1202–4); and Richard Armitage as Raymond de Merville, the sacrilegious son of an invading Norman lord.

The film opens in the year 55, in rural Cappadocia, Turkey, where a crowd of men brutally stone a fictionalized version of Saint Matthias the Apostle (d. *c.* 80), who wears a *chi rho* pendant indicating his Christian faith. As the leader of the group raises a large rock to strike the killing blow, thunder and lightning erupt overhead, signaling divine anger over the event. The rock itself becomes the central object in the film's narrative, as its physical contact with Saint Matthias and his blood render it a Christian relic, an item imbued with the holiness of a saint. Objects that touched the saint, as well as any remains (fingernails, skulls, hair, and blood), could become relics of the sainted individual. Furthermore, reliquaries, the receptacles that housed the saint's relics, could become sacred themselves because of their long-term contact with such holy objects.

After the gruesome scene of Saint Matthias's martyrdom, which establishes the existence of the relic, *Pilgrimage* then cuts to 1209 in Kilmannán, Ireland, where an isolated Benedictine monastery sits on the coastline.

A Cistercian monk, Brother Geraldus, arrives at the monastery with a request from Pope Innocent III (r. 1198–1216): he demands the monks' relic, the stone that martyred Saint Matthias, be brought to Rome to assist in the upcoming crusade for Jerusalem (that is, the Fifth Crusade, 1217–21).

Although *Pilgrimage*'s plot reflects the types of voyages taken by individuals moving relics during the Middle Ages, it does not present the translation, or movement, of Matthias's stone in a positive light. Through dramatic music, seemingly supernatural yet natural events, constant bloodshed, and the unease of the Benedictines throughout the film, it is clear that the removal of the relic from its "home" brings trouble. Indeed, shortly after leaving Kilmannán, Brother Geraldus (Stanley Weber) notes that the grizzled Irish escorts traveling with the monks seem to be afraid of the relic. "Of course they are," replies one of the Benedictines, "they know what happens to those who disturb the relic."

Disturbing any relic or removing a sacred object without approval carried severe consequences in medieval Europe. In particular, Christian clergy punished the unauthorized movement of devotional items through excommunication, which barred an individual from reception of the sacraments in life, and anathema, which also banned the person from heaven in death.[1] Through *Pilgrimage*, one can interrogate how anathema for removing sacred objects, including reliquaries, from their intended homes can be instructive in surveying the circumstances in which items were taken from churches, including the language surrounding the conditions for object removal. In so doing, this chapter contextualizes the use and the development of liturgical rites involving anathema and excommunication against church thieves in medieval sources.

Overall, *Pilgrimage* highlights not only the relationship between spiritual centers and peripheries in medieval Christian thought, but also the importance of movement—of both people and sacred objects—that connected Christians across time and space. The action surrounding the relic of Saint Matthias in *Pilgrimage* connects Cappadocia and Ireland, the shared beliefs and motivations of the church and ordinary believers, and associated Ireland with the prestige of Rome and, by extension, Jerusalem, a contested holy site during the many centuries of Christian crusading to the Holy Land.

PILGRIMAGES TO RELICS AND IRISH COLONIZATION

The film's title refers to the practice of journeying to a place to view and venerate holy relics and sites. Saint Matthias's relic's movement toward the "center" of Christendom, Rome, mirrors the hundreds of pilgrimages taken by medieval individuals to locations across Europe, Northern Africa, and the Levant. Medieval Christians frequently traveled to see and even touch saints' relics at local shrines or larger, more prestigious sites such as Canterbury in England (for the shrine of the martyr Saint Thomas Becket), Santiago de Compostela in Spain (for the shrine of Saint James the Apostle), Rome, and Jerusalem. As relics were traded, stolen, moved, or discovered, new shrines appeared and their custodians vied for legitimacy.[2]

Just as medieval relics brought together people from multiple backgrounds, the stone of Matthias in *Pilgrimage* links two different groups: the Irish and Anglo-Normans. Although all the men are Christians, they speak different languages based on their points of origin. The Irish speak Gaelic, while the "English" speak French, as the "English" here are in actuality the descendants of the Normans, invaders from northern France who conquered England in 1066 and enveloped it as part of their larger Angevin Empire, especially once King Henry II (r. 1154–89) assumed the English throne.[3] This detail—of the cultural and linguistic differences between the Irish natives and the Anglo-Norman invaders and settlers—is rare in medieval cinema. *Pilgrimage*, as a film partially funded by Ireland's government, makes plain to audiences this particular aspect of the English colonization of Ireland, which began in 1171 under Henry II.[4] By 1204, much of Ireland was at least nominally under the rule of his son, King John (r. 1199–1216).

After this initial invasion, tensions between the Irish and Anglo-Normans continued with violence frequently erupting, a history reflected in the film. By the sixteenth century, when a new conquest of Ireland was undertaken by King Henry VIII (r. 1509–47), many who had come from England and settled in Ireland in previous centuries, much to the disgust of contemporary English observers, were seen to have assimilated into the larger Irish population. Differences between these cultures in the Angevin period, however, are seen in the film, particularly with the types of tonsure (haircut) that the Irish monks and their Continental counterparts sport, as well as with the customs relating to the reliquary and its handling. These cultural differences between the Irish and Continental monks, as well as the

Angevin overlords, further exacerbate their conflicting views on the relic and its importance.

THE CULT OF RELICS AND IRISH MONASTICISM

The Christian cult of relics began when the first martyrs, or those considered to be the first saints, such as Saint Matthias, died for their faith in the immediate centuries after Christ's death.[5] Fellow believers hid and venerated the possessions and bodily remains, called corporeal relics, of individuals regarded as saints, as well as contact relics, or items that touched these saints. Relics of the martyrs and apostles were collected and distributed by the papacy, bringing Christians across Europe into direct contact with the sacred through holy remains.

The cult of relics grew drastically after the 787 Council of Nicaea declared that every church altar needed to house a relic, and after 1099, each wave of crusaders returned to Europe with new relics they obtained in the Levant, supplementing the collections of local saints with contact relics of Christ and the Virgin Mary. To properly house such precious objects, medieval Christians created reliquaries of various sizes, materials, and shapes. Reliquaries held both corporeal and contact relics and focused the veneration of pilgrims and the faithful onto the saints. Many medieval reliquaries were portable and intended to move beyond the confines of the church treasury or the main altar. Indeed, especially in Ireland, the design of shrines and reliquaries indicated that "relics were seen (and understood) primarily in motion."[6]

Other relics were more static and were incorporated into altars or large shrines, so could not be moved. While reliquaries often elevated the status and prestige of a relic, relics were the more spiritually valuable item of the two. Indeed, in a moment of desperation in *Pilgrimage*, the monks remove the rock from its reliquary, abandoning its golden chest in the woods. Although their attackers pried the gemstones off the reliquary and treated the chest as loot, the monks treasured the plain rock over material wealth.

The importance of the relic to the worldview of the monks and the action of the story is present in both the prologue and opening scenes of *Pilgrimage*. Although the monks welcome their fellow Christian brother, there is a slight tension between their orders. The Benedictines appear humble and accustomed to manual labor, while the Cistercian carries the authority of the pope and seems to hold more prestige, which parallels the Cistercians' elevated status that crystallized in the twelfth century and continued into the early thirteenth, the period of *Pilgrimage*'s story. The Cistercian Order sprang from reformers within the Benedictine Order, and its members were known for their spiritual rigor, ability to attract sizable donations from rich aristocrats, and considerable political influence, especially during the powerful leadership of the Second Crusade's most fiery instigator, the abbot Bernard of Clairvaux (1090–1153).

At sunset, the monks in the film reluctantly proceed to a nearby well and pull up from its depths a gold reliquary wrapped in sheepskin. Although most relics held by monks would be kept in the main altar of the church or the monastery's treasury, the monks of Kilmannán have hidden their treasure. The reliquary is loaded onto a cart as the abbot blesses the three monks and the novice who will transport the relic to Rome. With the mute laborer, the Cistercian, and two Irish guards, the monks set off on their journey, which is fraught with danger and deception. The relic itself is taken on a kind of pilgrimage; once it reaches Rome, it will aid in the larger Christian cause to retake control of Jerusalem, reflecting how, in the First Crusade, certain Christian nobles believed that the "discovery" of the Holy Lance, a relic thought to have once pierced Jesus's side during the Crucifixion, helped their successful and violent takeover of Antioch in 1098 and Jerusalem the following year.

The authorized removal of reliquaries and shrines from consecrated spaces, the incident that propels the plot in *Pilgrimage*, frequently occurred in ecclesiastical processions around churches, city walls, and open fields to protect the area and its inhabitants against famine, disease, natural disasters, foreign enemies, and demons. Most processional routes were a short circuit through a town and back to the church, but others were to local council meetings, where the presence of a saint's relics enhanced the authority of the ecclesiastical presiders. Processions of saints' relics and even liturgical books could promote civic identity, instill social order and local control, and enhance "social cohesion and legitimate internal differences" within a community.[7] In processing their reliquaries, shrines, and books from inside the walls of a church, clerics and monks merged their world with the outside in an attempt to bring Heaven to the people.

This was especially the case during the Peace of God movement (c. 990–1200) in Western Europe, in which the removal of relics from their church settings reminded the lay population that their Christian saints and holy dead were neither inactive nor immobile but involved in the community and worth venerating.[8] During the Peace of God, clergy attempted to curtail ongoing feuds and violence between nobles by instituting spiritual consequences. In particular, clergy desired to protect women, children, monks, and nuns, as well as their property, from the unchecked violence of local, powerful lords. The Peace of God, however, was not always about the practice of nonviolence. When Pope Urban II (r. 1088–99) called upon nobles from Western Europe to join what originally was known as a pilgrimage but became later recognized as the First Crusade, this also must be understood as part of the Peace of God movement. Urban II's call to action aimed to direct these Christian aristocrats' violent energies away from the church and each other toward Muslims who lived in the Holy Land.

To lend physical weight to threats of spiritual excommunication, priests and bishops often brought relics into a town square or proceeded with them around a contested area. Some clergy found this contentious, as it made the relics and reliquaries vulnerable to attack. Others, such as the abbot and monks of Lobbes in present-day Belgium, decided to take the relics of Saint Ursmer, the saint who had converted the Flemish to Christianity, on a tour through Flanders to influence the lords to return the monastic lands. To accomplish their goal of peace, the touring Lobbes monks frequently singled out the local feud leader and shamed him with the relics and rituals.[9] The feuding knights were gathered in the middle of the town, and Ursmer's relics were placed before them. The monks beseeched the knights to swear oaths of peace on the relics, and, under the pressure from the townspeople and the apparent disapproval of Ursmer, the lords promised to cease fighting and return lands.[10] In his *Histories*, Rodolfus Glaber (985–1047) describes similar scenes at Peace of God councils across the region of Burgundy, where relics were brought before everyone while statutes for peace were created (excerpted in appendix). The relics held mental and emotional influence and, without the saint physically present, the monks and clergy had little to no authority.

The public display of relics asserted the church's authority and gave lay individuals tangible evidence of divine influence in the secular world. Relic processions implied that ecclesiastical power could extend beyond the reach of the church and monastic walls. In the case of the Lobbes relic tour and other relic processions during the Peace of God, this notion served as a warning to feuding lords and a comfort to the people whose land and well-being were threatened. The removal of relics from their church settings reminded the lay population that their Christian saints lived on in their communities.

Unauthorized removal of objects from their church settings, or their abuse, occurred frequently in war-torn lands, where feuding noblemen and various armies attacked churches and carried off their treasures. Medieval chroniclers utilized such episodes to highlight the impiety of the perpetrators, who disrespected both the sanctity of the church interior and the holiness of the items inside by paralleling the crimes committed against church objects with violence against Christians. For instance, Thietmar of Merseburg lamented the sack of Brandenburg in 983 by Slavic troops "who stole all of the church's treasures and brutally spilled the blood of many."[11] For Thietmar and his audience of monks, the maltreatment of both persons and church objects demonstrated the full extent of the Slavs' evil nature.

ANATHEMA AND EXCOMMUNICATION

The removal of Saint Matthias's relic from Kilmannán in *Pilgrimage* does not constitute a theft per se, but the monks' reluctance to move the stone and the ensuing divine wrath signal that the relic should have been left alone. The relic, its reliquary, and its caretakers are safest in the monastery; once the relic is taken away, it becomes vulnerable. This tension in the film signals a historical reality: the existence of prescriptions for anathema against relic theft in medieval Europe.

The Christian concept of anathema, condemnation by God, derives from the New Testament. By the sixth century, it came to mean a full separation of the soul from God and Heaven in life and death. The practice of anathema and excommunication as punishment for the theft of church property was well-established by the eleventh century.[12] Between 906 and 913, the chronicler and theologian Regino of Prüm (d. 915) first used the phrase "let him be anathema" in his *De ecclesiasticis disciplinis* (*On Ecclesiastical Instructions*), a collection of canon law that included formulas for excommunication and reconciliation.[13] In Book Two, Canon 412, Regino declared separation from the "bosom of the church" and anathema against any individual who attacked church lands and serfs, harmed clergy, and stole their possessions.[14] Regino's formulas for anathema and excommunication of individuals who stole church objects influenced doctrine for centuries. Manuscripts that contained the rites performed by clergy who were bishops or of higher status, called pontificals, and other liturgical texts across medieval Europe in the eleventh and twelfth centuries included such formulas.

One eleventh-century pontifical, written in Bamberg, presented the excommunication of church thieves in the form of a papal letter directly from the pope to the clergy in Europe, which lent authority to the text.[15] Probably compiled under the direction of the German king Henry II (r. 1002–24) for his foundation at Bamberg, the pontifical includes several rites that enforced both earthly and eternal punishments on those who removed any items from a church treasury (excerpted in the appendix). Bamberg's clergy desired to maintain protection for their property. The threat of anathema for stealing any "possessions of Saint Peter," the apostle considered to be the first pope and to whom Bamberg Cathedral was dedicated, was intended to curtail any removal of church property.

The influence of Regino's prohibitions on the theft of church objects also materialized in monastic chronicles. In the *Annals of Hildesheim*, the 1022 consecration of the Church of St. Michael the Archangel included a reference to the bishop's authority against anyone who attacked the new church's property. The bans promised the perpetrators "would be under perpetual damnation and damned with perpetual anathema and erased from the world of the living."[16] The *Annals of Hildesheim* utilized the word *deleo* ("to erase") to describe the full consequence of anathema. Instead of indicating a simple removal from the Christian community, *deleo* contains a strong connotation of destruction, alongside erasure. The *Annals'* repetition of variations on *perpetuo* ("perpetual") and *damnatus* ("damned") further emphasized the eternal condemnation of anathema for the sinner.

Even when not documenting a ban or curse, chroniclers considered anathema a consequence for church theft. For example, when the monk Berthold of Reichenau (d. *c.* 1088) described such a theft, he called the perpetrator "that obstinate intruder, worthy of anathema" and referred to the man as "a sacrilegious thief" for his deeds.[17] As papal and ecclesiastical authority grew in the eleventh and twelfth centuries, more and more severe spiritual punishments awaited those who challenged the church in this way. In this respect, *Pilgrimage* shows how the fear of translating the relic from its home in Ireland to Rome becomes its own type of curse for the relic's reluctant caretakers.

CONCLUSION

The movement of Christian relics and their reliquaries was common throughout medieval Europe and beyond, especially during the time of the crusades (1095–1291). During this period, many relics made their way to Western Europe via Constantinople, which had its own impressive assortment of saintly remains. In 1204, the same year in which the action of *Pilgrimage* takes place, Western Christian crusaders looted many of Constantinople's reliquaries and churches, stealing valuable devotional objects for themselves. Pope Innocent III reprimanded the crusaders, declaring them excommunicated for the evils that they did at Constantinople, including taking the city's relics. Indeed, in *Pilgrimage*, Raymond de Merville guesses that the mute laborer of Kilmannán fought at Constantinople during the so-called Fourth Crusade, and the audience is left with the impression that the laborer's penance is in atonement for his sins in 1204.

The relic in *Pilgrimage* is ultimately lost, neither returning home to Kilmannán nor completing the journey to Rome. The film ends with the young novice alone and unsure of where to go, implying that even the most well-intentioned travels could be disrupted by greed, violence, and false belief. *Pilgrimage*'s relic, however, provides a bridge between the biblical past of Saint Matthias and the medieval "present" of a colonized Ireland. By the end, the relic helps transform the peripheral Ireland to the "center" and the lands beyond it, like Rome and Jerusalem, to the "periphery."

APPENDIX

Pilgrimage (2017)

RODOLFUS GLABER (985–1047), *HISTORIES* (C. 1026–1033)

Book 4, Chapter 5: A portion of a monastic chronicle that details how relics were used during the Peace of God movement.
Source: J. P. Migne, ed., *Patrologia Latina*, vol. 142, col. 678–79 (Paris, 1880). Original in Latin. Translated by Sarah C. Luginbill.

In the thousandth year of the Lord's Passion, following a time of scarcity and destruction . . . the joyful face of heaven began to brighten and began to blow an agreeable breeze of air and by gentle serenity to show the greatness of the Creator; also, the whole surface of the earth was favorably verdant [with] an abundance of fruits to indicate the banishment of want. Then, therefore, in parts of Aquitaine, for the first time, bishops and abbots and other men from the whole people . . . began to unite in meetings of councils, to which also many bodies of saints and innumerable reliquaries of holy relics were brought. Henceforth, throughout the province of Arles and also Lyons, and in this manner throughout all of Burgundy, even to the furthest parts of France, through all the bishoprics, it was proclaimed that, in certain places, the princes and magnates of the whole country should attend councils about reforming the peace and the principles of the sacred faith. And when the whole multitude of the people, the greatest [to] the middling to the least, they joyfully went and were ready to obey the commands of the shepherds of the Church no less than if a voice sent from heaven had spoken to men on earth.

PONTIFICAL SPONSORED BY HENRY II (R. 1002–1024),
EXCOMMUNICATION FORMULA (C. 1007–1024)

A transcription of a letter, allegedly from "Pope Leo" to his clergy, instructing them on how to anathematize, or curse, individuals who remove relics without authorization.
Source: Bamberg Staatsbibliothek Msc. Lit.53 fol. 191r–191v. Original in Latin. Translated by Sarah C. Luginbill.

Leo, bishop, servant of the servants of God, to the most beloved brothers and sons, the archbishops and their suffragans, the abbots and the congregations of monks living together in Francia: perpetual greetings.

. . . By the authority of the Lord the Father and his son, our Lord Jesus Christ, and the Holy Spirit, the Paraclete, and from the succession of blessed Peter, the apostle, and also the blessed Mary, mother of the Lord, and through the blessed angels and apostles, martyrs, confessors, virgins, we excommunicate and curse those who invade and remove the possessions of the servants of Saint Peter and whoever extends [aid] to them; may their share be with Dathan and Abiron[18] whom the earth devoured alive on account of their pride, and with Judas who for enrichment sold his lord for a price. Amen.

May their children become orphans and their wives [become] widows. May their children be carried off and may those begging be cast out from their homes.

May the moneylender scrutinize all of their resources and may strangers tear apart their works. And again, everyone who will have said "let us possess through inheritance the shrine of the Lord," may God set those men behind and before just as blades [of grass] before the wind. Amen. Just as fire which consumes a forest, and just as flame consumes mountains, so You will follow them in your storm and make them filled with disgrace so that they may be ashamed and confused and lost. Amen. These are the curses which the Lord promulgated upon the children through Moses, over those who have been entrusted with the goods and villages of Saint Peter, that they are cursed in the city, cursed in the field, and in every place. Amen. Cursed are their storehouses, cursed is the fruit of their stomach and the fruit of their earth. Amen.

Cursed are all that are of them and cursed are those going forth and returning. Amen. May the Lord swiftly ruin them from the earth. Amen.

May the Lord strike them with hunger and thirst, want, cold, and fever until they perish. Amen. May the Lord deliver them falling before their enemies. Amen. And may their corpses entice all flying [birds] of the sky and beasts of the earth. Amen. May the Lord strike them with sores of the worst itch and also with itching, madness, and blindness. Amen.

And may they grope [around] in mid-day just as a blind man feels in the darkness. Amen.

And just as the Lord gave to blessed Peter the apostle and his successors, whose succession we hold, however unworthy, the power that whatsoever they bind on earth shall be bound in heaven, and whatsoever they loose on earth shall be loosed in heaven. Thus, if they [the perpetrators] do not wish to make amends, we shut heaven and we deny earth for burial, and may they be cast into the lower Hell and may they pay for what they did without end. Amen.

If, however, they come to penance and amends, and if they make penance worthy of the consequence of the crime, God may turn away all that evil from them and we are prepared to receive [them] and pray for them. If, however, they do not wish to come to give amends, let them be anathema forever so that they may not enter the Lord's church, nor may they have the peace of the Christians, nor make any partaking. May they not take the body and blood of the Lord on the day of death but let them be delivered to eternal oblivion just as dust before of nature the wind, and may they be consigned with the devil and his angels to everlasting fires. And as this light is extinguished so may their souls be extinguished in the stench of Hell.

Amen.

Reading questions

- In this passage concerning the time of the Peace of God, describe how Glaber presents the movement of people and relics. What do you think were the reasons for churchmen wanting relics at these councils?
- How do the relics and councils unite the common people? Does the relic in *Pilgrimage* effect the same unity among its devotees? Why or why not?
- What punishments does the author of the pontifical envision for the accused? Can you compare these punishments to those of the characters in *Pilgrimage* for their roles in moving the relic of Saint Matthias?
- Why do you think the author of the pontifical formatted the excommunication formula as a papal letter from a specific pope? Do you think the curses in this text are similar to curses uttered in *Pilgrimage*?

NOTES

1. Bruce C. Brasington, "'Differentia est': A Twelfth-Century *Summula* on Anathema and Excommunication," in *Canon Law, Religion, and Politics: Liber Amicorum Robert Somerville*, ed. Uta-Renate Blumenthal, Anders Winroth, and Peter Landau (Washington, D.C.: The Catholic University of America Press, 2012).

2. For more on St. Thomas Becket, see Anthony Perron's chapter on *Becket* (1964) in this book.

3. "Angevin" refers to Anjou in France, a duchy under the control of Henry II.

4. See Brendan Smith, *Colonisation and Conquest in Medieval Ireland: The English in Louth, 1170–1330* (Cambridge: Cambridge University Press, 1999).

5. Niamh Wycherley, *The Cult of Relics in Early Medieval Ireland* (Turnhout: Brepols, 2015), 16.

6. Karen Eileen Overbey, *Sacral Geographies: Saints, Shrines and Territories in Medieval Ireland* (Turnhout: Brepols, 2012), 9.

7. Keith D. Lilley, "Cities of God? Medieval Urban Forms and Their Christian Symbolism," *Transactions of the Institute of British Geographers* 29, no. 3 (2004): 305; Kate M. Craig, *Mobile Saints: Relic Circulation, Devotion, and Conflict in the Central Middle Ages* (Abingdon: Oxon; New York: Routledge, 2021); Pamela Sheingorn and Kathleen M. Ashley, "Sainte Foy on the Loose, or, the Possibilities of Procession," in *Moving Subjects: Processional Performance in the Middle Ages and the Renaissance*, ed. Kathleen M. Ashley and Wim Hüskin (Amsterdam: Brill, 2001), 53–68.

8. See Hans-Werner Goetz, "Protection of the Church, Defense of the Law, and Reform," in *The Peace of God: Social Violence and Religious Response in France around the Year 1000*, ed. Thomas Head and Richard Landes (Ithaca, N.Y: Cornell University Press, 1992), 259–79; Thomas Head, "The Development of the Peace of God in Aquitaine (970-1005)," *Speculum* 74, no. 3 (1999): 656–86.

9. Geoffrey Koziol, "Monks, Feuds, and the Making of Peace in Eleventh-Century Flanders," in Head and Landes, *Peace of God*, 247.

10. For more on oath-taking, see Esther Liberman Cuenca's chapter on *Kingdom of Heaven* (2005) in this book.

11. David A. Warner, trans., *Ottonian Germany: The Chronicon of Thietmar of Merseburg* (Manchester: Manchester University Press, 2001), 141.

12. See Elisabeth Vodola, *Excommunication in the Middle Ages* (Berkeley: University of California Press, 1986).

13. Jacques-Paul Migne, ed., "Regino of Prüm," *Patrologia Latina* 132 (Paris, 1880), 360.

14. Migne, "Regino of Prüm," PL 132, 362; Sarah Hamilton, "Interpreting Diversity: Excommunication Rites in the Tenth and Eleventh Centuries," in *Understanding Medieval Liturgy: Essays in Interpretation*, ed. Helen Gittos and Sarah Hamilton (London: Routledge, 2016), 131.

15. Bamberg Staatsbibliothek Ms. Lit. 53 fol. 191r–91v.

16. Georg Waitz, ed., *Annales Hildesheimenses* (Hanover, 1878), 33. The original source uses "deletus," from which we get our word *delete*.

17. Ian S. Robinson, ed., *Monumenta Germaniae Historica: Scriptores Rerum Germanicarum*, New Series, vol. 14, *The Chronicle of Berthold of Reichenau* (Hannover: Hahnsche Buchhandlung, 2003), 209, 210.

18. In the book of Exodus, Dathan and Abiron continuously opposed Moses and attempted to undermine his authority with the Israelites.

CHAPTER THREE

THE CREATION OF THE FRANCISCAN RULE IN *FRANCESCO* (1989)

By Nathan Melson

While all medieval Christian religious orders had as their core principle the imitation of the life of Jesus—be it poverty, charity, or ministry—few placed as much emphasis on imitating the life of their founder as the Order of Friars Minor, better known as the Franciscans. To comprehend the order's history and its centuries-long struggle over how to live a life of true poverty, one therefore must also understand its founder, Saint Francis of Assisi (1181–1226). This search for understanding drives the narrative of *Francesco*, Liliana Cavani's 1989 biopic of the saint. The film follows Francis, played by Mickey Rourke, as he undergoes conversion from a member of Italy's mercantile class to a religious way of life, through the growth of his early brotherhood, and culminates in his struggle to found a new brotherhood that embraced poverty and ministry as its central program. Although Cavani (b. 1933) is perhaps best known for her 1974 film *The Night Porter*, *Francesco* is actually the second of three films she has written and directed exploring the saint's life. The first, *Francesco d'Assisi* (1966), was her first feature film; the third, also titled *Francesco* (2014), was, like the 1966 production, made for television.

In its treatment of Francis's life and ministry, Cavani's *Francesco* is a (sometimes violent) psychodrama that explores the outward manifestations of Francis's psychological and spiritual turmoil, and Rourke often seems to be emoting an inner dialogue to which the audience is not privy. When Francis abandons his well-off urban origins to embrace a mendicant, or "begging," lifestyle, he finds himself surrounded by the destitute poor of Assisi, who experience profound physical and mental illness. Seeing him embrace lepers and sit with a mother who has lost her infant child to starvation, Francis's family and contemporaries—and the film's audience—wonder whether he has also taken leave of his senses. Indeed, Cavani's directorial choices and her script, cowritten with Roberta Mazzoni, seem to imply that there is a fine line between sanctity and insanity.

Francesco's tone stands in stark contrast to other biographical films about the saint, most notably Franco Zeffirelli's *Brother Sun, Sister Moon* (1972), which depicts Francis and his early followers as medieval hippies, singing folk songs across the sun-dappled Italian countryside and ending with Pope Innocent III (r. 1198–1216, played by Alec Guinness) giving Francis and his brothers approval for their way of life in 1209. *Francesco*, on the other hand, is a much darker film, both in its cinematography and how it treats its subject. A color palette of dirty grays and earth tones dominates the film's aesthetic, and, unlike the brightly lit *Brother Sun, Sister Moon*, most of *Francesco*'s outdoor scenes are gray and overcast. While both films use extensive makeup to show the voluntarily poor friars as dirty, *Francesco* emphasizes their skin lesions and sores, caused by exposure to the elements and malnutrition. Supporting *Francesco*'s somber tone is a foreboding and synthesizer-heavy score by Vangelis, the Oscar-winning composer of the *Chariots of Fire* (1981) and *Blade Runner* (1982) soundtracks. *Francesco* also embraces a longer timeline than *Brother Sun, Sister Moon*, and the last quarter of the film is devoted to the struggles and tribulations Francis faced as his small group of poor brothers expanded in number after receiving papal approval.

This chapter argues that these elements of lighting, cinematography, and score are not just artistic choices; they set up the film's thesis, which interrogates why Francis's voluntary poverty was so attractive to those who chose to join him. Cavani seems to ask whether it was ever possible for Francis's lifestyle to be codified into a religious order without losing something in the process and whether his rejection of worldly trappings and structures was too radical to survive institutionalization unchanged. *Francesco* is, therefore, both the story of a man becoming a saint (in other words, a hagiography) and that of a close-knit brotherhood transforming into a large and popular religious order. While the film does make artistic alterations to the historical record, these changes reflect and are informed by the medieval hagiographic tradition. As Rourke's Francis sheds his mercantile-class youth and embraces absolute poverty, he finds peace, contentment, and joy. When compelled by the desires of his brothers for a communal rule, he becomes forlorn and falls into despair, forced to create a rule that negotiates between his idealism and the demands of his community.

THE LIFE AND LIVES OF FRANCIS OF ASSISI

Born in 1181 as the son of a cloth merchant in Assisi, Italy, Francesco di Bernardone had a short-lived military career before experiencing a religious transformation, which the film posits as the result of Francis finding a vernacular translation of the Gospels during a traumatic period of captivity amid a military conflict between Assisi and Perugia.[1] In his mid-twenties, Francis abandoned the future his family had planned for him, sold or gave away much of his father's stock (without permission), and began to lead the life of a begging handyman, doing odd jobs for food, giving away his money and possessions to the poor, and tending to a local leper colony. Eventually, Francis's father had him brought before the bishop of Assisi, where Francis renounced his inheritance, took off all his clothes, and stood naked before the bishop, who then wrapped Francis in his cloak.

Dressed in a simple tunic, Francis embraced extreme poverty and active ministry, a mode of life known as the *vita apostolica* ("apostolic life"), which sought to imitate the lifestyle of Christ and his apostles. Francis began to repair churches in and around Assisi and after several years was joined by other young men of the town, who were moved by his life of simple, voluntary poverty. In 1209, he sought and received papal approval from Pope Innocent III for his new brotherhood, the Order of Friars Minor. Over the following decade, the order grew to over a thousand brothers, but Francis continually resisted institutionalization or setting up a hierarchy and structure that would make the Friars Minor like other religious orders. He eventually left Italy and traveled to the Middle East, where he sought an audience with the Ayyubid sultan of Egypt, Al-Kamil (*c.* 1177–1238), whom he unsuccessfully attempted to convert to Christianity. On his return to Italy, he turned over management of the order to one of his early followers, Pietro Catani, who became "vicar-general" of the order.

In the final years of his life, Francis went into seclusion, at which point he reportedly received the wounds of Christ, or *stigmata*, in a vision, the first person ever to do so. His eyesight also began to degenerate as a result of an infection. Shortly before his death in 1226, he sensed that his brothers were moving away from the strict observance of poverty that he had originally envisioned, and so in his final days, he dictated a spiritual testament, encouraging the brothers not to abandon the principles of poverty and simplicity he had laid out in the order's Rule.[2]

Francesco opens with the body of Francis being brought into the chapel of San Damiano outside Assisi. It then cuts to a gathering of a handful of Francis's early followers, including Bernardo da Quintavalle (d. 1241, played by Diego Ribon), Rufino (Paco Reconti), Angelo (Matteo Corsini), and Chiara or Clare (1194–1253, played by Helena Bonham-Carter in one of her earliest film roles), who have gathered on a hillside in the country to reminisce and memorialize Francis, while one of the brothers, Leone (Fabio Bussotti), records the stories. The rest of the film then cuts back and forth between scenes from the life of Francis to this gathering of followers, creating a frame story structure for the movie.

Cavani and Mazzoni's script for *Francesco* seems heavily informed by the rich and varied biographies (or *vitae*) of Francis composed in the thirteenth and fourteenth centuries. Indeed, few medieval saints can boast as many official and unofficial biographies as Francis. The genre of hagiography—accounts of the lives and activities of those individuals venerated as saints—dates to the earliest centuries of the Christian faith. Many early Christian saints were martyrs who died during periods of persecution by the Roman government, and accounts of their lives were created and disseminated to provide encouragement and a model for steadfast devotion in the face of death. With the end of Roman persecution, most recognized saints were, rather than martyrs, individuals who lived remarkable pious and upright lives, again acting as role models and examples of devotion for the Christian faithful. Over time, the composition of a saint's *vita* became part of the process of recognizing someone as a saint, and their biography then gave rise to widespread recognition of their sanctity. Indeed, it was during Francis's own lifetime that canonization in the Western church was becoming a formalized process under the exclusive purview of the papacy.[3]

Accounts of Francis's life began to be compiled soon after his death in 1226. The first such account was composed by a Franciscan brother, Thomas of Celano (1200–60), who completed his work in 1229, the year after Francis's canonization by Pope Gregory IX (r. 1227–41), the former Ugolino di Conti, cardinal-protector of the Franciscan order (played by Mario Adorf in the film). But, as portrayed in *Francesco*'s frame story, a strong tradition of anecdotes told by those who had been Francis's companions, confidantes, and early followers also emerged. Therefore, in the 1230s and '40s, alternate versions of the life, such as a prose version by Julian of Speyer (d. *c.* 1250) and a verse form by Henri d'Avranches (d. 1260), were composed. More informal collections of stories about Francis as told by his companions likewise emerged, the best known of which are *The Legend of the Three Companions* and a compendium known variously as *The Writings of Leo, Rufino, and Angelo, Companions of St. Francis*; the *Anonymous of Perugia*; and the *Assisi Compilation*.[4] These story collections expand on various aspects of Francis's life, in turn prompting Thomas of Celano to revise his earlier *vita*. His new version, completed in 1247, is often called the *Vita Secunda*. Even this life, however, was surpassed by a third official version, composed by the then–Minister General of the Order, Bonaventure of Bagnoregio (1221–74), who was supposedly responding to a demand for a new, updated life made by the brothers at the 1260 General Chapter in Narbonne, France. Bonaventure's life, completed in 1267, draws on all the previous collections and lives.

The existence of so many (and sometimes contradictory) lives was not a problem for medieval Christians. Indeed, as historians like Aviad Kleinberg have argued, sainthood is not a static state recognized through formal canonization.[5] Rather, sainthood is a dialogue between a saint and his/her communities, both in life and after death. While they may behave piously, their status as saints is conferred on them by the Christian faithful. *Francesco* implicitly recognizes this reality through its frame story of the early brothers and Chiara gathering to compile their remembrances of Francis after his death. Francis the person is, from the first scene of the film, dead, and Francis the saint is brought to life and constructed by their collective remembrance of him. The film's narrative likewise draws from both the official lives and—in its structure and tone—from the more informal story collections.

THE FRANCISCAN RULE

In the first centuries of the Christian faith, its adherents began to explore a variety of avenues of religious devotion and expression, many of which centered on ascetic practices, living disciplined lives of renunciation and prayer. The earliest form of Christian ascetic practice was solitary, one in which the individual withdrew from public life and society to live alone in contemplation, often in the desert. But solitary living was difficult, and the mode that became far more popular was cenobitic monasticism, that of a "shared life" in a religious community. Unlike solitary eremitism, communal life necessitated guidelines for living together, as well as clear structures and obligations for members of the community. From the fourth century on, therefore, monastic rules (*regulae*) designed to govern behavior and define the responsibilities of members of Christian religious communities began to proliferate throughout the Mediterranean.[6] The most famous of these rules was composed by Benedict of Nursia (480–547) in the sixth century, and the Rule of Saint Benedict became the most widely followed monastic rule in Western Europe.[7]

Francis, however, rejected the use of any extant religious rule.[8] His brothers, or *friars* (from the Latin *frater*), were not monks. Monks retreated from the world to live quiet lives of contemplation, prayer, and labor. Francis wanted his brothers to be active and involved in the world, ministering and preaching to people directly rather than living a cloistered existence behind the walls of a monastery or abbey. Therefore, when Francis appeared before Innocent III in 1209 to seek approval for his brotherhood, he presented the pope with an extremely simple rule that reportedly consisted of little more than strung-together biblical quotations.

While Innocent gave his assent based on this Primitive Rule (*Regula primitiva*), the rapid growth of the order in the following decade necessitated a more extensive set of guidelines. *Francesco* shows this growth as brothers join from outside Italy and from more elite socioeconomic classes. When these brothers try to stay in a house that was donated for their use, Francis begins to dismantle the roof. In 1221, Francis composed a new rule, one that mandated strict and absolute poverty in imitation of Christ and his apostles. This edition, however, was never given papal approval and is thus known as the *Regula non bullata*, the "Rule without a [papal] bull." The film depicts the rejection of the *Regula non bullata* not as the work of the papal curia, but of a faction of "more delicate" and learned brothers led by Elias of Cortona (played by Stanko Molnar), who calls the 1221 rule a "suicide" owing to its strictness. In reality, as Heribert Holzapfel points out, this version of the Rule was rejected because of its "excessive length and confused arrangement of material."[9] It was not until November 1223 that the third and final iteration of the Rule was completed and approved by Pope Honorius III.

Compared to many other religious rules, the 1223 Franciscan Rule is shockingly brief, comprising just twelve chapters, shorter than even the 1221 version of the Rule, which contained extensive scriptural quotations and even prayers for the brothers.[10] Moreover, whereas the 1221 Rule contains lengthy exhortations and detailed rationales for its injunctions and requirements, the 1223 Rule is far more concise. Take, for instance, the 1221 Rule's chapter on the brothers and their relationship to money. After forbidding them from accepting money, the 1221 Rule assigns harsh social penalties:

If by chance, which God forbid, it happens that some brother is collecting or holding coin or money, unless it is only for the aforesaid needs of the sick, let all the brothers consider him a deceptive brother, an apostate, a thief, a robber, and as the one who held the money bag, unless he has sincerely repented.[11]

The 1223 Rule, by contrast, only forbids the brothers from accepting money, except in certain cases and conditions; the social castigation has been entirely removed (see the Rule excerpts in the appendix).[12] Even the 1223 version of the Rule, though, represented a severe adherence to poverty that, over the next century, created deep divisions among the friars about what it meant to imitate Christ's poverty and the degree to which a religious order could survive without owning anything.[13]

Another point of contrast between the Franciscan Rule and other religious orders is its approach to institutional hierarchy. Whereas most monastic rules, like the Rule of Saint Benedict, are precise and detailed in their description of organizational structures and responsibilities, the Franciscan Rule is remarkably vague. As early as 1217, Francis sent brothers north, across the Alps, which led to the expansion of the order outside Italy. This led to the Franciscans adopting, like other mendicant orders, a "provincial" organization, with each province headed by a provincial minister, who oversaw smaller divisions or custodies, overseen by a custodian.[14] The order was to be led by a Minister General, elected every three years during the General Chapter, a meeting of the provincial ministers and custodians. But this is the extent of organization as outlined in the Rule.

Yet by the time of Francis's death, the order was beginning to transition to a more traditional model based in convents, overseen by one of the brothers who was named "guardian," as opposed to an abbot or prior. The Franciscan Rule, however, does not mention convents or guardians. Indeed, in his *Testament*, Francis exhorted his brothers "not to receive in any way churches or poor dwellings or anything else built for them unless they are according to the holy poverty we have promised in the Rule," and they were to conduct themselves "guests" and "pilgrims and strangers" in any buildings they did receive. Nor were they to "ask any letter from the Roman Curia, either personally or through an intermediary, whether for a church or another place or under the pretext of preaching or the persecution of their bodies. But, wherever they have not been received, let them flee into another country to do penance with the blessing of God."[15] In other words, the brothers were to shun property even in cases where having a convent or place of refuge might provide them with safety. Francis's call for his brothers to follow a strict and absolute form of poverty thus ran up against an order that was increasingly becoming settled and institutional, and Pope Gregory IX declared in the bull *Quo elongati* (1230) that Francis's *Testament* was not binding on the order.

CONCLUSION

As an account of historical personages and events, *Francesco* is not without its errors and artistic liberties.[16] It conflates, for example, the Portiuncula, a small chapel just outside of Assisi that became a base of operations for the early Franciscans, with the church of San Damiano, another important Franciscan site located several miles outside of Assisi and the eventual home of a religious community headed by Chiara.

The most dramatic historical alteration is a scene toward the end of the film where Francis and Leone arrive in Perugia to get papal approval for the new, revised Rule, only to find that not only has Innocent III died, but the other cardinals and bishops have abandoned his body—now in full rigor—on the floor of the cathedral in order to rush back to Rome for a new electoral conclave. This, of course, never happened; not only did Innocent III die in 1216, seven years before the final version of the Rule was approved, but his body certainly would never have been left lying in an empty cathedral. This moment, however, hints at Cavani's thesis for the film. Francis's renunciation of the world (and its trappings of wealth and power) was fundamentally antithetical to what the institutional, hierarchical church had become. In the film, when Francis and his brothers seek approval for the Primitive Rule in their audience with Innocent III, the cardinals of the curia are dismissive and contemptuous of their efforts, because they claim that poverty gives way to vanity, and eventually those who promote extreme renunciation "proclaim themselves the 'true' Christians, the only apostles, and cover the throne of Peter with insults." The cardinals' hypocrisy in then abandoning Innocent's body therefore stands in stark contrast with the tenderness and dignity that Francis and Leone show the corpse as they move it off the floor. *Francesco* can therefore be considered a work of cinematic hagiography, depicting a model of sanctity that critiques institutional religious power and hierarchy.

APPENDIX

Francesco (1989)

THE RULE OF THE FRANCISCAN ORDER (1223)

Injunctions and obligations for the brothers concerning labor, poverty, and violations of the Rule.

Source: Paschal Robinson, OFM, ed., trans., *The Writings of Francis of Assisi* (Philadelphia: Dolphin Press, 1906), 64–66, 68–70. Original in Latin. Modernized by Nathan Melson.

Chapter 2: Of Those Who Wish to Embrace This Life and How They Ought to Be Received

If anyone wishes to embrace this life and come to our brothers, let them send them to their provincial ministers, who alone have the power of receiving brothers. But let the ministers diligently examine them regarding the Catholic faith and the sacraments of the church. And if they believe all these things, and if they will confess them faithfully and observe them firmly to the end, and if they have no wives, or, if they have and their wives have already entered a monastery, or have, with the authority of the diocesan bishop, given them permission after having made a vow of continence [sexual abstinence], and if the wives be of such an age that no suspicion may arise concerning them, let them [the ministers] say to them the word of the holy Gospel that they go and sell all their goods and strive to distribute them to the poor. If they are unable to do this, their good will suffices. And the brothers and their ministers must take care not to interfere with their temporal affairs, that they may freely do with their affairs whatsoever the Lord may inspire them [to do]. If, however, counsel should be required, the ministers shall have power of sending them to some God-fearing men by whose advice their goods may be distributed to the poor.

Afterwards, let them be given clothes of probation, that is, two tunics without a hood and a cord and breeches and a small cape reaching to the cord, unless at some time the same ministers may decide otherwise according to God. Once the year of probation is finished, they shall be received to obedience, promising to observe always this life and rule. And according to the command of the Lord Pope, they will in no way be allowed them to go out of this way of life, because, according to the holy Gospel: "No man putting his hand to the plough and looking back is fit for the kingdom of God." [Luke 9:62] And let those who have already promised obedience have one tunic with a hood, and if they wish it another without a hood. And those who are obliged by necessity may wear shoes. And let all the brothers be clothed in poor garments, and they may mend them with pieces of sackcloth and other things, with the blessing of God. I admonish and exhort them not to despise or judge men whom they see clothed in fine and showy garments using dainty meats and drinks, but rather let each one judge and despise himself.

Chapter 4: That the Brothers Must Not Receive Money
I strictly enjoin on all the brothers that in no way may they receive coins or money, either themselves or through an intermediary. Nevertheless, for the necessities of the sick and for clothing the other brothers, let the ministers and *custodes* [custodians] alone take watchful care through spiritual friends, according to locations, seasons, and cold climates, as they shall deem necessary, except always that, as has been said, they shall not receive coins or money.

Chapter 5: Of the Manner of Working
Let those brothers to whom the Lord has given the grace of working labor faithfully and devoutly, so that in banishing idleness, the enemy of the soul, they do not extinguish the spirit of holy prayer and devotion, to which all temporal things must be subservient. They may, however, receive as the reward of their labor, the things needful for the body for themselves and their brothers, with the exception of coins or money, and that humbly, as befits the servants of God and the followers of most holy poverty.

Chapter 6: That the Brothers Shall Appropriate Nothing to Themselves, and of Seeking Alms and of the Sick Brothers
The brothers shall appropriate nothing to themselves, neither a house nor place nor anything. And as pilgrims and strangers in this world, serving the Lord in poverty and humility, let them go confidently in quest of alms, and they should not be ashamed, because the Lord made Himself poor for us in this world. This, my dearest brothers, is the height of the most sublime

poverty which has made you heirs and kings of the kingdom of heaven: poor in goods, but exalted in virtue. Let that be your portion, for it leads to the land of the living; cleaving to it unreservedly, my best beloved brothers, for the Name of our Lord Jesus Christ, never desire to possess anything else under heaven.

And wheresoever the brothers are and may find themselves, let them mutually show among themselves that they are of one household. And let a brother make his needs known to another brother with confidence, for, if a mother nourishes and loves her carnal son, how much more earnestly ought one to love and nourish his spiritual brother! And if any of them should fall into illness, the other brothers must serve him as they would wish to be served themselves.

Chapter 7: Of the Penance to be Imposed on Brothers Who Sin

If any of the brothers, at the instigation of the enemy [Satan], sin mortally by those sins for which it has been decided among the brothers that recourse should be had to the provincial ministers alone, the aforesaid brothers must have recourse to them as soon as possible, without delay. But let the ministers themselves, if they are priests, impose penance on them with mercy; if however they are not priests, let them have it imposed by other priests of the Order, as it may seem to them most expedient, according to God. And they must beware lest they be angry or troubled on account of the sins of others, because anger and trouble impede charity in themselves and in others.

Reading questions

- Based on these chapters, what seem to be the chief ideals of the Franciscan order? How does it enforce or regulate a lifestyle based on those ideals? What practical issues or problems might arise for the friars trying to follow this rule?
- How does *Francesco* depict Francis and his brothers living out the manner of life outlined here?
- Why do you think that people were drawn to either join or support the Franciscans in their life and ministry?

NOTES

1. On Francis's life and the founding of the order, see John R. H. Moorman, *Saint Francis of Assisi* (London: SCM Press, 1950); John R. H. Moorman, *A History of the Franciscan Order from Its Origins to the Year 1517* (Oxford: Clarendon Press, 1968); Augustine Thompson, OP, *Francis of Assisi: A New Biography* (Ithaca, N.Y.: Cornell University Press, 2012); André Vauchez, *Francis of Assisi: The Life and Afterlife of a Medieval Saint* (New Haven, Conn.: Yale University Press, 2012).

2. For more on the debate about poverty in the Franciscan Order, see M. Christina Bruno's chapter on *The Name of the Rose* (1986) in this book.

3. On the high-to-late medieval evolution of the canonization process, see André Vauchez, *Sainthood in the Later Middle Ages* (Cambridge: Cambridge University Press, 1997), 22–57.

4. For a discussion of the issues surrounding the use of various hagiographic accounts of Francis's life, including the story collections, see Jaques Dalarun, *The Misadventure of Francis of Assisi* (St. Bonaventure, N.Y.: Franciscan Institute, 2002).

5. Aviad Kleinberg, *Prophets in Their Own Country: Living Saints and the Making of Sainthood in the Later Middle Ages* (Chicago: University of Chicago Press, 1992).

6. For an introduction to the emergence of monastic rules, see Albrecht Diem and Philip Rousseau, "Monastic Rules (Fourth to Ninth Century)," in *The Cambridge History of Medieval Monasticism in the Latin West*, ed. Isabelle Cochelin and Alison I. Beach (Cambridge: Cambridge University Press, 2020), 162–94.

7. For more on St. Benedict's rule as it applied to nuns, see Lucy Barnhouse's chapter on *Vision* (2009) in this book.

8. Moorman, *History of the Franciscan Order*, 54–56.

9. Heribert Holzapfel, OFM, *The History of the Franciscan Order*, trans. Antonine Tibesar, OFM, and Gervase Brinkman, OFM (2009), 18, https://franciscanstudies.com/2018/10/03/history-of-the-franciscan-order-by-heribert-holzapfel-ofm/.

10. See Michael Blastic, OFM, Jay Hammond, and Wayne Hellmann, OFM, eds., *The Writings of Francis of Assisi: Rules, Testament and Admonitions* (St. Bonaventure, N.Y.: Franciscan Institute, 2011).

11. Regis J. Armstrong, *Francis of Assisi, Early Documents*, vol. 1, *The Saint*, annotated ed. (New York: New City Press, 2002), 69–70.

12. For a discussion of the differences between the 1221 and 1223 Rules, see Ryan Thornton, "Defining Franciscan Poverty," in *Franciscan Poverty and Franciscan Economic Thought (1209–1348)* (Leiden: Brill, 2023), 26–70.

13. For a more in-depth discussion of the Franciscan Rule and its context, see Holly J. Grieco, "The Rule of Saint Francis," in *A Companion to Medieval Rules and Customaries*, ed. Krijn Pansters, Brill's Companions to the Christian Tradition, 93 (Leiden: Brill, 2020), 283–314.

14. On the use of provincial organization by mendicant orders, see Hans-Joachim Schmidt, "Establishing an Alternative Territorial Pattern: The Provinces of the Mendicant Orders," in *Franciscan Organization in the Mendicant Context: Formal and Informal Structures of the Friars' Lives and Ministry in the Middle Ages*, ed. Michael Robson and Jens Röhrkasten (Münster: LIT Verlag, 2010), 1–18.

15. Armstrong, *Francis of Assisi, Early Documents*, 1:126.

16. Cavani and Mazzoni's script also plays with the timeline of events, compressing together moments that happened years apart or in a different sequence. For instance, Clare of Assisi's vow and hair-cutting to show her adherence to Francis's way of life happened much later than as shown in the film. Moreover, she did not live among the brothers but was instead cloistered by Francis in a nearby Benedictine convent.

CHAPTER FOUR

POVERTY AND HERESY IN *THE NAME OF THE ROSE* (1986)

By M. Christina Bruno

Jean-Jacques Annaud's 1986 film adaptation of Umberto Eco's 1980 novel is just as complex, dark, and occasionally unsettling as its source material.[1] In his opening titles, Annaud calls the film a "palimpsest" of the novel. A palimpsest is a text superimposed over another obscured text. This gives the audience an immediate clue about what Annaud wanted to accomplish with his film. Eco's novel is a famous example of metanarrative, where the main action (a medieval murder mystery) takes place in a frame story (the narrator Adso of Melk's retelling of the story), which is itself framed by another story (the author finding a [fictional] manuscript containing Adso's tale). While Eco did not consult on the film and was ambivalent about what it was able to achieve, Annaud's reading of Eco's novel does bring across some of Eco's vision of the malleability and power of language and the way in which it reflects, reveals, or conceals the truth.[2]

The film opened to mixed reviews and a middling box office performance. Critics like Roger Ebert bemoaned everything from the film's pacing to how visually dark the film is; at certain points, especially if you're watching on a small screen, you may struggle to make out the action.[3] But it has since become something of a sleeper favorite for its evocative setting in real monasteries in Italy and West Germany and the rich performances of the international cast.

The film opens in 1327, as the Franciscans William of Baskerville (Sean Connery) and his novice Adso of Melk (Christian Slater) approach an unnamed abbey in the north of Italy, where they are to take part in a debate between members of the Franciscan Order and representatives of Pope John XXII (r. 1316–34) on the poverty of Christ. On their arrival, the inquisitive William (modeled on historical Franciscan philosopher William of Ockham and the fictional Sherlock Holmes) is asked to investigate a murder, initially thought to be a suicide, which turns into a series of murders in the abbey.

As he and Adso close in on the culprit, linking the murders to a mysterious book housed in the abbey's capacious but secret library, and as the poverty debate reaches its climax, the inquisitor, Bernardo Gui (F. Murray Abraham), arrives to undo William's investigation, eager to reach his own conclusions about the murders and to settle a personal score with William. William's investigation, which infers from the murders the existence of a copy of a lost fifth book of Aristotle's *Poetics* on comedy, is emblematic of the film's central premise: language and investigation construct the thing they hope to say or find, and the process by which the speaker or investigator proceeds can limit the outcome. William's investigation moves from evidence to conclusions, Bernardo's from conclusions to evidence, and the consequences are, naturally, very different.

The characters in Annaud's film, then, are in search of the truth according to their own methods. The film explores this relationship between language and truth. The law of the church is woven throughout the complex plot in the high-stakes debate with papal representatives that William and his brothers have come to attend and in the dramatic inquisitorial trial conducted by Bernardo Gui that dominates the film's third act. This chapter, while far from exhaustive, examines these two legal threads in the film, which seem separate but in fact are closely connected: first, the controversy over apostolic poverty that nearly tore the Franciscan Order apart; second, the process and institution of inquisition, which sought to identify, correct, and sometimes destroy believers and supporters of unorthodox belief.

POVERTY

While we are told at the beginning of the film that William and Adso have come to the abbey to participate in a debate on poverty, the audience may be forgiven for forgetting about this fact until the film is almost half over. The murder investigation occupies all our attention, and even when a group of Franciscans arrive, led by the historical head of the order, Michael of Cesena (d. 1342, played by Leopoldo Trieste), it feels like an afterthought. The meeting of Franciscans with papal representatives devolves into a shouting match:

> "Did Christ, or did he not, own the clothes that he wore?"
> "The Gospels state categorically that Christ carried a purse!"
> "The issue is not whether Christ was poor, but whether the Church should be poor!"

We, the audience, along with William of Baskerville, are at this point fidgeting uncomfortably in our chairs with our minds on the much more pressing matter of who is committing murders in the abbey. In fact, this is just the moment that the herbalist Severinus (Elya Baskin) tries to get William's attention to tell him the all-important book has been found. Why do the assembled Franciscans and papal representatives nearly come to blows over this apparently abstruse topic? The origins of this controversy lay in the framing of poverty as a legal concept, against the backdrop of a charismatic religious movement dedicated to poverty. The debate ultimately called into question the church's authority to decide what poverty meant and dictate the sort of life vowed religious were to lead.

The religious order founded by Francesco di Pietro di Bernardone, better known to posterity as St. Francis of Assisi (d. 1226), was a mendicant order, in contrast to earlier monastic orders.[4] Mendicants (from Latin *mendicare*, to beg) took vows of personal poverty. They were also not permitted to own property collectively, unlike traditional monastic orders with their settled lifestyle and often rich abbeys, such as the Benedictine abbey in which this film is set, with its bejeweled Abbot (Michael Lonsdale). Despite the initial suspicion of church authorities and the furious disapproval of his father, Francis and his early followers lived a life of apostolic poverty. *Apostolic* here means inspired by Christ and his apostles: living in common, preaching the Gospel, and owning nothing. As Francis's reputation for sanctity grew, his followers increased. He asked for formal recognition for his order from Pope Innocent III (r. 1198–1216). Innocent was initially hesitant, but in 1223 his successor Honorius III finally approved a Rule by which the order was to live.[5]

The heart of the controversy, already incipient in Francis's day, was the Franciscan understanding of poverty. Most medieval religious swore the three solemn vows: poverty, chastity, and obedience. Chastity (refraining from sexual contact) and obedience (subjugation of one's own will to one's superiors) were by this point uncontroversial, but poverty was difficult to pin down for Franciscans. While most monastic orders understood "poverty" as an injunction against personal possessions, Franciscans interpreted poverty as both personal and corporate—neither individual Franciscans nor the order itself could own property. This presented several logistical difficulties as the number of Franciscans increased and they began to live communally rather than begging and working sporadically. How were these communities to be fed and housed? How could Franciscans inhabit houses and churches without being accused of hypocrisy? What about sick brothers who could not beg or work for themselves? What if a Franciscan needed to get an expensive university education (as William clearly has in the film)?

In the century after Francis's death, the order underwent consolidation by brother-administrators, often with legal training, who had to face the thorny problem of how to translate Francis's charismatic vision into a universally applicable administrative solution. Differences of opinion, sometimes very subtle ones, emerged immediately. Scholars have tended to use a shorthand to refer to these two groups. The "Spirituals" advocated for a rigorous understanding of poverty that left almost no room for relaxations of the Rule. The "Conventuals" or "the Community" took a pragmatic stance to the Rule. They favored letting guardians, the heads of Franciscan convents, make exceptions based on their judgment. In fact, as David Burr and others have shown, there were many shades of opinion within this spectrum, and Franciscans at the time did not call themselves "Spiritual" or "Conventual."[6]

After Francis's death in 1226, a series of reformist popes sought to intervene and find a permanent solution to the problem of how Franciscans should interpret poverty, issuing bulls (papal pronouncements identified by their opening words in Latin) for the better part of a century. Beginning with Gregory IX in 1230, popes assumed formal ownership of the goods and property that were given to Franciscans for their use, creating the legal fiction that Franciscans technically owned nothing. The most controversial of these bulls was Nicholas III's *Exiit qui seminat* (1279), which allowed Franciscans the simple use of goods but further declared that a true imitation of Christ and the apostles had to include not just lack of ownership of the goods used, but also the slippery concept of the *usus pauper* (poor use).

Peter Olivi (d. 1298), a Provençal Franciscan who taught at the University of Paris, was the primary theorizer of the rigorist Franciscan camp and its understanding of the *usus pauper*.[7] If, as popes had already established, Franciscans could use goods technically owned by the papacy without owning them, what should that use look like? In Olivi's view, Franciscans were obligated to get by using the bare minimum that they could in each situation—that is, poor use. They could not dine off golden plates and ride horses (which would be *usus dives*, rich use) just because they did not technically own them. But this *usus* could be very difficult to pin down. If a Franciscan living in the chilly north of England used an extra cloak, that could be a necessity rather than a luxury, whereas for one who lived in the sunny south of France, perhaps it was a luxury. But more disturbingly, beyond the inherent fuzziness of the concept of *usus pauper*, when *Exiit qui seminat* declared that Christ and his apostles were absolutely poor, it meant that the rest of the church, apart from the very strictest of Franciscans, were interpreting poverty in an imperfect way.

The controversy we see in *The Name of the Rose* was precipitated when Pope John XXII reopened the discussion of *Exiit qui seminat* in 1322. A shrewd lawyer who was hostile to the rigorist position, he later declared the doctrine of the absolute poverty of Christ and the apostles to be heretical. Michael of Cesena eventually came to reject John XXII's right to make this pronouncement and, in turn, declared John a heretic, fleeing to the court of Emperor Louis of Bavaria, the Pope's rival.[8] Though perhaps not the main point for the Franciscan protagonists of this story, the moment during which John overturned his predecessor's decision in *Exiit qui seminat* and the controversy that followed foreshadowed much later debates on papal infallibility.[9]

Peter Olivi was posthumously declared a heretic, but his works remained influential among other Franciscans, notably his pupil Ubertino of Casale (d. 1329, the wizened and rather frightening elder Franciscan played by William Hickey in the film). The laity too was invested in the solution to this problem, and they were watching closely. Franciscans proved popular among the urban populace throughout Europe, but especially in central and northern Italy and in Provençe. As the laity sought to follow Franciscan teachings and adapt them for themselves, many of them came under suspicion of heresy, as Louisa Burnham has explored.[10] The line between Franciscans as orthodox believers and Franciscans as heretics could be blurred over the years as doctrine was negotiated. The danger of heresy, then, underlies much of the story of how the Franciscans struggled to define poverty. This danger was felt by the church and by those Franciscans identified as heretics. Heresy also underlies the film's third act, and so now we will ask: what (or who) is a heretic, and how do you go about finding out?

INQUISITION

Almost as soon as Bernardo Gui arrives on screen, we know that he means business. It's also personal: He and William have an unhappy past association, and Bernardo is out to get him. And we are also compelled to compare

Bernardo's investigative method with William's. Where William reasons deductively, allowing evidence to take him wherever it leads, Bernardo has come with the assumption that he will find someone deserving of prosecution; and so he does, interpreting the circumstances in which he finds Salvatore (Ron Perlman) and the nameless girl (Valentina Vargas) in the worst possible light. Bernardo's method of investigation—interrogation under torture leading to confession—sheds light on a feature scholars like John Arnold argue is characteristic of inquisition: while it seeks heretics, it also constructs the heretics it seeks.[11]

Scholars like R. I. Moore have pointed to the church's increasing preoccupation with orthodoxy, or correct belief, as a precondition for its preoccupation with heresy, or incorrect belief. Once correct belief was established with an unprecedented degree of precision, everything that fell outside it was, by default, unorthodox or heretical.[12] Papal inquisitors first appeared during the 1230s. By Bernard Gui's time in the fourteenth century, there was a clear procedure in place for the investigation of heresy.[13] The film's Bernardo Gui and his companions, clad in black and white, are members of the Dominican Order, founded by St. Dominic de Guzmán in 1216. Dominicans were from their inception dedicated to teaching and fighting heresy, but they also had much in common with their fellow mendicants, the Franciscans. Like the Franciscans, they were highly mobile, theoretically owned nothing, and were directly subject to the pope.

Despite regional variation, inquisition generally unfolded according to a prescribed procedure. In an area where heresy had never been suspected, the inquisitor arrived, usually at the request of a bishop or another prelate. Often, though not always, the inquisitor was a member of a mendicant order, subject to the pope and not beholden to the bishop or anyone else locally. This meant that he could function as a sort of special prosecutor, with limited ties to the community. And while he was often called upon to investigate one matter, many other matters came to light once he began digging into peoples' beliefs and behaviors.[14]

Inquisitors first preached a sermon exhorting people to repent of their sinful ways and beliefs. Following the sermon, in locales where there had never been an inquisition before, individuals were encouraged to come to the inquisitor and inform anonymously on their neighbors. These denunciations became the basis for interrogations, the part of the inquisitorial procedure with the most sinister reputation. These interrogations, undertaken under the threat of torture, often ended in confessions (abjurations) of heresy that were of questionable accuracy.[15] They often also led to cascading accusations of heresy, where the one confessing supplied the names of other members of his or her circle. At this point, there were several possible outcomes: an abjured heretic was given a penance, sometimes onerous, sometimes light, that involved public abjuration of heresy and often humiliation. If a convicted heretic later recanted (retracted) his or her confession, he or she could be burned at the stake. The punishment could sometimes also be commuted to life imprisonment.

At the end of the process, whatever the outcome, the inquisitor ended by preaching another sermon. Bookended by events intended for public edification, the sermons underscored that the inquisitorial procedure was not only a way for the church to exercise authority over wayward believers or correct and punish the guilty, but also a teaching moment for the entire laity.

Scholars have mined inquisitors' manuals and especially inquisitorial depositions for many years for the insight they give into the beliefs and behaviors of witnesses and their society. But what are we actually hearing in records drawn up by the inquisitors' scribes? Historian John Arnold has drawn attention to the importance of the inquisitor's confessing subjects, who were asked a series of formulaic questions laid out by manuals, threatened with imprisonment and torture, deprived of the right to know their accusers or even the crimes of which they were suspected. Their words are mediated by these circumstances and so must be read critically. Inquisition, then, became a "mechanism for producing knowledge" and "a system for interrogating and interpreting all kinds of subjects," one that continually increased in the complexity of its distinctions among different types of unorthodox belief and believers.[16]

The film underscores this point beautifully. During the climactic trial scene, two of the three people under interrogation do not speak at all in a meaningful way. The girl is silent and apparently disengaged from her surroundings, perhaps not understanding the language spoken to her (presumably Latin). Salvatore speaks his strange conglomerate of languages, though he can at least make himself understood. The cellarer Remigio (Helmut Qualtinger), for Bernardo the most frightening of the three, confronts him directly, admits his heretical past, and dares Bernardo to do his worst, knowing he will die. Even he, however, immediately crumples under the threat of torture and confesses—not to heresy, but to whatever will alleviate that threat. The trial scene, however, begs a question when compared with primary sources like Bernard Gui's manual (found in the appendix), which lays out heretical beliefs in painstaking and systematic detail: how did he know what heretics believed when questioning them led to answers given for all sorts of other reasons?

CONCLUSION

Just after Adso and William meet Salvatore for the first time, William, who was an inquisitor in the past, identifies Salvatore as a Dolcinite heretic by his cry of "Penitenziagite!" The Dolcinites or Dulcinians, followers of Fra Dolcino (d. 1307), were one of many Franciscan-adjacent sects that took a position on the church's wealth. Ultimately, they found themselves to be on the wrong side of orthodoxy, along with the Beguins of southern France and the *fraticelli* ("little brothers") of Italy. But when Adso asks William about them, he is told that they were "those who believed in the poverty of Christ." Adso, perplexed, exclaims, "But, so do we Franciscans!" This exchange highlights that, for the Franciscan Order, staying on the right side of orthodoxy was far from a foregone conclusion. Franciscans could find themselves on either side of the blurry line that separated the heretical from the orthodox as they attempted to work out what poverty meant for their order and for the church. Inquisitors like Bernard Gui were watching this line carefully, intricately categorizing beliefs that could be classified as heretical. Aligning a confessing subject's recorded words with the categories that appear in the inquisitor's manual, to say nothing of the truth of the confessing subject's own belief, is a difficult matter for us no less than for the inquisitor. But as the novel's William himself says, "Books are not made to be believed. They are made to be subjected to inquiry. When we consider a book, we mustn't consider what it says, but what it means."[17]

APPENDIX

The Name of the Rose (1986)

BERNARD GUI (D. 1331), *MANUAL ON THE INQUISITION OF HERETICAL DEPRAVITY* (14TH CENTURY)

Part V, Section 4: Bernard Gui details the heretical beliefs of the Beguins and provides questions to help draw them out.
Source: Célestin Douais, ed. *Practica Inquisitionis Heretice Pravitatis* (Paris, 1886), 267–68, 277–78, 286–87. Original in Latin. Translated by M. Christina Bruno.

5. On the Erroneous, Schismatic, Reckless, and False Articles of the Said Beguins and Their Followers

First, those commonly called Beguins say and assert that they themselves are called Poor Brothers of Penitence of the Third Order of St. Francis. They believe and hold that the Lord Jesus Christ (inasmuch as he was man) and his apostles held nothing either individually, or in common, since they were perfect paupers in this world. Also, they say that this is perfect evangelical poverty, i.e., to have nothing individually, or in common. Also, they say that to have anything in common diminishes the perfection of evangelical poverty. Also, that the apostles could not have held anything, either individually or in common, without diminishing their perfection and without sin. Also, they say that to believe or assert the contrary is heretical. Also, they say that St. Francis gave his brothers in the order a Rule about the abovementioned evangelical poverty, so that those who profess the said Rule can hold nothing individually or in common beyond the poor use [*usum pauperem*] necessary for life, which should always savor of the abjectness of poverty and nothing superfluous. . . . Also, they say that whoever in any way impugns or contradicts the Rule of St. Francis (which they say is the Gospel), impugns and contradicts the Gospel of Christ, and so they err and become heretics if they persevere in it. Also, they say that just as neither the Pope nor anyone else can change, add, or subtract anything in the Gospel of Christ, so he cannot change anything in the said Rule of St. Francis, nor add nor subtract anything from the vows, or the evangelical counsels, or the precepts contained in it. . . .

7. Questions Appropriate for the Beguins of Modern Times

First, the one being examined should be asked when and where and by what minister of the order he was received into the order and professed. Also, if he was examined about the faith by the ordinary of the place, or anyone else in his stead during his reception, since the lord Pope John XXII has decreed and ordained that an examination or reception done in any other way is not valid, and is completely void and worthless. Also, with whom he associated, and where. Also, if the one examined is not a Beguin, but a great believer and friend of the Beguins, and suspected of their errors, he should be asked when he began to believe in them and adhere to them. Also, the one examined should be asked if he heard others teaching and asserting that Christ and the apostles had nothing individually or in common. Also, if he has heard it said that to hold or believe the contrary is heretical. Also, if he has heard it taught that to have anything in common diminishes the perfection of evangelical poverty. Also, if he has heard it said or taught, and if he believed and believes, that the Rule of St. Francis is one and the same as the Gospel of Christ, or that it is the Gospel of Christ. Also, if he believed or believes that, just as the pope cannot change anything in the Gospel, nor add, nor subtract anything, so he cannot change anything in the Rule of St. Francis, nor subtract, nor add anything regarding the vows or evangelical counsels or precepts contained in the said Rule. . . .

11. Instruction against the Treachery and Deceit of Those Who Respond Ambiguously, Obscurely, or Equivocally, Because They Do Not Wish to Respond Clearly and Lucidly

There are some among them who are so malicious and treacherous that, in order to obscure the truth and protect themselves and their accomplices and hide them, lest their error and falseness be known, they respond ambiguously, or obscurely, and so vaguely and unclearly to the questions asked, that it is not possible to gather the truth from their responses. Thence, asked what they believe about a proposed article, they respond: I believe about this what the holy Church of God believes; they do not wish to declare themselves explicitly, nor to respond in any other way, even when asked repeatedly. In this case, to counteract the deceit they use, or rather abuse, in the name of the Church of God, they must be interrogated diligently, subtly, and persistently about what they mean by the Church of God, whether they mean the Church of God or what *they* understand to be the Church of God, since they equivocate about the Church of God, as is obvious from their errors, since they and their accomplices and believers call themselves the Church of God. But those who hold and believe the contrary they do not hold to be the Church of God. . . .

Reading questions

- How does Bernard Gui know what the Beguins believe?
- What methods does he advocate for discovering whether the accused is a Beguin?
- What, for the inquisitor, is the most frightening aspect of the Beguin heresy?
- In *The Name of the Rose*, how might Remigio, Salvatore, or the girl answer the previous questions?

NOTES

1. Umberto Eco, *Il nome della rosa* (Milan: Bompiani, 1980), trans. William Weaver (San Diego: Harcourt Brace Jovanovich, 1983). For a discussion of how the film adapts the novel, see Robert Bartlett's chapter on the film in *The Middle Ages and the Movies: Eight Key Films* (London: Reaktion Books, 2022), 49–75.

2. Eco spoke with Annaud about the film but was not involved directly in production. See Stefano Rossi, "A Correspondence with Umberto Eco, Genova-Bologna-Binghamton-Bloomington, August–September, 1982, March–April, 1983," *boundary 2* 12, no. 1 (1983): 1–13, 10.

3. Roger Ebert, "The Name of the Rose," October 24, 1986, https://www.rogerebert.com/reviews/the-name-of-the-rose-1986 (accessed February 16, 2022).

4. On Francis's life and early experiments with poverty, see André Vauchez, *St. Francis of Assisi: The Life and Afterlife of a Medieval Saint*, trans. Michael Cusato (New Haven, Conn.: Yale University Press, 2012).

5. On the struggle to get the Rule approved and the controversy over poverty that followed, see M. D. Lambert, *Franciscan Poverty: The Doctrine of the Absolute Poverty of Christ and the Apostles, 1210–1323* (St. Bonaventure, N.Y.: Franciscan Institute, 1998), rev. ed. For Bartlett's take on poverty and heresy in the film, see *Middle Ages and the Movies*, 55–58.

6. See David Burr, *The Spiritual Franciscans: From Protest to Persecution in the Century After Saint Francis* (University Park: Pennsylvania State University Press, 2001); Michael Cusato, "Whence 'the Community'?" *Franciscan Studies* 6, no. 1 (2003): 39–92.

7. See David Burr, *Olivi and Franciscan Poverty: The Origins of the Usus Pauper Controversy* (University Park: Pennsylvania State University Press, 1989).

8. On the Michaelist controversy over papal authority, see Patrick Nold, *Pope John XXII and his Franciscan Cardinal: Bertrand de la Tour and the Apostolic Poverty Controversy* (Oxford: Clarendon Press, 2003).

9. See Brian Tierney, "Origins of Papal Infallibility," in *Rights, Laws, and Infallibility in Medieval Thought*, ed. Brian Tierney (Aldershot: Variorum, 1997).

10. Louisa Burnham, *So Great a Light, So Great a Smoke: The Beguin Heretics of Languedoc* (Ithaca, N.Y.: Cornell University Press, 2007).

11. See John Arnold, *Inquisition and Power: Catharism and the Confessing Subject in Medieval Languedoc* (Philadelphia: University of Pennsylvania Press, 2001).

12. See R. I. Moore, *The Formation of a Persecuting Society: Authority and Deviance in Western Europe 950–1250*, rev. ed. (Malden, Mass.: Blackwell, 2007).

13. On Bernard Gui, see Derek Hill, *Inquisition in the Fourteenth Century: The Manuals of Bernard Gui and Nicholas Eymerich* (Woodbridge: Boydell Press, 2019).

14. For a discussion of procedure and personnel involved in inquisition, see Jill Moore, *Inquisition and Its Organisation in Italy, 1250–1350* (Woodbridge: Boydell Press, 2019).

15. See Henry Ansgar Kelly, "Judicial Torture in Canon Law and Church Tribunals: From Gratian to Galileo," *Catholic Historical Review* 101, no. 4 (2015): 754–93.

16. Arnold, *Inquisition and Power*, 55.

17. Eco, *Name of the Rose*, 316.

CHAPTER FIVE

JOAN OF ARC'S INQUISITORIAL TRIAL OF FAITH IN *THE PASSION OF JOAN OF ARC* (1928)

By Henry Ansgar Kelly

Joan of Arc came out of nowhere twice: first, in 1429, when she was only seventeen, as a national champion of France during the Hundred Years' War (1337–1453); and second, much later, as a saint. Her enemies executed her in 1431 on far-fetched charges of heresy. After her mother and brothers sued for damages twenty-five years later, in a trial mandated by the pope at their supplication, these charges were repudiated, and she was restored to her original fame. But nothing more. There was no sign of venerating her as a saint until four centuries on, after the acts of her trials were published in the 1840s. In 1920 she was canonized as a saint—but not as a martyr ("witness") who died for the Christian faith.

The first significant dramatization of Joan after her canonization reflected her new sainthood in its title: George Bernard Shaw's 1923 play, *Saint Joan*.[1] In 1928, film director Carl Theodor Dreyer also saw her as a saint, which undoubtedly accounts for the seemingly other-worldly detachment Joan shows in his version of her trial. But he also went one step further and presented her as a martyr. Dreyer released his silent film of her prosecution under the title of *La Passion de Jeanne d'Arc*, "The Passion of Joan of Arc."[2] The word "passion" here means "suffering and death of a martyr." The premier passion of all time, of course, was that of Jesus, as popularized more recently in Mel Gibson's retelling, *The Passion of the Christ* (2004). Christ's passion took place in less than a day, from his agony in the garden and three trials (before the Sanhedrin, King Herod, and Pilate) to his crucifixion and burial. Dreyer mirrors this economy by compressing the action of months in Joan's ordeal to a single day. And, just as the four Gospels present different perspectives—from the "Man of Sorrows" in Matthew and Mark to serenity in Luke and confident control in John—different takes of Joan's tragedy can be found. Whereas Ingrid Bergman's calm and firm Joan reflects the Jesus of Luke and John in Victor Fleming's 1948 film *Joan of Arc*, Renée

Falconetti as Joan in Dreyer's *Passion* replicates the sense of overwhelming dread seen in Matthew and Mark's portrayal of Jesus. And Christ's example gives her strength: she is comforted by "signs" of the cross in her cell and a physical cross at the end.

To provide a proper understanding of Dreyer's cinematic retelling of this historic event, this chapter first explains the rules of due process in the inquisitorial system and how they were sometimes flaunted by Joan's time, especially in "trials of faith" (heresy trials), and then it recounts what actually happened in Joan's trial. Next, in reviewing the action of the film and Dreyer's changes in the story, especially his compressing the timeline and modeling Joan's death on Christ's, the chapter analyzes how he transformed her from a mere saint who lived a holy life into a martyr of faith. In his version, Joan is a martyr not only to the Christian faith (a faith she was accused of denying and for which she was executed), but also to her own faith in God and his revelations to her and, in consequence, a martyr to her faith in the nationalist struggle for the liberation of France.

GOOD AND BAD INQUISITIONS

Like all criminal trials of the time, the action against Joan of Arc was supposed to follow inquisitorial procedure. Inquisition was a form of trial-conduct instituted by Pope Innocent III at the Fourth Lateran Council in 1215. This was the very year in which the first Magna Carta was signed in England. Innocent's decree setting out the rules of inquisition, *Qualiter et Quando*, can be considered the church's Magna Carta.[3]

Inquisitions were supposed to work like this: when *fama publica* (general public belief) held that a certain crime was committed by a certain person, a bishop or some other church judge could use that *fama* as probable cause to start a trial (inquisition) against the person. The judge (now an inquisitor) would summon the suspect, explain the charge, and require him or her to plead guilty or not guilty, under oath, and be questioned on it. If the defendant said not guilty, he or she was to be allowed to have lawyers and call witnesses against the inquisitor's witnesses or other proofs. If these rights were violated, the defendant could instantly appeal to a higher judge—even to the pope. The purpose of the trials was to determine the truth of public accusations and either exonerate the suspects or convict and punish them (and, implicitly, correct or rehabilitate them).

When the method was adopted by the new heresy inquisitors in France twenty years later, they largely followed these rules for the first generation or so, but then they started to use a shortcut (doubtless with the excuse of safeguarding the community from dangerous doctrines). Instead of bothering with *fama*, they simply put suspects under oath and started interrogating them, not even telling them what crimes they were suspected of. If they mentioned something wrong, or said something wrong, it became immediately notorious, so there was no need for *fama*. They had confessed.

It was still true that the defendants had the right to remain silent—that is, to refuse to submit to pretrial interrogation—and to know the charges, and to see proofs of *fama*, and to have an attorney, and to enter appeals. Most of them, however, did not know that they had these rights. There was no *Miranda* law in place. If they did know the law, unscrupulous judges could simply refuse to honor it. This was the situation that Joan found herself in.[4]

A HERESY CONVICTION SOUGHT FOR JOAN

Joan of Arc was finally captured at Compiègne in the diocese of Beauvais, fifty miles north of Paris, on May 23, 1430, by Burgundians soldiers, in league with the occupying English. It was decided, doubtless at the urging of the now pro-English University of Paris, that she should not be treated as a prisoner of war but should be convicted in a church court and put to death. The charge would have to be heresy, in a trial of faith, because heresy was the only religious crime that entailed a death penalty.

In France, a heresy trial could be held either by the regional heresy inquisitor, by the suspect's bishop, or by both together. When Joan was captured, a sub-inquisitor stationed at the University of Paris applied for the job immediately, but the English authorities assigned the inquisition instead to the bishop of Beauvais, Pierre Cauchon (r. 1420–32), who was in their pay. He eagerly accepted, but, perhaps because his jurisdiction over Joan was questionable, he wished the "Holy Inquisition" to share the responsibility. Therefore, he co-opted the local Rouen sub-inquisitor, Jean Lemaistre, prior of the city's Dominican friars. Lemaistre was clearly reluctant and participated only out of fear. He refused to sit as judge until permission came through from his superior three weeks after Joan first appeared in court. Cauchon also appointed the "promotor" or prosecutor from his diocese, a priest named Jean Estivet, to be his promotor here. Official notaries recorded the original "French Record," but after the trial Cauchon had one of his chief allies among the consultants, Thomas Courcelles (1400–1469), a theology professor from the university, compile the "Latin Record," which was full of sly distortions.[5]

A letter in the Latin Record, in the name of the ten-year-old King Henry VI of England (r. 1422–61, 1470–71), states that Joan was turned over to Cauchon for trial on January 3, 1431, in Rouen in Normandy. She was not put in church custody but was held chained in a prison cell at Rouen Castle, guarded by English soldiers. The courtroom was the Castle chapel, which was declared temporary Beauvais territory. She first appeared there seven weeks later, on February 21, with her shackles still on, brought in by the priest Jean Massieu, the urban dean of Rouen. Judge-Inquisitor Cauchon was seated there, surrounded by nine consultants, including Courcelles (Courcelles expanded this to forty-one in his Latin Record, but left himself out).

By law, Estivet was supposed to present the charges against Joan immediately, so that she could deny them and defend herself. Instead, he simply delivered her to Cauchon to be put under oath and questioned, which went on for weeks. Cauchon soon appointed another Paris theologian, Jean Beaupère, to assist him. At each session Cauchon tried to make her swear a blanket oath to respond to all his questions, but Joan resisted him forcefully each time. The records frequently show Joan objecting that the questions had nothing to do with their case against her. At one point, she insisted that the consultants be polled on the subject. But they all agreed that it was relevant (see the primary text from the Latin Record included in the appendix to this chapter). From Cauchon's point of view, anything was relevant that could be used or twisted against her. Legally, nothing was relevant until she was charged, and even then, only the charges would be up for interrogation. Joan was interrogated in open sessions six times during the first two weeks, and then, after a week, in her prison cell, for nine more sessions over eight days (March 10–17), with just a few university consultants present. During this latter time, Lemaistre took his place as official co-judge.

Then, however, Jean Lohier, a noted jurist of the Rouen diocese who was passing through the city, a judge at the papal court in Rome, threw a wrench into the proceedings, saying that what they had done so far was illegal and invalid. Cauchon ignored most of his strictures (e.g., the hostile make-up of the court, no counsel for Joan), but he did remedy one defect. Lohier had pointed out that no charges had yet been made against her. Cauchon scheduled two days (March 27–28) for Estivet to present his "book" against her, and Joan pleaded not guilty to everything. This "contesting of the case" was the beginning of the actual trial.

But it made little difference to Cauchon's plan. Even before Estivet delivered his charges, Cauchon had ordered yet another Paris theologian, Nicholas Midi, to make a digest of Joan's previous answers. The resulting "Twelve Articles" distorted her responses—for instance, having her admit to foretelling the future and refusing to submit to the church. These articles were sent out to experts for comment, notably those at the University of Paris, many of whose professors had served as consultants at the trial, as we have seen. The university responded that she should be convicted of heresy. They identified no heresy committed by her, but did say, unprecedentedly, that wearing male clothes was an error in faith.

In the meantime, Cauchon set up three more sessions with Joan in April and May. The first two were ostensibly designed to persuade her to see the light and agree with them (in the first she was very ill, and doctors were brought to her). In the third encounter, she was threatened with torture if she did not answer more fully. Joan remained completely undaunted, and it was decided that there was already enough to condemn her. Sentence was set for May 24, to be delivered in the public square.

On the scaffold, Joan repeated her appeal to the pope that she had made earlier. Cauchon rejected it, saying the pope was too far away. He began to read the sentence, convicting her of such things as divination, concocting visions, cruelty, and making errors of faith (no word of heresy). At this point, Joan faltered in her resolve for fear of the fire that awaited her and agreed to go along with the judges, renouncing her visions and submitting to the church as they wished. Massieu read to her a short abjuration of a few lines, to which she agreed, and then Cauchon sentenced her to perpetual prison.

Four days later, Cauchon and Lemaistre confronted her in her cell, finding her dressed again in male clothes and affirming her visions, and they took this as signs that she had relapsed into heresy. There was supposed to be another trial on this new charge, and the consultants urged it. However, Cauchon sentenced her on the next day without further ado, convicting her of relapse into "many errors and crimes," such as schism, idolatry, and invoking demons. She was immediately burned at the stake.

DREYER'S CINEMATIC INTERPRETATION OF THE PROCEEDINGS

Dreyer indicates that his account will be true to history by showing hands flipping through the Latin Record at the beginning of the film. He then shows the beginning of Joan's interrogation, in the Rouen Castle chapel, with twenty or so clergymen taking their seats; they are all identified as judges, rather than as consultants. Cauchon (Eugène Silvain) is shown in the middle, very busy. The jovial sub-inquisitor Lemaistre (Gilbert Dalleu), in his Dominican habit, is already in place beside him, on his left. The hawk-nosed judge who first appears at Cauchon's right is Nicolas Loiseleur (or l'Oiseleur, "the Birdcatcher," played by Maurice Schutz). Historically, he was a sinister but minor player who, before he started to show up as a consultant, had pretended to be a prisoner from Joan's home region—he even heard her confessions, which were spied upon and recorded. Dreyer turns him into the mastermind behind the whole proceedings, serving as "dramaturge" and liaison. He is the only one who confers with the English occupiers: namely, the Earl of Warwick (Camille Bardou), governor of Rouen, who appears briefly on the left, and the soldier guards, wearing World War I helmets (reminding the 1928 audience of recent enmities).

The urban dean, Jean Massieu (Antonin Artaud), played here as a young monk, ushers in the shackled Joan and is very protective of her, here and elsewhere in the film. Joan, seeming at first a quite pathetic and vulnerable creature, makes no trouble about the oath, and Cauchon starts to ask her about herself and her age. He smiles contemptuously as she counts out her years on her fingers. He asks if she can say the Our Father, and who taught it to her. Joan, looking dazed and almost stupefied throughout, sheds a tear, and answers, "My mother." Beaupère (Louis Ravet), seated in front of Lemaistre, asks about her mission, and she hesitantly says that she was sent to save France. When she says that the English will be driven out, except those who die here, there is an uproar among the judges and the guards—and the latter are settled down by Loiseleur.

Dreyer does not use panning shots, but only start-stops and closeups, often with blank backgrounds. It produces a disorienting effect, reflected in Joan's bewildered glances. Cauchon leads the quizzing about the clothing of St. Michael in her visions, and the other judges shout out questions. A query about her male clothes gets passed along by Cauchon through Lemaistre to

Beaupère, and he asks, "Did God command it?" When another question—"What reward do you expect?"—is passed through to the corpulent Estivet (André Berley), a sympathetic judge is flashed on the screen, warning her not to answer by drawing his finger across his mouth. When she responds, "The salvation of my soul," Estivet, after a double take, accuses her of blasphemy and comes over and spits in her face. Another sympathizer, Nicolas Houppeville (Jean d'Yd), objects to all this, declaring that he considers her a saint, and kneels down at Joan's feet. He then leaves the courtroom. Loiseleur and Warwick confer, and a troop of soldiers go out after him.

Cauchon calms the courtroom and resumes the effort to get Joan to incriminate herself. Here, Dreyer presents his version of the fifth day of questioning, which should be contrasted with the actual record given in this chapter's appendix. He asks Joan to say what God promised her. She responds that that has nothing to do with their trial. Cauchon very genially maintains the contrary, and, instead of Joan demanding to hear the opinion of the consultants, as in the record, Cauchon himself calls for a vote from the "judges." Hands go up for the yeas, with only young Martin Ladvenu in the back hesitating. But with a sharp glance from Cauchon, he too raises his hand. Cauchon gets Joan to admit that God promised her escape, but when she says that she does not know when, he impatiently ends the session and sends her to her cell.

The overt sympathy of Massieu and the actions of Houppeville and Ladvenu are not historical. Houppeville was never seated in the court, but rather had been sent to prison by Cauchon for speaking in defense of Joan (though not before he observed the fear of his friend, co-judge Lemaistre). Dreyer puts him here to stress his theme that Joan was regarded as a saint in her own day. Ladvenu, Joan's confessor later on, does service at this point in the film for his fellow friar, Isambart Lapierre, who, according to retrial testimony, tried to signal to Joan one time when he was seated next to her and was furiously rebuked for it by Warwick.

Much of the action that follows is also invented business. After Joan is taken out of court, we see Loiseleur conferring with the English captain of the guards, telling him that they will not get her to confess unless they use wiles. We next see him in her cell gaining her confidence with a forged letter from King Charles (this establishes that she can't read). She is then interrogated briefly by Cauchon and Lemaistre in her cell and is soon brought to the torture chamber. In the original screenplay, Cauchon finally presented the charges against her in this climactic scene, reading them from a parchment sheet, and she rejected them. But in the film, she is never told the charges, but simply urged by the judges to sign an abjuration sheet, after being told by Beaupère and others that her visions were not from God but from the Devil. The sheet, flashed several times on the screen, has her confess only to making up her visions. When she refuses to sign, she is threatened with the torture instruments, which start spinning, causing her to faint and become deathly ill. The captain is concerned that she not die a natural death, and a doctor bleeds her. At her continued refusal, even after she is offered Communion in exchange, Cauchon summons the executioner.

On the scaffold, the preacher tells her that her king is a heretic and urges her to sign the abjuration. Loiseleur whispers to her to sign and to live to fight on for her king, and guides her hand in signing it. He then hands it to the captain, who indignantly throws it away. We are doubtless meant to see that Loiseleur has achieved the judges' real goal, which is not Joan's death, but her conviction and imprisonment. This is an interesting twist on Dreyer's part, to some extent redeeming the judges.

Back in prison, after her hair is cut off, Joan bitterly regrets her submission, which was done out of fear, and sends for the judges. They ask, does she still believe that she was sent by God? She says yes. This seals her death, as Massieu realizes. Cauchon and Loiseleur and the other judges present are genuinely sorrowful at what she, and they, have done.

But now Joan is energized. She tells Massieu that her victory will be her martyrdom. She goes to confession to him (during which a sign is nailed to the stake: RELAPSED HERETIC, APOSTATE, IDOLATER), and she receives Communion, while Loiseleur sadly looks on. At the stake, Joan accepts her death, embracing a cross, praying God to make it soon. When someone in the crowd shouts, "You have burned a saint!," a riot erupts. The film ends with a scroll saying that Joan will always be honored by France. She has won, in heaven and on earth; her martyrdom is complete.

CONCLUSION

Joan of Arc's death was a judicial murder. It was facilitated by the inroads that had been made upon inquisitorial procedure, especially in tolerating pretrial interrogation. The chief villain in the matter, apart from the English occupiers of France, was Bishop Cauchon. Efforts have been made to excuse him: the playwright George Bernard Shaw, for instance, thought he was sincere, according to his "lights."⁶

Dreyer made a similar judgment in the film's Preface, blaming Joan's fate on "blinded theologians." Historically, "biased and malicious" might have been more accurate, given the role of the Paris professors. But in the film, Cauchon and Loiseleur and their cronies seem more conniving than either misguided or outrightly ill-willed toward Joan. They want to trick or force her into confessing what they consider her real offenses, but they also wish her to save herself by abjuring. The historical Cauchon often expressed charitable intentions toward Joan in the proceedings. But the consensus and verdict of history are undoubtedly correct: Cauchon was a venally motivated "hanging judge," whereas Joan was completely innocent—and perhaps even more: a saint.

APPENDIX

The Passion of Joan of Arc (1928)

THE LATIN RECORD, JOAN'S FIFTH DAY IN COURT (MARCH 1, 1431)

Thomas Courcelles's Latinizing and reworking of the French Record of the trial, presented as an open letter from the judges, Bishop Cauchon and Vice-Inquisitor Lemaistre.

Source: Pierre Tisset, ed., *Procès de condemnation de Jeanne d'Arc* (Paris: Société de l'Histoire de France, 1960),1:85–88. Original in Latin. Translated by Henry Ansgar Kelly.

Asked whether Saints Margaret and Catherine spoke to her under that tree, she said, "I don't remember."

Asked if the saints spoke with her at the fountain next to the tree, she replied, yes, she did hear them there, but no longer remembered what they said.

Asked what the saints promised her, there or elsewhere, she replied that any promises they made were with God's permission.

Asked what sort of promises they made, she replied, "That has nothing to do with your case against me here." She added, however, that one of the things they told her was that her king would be restored to his kingdom, whether his enemies liked it or not. She also said that the saints answered her prayer to accompany her into paradise.

Asked if they made another promise, she said yes, but she would not say what it was, and it had no relevance to their case. But then she said that she would say what the promise was in three months' time.

Asked if the voices said that she would be freed from prison within three months, she said, "That doesn't concern your case. Besides, I don't know when I'll be freed." She added that those who wished to remove her from this world might very well leave it before she did.

Asked if her saints would tell her if she would be freed from her present prison, she said, "Ask me again in three months and I'll tell you about it."

Then she said, "Have the consultants say on their oath whether this concerns the case."

The consultants deliberated on the matter, and they all concluded that it was pertinent to the case.

She then said, "I've always well and truly told you that I won't tell you everything. It's a sure thing that I'll be freed sometime. But I need permission to talk about it—that's why I've asked for a delay."

Asked if her voices forbade her to tell the truth, she replied, "You want me to tell you what will happen to the king of France? That and lots of other things don't concern your case here." She said that she knew for sure that her king would get his kingdom back, just as sure as she knew that we [i.e., Bishop Cauchon] were there before her in court. She added that she would be dead now if it were not for the revelations that comforted her every day.

Asked what she did with her mandrake [plant with alleged man-shaped root], she answered that she never had a mandrake. She did hear that there was one near her village, but she had never seen any. She also heard that it was dangerous and bad to keep. But she did not know what it was for.

Asked where the mandrake was that she had heard about, she said it was supposedly near that tree they talked about but was not sure exactly where. She also heard that there was a hazel tree over it.

Asked what she heard the mandrake was used for, she said that it was supposed to make money, but she didn't believe a word of it. Also, her voices never spoke about it.

Asked what shape St. Michael appeared in, she said she saw no crown and remembered nothing about his clothing.

Asked if he was naked, she said, "Do you think God can't find clothes for him?"

Asked if he had hair, she said, "Why would it be cut off?" She said that she had not seen St. Michael since she left the castle of Cotroy—and in fact she never did see him very often. She finally said that she did not remember if he had hair.

Asked if he had his pair of scales, she said, "I don't remember." She also said that she was always very happy when she saw him, since it seemed clear to her then that she was not in the state of mortal sin. She said that Saints Margaret and Catherine liked to make her go to confession to them, each in turn. If she was in mortal sin, she said, she did not know it.

Asked if, when she went to confession, she believed that she was in mortal sin, she said that she did not know, but believed that she had never committed anything to make her so. "Please God," she said, "I may never do such things, and please God I have never burdened my soul with them."

Asked what sign she gave her king when she came to him "from God," she said, "I keep telling you that you'll never pry that from my mouth! Go ask him!"

Asked, did she not swear to tell everything connected with this case that was asked of her, she said, "You won't get that from me!" As for being connected to the case, she said, "You won't get anything from me that I promised to keep secret. I can't break my promise about this and tell you without committing perjury."

Reading questions

- In this excerpt, what are the questioners after? How does Dreyer's *Passion of Joan of Arc* mirror the type of questioning found in this medieval source?
- Why does Joan refuse to answer some questions? In what ways does the film reflect this resistance through its imagery, Falconetti's performance as Joan, and/or dialogue (in the intertitles)?
- Do you think the questions in this source actually concern her case (i.e., heresy)? Why or why not?

NOTES

1. Shaw's play was adapted by Graham Greene for Otto Preminger's 1957 film *Saint Joan*, with Jean Seberg. See Kevin J. Harty, "Jeanne au cinéma," in *Fresh Verdicts on Joan of Arc*, ed. Bonnie Wheeler and Charles T. Wood (New York: Garland, 1996), 253–55.

2. For the much different original screenplay, see Carl Theodor Dreyer, *Four Screenplays* (Bloomington: Indiana University Press, 1970).

3. Henry Ansgar Kelly, *Criminal-Inquisitorial Trials in English Church Courts* (Washington, D.C.: The Catholic University of America Press, 2023), 419.

4. Henry Ansgar Kelly, "The Right to Remain Silent: Before and After Joan of Arc," *Speculum* 68, no. 4 (1993): 992–1026.

5. Pierre Tisset, ed., *Procès de condemnation de Jeanne d'Arc* (Paris: Societé de L'histoire de France, 1960–71), vol. 1. For an abridged translation, see Daniel Hobbins, *The Trial of Joan of Arc* (Cambridge, Mass: Harvard University Press, 2005); for W. P. Barrett's complete 1932 translation, see https://sourcebooks.fordham.edu/basis/joanofarc-trial.asp.

6. Much the same verdict is given by Hobbins in the introduction to his translation. For comment, see Henry Ansgar Kelly, "Questions of Due Process and Conviction in the Trial of Joan of Arc," in *Religion, Power, and Resistance from the Eleventh to the Sixteenth Centuries*, ed. Karen Bollerman et al. (New York: Palgrave Macmillan, 2014), 81–100.

"FEUDAL" LAW AND THE CUSTOMS OF LORDSHIP

CHAPTER SIX

THE CHIVALRIC CODE IN *THE GREEN KNIGHT* (2021)

By Coral Lumbley

"Honor? ... Honor. That is why a knight does what he does." So stammers Gawain, a young would-be knight with lofty aspirations, as portrayed by Dev Patel in David Lowery's 2021 film *The Green Knight*. Lowery made the creative decision to adapt the medieval English story of *Sir Gawain and the Green Knight* (written by an anonymous author just before 1400) not as a mainstream action or fantasy film, but an arthouse film. It thus privileges aesthetic elements like visual images, emotional impressions, and atmosphere over conventional elements like plot, character development, and resolution. Viewers know that the film will be unusual from the very start. Five minutes into the movie, a series of intertitles appear on screen. These lines do not reveal the title of the film. Instead, they read, "a Filmed Adaptation of / the Chivalric Romance / by Anonymous / Sir Gawain and . . ." This unfinished announcement is only completed in the final shot of the film, with text reading, "The Green Knight."

Lowery wants his contemporary audience to know that the movie has a medieval origin, and he communicates this in a manner that shows us it will be a strange and mysterious viewing experience. In many ways, Lowery's film is true to the genre of medieval chivalric romance, a type of narrative that typically features knightly quests, mysterious and magical ladies, and terrifying beasts or monsters. Both the film and medieval romance are cyclical narratives about magic and adventure, chivalric placidity in the face of horrors, and the inevitability of human weakness among the greatest of societies and individuals.

The Green Knight is a highly divisive film, and audiences tend to love or hate Lowery's art-focused, alternative approach. The film was warmly received by critics. Brian Tallerico of RogerEbert.com admired its "surreal tone" and "poetic eye," praising how it transported the audience: "We're all just sitting in that banquet hall, listening to the story requested by King Arthur, told by a master storyteller."[1] A. O. Scott of the *New York Times* called the film "sumptuous, ragged and inventive," and Peter Bradshaw of the *Guardian* noted the "visual brilliance of this film combine[d] . . . shroomy toxicity and inexplicable moral grandeur: what a stunning experience."[2] Mainstream audiences, however, were more divided. As of May 2023, the film has a 50 percent "Fresh" rating on RottenTomatoes.com, with many critics characterizing the film as slow, confusing, inaccessible, or pretentious.[3] Some viewers claimed that you have to know the medieval story to appreciate the film. Others claimed that knowing and loving the medieval story makes it impossible to appreciate the film, which they saw as an unfaithful adaptation.

"Faithful" or not, Lowery delivers a coming-of-age story in which young Gawain takes the audience on a quest to discover what it means to be honorable, what it means to be a knight. In medieval Europe, chivalry was a code of behavior that delimited and legalized certain forms of violence and social control, regulating how warriors engaged in warfare, love and sex, and religion. "Chivalric texts," observed Richard Kaeuper, "urged mercy for helpless, defeated opponents, yet vengeance, a particularly prickly sense of honor, and [the] unrestrained joy in the skilled and vigorous use of edged weaponry [also] animated chivalric ideology."[4] This chapter analyzes two critical aspects of the so-called chivalric code as interpreted in the film's narrative: first, the concept of chivalry itself and, second, its deconstruction of "honor," which provides a new perspective on the medieval source text. In fact, the film's happy ending features Gawain as a knight—not one knighted by a king, but one who has achieved internal honor. Honor, divorced from status, is the prize Gawain wins on his quest.

CHIVALRY

Chivalry is so significant in western European cultural history that it has been called "the ideological framework for lay society for nearly five centuries."[5] In the twenty-first century, the word "chivalry" typically refers to social etiquette derived from traditional gender roles. Men who insist on opening doors or doing small favors for women may be referred to as "chivalrous," and this gender-based behavior is often seen as insulting or patronizing. This new use of the term is actually a great simplification of its original use, in which it referred to a social and legal system that regulated the behavior of upper-class male warriors. An international culture of refined, courtly behavior arose in Britain and France in the twelfth century. Within this new culture, warriors had to uphold courteous, chivalrous behavior to be considered knights.

The Old English word *cniht* (pronounced kuh-neekt) originally referred to a young male servant, akin to what modern English speakers might call a "squire," or a knight's apprentice. But around 1100, *cniht* came to refer to a loyal champion of a king or lady, and the concept of knighthood (a vocation or job) became inseparable from the chivalric code (a form of upper-class etiquette).[6] In the broadest terms, chivalry was a medieval worldview and performative code of conduct in which certain men were expected to embody four major values: military strength and bravery; spiritual humility and piety; gallantry in their treatment of women; and personal honor and virtue.[7] This courtly behavior became standard in the 1100s, but the word "chivalry" did not enter the English language until the fourteenth century, when it was borrowed from the Old French term *chevalerie* during the violent Hundred Years' War (1337–1453) between England and France.[8] Just as modern audiences enjoy stories about great warriors and superheroes, medieval audiences loved tales of great *chevaliers* (knights) like Sir Gawain, King Arthur's nephew and a famously chivalrous knight. In Welsh, he appeared as Gwalchmei, a hero in the first full-length tale about King Arthur, in *Culhwch and Olwen* (c. 1100). He gained popularity in the Latin *History of the Kings of Britain* (1136) and *De Ortu Waluuanii* (*The Rise of Gawain*, twelfth century), and he became especially beloved by English readers, appearing in tales like *Sir Gawain and the Carl of Carlisle* (c. 1400), *The Wedding of Sir Gawain and Dame Ragnell* (fifteenth century), and *Sir Gawain and the Green Knight* (c. 1400), a selection from which can be found in this chapter's appendix.

Sir Gawain and the Green Knight is considered one of the greatest works of medieval English literature.[9] This chivalric romance explores questions of perfection and fallibility, with Sir Gawain attempting—and failing—to achieve perfection as a knight. Taking place during the early years of King Arthur's rule, this narrative poem tells the story of a supernatural Green Knight who appears in Camelot. He offers to receive a strike to the neck if a brave knight will agree to receive one in turn. Gawain bravely accepts this deal and chops off the Green Knight's head with the knight's own axe. One year later, Gawain takes the axe on a quest to find the Green Chapel and receive his end of the deal. On the way, Gawain visits a mysterious castle in the forest, where the lord Sir Bertilak proposes a Game of Winnings. For three days, each man will give the other what he wins during that day. Much to Gawain's surprise, the lord's wife attempts to seduce him every day while her husband is out hunting. To uphold the chivalric code, Gawain must find a way to refuse her advances but not cause her offense. This results in Lord Bertilak bringing animal pelts to Gawain and Gawain giving kisses to the Lord. However, Gawain commits one act of dishonor: on the final day, the Lady gives him a magic green girdle that will protect him from the Green Knight. Afraid for his life, Gawain keeps this a secret from Lord Bertilak. When Gawain arrives for the Beheading Game, the Green Knight reveals his own secret: he himself is Lord Bertilak, he told his wife to tempt Gawain, and this whole plot was devised by the sorceress Morgan le Fay to frighten Queen Guinevere! Gawain is humiliated and furious. However, the Green Knight/Sir Bertilak forgives Gawain and sends the knight back home to Camelot, a little worse for wear.

Lowery's version of Gawain differs greatly from the medieval source material, not least due to the casting of Patel, a British Indian actor, as the protagonist.[10] Far from being chivalrous or heroic, Patel's Gawain is lazy and cowardly. The film's main action opens on a fire raging outside the castle walls, with Gawain sleeping peacefully despite the conflict. This is a key point for the film's depiction of chivalry: this code's military dimension involved requiring battle on horseback, or participating in the cavalry (that is, among other horse-riding warriors). Although Gawain, the nephew of the King, should be riding into the battle, we instead see an unnamed soldier performing valiant deeds. The soldier unsheathes his sword, puts a woman on horseback and sends her to safety, then runs into the fray alone. This form of bravery and selflessness is expected of a knight, and the credits reveal that these events unfold in Gawain's dreams. In his dreams, he witnesses great deeds, but does not perform them.[11] Indeed, Gawain wakes and goes to a feast, showing that he coasts through life depending on inherited wealth and undeserved status.

Historically, knighthood did require a measure of wealth. A warrior had to manage the expense and upkeep of a complicated, valuable military kit.[12] When Gawain sallies forth from Camelot on horseback with arms and armor, he displays this level of social privilege for all to see; hence, the observations of the young Scavenger (Barry Keoghan) that Gawain looks and smells like a knight. When the Scavenger and his friends ambush Gawain, saying that because Gawain would not render charity to them, they'll take it by force, Gawain's external appearance begins to match his internal status. He is literally unhorsed, stripped of his *cheval* as well as his axe, tied up, and left for dead. As the camera pans around in a full circle, Gawain and the audience contemplate his future as a skeleton, forever lying on the forest floor. This spurs Gawain to make an effort, perhaps for the first time in his life. He bravely slices the ropes off his wrists, slicing his hands open on a sword, and survives to continue the quest.

When Gawain encounters a strange and ghostly woman based on St. Winifred (Erin Kellyman), he agrees to retrieve her head, which is at the bottom of a lake. This is an opportunity for Gawain to prove his worth, to show that the image of the Virgin Mary on his shield represents true internal piety. However, Gawain pauses and asks, "If I go in there and find it, what would you offer me in exchange?" Winifred is shocked: "Why would you ask me that? Why would you ever ask me that?" No properly chivalrous knight would demand rewards of a young female saint in distress, and Gawain has almost failed his second major test. Humbled, he retrieves the head with no promise of reward. Still, his axe is magically returned to him by Winifred. According to the film, Gawain is beginning to learn what it means to be a knight: to perform dangerous deeds for a righteous cause.

Of course, it was not enough for a chivalric hero to be a great fighter; he also had to be a great lover. This particular aspect of chivalric identity has come to be known as "courtly love," a system of romantic behavior still legendary today. Courtly love was, most importantly, expected to ennoble the lover and provide a system to regulate sexual desire. After the so-called Norman Conquest of 1066, the new French aristocracy brought their language and culture to Britain, cultivating refined modes of courtship. Around 1190, Andreas Capellanus wrote a text called *De Amore* (*On Love*), noting that "love is a certain inborn suffering derived from the sight of and excessive meditation upon the beauty of the opposite sex, which causes each one to wish above all things the embraces of the other."[13] Performative, heterosexual desire—often without sexual consummation—was key to chivalric identity.

To his own detriment, Gawain is a poor lover. In fact, his relationship with the sex worker Essel (Alicia Vikander) becomes a key indication of his internal growth as a knight. When Gawain awakens in the brothel, it becomes clear that he is friendly with many of the sex workers and that he visits Essel frequently. When Essel says she wants to become Gawain's Lady, meaning his wife, he highlights their class difference, saying, "I could give you more gold than any Lady has." Gawain essentially tells Essel that since he can purchase her body, she should be content with their relationship. Undeterred, Essel tells Gawain exactly what she wishes he would say to her: "You may have my ear and my hand and heart. And I will be king and you my queen." Gawain never speaks these words. Instead, he goes on his quest (against Essel's wishes) and accepts the secret gifts and sexual overtures of an aristocratic Lady (also played by Alicia Vikander), the wife of the Lord (Joel Edgerton) in a mysterious forest castle.[14]

To his credit, Gawain begins to deeply reconsider his romantic and sexual habits as his own death looms closer. In the film's climax, he imagines an alternative future in which he runs away from the Green Knight's final blow, breaking his agreement and losing honor. This act of cowardice creates a trajectory in which Gawain's whole life is dishonorable. This alternate Gawain gets Essel pregnant, then rips her baby away minutes after she gives birth. He raises the bastard child as a soldier. Essel grows old alone while Gawain marries a delicate, porcelain-skinned princess from another land. These self-serving actions ultimately do little good; he ends his life as the lonely, hated king of a defeated realm. This vision leads Gawain to a resolute determination to live honorably, even if this leads to his death. In this way, Lowery's depiction of romantic love follows the pattern of the chivalric romance genre. Romantic love—and his realization that his treatment of women is dishonorable—ennobles Gawain to become a chivalric hero.

HONOR

These three values of chivalry—military prowess, spiritual purity, and romantic idealism—are often external performances. A knight undertook these performances to convince others—and perhaps himself—that he was a man of honor. But honor, the intangible target of Gawain's quest, was the key trait that a chivalric knight had to cultivate, and the one most important to the value system presented in the film. Texts like the *Book of Chivalry*, by Geoffroi de Charny (1306–56), a French knight with over two decades of battle experience, testify to the importance of gaining honor, with those who have the "greatest heart" winning the highest honor.[15]

When the Lord of the forest castle asks what Gawain hopes to gain from his encounter with the Green Knight, Gawain responds as though he is being quizzed. "Honor?" he says without confidence, and the Lord is surprised. "Are you asking me?" he responds. Gawain tries to muster confidence, and states, "Honor. That is why a knight does what he does." Through his friendly questioning, the Lord gets Gawain to articulate the crux of the film:

> LORD: And this is what you want most in life?
>
> GAWAIN: To be a knight.
>
> LORD: No, honor. [Chuckles]. You are not very good with questions.

It is clear that Gawain has neither thought about nor discussed these topics in depth. He unwittingly admits that he wants the trappings of knighthood—fame, reputation, and admiration—without having to live with honor. Furthermore, Gawain does not even seem sure that he wants these things; perhaps he only wants to want them. The Lord continues to ask if this single quest will lead to the life Gawain wants:

> LORD: "You'll do this one thing, you return home a changed man, an honorable man? Just like that?"
>
> GAWAIN: Yes.
>
> LORD: "Oh, I wish I could see the new you. . . . But perhaps we will miss our old friend and our fun and our games."

The Lord calls the quest itself into question, as do Essel and the Lady. Gawain hopes to attain knighthood, a seat among the other knights of Arthur's court, but he is unsure of how to do so. In this way, Lowery invites critique of the chivalric system itself. Yes, the system asks men to cultivate honor, but as we see with Gawain—and even Arthur himself—the system is prone to corruption and weakness. It takes itself quite seriously, but it can be easily manipulated by magic and nature, as we see in the spells of Gawain's mother (Sarita Choudhury) and in the speech on "green" by the Lady.

Gawain tries over and over to gain the honor that will allow him to claim the title of "knight," a praiseworthy champion of the chivalric code. This is difficult because he is not quite sure what honor really is. In a fumbled attempt to gain honor, he beheads the Green Knight in Arthur's court, hoping that this hyper-violent deed will gain him fame and notoriety. This needless deed leads to a grueling quest that challenges him to undertake other impressive feats of arms. It is not until the film's ending that Gawain is able to perform impressive *internal* tasks, ones that demonstrate the true honor in the world of the film. When Gawain takes off his magical protective belt and stoically kneels to have his head chopped off, the Green Knight gently says, "Well done, my brave knight." Gawain receives no fanfare, no crown, and no celebrity. Along with the audience, Gawain comes to understand that knighthood is about internal honor. It is not about knighting ceremonies, castle feasting, or widespread fame. Only by rejecting these external signs of knighthood and relying on internal honor can Gawain become a true knight.

CONCLUSION

Fittingly for a story featuring doubles (Mother/Sightless Woman, Essel/Lady, Lord/Green Knight), this film inverts the medieval text. In the modern film, Gawain is a layabout who finally becomes a knight, delivering a story about the importance of internal honor. In the medieval text, Sir Gawain is an already-famous knight who slips up and commits an embarrassing act of dishonor, creating a tale about the natural imperfection of even the greatest of humans. The medieval text also features an ending that does not appear in the film. The Green Knight reveals himself to be the Lord Bertilak, who knows that Gawain is wrongfully wearing a secret, magical green girdle given by Bertilak's wife. Gawain returns to Camelot and shows the girdle to the whole court in repentance, saying:

> This is the token of the dishonesty I was caught committing
> and I must wear it for the rest of my life;
> for a man may hide his mistake, but never undo it,
> for once it has taken root it will never come out.[16]

The film alludes to these lines in Gawain's alternative future. In that future, Gawain never takes off his green girdle, made by his mother. It literally takes root in his body, absorbing into his abdomen until he rips it out, causing his own head to roll from his shoulders. His dishonor is his undoing.

In some ways, the medieval text is far gentler than the film. The medieval court laughs at Gawain's embarrassment, encourages him not to take it too seriously, and decides to wear green girdles in his honor. "And he who wears it is honored for evermore," says the anonymous author of *Sir Gawain and the Green Knight*.[17] In contrast, Lowery's ending refuses to turn back to Arthur's court, to the chivalric system into which Gawain has imbricated himself. Honor must be tried and measured outside of public systems, and even in the face of inevitable failure and death, we should—we must—try our very hardest to do good along the way. Lowery opts for an ambiguous end for Gawain; when the Green Knight smiles and says, "Now, off with your head," does he mean that Gawain should be off, intact, or that he will now chop Gawain's head off?

This is for the audience to decide. The point is not whether Gawain lives or dies in the end, for we all die in the end. The point is that finally, if only for a moment, he lived with honor.

APPENDIX

The Green Knight (2021)

ANONYMOUS, KNOWN AS THE GAWAIN-POET OR PEARL-POET, *SIR GAWAIN AND THE GREEN KNIGHT* (C. 1400)

Gawain and the Green Knight meet and play a game.

Source: James Winny, ed., *Sir Gawain and the Green Knight* (Toronto: Broadview Press, 1992), Fitt 4, Lines 2309–73 and 2388–2415. Original in Middle English. Translated by Coral Lumbley.

Lines 2309–2373:

In the Lord's castle, Gawain agrees to a game, an exchange of winnings: and the Lord Bertilak will give each other what they get for three days. Gawain upholds the bargain for two days but keeps the Lady's magic protective green girdle on Day 3. Later, the Green Knight feints twice, then prepares to deal the third and final blow:

> He deftly lifts his ax and lets it fall down
> with the blade's edge biting at the bare neck;
> though he hammered harshly, it didn't harm [Gawain] any more
> than a slight slash that sliced the skin on that side.
> The blade cut the flesh of the delicate neck,
> so that bright blood spurted over his shoulder onto the earth.
> And when [Gawain] saw the blood splatter onto the snow,
> he leapt away with both feet, more than a spear length,
> seized his helmet, and jammed it on his head,
> darted down with shoulders under his shield,
> brought forth a bright sword, and fiercely speaks—
> never since he was born of his mother
> was a man in this wide world half so relieved.
> "Desist, man, from your attack, you command me no more!
> I have taken a strike without any resistance,
> and if you come at me anymore, I will readily pay you back,
> and return it right away—and trust that for sure—
>   and with force.
>   Only one stroke is due to me.
>   The agreement says so,

> formed in Arthur's hall,
> and therefore, take it, and go!

The [Green] knight stood a ways away, and rested on his axe,
set the shaft on the ground and leaned on the blade,
and looked at the young man who stood in the glade.
How that doughty, fearless, aggrieved man stood there
armed and undaunted. He liked him in his heart.
Then [the Green Knight] spoke merrily with a loud voice,
and with this resounding voice he said to the knight,
"Bold knight, in this place do not be so angry.
No man here has ill-treated you,
nor acted contrary to the agreement that was made at the king's court.
I promised you a stroke and you've had it, consider yourself well paid.
I release you from the remainder of all my other rights.
If I had been more unrestrained, perhaps a blow
I could have given you wrathfully, to rouse your anger.
But first, I playfully scared you with a fake blow,
and gave you no wound, rightly doing so
for the agreement we made on the first night,
when you faithfully and truthfully held up our troth
and gave me all your winnings, as a good man should.
The second fake blow I gave you, sir, was for the next morning
when you kissed my lovely wife—you rightly gave me those kisses.
For both these events I gave you just two harmless "blows"
> without injury.
> True man repays truly,
> and he need not fear.
> On the third day you failed,
> and therefore you took that tap.

For it is my belt you are wearing, that same woven girdle.
My own wife gave it to you, I know it well and truly.
I know all about your kisses, as well as your courtesies
and the wooing by my wife. I arranged it myself.
I sent her to test you, and truly I think
you are the most faultless man who ever walked the earth.
As pearls are of greater price than white peas,

so is Gawain, in good faith, before other gay knights.
Only here you failed a little, sir, and lacked loyalty,
but that was not because of wiles, nor wooing,
but only because you loved life, and so I blame you the least."
The other brave man stood there studying [the Green Knight] a long while.
[Gawain] was so aggrieved and angry he shuddered within.
All the blood in his breast burned in his face.
He shrank with shame at what the man had said.

Lines 2388–2415:
Then the other man [Bertilak] laughed, and lovingly said,
"I consider it entirely gone, the wrong you gave me.
You have confessed so completely, admitted your mistakes,
and have done penance on the edge of my axe.
I consider you absolved of that sin, and pure and clean
as though you had never committed a sin since you were born,
and I give you, sir, the gold-hemmed girdle.
Because it is as green as my clothes, Sir Gawain, you may
think upon this meeting, when you go forth
among high-ranked princes. It will be a true token
of the adventure of the Green Chapel among chivalrous knights.
And you shall come back to my castle this New Year,
and we will enjoy revels for the remainder of this high feast
>					with great joy."
>				He took [Gawain] fast by the hand
>				and said, "With my wife, I know
>				we'll get you reconciled,
>				though she was your keen enemy."

"No, indeed," said the knight, and seized his helmet
and took it off handily, and thanked the noble man.
"I have sojourned too long: good tidings be with you,
and may He who dispenses all honors send you rewards!
And commend me to that courteous one, your comely wife,
both that one and the other, the honored ladies
who have beguiled this knight with their game.
It is no wonder if a fool acts madly
and gets tricked into sorrow by the wiles of women. . . ."

Reading questions

- How do ideas of fairness and repayment operate in the medieval text and in the film *The Green Knight*?
- What is the role of women in the chivalric system of the medieval text? Compare and contrast this role with how women are portrayed in the film.
- In the text, the Green Knight is Sir Bertilak in disguise. In the film, the identities of the two figures are much more ambiguous. Why do you think the filmmakers made this change?
- Is fear of death more acceptable in the medieval text or in the film?

NOTES

1. Brian Tallerico, "The Green Knight," *RogerEbert.com* (July 20, 2021), https://www.rogerebert.com/reviews/the-green-knight-movie-review-2021.

2. A. O. Scott, "*The Green Knight* Review: Monty Python and the Seventh Seal," *New York Times* (July 29, 2021), https://www.nytimes.com/2021/07/29/movies/the-green-knight-review.html; Peter Bradshaw, "*The Green Knight* Review—Dev Patel Rides High on Sublimely Beautiful Quest," *Guardian* (September 24, 2021), https://www.theguardian.com/film/2021/sep/24/the-green-knight-review-dev-patel.

3. "The Green Knight," https://www.rottentomatoes.com/m/the_green_knight.

4. Richard W. Kaeuper, *Holy Warriors: The Religious Ideology of Chivalry* (Philadelphia: University of Pennsylvania Press, 2012), 6.

5. Elspeth Kennedy and Richard W. Kaeuper, "Historical Introduction," in *A Knight's Own Book of Chivalry*, by Geoffroi de Charny (Philadelphia: University of Pennsylvania Press, 2013), 2.

6. *Oxford English Dictionary*, s.v. "knight, n.," April 2023, https://doi.org/10.1093/OED/3926635212.

7. On chivalry as a theatrical performance, see Peter Sposato and Samuel Claussen, "Chivalric Violence," in *A Companion to Chivalry*, ed. Robert W. Jones and Peter Coss (Woodbridge and Rochester, N.Y.: Boydell Press, 2019), 99–117.

8. *Oxford English Dictionary*, s.v. "chivalry, n.," July 2023, https://doi.org/10.1093/OED/1047172768.

9. There are several excellent modern English translations and Middle English editions of the poem. See, for example, Marie Borroff, ed., *Sir Gawain and the Green Knight: A New Verse Translation* (New York: W. W. Norton, 1967) and James Winny, ed., *Sir Gawain and the Green Knight* (Toronto: Broadview Press, 1992).

10. On the film's treatment of Patel's race, see Tirumular (Drew) Narayanan, "'Why Is He Indian?': Missed Opportunities for Discussing Race in David Lowery's *The Green Knight* (2021)," *Arthuriana* 33, no. 3 (2023): 36–59.

11. The credits also establish the figures as the ancient Helen of Troy and Paris. See Tasha Robinson, "*The Green Knight's* DP Clears Up One of the Movie's Big-

gest Mysteries," *Polygon* (August 28, 2021), https://www.polygon.com/interviews/22645517/green-knight-interview-colors-meaning-easter-eggs-helen-of-troy.

12. See Peter Coss, "The Origins and Diffusion of Chivalry," in Jones and Coss, *Companion to Chivalry*, 1–32; Ralph Moffat, "Arms and Armour," in Jones and Coss, *Companion to Chivalry*, 159–85.

13. Andreas Capellanus, *De Amore*, trans. J. J. Parry (New York: Ungar, 1959), 28. See also, in this book, Lorraine Stock's chapter on *Braveheart* (1995) and its appendix source for more discussion on *De Amore*.

14. On Lowery's framing of the seduction scene, see Tison Pugh, "Seminal Semiotics and Pornographic Displeasures in David Lowery's *The Green Knight* (2021)," *Arthuriana* 32, no. 3 (2022): 47–57.

15. De Charny, *Knight's Own Book of Chivalry*, 1:1 –5.

16. James Winny, ed., *Sir Gawain and the Green Knight*, trans. Coral Lumbley (Toronto: Broadview Press, 1992), lines 2509–12.

17. Ibid., 2520.

CHAPTER SEVEN
CRUSADING AND OATH-TAKING IN *KINGDOM OF HEAVEN* (2005)

By Esther Liberman Cuenca

Kingdom of Heaven is a loose adaptation of medieval chronicle sources that tell the story of Balian of Ibelin's defense of Jerusalem and his eventual surrender of the city to the larger-than-life general and sultan Saladin (r. 1174–93), who offered Latin Christians safe passage following his victory at the Battle of Hattin in 1187.[1] Directed by the prolific Ridley Scott, it was released at the beginning of the second Iraq War (2003–11), a series of hostilities that originated with President George W. Bush administration's erroneous claims that Iraq's president, Saddam Hussein, intended to use weapons of mass destruction against the United States and was harboring al-Qaeda, the terror organization responsible for the attacks on the World Trade Center and Pentagon on September 11, 2001. The invasion of Afghanistan in 2001 and then Iraq signaled the beginning of a larger "Global War on Terrorism."

Kingdom of Heaven was a financial risk, given its hefty price tag and heavy subject matter for a summer movie, but executives at Twentieth Century Fox Studios likely had several reasons for feeling confident about its box office prospects. Scott had made the wildly successful historical epic *Gladiator* (2000) five years earlier, winning Best Picture at the Academy Awards.[2] The following year, Scott made the rapturously received war thriller *Black Hawk Down* (2001), which depicted, through gritty and propulsive action, the futility of one American military operation in Somalia in 1993.[3] In that same period, the now-iconic *Lord of the Rings* trilogy (2001–3), directed by Peter Jackson, popularized large-scale war films set in a recognizably medieval setting. If Scott and writer William Monahan were going to make a $130 million medieval war film that served as a commentary on terrorism, religious fundamentalism, and the elusiveness of peace in the Middle East, then this was the time to do it. Yet, despite its timely subject matter and well-known cast, the film was a box office disappointment, and its critical reception was mixed.

Following its release, much was made of the film's politics, including one article that commented on the clash between Western powers and Islamic "fundamentalism" during the "war on terror."[4] A famous crusades historian, Jonathan Riley-Smith, condemned the film's framing of the conflict between Christians and Muslims as deeply ahistorical in a way that could be politically damaging.[5] Historian Thomas Madden lodged several complaints about the film in the conservative *National Review*, one of which was Scott's sterilization of medieval religion—a cinematic Jerusalem nearly absent of crucifixes, clergy, sacred icons, and Muslims or Christians at prayer.[6] The film, in his view, secularizes the lives of medieval people, who appear modern and irreligious.

The tension between the secular and religious worlds, however, was always a point of contention in the Middle Ages, though perhaps not in the way Scott depicts in his film. This chapter highlights two dramatic scenes in the film involving oath-taking—a ritual that understandably reads as "medieval" and religious to popular audiences but was, in fact, often used for secular matters. As legal practice, oaths could be unmoored from the sacred and outright broken if deemed too difficult to keep. Oath-taking, both in the Middle Ages and *Kingdom of Heaven*, intertwined the religious with the secular, and the tension between the two also illuminates the film's broader theme, which is the seeming irreconcilability between religious faith and secular politics that can promote peace.

OATH-TAKING IN MEDIEVAL EUROPE

Oath-taking is an ancient legal procedure that has survived into the present day. Oaths are religious in nature but used in secular matters. We take oaths when we become new citizens, are sworn in as witnesses, and, if elected to serve, assume political office. Like people in the Middle Ages, we swear an oath by touching a holy object, usually a Bible, in a ceremony that invokes the divine. Witnesses are to believe that our word is our bond. Oath-taking can involve rites of initiation, as well as rituals that affirm our places within our communities and our words as truthful. Oath-taking predates the Middle Ages, and evidence for people swearing oaths dates to written records of early civilizations in western Asia. "Oath" is a Germanic word originally, entering English, in written form, during the early Middle Ages. Its first documented use in early English was in the anonymous eighth-century epic *Beowulf*.[7]

In the Middle Ages, rituals involving oath-taking were not only crucial to the smooth operation of courts in which crime and other legal matters were adjudged, but also foundational to the social contract that governed the mutual obligations owed between rulers and their subjects, lords and vassals, and litigants and their communities. Oaths served two functions. They could be *assertory* statements, a declaration or *assertion* about a condition or fact that oath-takers knew to be true. For example, in the sixth-century law of the Germanic-speaking peoples known as the Salian Franks who once inhabited present-day Belgium, a convicted killer who had given up all his property in restitution and had not been able to render the full payment for his crime was to take an assertory oath. This oath required twelve sworn witnesses, who then took oaths that the convict had no other property to give up. Then he was to throw dust in the direction of his kin, who were liable for making up the financial deficit.[8] This may sound primitive, but rituals like these allowed communities then, as now, to bear witness to oath-takers swearing to what they know. The oath-takers' professed truthfulness could be recorded, if not in writing, then in the consensus of a shared public memory of the event. Oath-takers were not only responsible for their words not endangering their souls, but also for their testimonies strengthening the community's consensus on a potentially divisive matter.

The most common oaths found in medieval narratives from which we gather so many of our popular images of crusading are the second kind, *promissory*. Here, oath-takers *promised* publicly that they would fulfill some obligation in the future.[9] In medieval chronicles and literature, promissory oaths could take on different forms and reflect many social arrangements. When it came to the aristocratic world of warriors and kings, men-at-arms took oaths to their chieftains or rulers to profess their loyalty, and kings swore oaths to each other to seal military or dynastic alliances. Oath-taking could also be weaponized against individuals or populations, who swore oaths in subjugation to conquerors and bound themselves to new rulers to prevent further warfare and violence.

PENANCE, CRUSADES, AND OATH-TAKING

The events known popularly as the "Crusades" can be best understood as part of a larger cultural shift, especially after the first millennium CE, toward spiritual and moral purification, and heightened concerns about personal salvation. Popular movements and rituals abounded with distinct interpretations about what it meant to be a good Christian and what one needed to do to get to heaven (or at least spend as little time as possible in the cleansing fires of purgatory). One Christian sacrament gained immense spiritual importance in this period. Penance, which constituted a variety of practices, was not punishment per se but an act of contrition that allowed the sinner to rectify her or his sins against God and the community. With penance, sinners could formally reintegrate themselves into the community of the faithful.

One form of penance was pilgrimage. The church held jurisdiction over crusading because crusading was, in essence, an armed pilgrimage, allowing Christian knights to channel their warlike energies into a penitentiary movement, which took on all the burdens of pilgrimage to fulfill the sacrament of penance. In fact, the word "crusade" does not enter the English vernacular until the thirteenth century, or about a century after the First Crusade (1096–99).[10] Oath-taking during the crusading movement was important from the time crusading began in the eleventh century. Those who intended to go on crusade swore an oath, or vow, that bound them to their mission, which was governed under the rules of canon (or church) law. In swearing oaths, crusaders were not only bound by promises to embark on their pilgrimages, but also to behave with the moral rectitude expected of Christian pilgrims.[11] Crusading oaths, however, also guaranteed crusaders certain protections and privileges. Pilgrims and crusaders, as made clear by some canon law jurists in the twelfth and thirteenth centuries, were not to be harassed, were subject to receive charity or housing, and were allowed confession even in places under interdict (that is, when people of a certain region have been excommunicated and barred from receiving sacraments).[12]

Without a doubt, the most famous of such oaths during the crusades were the ones sworn to Byzantine emperor Alexios I Komnenos (r. 1081–1118) at the beginning of the First Crusade, which was arguably the only "successful" crusade because aristocrats from Western Europe achieved Pope Urban II's objective: the conquest of the Holy Land. At the time, the Byzantine emperor and Pope Urban II (r. 1088–99) sought to heal a political rift between Rome and Constantinople. Alexios also sought Urban II's assistance to recapture parts of Asia Minor (Turkey) that were lost in battle to the Seljuk Turks in decades prior. Alexios implied that he wanted mercenary fighters sent his way, but the pope had other plans. The expedition known as the First Crusade was a collection of several aristocratic, not mercenary, armies mainly from Francia (France). When these armies arrived in Byzantium, Alexios was suspicious of their intentions.[13]

A famous account of Alexios's encounters with the Franks appears in his biography *The Alexiad*, written by his daughter, Anna Komnene (1083–1153). According to the Byzantine princess, the Frankish knights had stopped in Constantinople as envoys and heads of armies, answering Urban II's call for an armed pilgrimage to Jerusalem. Seeing the Franks as uncultured, brutish, and untrustworthy, Anna relates how her father extracted fealty oaths from them, and the Franks broke their oaths as soon as it was politically convenient. Anna details many instances of oath-taking in her book. In her estimation, oaths taken by these Franks were "worthless" and "amounted to no more than words."[14] This was not Anna's condemnation of oath-taking as an unreliable practice, but rather her extremely low opinion of the Franks, who besmirched their own honor when they broke their oaths.

It was during the Second Crusade (1147–50) that another pope, Eugenius III (r. 1145–53), outlined more firmly the spiritual rewards crusaders would find when they promised to embark on their journeys. Eugenius III issued the papal bull *Quantum praedecessores* (1146) in response to the fall of one of the crusader states, the County of Edessa. Addressing King Louis VII of France (r. 1137–80), the pope promised the crusaders protection of their property, and stated that all those who went on crusade would garner formal remission for their sins, continuing the tradition that his predecessor Urban II had informally established.[15] The spectacular failure of the Second Crusade—the inability to recapture Edessa—and the rivalries between the other crusader states (Tripoli, Jerusalem, and Antioch) serve as the political backdrop of the events depicted in *Kingdom of Heaven*.

A KINGDOM OF HEAVEN, COLONIALISM, AND OATH-TAKING

The term "kingdom of heaven" has multiple meanings. It refers to the destination believed to await those who have waged holy war and died in a state of grace, but also the fundamental assumption that political structures on

Earth can or should mirror those in heaven. According to Christian theology, God the Father, Jesus, angels, and saints rule over a kingdom in heaven, and the "natural" order on Earth, with its kings and princes at the top of the hierarchy, reflects this ideal sacred order. The action of the film centers on the Kingdom of Jerusalem as the ironic emblem of this ideal: Even in the holiest of cities there is war and social unrest—anything but the peace that is promised in a kingdom of heaven. The film's focus on Jerusalem as a place of potential religious harmony for the followers of two major world religions, Christianity and Islam, acknowledges the city's central place in these religions' origins, though of course Jerusalem plays a different role in each. Because the film's action takes place mainly before Saladin's conquest, which triggered a Third Crusade (1187–92) to take it back from his control, the film is attempting to make a larger point about the cyclical nature of religious warfare. The film is arguing that there are figures in history, like Balian of Ibelin (Orlando Bloom) and Saladin (Ghassan Massoud), who try to break this cycle of violence, and then there are villains driven by greed, power, and bloodlust, like Guy of Lusignan (Marton Csokas) and Raynald of Châtillon (Brendan Gleeson), who would happily continue it.

The scholar Matthew Schlimm argued that the film is a representation of "neocolonialism," which can often appear to be condemning colonialism but is perpetuating damaging stereotypes of the East that justify Western military intervention. Schlimm observed that *Kingdom of Heaven* establishes characters like Raynald and Guy as examples of "bad" colonialism and celebrates figures of "good" colonialism, such as Balian, as representing its most "positive" aspects.[16] But was the crusading movement itself an example of colonialism? There has been scholarly debate about this ever since European imperialism and nationalism began to dominate world politics in the nineteenth century. As crusades historians have observed, aristocratic crusaders stood to make a very small financial gain, if at all, from engaging in expensive military campaigns in the Middle East. Thus, some have argued, critiques of medieval crusading as an effort to subjugate the region through colonization is not a correct interpretation; the crusades were costly and had a spiritual purpose, and the crusader states were not necessarily colonial outposts for any one centralized power in Europe. Other scholars, however, have contended that the crusading movement—its members responsible for the slaughter of Jerusalem's inhabitants in 1099—placed Jerusalem under military and political occupation by outsiders from Western

Europe well into the twelfth century.[17] Either way, it is not difficult to see how histories of crusading can be rich texts for discussions of religious and ethnic conflict in the modern era.[18] The film's depiction of Jerusalem as a place in which men can remake themselves and find new lands to cultivate draws a clear parallel between romantic notions of modern colonialism and medieval lordship.

The film's protagonist, Balian of Ibelin (c. 1143–93), is based on a real person, though the movie takes substantial liberties with Balian's biography. Balian was born in the Holy Land and was a great lord in *Outremer* (the Old French term for the crusader states), but in the movie he is a humble blacksmith from France. Balian, unlike his cinematic counterpart, had also married into a powerful family. His wife, Maria Komnene (c. 1154–1217), had been queen consort in Jerusalem from 1167 to 1174 and was the grandniece of a Byzantine emperor. Much of what we know of Balian's life comes from medieval chronicles. The short, Latin-language *Libellus de expugnatione Terrae Sanctae per Saladinum* (or: *Little Book on the Conquest of the Holy Land by Saladin*) describes Balian of Nablus, as he was also known, fleeing the Battle of Hattin so quickly that he ended up trampling other Christians underfoot. (The Battle of Hattin in *Kingdom of Heaven*, you will notice, is excised from the film; only its aftermath is shown, likely because the last set piece, Saladin's siege of Jerusalem, was very costly to film.) There are far more flattering portraits of Balian elsewhere. He appears most memorably in a chronicle known as William of Tyre's *Old French Continuation*, which recounts Balian's various deeds in mostly positive terms.[19]

Near the end of the first act of *Kingdom of Heaven*, Balian enters a candlelit chapel to take a solemn oath in front of his dying father (Liam Neeson), who ends the ritual dramatically by slapping Balian's face, telling him to remember his oath to defend the Holy Land and the people within the walls of Jerusalem. In this moment, Balian undergoes a rite of passage, taking a promissory oath pledging himself to the cause. This oath-taking ceremony in the first act of the film also foreshadows the oath-taking scene at the end of the film, when Balian bestows knighthood to all defenders of Jerusalem. In this scene, oath-taking no longer signifies merely a personal transformation but a ritual that binds Jerusalem's inhabitants together in the military, if not spiritual, defense of the city.

This scene is a cinematic version of events told in several chronicles, especially the Old French *Chronique d'Ernoul et de Bernard le Trésorier* (or: *The*

Chronicle of Ernoul and of Bernard the Treasurer, an excerpt from which can be found in the appendix). A certain Ernoul, who may have been a squire in Balian's service, perhaps compiled this work in collaboration with a monk named Bernard, who was the treasurer of Corbie abbey in the thirteenth century.[20] The *Chronique* was adapted from William's *Continuation* and provides an account of oath-taking that crossed religious boundaries, a practice not uncommon in the Middle Ages. The *Chronique* describes several events adapted in the film, including Saladin's decapitation of Raynald of Châtillon for being insolent, though the film suggests Saladin executes Raynald for also killing his sister (which never happened). In the *Chronique*, the patriarch of Jerusalem (who in the film, as played by Jon Finch, is craven) insists that Balian was not bound to keep his oath to Saladin, to whom he promised a truce. The patriarch then formally relieves Balian of his obligation to honor his oath. According to the chronicler, Balian breaking his oath to Saladin allowed him to take charge of the city, prepare for the defense of Jerusalem, and grant knighthood to sixty men. The latter move is somewhat reflected at the end of the film in the triumphant oath-taking scene, though here Balian's bestowal of knighthood on all the foot soldiers signals a democratization of heroism, reflecting his role in the film as the everyman leader.

CONCLUSION

Oath-taking in the medieval world permeated almost every interaction that involved promises and testimonies in a formal setting. All legal business in the Middle Ages was public in nature, and oaths even more so, given that they had to be sworn in front of witnesses to be legally binding. Oath-taking, solemn promises, and vows are frequently depicted in medieval movies and TV shows. They often show how characters build relationships of trust and how political alliances are formed. For the viewer, breaking an oath usually signifies the creation of conflict and the breakdown of social bonds. In much the same way, the evidence for taking oaths found in medieval sources shows how people forged connections to each other—in friendship, uneasy truces, formal allegiances, and through subjugation. But people in the Middle Ages frequently broke these connections if the occasion arose. Despite oath-taking being a public and religious act, sworn on Bibles or relics and in front of witnesses, it was fundamentally a flexible contract, subject to changing circumstances and the whims of the people who swore them.

APPENDIX

Kingdom of Heaven (2005)

THE CHRONICLE OF ERNOUL AND OF BERNARD THE
TREASURER (MID-13TH CENTURY)

Chapter XV: Saladin beheads Raynald of Châtillon, and Balian of Ibelin prepares for Jerusalem's defense after being relieved of his oath.
Source: L. de Mas Latrie, ed., *Chronique d'Ernoul et de Bernard le Trésorier* (Paris: Jules Renouard, 1871), 172–76. Original in Old French. Translated by Esther Liberman Cuenca.

Now we will tell you about the [Muslims] who defeated the Christians and captured them. They made camp, and Saladin gave thanks to our lord for the honor which he had given him. And he sent an order to the army for all the captured knights to be brought to his tent, and they were brought to him. It was commanded that all the barons be brought and placed before him in a tent so that he could see them, and the others left outside. The king was brought to him. Saladin had the king [Guy of Lusignan] seated before him. Prince Raynald of Châtillon was brought in afterward, then Humphrey his stepson, then the Master of the Temple, then the Marquis Boniface of Montferrat, then Count Joscelin, then the constable Aimery (whose brother was king), then the king's marshal. All these great men were taken with the king in the battle. This day was Saturday and the feast of Saint Martin le Bouillant before August.

When Saladin saw the king and his barons at his mercy before him, he was greatly overjoyed. And he saw that the king was hot, so he knew he would drink gladly. The king was fetched a plain cup of syrup to drink and cool down. When the king had drunk, he extended the cup to Prince Raynald of Châtillon, who was beside him. When Saladin saw before him that the king had given a drink to Prince Raynald, the man he hated most in the world, Saladin was greatly upset.

Saladin then told the king that he regretted that they had given [Reynald] to drink, but because they had, he should drink well, [for] he would never drink again as he would not let him live for all the possible wealth they could give [Saladin]. Instead, he would cut off his head with his own hand, for he had neither faith nor belief in any truce that he had given.

When Prince Raynald had drunk, Saladin took him out of his tent and demanded a sword. They brought one to him, he took it and cut off Prince Raynald's head. And he had the head picked up and ordered that it be dragged through all the castles and the cities of his lands. And so it was.

After Saladin cut off Prince Raynald's head, he took the king and all his prisoners and sent them to prison in Damascus. And he left that place and went to stay near Tiberius. When the countess [Eschiva de Bures] saw that the king had been taken prisoner, and that the Christians had been defeated, she surrendered Tiberius to Saladin to save her life. And that same day Saladin sent his men to Nazareth, which surrendered to him. On the same day as the Christian defeat, two cities surrendered, Tiberius and Nazareth. On Wednesday, he went to Acre, which surrendered to him. After, he headed to Tyre, but he did not want to lay siege because the cavalry was still inside, as well as the barons and the knights, who had escaped from the battle.

Now came Balian of Ibelin, who was within Tyre, and sent a message to ask Saladin for permission to go to Jerusalem, to bring the queen his wife and his children. And [Saladin] gave [Balian] leave willingly, so that in Jerusalem he would stay only one night, and no arms would be borne against him. When Balian came to Jerusalem, the people of the city were very happy, and there was great joy on his arrival. And they surrendered the city. They prayed to God that [Balian] protect [the city] and be its ruler. He said that he could not stay long. He promised Saladin that he would only stay one night, that he could neither stay nor protect the city. But the Patriarch [of Jerusalem] came to him and said: "Sire, I absolve you of the sin and of the oath that you have given Saladin. And I say to you that the greater sin would be in keeping, rather than breaking, the oath you swore because great shame [and great reproach] would come to you and your heirs if you left the city of Jerusalem in such a state. You will not have honor nor any truth [if you were to flee]."

So, Balian promised he would stay. All the people of the city paid him homage and acknowledged him as lord. Queen [Sibylla], the wife of King Guy, was still in Jerusalem. Now, there was no one in the whole city of Jerusalem except two knights—they had escaped from the battle. Balian then took as many as sixty sons of townsmen and made them knights. And I tell you that, truly, the city was still full of people, of women and children who fled into the city when they heard the king had been captured and the Christians defeated. I tell you, truly, that there were so many [people] they could not even fit inside the houses, so they spilled into the streets.

Then the Patriarch went to Balian to have the monument on the Sepulcher uncovered. It was all made of silver. He had it brought out and minted money to give to the knights and soldiers, each day, for wages. [Every day] the knights and the soldiers surrounded the city [and] brought whatever food they could find into the city, for they knew very well that they would be besieged.

Reading questions

- In *Kingdom of Heaven*, the Patriarch of Jerusalem suggests to Balian that he and others could save themselves by converting to Islam, which they can later reject. How does that version of oath-taking compare with Balian's in the film?
- How does the film's version of oath-taking compare with Balian, Saladin, and the Patriarch's attitudes toward oath-taking as described in *The Chronicle of Ernoul*?
- How does *Kingdom of Heaven* and *The Chronicle of Ernoul* compare in their depictions of the medieval world's social and religious classes?
- How do you think Saladin is portrayed in *Kingdom of Heaven*? Does he compare more favorably in the film or in *The Chronicle of Ernoul*? Why or why not?

NOTES

1. Nickolas Haydock and E. L. Risden, eds., *Hollywood in the Holy Land: Essays on Film Depictions of the Crusades and Christian-Muslim Clashes* (Jefferson, N.C.: McFarland, 2008).

2. For other "medieval" films directed by Ridley Scott, see the chapters on *1492* (1992) and *The Last Duel* (2021) in this book.

3. Simon Dalby, "Warrior Geopolitics: *Gladiator, Black Hawk Down* and *The Kingdom of Heaven*," *Political Geography* 27 (2008): 439–55.

4. John Aberth, "Kingdom of Heaven," *American Historical Review* 110, no. 4 (2005): 1235–36.

5. Jonathan Riley-Smith, "Truth Is the First Victim," *Times* (May 5, 2005), https://www.thetimes.co.uk/article/truth-is-the-first-victim-p9zsd2d7nsb.

6. Thomas F. Madden, "Onward PC Soldiers: Ridley Scott's *Kingdom of Heaven*," *National Review* (May 27, 2005), https://www.nationalreview.com/2005/05/onward-pc-soldiers-thomas-f-madden/.

7. "Oath, n.," *Oxford English Dictionary* Online, last updated December 2021.

8. Paul Halsall, "The Law of the Salian Franks," *Internet Medieval Sourcebook*, https://sourcebooks.web.fordham.edu/source/salic-law.asp, accessed March 12, 2024.

9. Ole-Albert Rønning Nordby, "The Judicial Oath in Medieval Norway: Compurgation, Community and Knowledge in the Thirteenth Century," Ph.D. diss., University of Oslo, 2018, 1–8.

10. "Crusade, n.," *Oxford English Dictionary Online*, last updated September 2021.

11. Andrew Holt, ed., "Oaths," in *The World of the Crusades: A Daily Life Encyclopedia* (Santa Barbara, Calif.: Greenwood, 2019), 2:545–46.

12. Atria A. Larson, "From Protections for *Miserabiles Personae* to Legal Privileges for International Travellers: The Historical Development of the Medieval Canon Law regarding Pilgrims," *GLOSSAE: European Journal of Legal History* 16 (2019): 167–87.

13. Jill N. Claster, *Sacred Violence: The European Crusades to the Middle East, 1095–1396* (Toronto: University Press, 2009), 35–37.

14. Elizabeth A. Dawes, ed., *The Alexiad, by Anna Comnena* (London: K. Paul and Trench, Trubner, 1928), 35.

15. Jonathan Phillips, *The Second Crusade: Extending the Frontiers of Christendom* (New Haven: Yale University Press, 2007), Chapter 3.

16. Matthew Schlimm, "The Necessity of Permanent Criticism: A Postcolonial Critique of Ridley Scott's *Kingdom of Heaven*," *Journal of Media and Religion* 9 (2010): 129–49.

17. Christopher Tyerman, *The Debate on the Crusades* (Manchester: Manchester University Press, 2015), esp. Chapter 6. See also Sylvia Throop, *The Crusades: An Epitome* (Leeds: Kismet Press, 2018), esp. Conclusion.

18. Nicholas L. Paul, "Modern Intolerance and the Medieval Crusades," in *Whose Middle Ages? Teachable Moments for an Ill-Used Past*, ed. Andrew Albin, Mary C. Erler, Thomas O'Donnell, Nicholas L. Paul, and Nina Rowe (New York: Fordham University Press, 2019).

19. Graham A. Loud, ed., "The Conquest of the Holy Land by Saladin," in *Medieval History Texts in Translation* (University of Leeds: Institute for Medieval Studies, 2010), https://ims.leeds.ac.uk/archives/translations/ (accessed November 22, 2024). For the *Old French Continuation of William of Tyre*, see Peter W. Edbury, ed., *The Conquest of Jerusalem and the Third Crusade: Sources in Translation* (Brookfield, Vt.: Scolar Press, 1996).

20. "Chronique d'Ernoul et de Bernard le Trésorier," *French of Outremer*, https://frenchofoutremer.ace.fordham.edu/index-of-sources/alphabetical-listing/chronique-dernoul-et-de-bernard-le-tresorier/ (accessed March 12, 2024).

CHAPTER EIGHT

FOREST LAW IN *THE ADVENTURES OF ROBIN HOOD* (1938)

By Casey Ireland

he Adventures of Robin Hood is the first full-length film adaptation of Robin Hood with sound, following the silent feature *Robin Hood* (1922) and five short films in the 1910s. In *Adventures*, directed by Michael Curtiz and William Keighley, Sir Robin of Locksley (Errol Flynn) is a Saxon knight who rebels against the treasonous Norman prince John (Claude Rains) and his henchman, Sir Guy of Gisbourne (Basil Rathbone), to protect the Saxon underclass. Robin uses Sherwood Forest as a base from which to recruit fighters, woo Lady Marian Fitzwalter (Olivia de Havilland), and eventually restore King Richard (Ian Hunter) to his throne. A charismatic, athletic Flynn as Robin defined the role, and the film itself was a commercial and critical success. No subsequent Robin Hood film has yet unseated *Adventures* from its place as "the definitive Robin picture."[1]

The film is set in 1191 during the Third Crusade, a time supposedly marked by intense Norman and Saxon conflict in England. But the date of 1191 overshoots that conflict by one century and predates the Robin Hood source texts by two. The writers of the film harnessed the tumult of the Angevin kings (*c.* 1154–1216) to create a stratified, precarious society divided into Norman/Saxon and just/unjust binaries that reflected contemporary Depression-era politics and New Deal policies of the 1930s.[2] Yet the social inequalities of the Angevin period, exemplified by rigid forest laws and the creation of the Magna Carta (1215) as a type of corrective, was not between "Norman" greed and "Saxon" labor, as in *Adventures*, but between aristocratic customs and monarchical overreach.

King William I (r. 1066–87) brought forest law, or *foresta* (the Latin term from which "forest" derives) to England from Normandy when he invaded in 1066. While there had been some hunting prerogatives for early English rulers prior to the Conquest, forest law was seen as an unprecedented restriction on the territory and movements of English nobility. By the late twelfth century—the period depicted in *Adventures*—forest law had codified strict parameters for use, and punishment for misuse, of royal Forests.[3] The laws were administered by a network of officials who monitored the continuously expanding territory that was legally considered Forest. And though forest laws were a concern in the fifteenth century when the Robin Hood ballads originated, anxieties at that time related to lower-class access to protected hunting areas rather than the harshness of the rules more generally.

This chapter sees *Adventures* engaging with medieval forest law in two ways: first, the film demonstrates the laws' severity and the arbitrariness with which rulers and administrators enforced them; second, *Adventures* can establish a broader understanding of the medieval forest as a royal territory with a distinct jurisdiction, the importance of poaching, and the selective application of punishment for violations of forest law. *Adventures* sought to illustrate the injustice of Norman rule; when characters poach, they balance the scales—hungry people get to eat, and harassed Saxons correct Norman overreach. *Adventures* inextricably links the rights of "free born Englishmen" with the forest, imagining that forest law—and, by extension, the royal privileges it upheld—was an aberration, rather than a normative aspect, of English law.

FORESTS AS ROYAL TERRITORY

One of the earliest scenes in the film is a hunt in Sherwood Forest. A colorful, orderly group of men, dogs, and horses chase a deer through lush, close woodland, filmed not in Nottingham Forest but in southern California. There is no attempt at camouflage or subterfuge; instead, the drama of the hunt seems as important as the eventual slaughter of the deer. This kind of hunting—ritualized and formal, with waving banners held by a massive entourage—is a classic image of the Middle Ages and one introduced to England during the Norman Conquest. Old English texts such as saints' lives and chronicles indicate that early medieval English nobility and rulers hunted, both alone and in groups, but there is no indication of the scale and pageantry we see in the hunt scene in *Adventures*. By the time of Richard I (r. 1189–99), close to one-third of England was considered royal Forest, subject to its own legal protections, courts, and administrators.[4] In this scene, we first see the distinction between kingswood and greenwood—between Forests as protected territory and forests as idealized physical spaces.

Sherwood Forest in *Adventures* is not an untouched wilderness, but it also is not a theme park. There are cleared open spaces and dense wooded areas—places to hide, hunt, and meet. We usually think of forests as spaces with heavy tree cover, but not all the land Norman rulers considered Forests fit this criterion. The Franks introduced the term *foresta* (stemming from the Latin *foris*, or "outside of") in the Merovingian period (*c.* 450–750) to separate royal hunting grounds from *nemus*, the more commonly used word for woodlands.[5] "Forest," then, belongs to an administrative legal lexicon that refers to "land that had been placed off-limits by royal decree [that once] 'afforested,' or declared a forest . . . could not be cultivated, exploited, or encroached upon."[6] Post-Norman Forests included areas with more or less tree cover; they also might include villages and arable land. For forest law, the more useful definition of Forest is a landscape that provided both controlled access to game and tax revenue for rulers.

His establishment of royal Forests was not well received by William I's new subjects. An Old English epitaph of the king included in the 1087 entry of the Peterborough Chronicle famously derided the ruler as one who "loved the deer as if he were their father."[7] The writer of the *Rime of King William* equates misrule with forest law (simplified as *laga*, or "law," in Old English) in noting how William "established a great deer park and he instituted laws therewith / That whosoever slew hart or hind, that he should be blinded."[8] These protections, which also extended to boar and rabbits, all but ensured that, according to the *Rime*, "his rich men complained about it and his poor men murmured about it . . . but they must all obey the king's will if they would live or have land, / Land or possessions or indeed, his friendship."[9] As we see in *Adventures*, forest law impacted both commoners and nobility—though one group could voice their opposition louder than the other. Status, life, and livelihood all depended upon acquiescence to forest law.

Adventures takes place in 1191, not during the initial establishment of the Forests but a century later. Yet the ballads that established the Robin Hood tradition first circulated in the fifteenth century, not the twelfth, and provided the blueprint for continuous adaptations throughout the following centuries. As the opening credits of *Adventures* roll (in medieval-looking script on an aged parchment background), the audience learns that the film is "based upon ancient Robin Hood legends." What "ancient" means, in this case, is late medieval by way of the early modern period, which begins around the ascension of the Tudor monarchs in the sixteenth century. There was no medieval historian consulted on the film. An early modern scholar, F. M. Padelford, gave guidance to the filmmakers and based his version of Robin Hood on his reading of seventeenth-century "garlands," or collections of popular stories that replaced earlier printed broadsides, rather than medieval ballads.[10] These garlands relay a fundamentally different Robin Hood from the ballads, one who acts as a hero rather than simply a protagonist.

The first written reference to Robin Hood is found in William Langland's late fourteenth-century poem *Piers Plowman* (*c.* 1377), which includes a lazy priest who cannot say his prayers but *does* know the "rymes of Robyn Hood," indicating that the existence and popularity of the Robin Hood legend goes back earlier than the late fourteenth century.[11] The two earliest known Robin Hood ballads, *A Gest of Robyn Hode* and *Robin Hood and the Monk*, emphasize the organized crime element to Robin's outlawry. There are no starved and suffering "Saxons"—or Maid Marian, for that matter. The Sheriff of Nottingham, rather than Guy of Gisbourne, is the main villain, and the hero himself is not an aristocrat but an opportunistic yeoman of indeterminate social status using the Forest for personal financial gain.[12]

A Gest of Robyn Hode (*c.* 1450) has Robin running Sherwood Forest as a grifter, extracting payments from passersby in the guise of seeking entertainment from interesting travelers. He spares yeomen, plowmen, and "good" knights and squires, but targets high-ranking clergy like archbishops and bishops, as well as the Sheriff of Nottingham. The stakes are not political; Robin eats poached deer as part of his lifestyle and ultimately kills the Sheriff out of personal animosity. Although this character may have been less useful for filmmakers invested in the moral stakes of economic hardship, there is still a narrative appeal to a less-noble outlaw. In assessing contemporary reception to the ballads, the historian Barbara Hanawalt acknowledges how "late Medieval English audiences were very much like modern ones who enjoy the numerous films about the Mafia, but nonetheless feel that such criminals must ultimately be brought to justice."[13] Medieval audiences would not necessarily have viewed Robin Hood's commandeering of the Forest as aspirational, but they would certainly have seen it as cunning and compelling.

POACHING

In both the film and ballads, Robin Hood and his companions commit crimes that were very real, including poaching, jail breaking, theft, extortion, robbery, and murder.[14] But *Adventures* shifts the criminal burden of poaching from Robin onto Much the Miller's Son, even though Robin claims the act as his own. The scene in which we see Guy of Gisbourne hunting with his men cuts to a parallel scene in which a single camouflaged hunter watches a deer—the same deer chased by Guy's party. This solitary hunter is stealthy and careful, the visual and physical opposite of the mass of hunters coming toward him. The two scenes converge when the hunting party catches the deer, only to see it killed by a single arrow shot from the poacher's bow. Guy and his men apprehend the poacher, who identifies himself as Much the Miller's Son (a "Saxon"):

Guy: "Don't you know it's death to kill the king's deer?"
Much: "Yes, and death from hunger if I don't, thanks to you and the rest of you Norman cutthroats at Nottingham castle."

Much, of course, is less concerned with the legality of his actions than their physical necessity.

Despite the familiarity of this image, there was no standard poacher in the Middle Ages. *Adventures* shows two variants—the poor man poaching out of desperation and the nobleman poaching out of resentment—but there were many other types of people who hunted unlawfully in medieval England. In *A Gest of Robyn Hode*, both the outlaw Robin and the Sheriff of Nottingham poach deer. Legal records show noblemen, court officials, gentry, craftspeople, peasants, and clergy accused of and punished for poaching. Even foresters, whose green uniforms were similar to those worn by Robin and his company, took part in unlawful hunting. At the court for Staffordshire Forest in 1286, a knight named Alfred de Solny was accused of poaching in a group consisting of his squire, two foresters, a clerk, and two others, including the illegitimate son of a local lord.[15] A group such as this might be closer to a criminal association, but a different group of poachers might see the hunt as a largely social occasion—or a form of political protest.[16]

On parchment, the consequences for poaching in the twelfth century look grim. In the 1184 Assize of the Forest, the first codified forest law, King Henry II (r. 1154–89) "forbids that anyone shall offend in regard to his venison or his forests in any respect" and that if an offense results in conviction, "he wills that full justice be exacted as was done in the time of king Henry [Henry I, r. 1100–35], his grandfather."[17] The Assize, excerpted in the appendix of this chapter, does not specify what justice under Henry I looked like, but contemporary sources indicated, as Judith Green argues, that "Henry I was said to have punished those who killed deer as severely as those who killed men."[18] Whether or not Henry I did, in fact, demand capital punishment for offenses that may have robbed him of venison is not certain. What is clear, however, is that Henry II could marshal his grandfather's reputation in order to intimidate would-be offenders.

The audience knows it is Much the Miller's Son, not Robin, who shoots the king's deer. Robin's decision to claim the act as his own allows him to embody the role of poacher for the Norman nobility. Chroniclers in the sixteenth century elevated Robin Hood from the "gode yeman" (good yeoman) of ballads to a conscience-stricken nobleman in a process that Stephen Knight and Thomas H. Ohlgren refer to as "literary gentrification."[19] *Adventures* takes part in this tradition by having Sir Robin of Locksley assume the crime of poaching to spare Much. For Guy, the killing of the king's deer is now about the protest of Saxon elites rather than the starvation of Saxon peasants.

ENFORCEMENT

But before Robin of Locksley takes responsibility for Much the Miller's criminal act, Guy of Gisbourne moves to execute the poacher. Robin and Will Scarlett interrupt Guy before he can strike Much. Enraged at the disruption, Guy asks Robin, "By what right do you interfere with the king's justice?" Robin replies, "I have better right than you have to misuse it." Here, Guy of Gisbourne is judge, jury, and would-be executioner for Much the Miller's Son. As Prince John's aide and a Norman noble, Guy is an extension of John's power and an enforcer of forest law.

Neither Robin nor Guy is an actual administrator of the king's justice—or of forest law, for that matter. Guy's cruel legalism does not actually exemplify the letter of forest law, and Henry II did not actually list execution as a possible punishment for Forest offenses in his Assize. In reality, the administration of forest law was often a drawn-out, bureaucratic process, adjudicated in select years by traveling courts known as forest eyres. Just as forest law was distinct from common law and subject to its own courts, Forests had their own law enforcement, including forest eyre justices, sheriffs, bailiffs, foresters, and lower-ranking nobility responsible for maintaining the "vert and venison"—the Forest landscape and the animals supported by it. Rulers depended upon this system of law and its administrators for consistent hunting conditions, but also for providing revenue for the royal treasury. Henry II used forests for generating income through fees, fines, and physical resources. Legal historian Ryan Rowberry cites King John's "savage overexploitation" of forests' economic potential in the first decade of the thirteenth century as a major contributing factor to the drafting of the Magna Carta in 1215.[20]

Most of the punishments for offenses against the Forest were in the form of amercements, or fines; the poverty of some lower-status offenders might have gained them a pardon; repeat offenders, however, could be imprisoned.[21] Of Alfred de Solny's party in Staffordshire, five were imprisoned and released for fines. Two had fled. In charge of producing these offenders was the sheriff, who was neither the bumbling, complacent Sheriff of *Adventures* nor the corrupt villain of medieval ballads. Medieval sheriffs were administrators appointed by the king to exercise oversight in specific districts (or shires), including tax collection. Many sheriffs went on to become forest eyre justices, whose appointments were not dissimilar to common law justices.[22] These eyre justices were toward the top of a network of local administrators and officials who heard pleas or adjudicated cases that came to their courts. Forest eyre justices did not preside over juries, but largely dismissed or meted out amercements for offenses brought before them (see the examples of cases in the appendix).[23]

Adventures shows that the boundaries between pardonable and punishable Forest offenses are thin. According to the legal evidence, the difference between the two could depend on the status of the accused poacher.[24] To protect Much from Gisbourne's final attempt at apprehending him, Robin insists, "I killed that deer. This man is my servant." Gisbourne then responds, "I suppose you realize the penalty for killing the king's deer is death, whether for serf or noble?" While drawing his bow, Robin asks wryly, "Really? Are there no exceptions?" The Normans retreat, and the question is left unanswered. Robin's question is more of a statement, one that cuts to the core of the arbitrariness of medieval forest law, as well as its potential for misuse and selective application.

CONCLUSION

After incorporating Much into his group of outlaws, Robin decides to address the unjust taxation and treatment of Saxons in a visit to Nottingham Castle—Gisbourne's seat and the current residence of Prince John—with the slain deer slung over his shoulders. Rather than hang Robin, as promised before his arrival, Prince John delights in the "bold rascal." But the mood shifts when John announces his takeover as regent of England and asks the noblemen present for their support. Robin spits out a mouthful of meat.

> "What's the matter, have you no stomach for honest meat?" Prince John asks him.
> "For honest meat, yes," Robin replies, "but I've no stomach for traitors."

For Sir Robin of Locksley, it is better to eat poached meat as an outlaw than to eat "honest meat" as a traitor. Restricting access to forested space and to the animals within it is a crime committed by the ruler rather than the subject. In the other feast scene in *Adventures*, Robin hosts an open-air celebration in Sherwood Forest that is the inverse of the claustrophobic, hierarchical banquet in Nottingham Castle. And Robin Hood, whether in ballad form or onscreen, makes forest-dwelling into a lifestyle. But *Adventures*, in setting the plot in the Angevin period, makes the protest of such a restriction an issue of principle rather than lifestyle. Although the forest offers restoration, forest law restricts access to that restorative space.

APPENDIX

The Adventures of Robin Hood (1938)

ASSIZE OF THE FOREST (1184)

Laws issued by King Henry II (r. 1154–89) for royal forests in England.
Source: George Burton Adams and H. Morse Stephens, eds., trans., *Select Documents of English Constitutional History* (New York: Macmillan, 1901), 25–27. Original in Latin. Modernized by Casey Ireland.

Here begins the assize of the Forest of the lord Henry the king.

This is the assize of lord Henry the king, the son of Matilda, in England, concerning the forest and his venison, by the advice and assent of the archbishops, bishops and barons, earls and nobles of England, at Woodstock.

[1] First, he forbids that anyone shall offend in regard to his venison or his forests in any respect: and he asks that no prior violator expect leniency due to previous treatment upon those who had offended in regard to his venison and his forests. For if any one hereafter shall offend and be convicted, he wills that full justice be exacted as was done in the time of king Henry [I, r. 1100–35], his grandfather.

[2] Also, he forbids anyone to have bows or arrows, or hounds, or harriers in his forests unless by the authority of the king.

[3] Also, he forbids that anyone shall give or sell anything to waste [cut down more than needed] or destroy the woods which are within the forest of king Henry: he grants fully that they may take from their woods what shall be necessary for them (i.e., firewood), without wasting, and this under the supervision of the royal forester. . . .

[5] Also, the lord king orders that his foresters shall take care concerning the forests of knights and others who have woods within the bounds of the royal forest, that the woods be not destroyed; for if in spite of this they shall have been destroyed, let those whose woods have been destroyed know well that redress will be exacted from [the destroyers'] persons or their lands and not from another. . . .

[7] Also, the king orders that in every county in which he has venison, twelve knights shall be appointed for guarding his vert[25] and venison with the forest; and that four knights shall be appointed to agist[26] his woods and to receive and keep his pasture rents; and the king forbids that any one shall

agist his woods within the bounds of the forest before the king's own woods have been agisted, and the lord king's period for agisting the forest shall begin fifteen days before Michaelmas [September 29] and shall last fifteen days after Michaelmas.

[12] At Woodstock the king orders that from whoever has offended in regard to his forests for the first time, good sureties [pledges against further liability] shall be taken; and if he shall offend a second time, likewise; but if he shall offend a third time, for the third offence no other sureties shall be taken from him, nor anything else except the very person of the offender [i.e., to prison].

[13] Also, he orders that every man of twelve years of age, remaining within the hunting reserve, and clerks holding a non-ecclesiastical piece of land shall take an oath to keep his peace.

[14] Also, he orders that the lawing [mutilation of dogs' paws to prevent their running] of mastiffs shall be performed wherever his wild animals have peace or are accustomed to have it.

[15] Also, he orders that no tanner or bleacher of hides shall dwell in his forests outside of a borough.[27]

[16] Also the king orders that no one for the future shall chase in any manner to capture wild animals by night within or without the forest, wherever his wild animals frequent or are accustomed to have peace, under penalty of imprisonment for one year and of paying a fine or ransom at the king's pleasure, and that no one, under the same penalty, shall make any obstruction . . . against his wild animals in his forests and woods or in other places disafforested [removed from consideration as royal Forest] by himself or his predecessors.

PLEAS OF THE FOREST FOR NOTTINGHAMSHIRE (1287, 1334)

Two cases brought before the justices of the forest eyre, a traveling court which convened infrequently, during the time of Edward I (r. 1272–1307) and Edward III (r. 1327–77).

Source: G. J. Turner, ed., trans., Select Pleas of the Forest (London: B. Quaritch, 1901), 62, 65–66. Original in Latin.

[1287]: Pleas of the Forest of Sherwood at Nottingham before Sirs William de Yescy, Thomas de Normanville, and Richard of Creeping, justices in eyre of the Lord King for pleas of the same forest, on the morrow of St. Hilary in the fifteenth year of the reign of King Edward by the foresters and verderers named below, to wit by: . . . It is presented, etc., that Alan of Leverton, the clerk of the forest of Sherwood, with Adam of Everingham, and Robillard his page took a doe in the park of Clipston on the Friday before Ascension Day in the seventh year of the reign [1279] of king Edward with a red greyhound. And the doe was eaten by the pigs, because it was taken so late in the evening that it could not be found. And the aforesaid Alan came before the justices, and being convicted of this is sent to prison. And the aforesaid Robillard does not come, nor is he found . . . therefore, let him be found. And the aforesaid Alan is ransomed at half a mark. And he finds pledges [people acting as sureties for the accused] as appears, etc.

[1334]: Pleas of the Forest of Sherwood held at Nottingham on the Monday next after the Feast of St. George in the eighth year of the reign of King Edward, the Third after the Conquest, before Ralph de Neville, Richard of Aldborough, and Peter of Middleton, justices of the lord king in eyre for Pleas of the Forest by the mandate of the lord king in these words: . . . It is presented and proved by the same persons that Hugh of Wotehale of Woodborough, William Hyend, Wilcock, formerly the servant of the parson of Clifton and Stephen Fleming of Nottingham, on the Thursday after the feast of St. William the archbishop, in the eighteenth year [1325] of the reign of king Edward [II], the son of king Edward [I], were in the wood of Arnold, in the place which is called *Throwys*, with bows and arrows. And they shot a hart so that it died. And its flesh was found putrid and devoured by vermin in a place which is called *Thweycehilli*. And the arrow was found in the said hart, wherewith it was shot. And the aforesaid Hugh came before the justices and is sent to prison. And the aforesaid William and Wilcock are not found. Nor have they been seen . . . therefore, let them be exacted. And the aforesaid Stephen Fleming is dead; therefore, nothing of him. And afterwards the aforesaid Hugh is brought out of prison and is pardoned because he is poor. And the aforesaid William and Wilcock were exacted in the county and did not appear; therefore, they are outlawed.

Reading questions

- An important plot point of *Adventures of Robin Hood* is the punishment of poachers by death, regardless of class. How would you compare this punishment with the penalties outlined in the Assize of 1184 and in the Nottinghamshire cases from 1287 and 1334? Are there different punishments for different social groups?

- What would you identify as the primary objective of this Assize of 1184, and how does it compare to the representation of forest law in *Adventures*?
- What kind of boundaries does the Assize of 1184 place on forest use? How was the forest policed?
- What do these two cases in Nottinghamshire show us about the practical application of forest law? Does the law apply equally to all parties?
- The 1287 and 1334 cases occurred more than a century after the Assize of the Forest. Does the legality of poaching in this later period differ from the late twelfth-century legal landscape, as depicted in either the fictional *Adventures* or the historical Assize of 1184? If so, how?

NOTES

1. John Aberth, "Splendid in Spandex," in *A Knight at the Movies: Medieval History on Film* (New York: Routledge, 2005), 167.

2. Esther Liberman Cuenca, "'Normans' vs. 'Saxons': Cinematic Imaginaries of Race and Nation in Angevin England, 1938–1964," *Open Library of Humanities* 9, no. 1 (2023): 1–20.

3. To differentiate between woodlands and royal Forests, this chapter follows John H. Baker's lead in capitalizing Forest when referring to legally protected royal territory. See Baker, *The Oxford History of the Laws of England* (Oxford: Oxford University Press, 2004), 2:455.

4. Ibid.

5. Robert Pogue Harrison, *Forests: The Shadow of Civilization* (Chicago: University of Chicago Press, 1992), 69.

6. Ibid.

7. *The Rime of King William*, "He lufode þa headeor swilce he waere heora faeder," in *The Anglo-Saxon Chronicle: A Collaborative Edition*, ed. Susan Irvine (Cambridge: D. S. Brewer, 2004), 7:97, line 13 (my translation).

8. Ibid.

9. Ibid.

10. Aberth, "Splendid in Spandex," 167; R. B. Dobson and J. Taylor, *Rymes of Robin Hood: An Introduction to the English Outlaw* (Pittsburgh: University of Pittsburgh Press, 1976), 51–52.

11. Derek Pearsall, ed., *Piers Plowman by William Langland: An Edition of the C-Text* (Berkeley and Los Angeles: University of California Press, 1978), 129 (*passus* VII, line 11).

12. By the fifteenth century, yeomanry included a broader swath of what we could consider the middle class. A yeoman might be a forester, a tradesman, or a petty landowner.

13. Barbara A. Hanawalt, "Ballads and Bandits: Fourteenth-Century Outlaws and the Robin Hood Poems," in *Chaucer's England: Literature in Historical Context*, ed. Barbara Hanawalt (Minneapolis and London: University of Minnesota Press, 1992), 155.

14. Thomas H. Olgren, "Introduction," in *A Gest of Robyn Hode*, in *Medieval Outlaws: Ten Tales in Modern English*, ed. Thomas H. Olgren (Stroud: Sutton, 1998), 216.

15. G. Wrottesley, ed., "Staffordshire Forest Pleas: 14 Edward I," in *Staffordshire Historical Collections* 1 (London, 1884), 5:161.

16. Jean Birrell, "Who Poached the King's Deer? A Study in Thirteenth Century Crime," *Midland History* 7, no. 1 (1982): 12.

17. George Burton Adams and H. Morse Stephens, eds., trans., *Select Documents of English Constitutional History* (New York: Macmillan, 1901), 25.

18. Judith Green, "Forest Laws in England and Normandy in the Twelfth Century," *Historical Research* 86, no. 233 (2013): 421.

19. Stephen Knight and Thomas H. Ohlgren, eds., *A Gest of Robyn Hode*, in *Robin Hood and Other Outlaw Tales* (Kalamazoo: Medieval Institute, Western Michigan University, 1997), line 3, https://d.lib.rochester.edu/teams/text/gest-of-robyn-hode. See also Knight and Ohlren's "General Introduction" in *Robin Hood and Other Outlaw Tales*.

20. Ryan Rowberry, "Forest Eyre Justices in the Reign of Henry III (1216–1272)," *William & Mary Bill of Rights Journal* 25, no. 2 (2016): 519.

21. Jean Birrell, "Peasant Deer Poachers in the Medieval Forest," in *Progress and Problems in Medieval England: Essays in Honour of Edward Miller*, ed. Richard Britnell and John Hatcher (Cambridge: Cambridge University Press, 1996), 82.

22. Rowberry, "Forest Eyre Justices," 515.

23. Charles R. Young, "The Forest Eyre in England during the Thirteenth Century," *American Journal of Legal History* 18, no. 4 (1974): 323.

24. G. J. Turner, ed., trans., *Select Pleas of the Forest* (London: B. Quaritch, 1901), 66.

25. Trees, shrubs, and other plant growth that protect and feed wildlife.

26. The right to pasture cattle in forest land for a fee.

27. Tanning was considered a foul-smelling and dirty trade.

CHAPTER NINE

TRIAL BY BATTLE AND GENDERED MEDIEVALISMS IN *THE LAST DUEL* (2021)

By Sara McDougall and David M. Perry

The *Last Duel*, directed by Ridley Scott, offers a gorgeous, vibrant, and devastatingly dark rendering of an actual trial by combat held in Paris in 1386. It is a story of male violence against women and against one another, with the Middle Ages as backdrop. The fight to the death at the story's core was engaged in as an attempt to resolve a legal dispute over an alleged rape. The knight, Jean de Carrouges (Matt Damon) claimed that the squire Jacques Le Gris (Adam Driver) had raped Jean's wife, Marguerite de Thibouville (Jodie Comer). Based on the 2004 bestselling book by Eric Jager, the film *The Last Duel* tells the same story from three perspectives—that of Carrouges, Le Gris, and, ostensibly, Marguerite.[1] The film's approach to showing these competing points of view is an attempt to reflect competing claims from the historical record and, by adding in "Marguerite's version of events," a well-meant if grossly mishandled effort to tell the woman's "side of the story." It is also an evident homage to Akira Kurosawa's cinematic classic *Rashomon* (1950).[2]

The movie brings to life the many ways that patriarchy, as it existed in medieval Europe, was bad for men and even worse for women. In this case, after years of feuding two men brutally fight to the death before a massive crowd of spectators, all to resolve whether one man had raped the other's wife. The customs of medieval European patriarchy, however, were not as simple as the movie suggests. In particular, the film does medieval women no favors. Women living in the Middle Ages were neither quite as objectified nor as oppressed as the movie portrays them. They were also, moreover, not modernized women seeking a "Me Too" moment, a movement that began in the late 2010s that led to greater recognition of the sexual violence and harassment that women often face.[3]

There is nothing wrong, necessarily, with movies engaging with modern audiences' possible medieval interests. Trial by battle, at least, was certainly medieval and has been a staple of cinematic representations of medieval legal culture, most likely because of its association with aristocratic culture and honor—two popular motifs found in modern literature about this period. Sir Walter Scott (1771–1832), the famous novelist whose influence on modern perceptions of the medieval period remains immeasurable, relied on judicial combat to frame the climax of two of his most popular novels, *Ivanhoe* (1820) and *The Fair Maid of Perth* (1828). More recently, judicial combat was seen in several episodes throughout the run of the HBO television series *Game of Thrones* (2011–19). Trials by combat and duels are a source of ongoing fascination for modern audiences. There was clearly ample appetite, too, for watching men dare each other to fight to the death in the Middle Ages, even while medieval theologians and secular authorities alike condemned and outlawed this judicial violence and deplored its ongoing practice.

This chapter approaches *The Last Duel* from two angles, both calculated originally to serve a national media audience in *Slate*. First, this chapter argues that, while effectively depicting the violence embedded in medieval ideas of elite masculinity, the film takes historical liberties in portraying the implications of that violence against women, as well as the circumstances of women in the Middle Ages more generally. Specifically, the film invents anachronistic modern repercussions faced by women who come forward to charge men with rape. The mistake here is particularly critical to scholars of medieval law because of its failure to recognize the intentional gap in many medieval legal systems between the letter of the law and the way that law was carried out. Second, the film plays with the gender anxieties of medieval aristocratic culture as manifested in the sartorial choices of its main protagonists—Carrouges, Le Gris, and Marguerite—specifically, their hairstyles. This chapter, thus, takes stock of this good, bad, and fun, highlighting the way in which the movie does and does not reflect medieval expressions and experiences of patriarchy and the intersections of gender and justice.

MEDIEVAL JUSTICE AND TRIAL BY COMBAT

Historians have a relative wealth of evidence for this disturbing tale of lust and violence. We can reconstruct a basic timeline of the history from medieval sources, including chronicles, some of the actual litigation, court records, legal documents, and a sort of memo—written after the fact and excerpted in the appendix—from Jean Le Coq, one of the lawyers involved.

In 1386, in Normandy, a knight and nobleman, Jean de Carrouges (d. 1396), accused the squire Jacques Le Gris (d. 1386) of having raped Carrouges's wife at Carrouges's mother's home. At the time, Carrouges had been in Paris seeking to collect money he needed after a failed military expedition. Le Gris denied the accusation, claiming he had only seen Marguerite once in his life, and had several noble witnesses who could provide an alibi. He further claimed that Carrouges hated him because he had obtained lands and titles that once belonged to Carrouges's father and father-in-law. Additionally, Le Gris charged that Carrouges tried to coerce his first wife to make a false rape accusation. Unable to prove his case and unable to find other resolution to the dispute, Carrouges demanded that King Charles VI (r. 1380–1422) permit him to prove his claim was just via trial by combat. They fought, Carrouges won, and he spent the few remaining years of his life as something of a celebrity among the companions of the king. Carrouges was also a leader of several military expeditions abroad and well-rewarded for his services.

Trials by combat such as this one had a role in medieval justice but were rare, frequently condemned, and regularly declared illegal. Judicial combats stem historically from early medieval legal culture, which allowed aggrieved parties to settle the public issue of their guilt or innocence by undergoing ordeals of water or fire. These trials by ordeal placed disputes between two parties before God's judgment, whose intervention on behalf of the innocent party would settle the matter.[4] Such ordeals were often demanded, but sometimes the demand was enough to lead to a peaceful resolution.[5] In the early thirteenth century, most ordeals, notably those involving trial by fire and water, were declared illegal. Trial by combat followed a somewhat different course. Though enterprising rulers like Louis IX of France (r. 1226–70) tried to limit the use of duels, they persisted as a mark of aristocratic privilege, as Frederick II (r. 1220–50) conceded in his laws for Sicily in 1234.[6]

As with other types of ordeals, when men, and some women, obtained judicial permission to engage in trial by combat, they or their designated champions only rarely followed through, instead finding ways to reconcile or put an end to the proceedings. And when they *did* fight, they rarely chose, or were permitted, to fight all the way to the death. This gap between the letter of the law and what actually happened is a major feature of medieval justice on a broad scale, and knowledge of that gap is vital to our present-day attempts to distinguish between what medieval laws said and how they functioned in society. The law often threatened the harshest of punishments, but these were rarely carried out.

In the film, as in Jager's book, not only are the men fighting to the death, but Marguerite's life is at risk, too. If her husband loses, then the rape accusation will be adjudicated to be false, which merits death by burning at the stake according to the film and the book. This was, however, unlikely to have ever happened in medieval France, let alone in this case. The closest evidence we have to eyewitness accounts of the duel come from a royal chronicler who was likely there, and from one of Le Gris's lawyers, who later voiced his doubts about the trial. Both make no mention of Marguerite being at risk of execution. The idea that Marguerite's life depended on the outcome of the trial is bound if anything to the idea that she, not her husband, was the accuser. This misses a key feature of medieval justice, which typically favored men as both plaintiffs and defendant, but also as the accused and culpable. This is one way in which patriarchy operated as a paternalistic shield that both protected and excluded women from criminal prosecution and its consequences. It was Marguerite's husband who made the accusation and Marguerite's husband whose life was at risk.

To be sure, the filmmakers and Jager did not invent this idea; they just did not know how carefully they needed to interpret medieval sources. The chronicler Jean Froissart (c. 1337–c. 1405) mentioned the threat of burning for Marguerite if her husband lost the combat. But Froissart was in Flanders at the time of the combat and did not see it firsthand. Moreover, the chronicler clearly enjoyed dramatization in his storytelling across his many works, and he got many of the other facts about this episode wrong, such as the location where the combat took place.[7] In inventing this fate for Marguerite, Froissart likely drew from old crusader laws that declared a woman who sought trial by combat and whose champion lost would be executed at the stake, but there is no evidence that anyone ever implemented this rule, even in the Crusader States, let alone in France. It seems to have been intended primarily as a deterrent to false or frivolous accusations.

Indeed, false accusations were a concern, especially in cases where conviction carried with it the risk of execution, as with rape. Women who made a rape accusation and then admitted they lied might be punished by whipping or beating under French custom. That kind of punishment was carried out in a few cases that we know about from surviving court records. On the whole, however, executions were rare for most crimes, including rape, and punishments for false accusations were rarer still. Justice was relatively weak; it was patriarchy that was strong.

ARISTOCRATIC MEN AND THE CUSTOMS OF MASCULINITY

If *The Last Duel* gets the details of medieval law incorrect in ways that misread women's circumstances, it is much better at representing how medieval ideas about masculinity encouraged and enabled men to do terrible things to one another and those in their power. The drive to improve their social status, be regarded as courageous and honorable, have a wife with a spotless reputation, father as many children as possible, and never permit disrespect—all of these could indeed come together at the elite levels of society to create the potential for violence. In the film, the moral but intolerant Carrouges, who disdains anyone less courageous and steadfastly loyal than he is (never mind his frequent acts of defiance to his own lord), seeks to confine and dominate his wife, bully his onetime friend, and fight his way to fame, fortune, and higher status. Meanwhile, Le Gris, who seduces women and extorts money, makes use of his training in Ovid and the art of making love to impress his lord. These are both types of masculinity that appear in both literary and nonliterary medieval sources.

Questions of masculinity are also at stake in the way the film visually presents its male protagonists. Every film set in the Middle Ages, of course, has to make choices about portraying a world centuries in the past, and this one is a complicated blend of medieval, modern, and something in between for men's hair. In the twelfth century, the often-cranky English monk Orderic Vitalis (1075– c. 1142) issued two laments in his *Ecclesiastical History* about the hairstyles of elite noblemen. One set, he moaned, "parted their hair from the crown of the head to the forehead, grew long and luxurious locks like women." The others "shave the front part of their head, like thieves, and let their hair grow very long in the back, like harlots."[8] The film's effort to use hair to define status and character, especially the hair of the male protagonists, actually does have an important medieval basis. Many people in the Middle Ages, not just Orderic Vitalis, were obsessed with hairstyles and their gendered meanings.

In *The Last Duel*, the leads go to these two extremes and, in so doing, suggest the masculine qualities that they are supposed to embody. We get one libertine, Le Gris, with his long, wavy locks, and one man, Carrouges, who looks at the same time both austere and uncouth, with a mullet. Le Gris, a squire who indulged in the art of seduction by recourse to Latin double-entendre, seems to take his cues from manuals on courtly love.

From a medieval perspective, the character's long hair appropriately reflects his interest in dalliances with the fair sex and in social climbing. Historically, by the time the trial by combat happened, Le Gris was probably already over fifty years old and no longer, according to his lawyers, up for amorous adventures and midnight orgies, but *The Last Duel* adds in this behavior to go with the hair.

Despite a long tradition of powerful men cultivating luscious, long locks in the Middle Ages, some people, especially churchmen, worried that long hair for men meant trouble. Bernard of Clairvaux, for example, praised the early Templars for their short (and dirty) hair, in contrast to the flowing locks of secular knights. Such an affectation was, he said, against the precepts of the Apostle Paul and more suited for women than warriors.[9] A woman's long hair, meanwhile, "is her glory," a glory that posed no small risks for her because it was thought to incite male lust.[10] But long hair for women, if dangerous, was appropriate. Between the time when Paul wrote and the time of *The Last Duel*, long hair was a critical marker of difference. Anything that blurred this distinction, that made men look like women, risked gender-bending, making women of men. In the eyes of some, long hair made men womanly and therefore lascivious, too weak to resist the temptation to sin. As with everything, what medieval norms proposed and what people actually did and thought are not the same. Often condemned, long hair was nonetheless popular and coveted. This was particularly true among the male nobility, who were often fond of flouting the rules.

ARISTOCRATIC WOMEN AND MEDIEVALISMS ABOUNDING

The film's Marguerite de Thibouville wears her glorious hair free-flowing, in the loosely braided locks of a girl, or in the flawless bejeweled crown of braids of a noble wife, expressing the ideal of medieval female beauty. Medieval religious teachings and society's moral code stressed modesty for women, who should cover their hair, especially in church. They were not supposed to *try* to be beautiful but were supposed to *be* beautiful to attract and keep husbands—at once pure and virginal *and* objects of desire. Jodie Comer's blond hair, bound in jewel-studded, proto-Leia buns (of *Star Wars* fame) on either side of her head, sends that signal perfectly.

Once we get past the external, though, the real problems with the film's handling of its protagonist start. The Last Duel makes many changes in the representation of medieval ideas about sex and pregnancy, particularly in Marguerite's circumstances, to raise the story's stakes during the trial scenes. The historical Marguerite was the heiress of a venerable Norman noble family, was probably young when she became Carrouges's second wife, and was, after the fact, enriched by her husband's fame and fortune in his role as celebrated hero of the "last duel." She had at least three children with Carrouges before he died during a military excursion in 1396. She herself most likely died between 1417 and 1419. That is fairly thin material on which the movie constructs a fully fleshed-out character, necessarily fictionalized because of the lack of sources, but fictionalized in ways that perpetuate modern stereotypes about the Middle Ages.

The movie turns Marguerite into a modern heroine, trapped in a medieval world between two awful men. She is forced to contend with a society that required obedience and fecundity and one that blamed the victim if she made a rape accusation. Viewers are supposed to believe Marguerite and side with her. But there is no evidence from medieval sources that making the accusation was her idea. We have not even one line of testimony from her. If you were writing this story based only on the documents we have, it would be not *"he said/she said,"* but *"he said/he said,"* with her voice silenced.

When Marguerite speaks in the film, she is either saying something that the screenwriters invented in their efforts to tell her story or, more troublingly, saying lines recognized as coming from the case her historical husband made in his demand for trial by combat. The film, in fact, perpetuates its own kind of silencing by assuming that she did, said, and thought what her husband's lawyers said. Reading the historical record, it is not possible to know if this is true. Carrouges may have forced his wife to play the role she did, resulting in a vicious fight to the death.

The film also distorts what we know of women's lives and their real problems in the Middle Ages by inventing an infertility problem for Marguerite as a major plot point in a well-meant effort to explore what sex and pregnancy might have been like for her and to engage with medieval ideas about reproduction. For example, Marguerite is presented as unable to become pregnant until after the rape. But there is no historical evidence to support this plot point. She may or may not have been pregnant during the trial or in the months before the trial. The assumptions made by the filmmakers and in the book indicate how much more care needs to be taken when trying to represent medieval women, children, and reproduction.

The Last Duel mishandles a medieval medical idea that women had to feel pleasure to conceive, an idea that could have dangerous application when pregnancy followed an alleged rape. The movie jumps from this idea about conception into an anachronistic and invented interrogation of a kind that would never have occurred at this time but would be familiar to present-day viewers of television court procedurals like *Law and Order* in which Marguerite is asked again and again if she enjoyed sex with her husband.

Here, the filmmakers apply modern concerns about female frigidity, as if medieval people were worried about whether women enjoyed sex. The concern embedded in medieval patriarchal culture was the opposite: that women enjoyed sex *too much*.[11] Women were depicted in literary and religious texts as weak and prone to temptation, too able to feel pleasure, even when they did not consent to sex. This idea appears with agonizing regularity in medieval culture, in songs, schoolbooks, and conduct literature, ample evidence of the real problems with which medieval women had to contend.

CONCLUSION

Although this was not actually the "last duel" in history or even technically a duel at all (duels are extrajudicial, operating outside the law; this trial by combat was, if awful, legal), *The Last Duel* dramatizes a true late-medieval story preserved from multiple perspectives in both legal documents and narrative accounts. A mix of history and fiction, *The Last Duel* was made immediately in the years following a public reckoning in American culture with the prevalence of violence against women. As such, the filmmakers opted to shape the historical account as a response to this heightened awareness of sexual violence. The film thus attempts to ascribe legal agency to Marguerite de Thibouville, despite the fact that doing so stretches the limits of the medieval evidence for the trial and, in giving voice to Marguerite only through her husband's claims, risks doubly silencing her. In its visualization of the trial by battle and aristocratic ideas about masculinity, *The Last Duel* does some justice to the Middle Ages, whose men could be quite as awful as the film implies, with the hair to match. When it comes to depicting medieval women and medieval systems of justice, *The Last Duel*, however, replaces the malevolence of medieval patriarchy with modern problems and preoccupations.

APPENDIX

The Last Duel (2021)

JEAN LE COQ (JOHANNES GALLUS), "COMMENT ON THE TRIAL BY COMBAT OF JACQUES LE GRIS" (LATE 14TH CENTURY)

Le Coq's memo about the trial.

Source: Jean Le Coq, *Questiones Johannis Galli*, ed. Marguerite Boulet (Paris: E. de Boccard, 1944), 110–12. Original in Latin. Translated by Anthony Perron and Sara McDougall.

Note that on the Saturday after Christmas, in the year 1386, which was the feast day of St. Thomas [Becket, December 29], a judicial duel was held between Jacques le Gris and lord Jean de Carrouge behind the walls of Saint-Martin-des-Champs. The said Jacques was defeated and killed, and I worry somewhat that it was the vengeance of God, and so it seemed to most of those who saw this duel, for the said Jacques, against the advice of his counselors, did not wish to avail himself of clerical privilege, although he was an unmarried cleric and the defendant. And this I know because I was part of his counsel. Moreover, it seemed to them that this happened by God's vengeance, since everyone was saying together that he was aware of his guilt in the crime on account of which the duel was decreed by law. Nonetheless, quite a lot of people assert the opposite of this, by virtue of Jacques's oath, namely that it [the rape] never happened nor was he aware of having any guilt, which I leave to his conscience.

■

The following are the grounds against the said Jacques le Gris, which I and many others had:

First, that when he came to Paris, he asked me whether, with this duel challenged and won by him, there could afterwards be proceedings against him through ordinary process and legal arguments. Second, whether there ought to be a hearing elsewhere in a matter of this kind.[12] Third, concerning the day on which his adversary reportedly said the crime had been committed, whether his adversary could alter it or make a change in it. Fourth, after the wager of battle had been decreed by law, he became ill. Fifth, that shortly before entering the field of battle, he had himself made a knight. Sixth, that despite being the defendant, he attacked his adversary very cruelly, and on foot, although he would have had the upper hand if he had been on horseback. Seventh, that although Carrouge was weak on account of fevers, which the said Carrouge was suffering from for a long time, and it appeared that lord Jacques was healthy, nonetheless he was defeated, miraculously as it were, since the said Carrouge was not able to help himself.[13] Eighth, that the wife of Carrouge was always steadfast in saying that the deed had taken place, both while in childbirth and on the day of the duel, to which duel she was brought on a carriage, but straightaway sent back by order of the king. Ninth, that he spoke feebly to those present who were speaking with him about a settlement. Tenth, that he once asked me whether I had any hesitation concerning law or fact in his case, because he saw me thinking. Eleventh, that he said to me that, when he heard the rumor that Carrouge wanted to prosecute him concerning this case, he quickly confessed to a priest.

The following are the grounds in his favor:

First, that he always asserted and swore that he had never done it and beseeched God to help in this affair, given that he was in the right and given that he was innocent of that deed and that he had never done it, not then nor at any other time, and I saw him do this twenty times and he did it on the day of the duel. Second, that he had prayers said in all the houses of worship in Paris, such that they were to pray to God on his behalf, in order that He might want to help him, given that he was in the right and given that he was innocent of that deed and that he had never done it, not then nor at any other time, and he did so on the day of the duel. Third, that he was a man of good class and an honorable man. Fourth, that he is not heedless of his own salvation.[14] Fifth, that the lord de Alençon had written to the king and to his uncles, also lords, that the said Jacques was not guilty. Sixth, a number of knights asserted that he had been with the lord de Alençon constantly on the whole day on which his adversary said the deed had happened, and for several days without interruption right before that time. Seventh, that Adam Lovel, who was said to be an accessory to this crime, had been questioned, etc.,[15] that young woman[16] who was said to have been in the home of Carrouge on that day, and they had confessed nothing. Some said that he[17] was unwilling to admit any guilt, both because he had made his confession concerning that deed[18] and was not bound to admit anything more, and because it would have been an insult to his children and friends, and in a certain way he would be speaking against the statement of the lord de Alençon, who had stated that the said Jacques was not guilty of this deed.

Despite all this, the truth about that deed was never known.

Reading questions

- Do you think Le Coq believed his client was innocent or guilty, why? Despite it being told from three points of view, in what way do you think the film *The Last Duel* leans on the matter of Le Gris's guilt or innocence?
- Do you recognize any of the reasons Le Coq gave for considering Le Gris more or less likely to have been innocent or guilty as also appearing in *The Last Duel*? Give a few examples and assess the use of the information in the film.
- The film and the book that inspired it both make a great deal of the idea that Marguerite de Thibouville might have been pregnant as a result of the alleged rape. The reference to her maintaining her account of an assault by Jacques Le Gris with the help of Adam Louvel while in childbirth, mentioned in this source, is the only evidence of this pregnancy. Does this interpretation of her pregnancy as a possible result of rape seem plausible to you? Why might that be problematic?

NOTES

1. Eric Jager, *The Last Duel: A True Story of Crime, Scandal, and Trial by Combat in Medieval France* (New York: Broadway Books, 2004).
2. A. A. Dowd, "Ridley Scott Offers His Own Rashomon with the Star-Studded Period Piece *The Last Duel*," *AV Club* (October 12, 2021), https://www.avclub.com/ridley-scott-offers-his-own-rashomon-with-the-star-stud-1847850421.
3. Justin Chang, "'The Last Duel' Is a 'Rashomon'-Style #MeToo Story," *NPR* (October 14, 2021), https://www.npr.org/2021/10/15/1045633461/the-last-duel-movie-review.
4. Robert Bartlett, *Trial by Fire and Water: The Medieval Judicial Ordeal* (Oxford: Clarendon Press, 1986).
5. Stephen D. White, "Proposing the Ordeal and Avoiding It: Strategy and Power in Western French Litigation, 1050–1110," in *Cultures of Power: Lordship, Status, and Process in Twelfth-Century Europe*, ed. Thomas N. Bisson (Philadelphia: University of Pennsylvania Press, 1995), 89–123.
6. R. C. Van Caenegem, "The Borough Charter of Saint-Omer of 1127 Granted by William Clito, Count of Flanders," in *Legal History: A European Perspective* (London: Hambledon Press, 1991), 61–70; *Etablissements de Saint Louis*, trans.

F. R. P. Akehurst (Philadelphia: University of Pennsylvania Press, 1996), 10; Frederick II, *Liber Augustalis (Constitutions of Melfi)*, trans. James M. Powell (Syracuse: Syracuse University Press, 1971), 90–93.

7. John Froissart, *Chronicles of England, France, Spain, and the Adjoining Countries: From the Latter Part of the Reign of Edward II to the Coronation of Henry IV*, ed. Thomas Johnes (London, 1844), 2:203–6.

8. John Block Friedman, "Hair and Social Class," in *Ambiguous Locks: An Iconology of Hair in Medieval Art and Literature*, ed. Roberta Milliken (Jefferson, N.C.: McFarland, 2012), 2:138.

9. Andrew Holt, "Between Warrior and Priest: The Creation of a New Masculine Identity during the Crusades," in *Negotiating Clerical Identities: Priests, Monks and Masculinity in the Middle Ages*, ed. Jennifer Thibodeaux (New York: Palgrave Macmillan, 2010), 185, 191.

10. Martha Easton, "Gender and Sexuality," in *Ambiguous Locks: An Iconology of Hair in Medieval Art and Literature*, ed. Roberta Milliken (Jefferson, N.C. McFarland, 2012), 2:108.

11. Ruth Mazo Karras, *Sexuality in Medieval Europe: Doing unto Others*, 3rd ed. (London and New York: Routledge, 2017), 118.

12. This is one of many interesting (and difficult to translate with certainty) passages. It could mean that Carrouges wondered about his alibi; it could be about jurisdiction and venue; it could even be about what lawyer or lawyers he should be using.

13. The sentence in Boulet's edition is incomplete. It reads, "Septimo, quia licet *Carrouge* esset debilis propter febres, quas se dictus *Carrouge* juvare." But the original manuscript (Paris, BnF, Ms. lat. 4645, fol. 48r) includes the following text between "quas" and "se," which completes the meaning of the sentence quite clearly: ". . . longo tempore habuerat et apparebat seu appareret Dominus Jacobus Robustus tamen deuictus fuit quasi miraculose quia non poterat. . . ." The digitized manuscript can be found here: https://gallica.bnf.fr/ark:/12148/btv1b90809137.

14. Boulet's edition reads "quia nemo immemor sue saluti" ("no one is heedless of their own salvation"). The manuscript (fol. 48v) has ". . . qui non immemor sue salutis" and thus would appear clearly to refer specifically to Jacques.

15. There seems to be a lacuna in the manuscript here.

16. The word used here, *domicella*, could refer to a domestic worker, as it is usually interpreted in the secondary work on the trial, or a young noblewoman, perhaps an attendant of some kind.

17. Presumably Jacques Le Gris.

18. To a priest, that is, as Jean Le Coq mentioned previously. The issue here is a second confession under the law.

CHAPTER TEN

ANIMAL TRIALS IN *THE ADVOCATE* (1993)

By Julie K. Chamberlin

The 1993 film *The Advocate* (also known as *The Hour of the Pig*) dramatizes medieval animal trials from the perspective of a "big city" lawyer from Paris who finds himself defending a pig against murder charges in the rural village of Abbeville in 1452. As the protagonist, Richard Courtois (Colin Firth), confronts the challenges of his new position, he unravels the mystery behind the murder of a local child. Courtois discovers that the villagers have found an easy scapegoat for the crime: a pig owned by a group of foreigners from "little Egypt." Although the historical record indicates free-roaming pigs were not only capable of maiming and even killing human children but were also tried for such crimes in medieval France, the film's grand reveal proves the pig innocent. The true culprit is a local lord's son, whose murderous tendencies have been enabled by corruption among village officials and the villagers' superstitions. In the end, Courtois is unable to pin the murder on the real offender. Instead, he performs a sleight-of-hand trick that shifts the blame onto a different pig, allowing the foreigners to retain ownership of their valuable asset. The film concludes with Courtois leaving Abbeville to return to Paris just before the plague arrives to decimate the village's population.

This chapter examines the attitude toward medieval law and culture that *The Advocate* impresses upon modern viewers, as well as how the film engages with its supposedly medieval source material. Modern viewers may be surprised to learn that the film is based on "historical fact." The film, however, apparently uses as its primary source an early twentieth-century account of medieval animal trials: E. P. Evans's 1906 *The Criminal Prosecution and Capital Punishment of Animals*, which cites a list of 191 incidents of animal prosecutions in medieval Europe.[1] Though Evans's account is problematic, given his disdainful attitude toward the medieval period, medieval legal evidence confirms that animal trials *did* occur in France. Several important sources for medieval customary law mention animal trials, and records of such trials occurring in northern France from the thirteenth to the sixteenth centuries can be found in medieval accounting ledgers.

The Advocate is a convoluted—and at times baffling—meditation on medieval culture. Courtois is an educated outsider in a medieval village, and the film encourages its audience to view its inhabitants from Courtois's enlightened perspective. Filmmakers allow for nuance in the depiction of other educated male figures—namely, the local *seigneur* and priest—yet reduce lower-class and female characters to stereotypes. *The Advocate*, this chapter argues, is never truly interested in considering why medieval people tried nonhuman animals or attempted to enact justice through these trials. Instead, the film portrays animal trials as borne out of ignorance, corruption, and superstition—missing the opportunity to reflect on the ways in which medieval understandings of animal agency differed from our own.

MEDIEVAL ANIMAL TRIALS: FACT OR FICTION?

Criminal trials of nonhuman animals did, in fact, occur in medieval Europe.[2] Philippe de Beaumanoir (d. 1296), a French jurist, alludes to animal trials in his customary lawbook (excerpted in the appendix), the *Coutumes de Beauvaisis*.[3] In the *Coutumes*, Philippe acknowledges that capital punishments such as drawing and hanging should not be used because animals cannot comprehend the spectacle of execution. However, if an animal is responsible for killing or maiming a human, Philippe concedes that it is best to kill the animal to prevent such an incident from recurring. If the animal committed a lesser crime, the creature might be simply forfeited to the local lord on whose lands the offense occurred. The owner of the animal would be liable to pay damages or answer for the crime in the event that the owner caused the animal to kill or injure someone. Philippe's assessment of animal culpability echoes not only Roman civil law,[4] but also modern legal practice in civil courts, which assign responsibility and assess damages but would not attempt to prove criminal intent in the way of criminal trials.

Another form of animal trial occurred in ecclesiastical courts. These trials typically involved pests that could not easily be brought to court or punished. A swarm of locusts, for instance, could not be summoned to trial for destroying an entire village's crops; instead, medieval justice-seekers resorted to supernatural means of vanquishing these creatures. French jurist Bartholomew Chassenée's (1480–1541) treatise on the excommunication of animals and insects, the sixteenth-century *Consilium primum*, describes a scenario in which the people of Beaune sought a remedy for a plague of insects that were laying waste to the once-fertile province (excerpted in the appendix).[5] In these types of cases, a bishop could summon the offending vermin to court and, when the vermin failed to acquiesce to the summons, afflict the vermin with a perpetual curse, or *anathema*, until they left the area or ceased causing damage. Though religious trials of pest animals may certainly rankle modern sensibilities, one can imagine medieval people's desperation, brought on by the threat of starvation, compelling them to seek divine intervention in the absence of practical remedies.

Why medieval people tried nonhuman animals is a subject of much debate that has few conclusive answers. One theory couches the practice in medieval superstition governed by religious belief and a rudimentary understanding of justice. Victorian-era animal rights advocates, like Evans, found interest in medieval animal trials on this basis and proffered the practice as evidence of historical mistreatment of animals. But the impulse to view medieval approaches to law and order as infantile fails to explain the precedent for animal trials in Roman law, or indeed why similar practices continued hundreds of years later. Others have noted the similarities between animal trials and trials of religious "others" and heretics, including Jews and accused witches.[6] These trials represent complex, if misguided, attempts to understand individual culpability and reconcile earthly justice with a Christian worldview that promises judgment in the afterlife. More recently, scholars have revisited the animal trials as evidence of premodern attempts to grapple with animal agency within the existing legal system. The 2011 trial and eventual execution of a grizzly bear at Yellowstone Park for killing park visitors, for instance, shows that animal trials were not just legal chicanery of a "backward" age. Rather, the practice of trying animals for crimes against humans persists in our modern legal system.[7]

INFLUENCE OF MODERN SCHOLARSHIP ON MEDIEVAL ANIMAL TRIALS

The Advocate portrays nonhuman animals involved in trials in three separate instances, all lifted from E. P. Evans's *The Criminal Prosecution and Capital Punishment of Animals*. In the opening scene, a man and a donkey are set to be hanged for bestiality.⁸ At the last moment, the donkey is saved from the gallows on grounds of its inability to consent. Later, Courtois defends a woman accused of bewitching rats. Her courtroom defense scene incorporates elements of a rat trial case Evans describes in detail.⁹ The pig trial, meanwhile, seems to be based on an incident in which a sow was tried and executed for killing a child in Falaise in 1386.¹⁰ The setting for *The Advocate*—the town of Abbeville in 1452—also comes out of Evans's work. Evans cites Abbeville as the location of pig trials in 1414, 1418, 1479, and 1490.¹¹ The filmmakers may have chosen 1452 as the date for the film because it is the median of these four dates. Of course, by placing three animal trials in the span of a single year, *The Advocate* implies that these sensational trials were far more frequent than the seventy-six-year span Evans reports in his work.

Evans corroborates *The Advocate*'s claims of historical fact in the film's opening text. Nonetheless, Evans's book is not a medieval source. Evans claims the writings of Chassenée, the historical figure on whom *The Advocate*'s Richard Courtois is based, as one of his primary sources. Chassenée does not appear to have ever defended a pig framed for murder as depicted in the film, but like the film's Courtois, he was educated in Roman law and took up legal practice in a northern French town. It is clear that Chassenée took animal trials seriously enough to discuss the topic first in a text intended to advise other jurists on wide-ranging legal matters. There is considerable doubt, however, whether Chassenée participated in all the instances that Evans and others have attributed to him. A trial often referred to as the "Rats of Autun," in which Chassenée is said to have launched a famous argument in defense of the rats, has been cited by Evans and other numerous scholars as fact.¹² Mention of such a trial, however, is conspicuously absent from the *Consilium primum*, and the earliest known source that describes the trial is a text on French martyrs that straddles the line between history, religious account, and fiction.¹³ Evans furthermore spins these supposedly factual narratives to support his own biases, expounding on medieval lawmakers' "childish disposition to punish irrational creatures" and even making an argument in favor of eugenics.¹⁴ Though Evans's text remains the most prominently cited source in the study of medieval animal trials, it is nonetheless important that budding historians remain vigilant in critically assessing Evans's citation practices and untangling historical truth from his personal agenda.

ANIMAL TRIALS AND CINEMATIC PERSPECTIVES OF MEDIEVAL LAW AND ORDER

The Advocate's Richard Courtois is more educated and worldly than the residents of Abbeville, and he brings an enlightened attitude to a village that is otherwise in the grips of corruption and superstition. Thus, the film places the audience at a similar vantage, observing villagers' "backward" ways from the viewpoint of a better-educated outsider. This perspective is established at the outset, in which a man is hanged for bestiality. While the filmmakers borrow the bestiality trial from the historical record, other choices—such as the reveal that the inn where Courtois stays is really a brothel—were seemingly devised to show the regressive and hypersexualized nature of the village's lower-class inhabitants, especially women.

Other male characters, meanwhile, debate Courtois on the matter of local custom. Following Courtois's failure to successfully defend a woman accused of witchcraft from the gallows, he laments that the sentence handed down by the judge is "nowhere in Roman law." To this, the prosecutor, Maître Pincheon (Donald Pleasence), replies, "Custom and practice." Pincheon's title, *maître*, indicates that he, like Courtois, has a legal education. Unlike the new recruit from Paris, however, Pincheon has grown cynical from his experiences in Abbeville and has resigned himself to placating the whims of the less-educated members of society. Courtois's inability to reconcile his knowledge of Roman law with local practice also highlights a real tension in medieval legal culture. While lawmakers in France had begun to issue statutes and codify legal practice, the local *coutumes*, or customary laws, that had preceded Roman law still held sway in rural villages such as Abbeville.[15] Moreover, in 1452, Abbeville would have been part of Ponthieu, which fell under the jurisdiction of English kings. This meant that regions such as Ponthieu, while geographically part of modern-day France, were not subject to any centralized French law. In moments of friction between Courtois and Pincheon, the filmmakers manage to capture some of the complexities that underlay legal jurisdictions during the Hundred Years' War (1337–1453) between England and France, as well as the cultural divide between educated lawyers' perspectives on the legal system and those of the rural people they served.

The filmmakers accurately depict the clergy and local aristocracy as imbricated in medieval village life. These figures each give voice to different and often competing perspectives on law and order. Father Albertus (Ian Holm) brings a philosophical, if morally gray, attitude to questions of justice. He advises Courtois, "In a world where nothing is reasonable, nothing can be truly mad." Through Father Albertus, the filmmakers imply that practices that seem irrational to modern audiences were genuine, if misguided, attempts to deal with a world in which senseless hardship abounded. Later, the priest's ethics are called into question when he admits to using his position of religious authority to seduce women. The complexity of characters like Father Albertus suggests that medieval attitudes toward law and order were not a monolith. Nonetheless, the film does not address the separation between canon law, governed by the church, and civil law, governed by secular authorities. In fact, Chassenée's alleged "rat defense," which filmmakers integrate into the witch trial scene, would have been heard in an ecclesiastical court before a bishop, not a secular court as depicted in the film. This important distinction, which explains some of the key differences in types of animal trials and differing approaches to trying animals, is nonexistent in *The Advocate*.

Seigneur Jehan d'Auferre (Nicol Williamson), meanwhile, uses local superstition and ignorance to cover up his son's murderous tendencies. He steps in as judge during the pig trial, which would have been his right as lord, aware that Courtois is beginning to unravel the mystery behind the series of murders. The seigneur's motivations are relatable—he wants to maintain order and secure his children's futures—but his unquestioned authority facilitates abuses of justice. Rather than allow his son to answer for his crimes, d'Auferre ships his son off to England and encourages the pig trial in order to displace scrutiny. In one of the film's many loosely integrated subplots, Courtois observes d'Auferre participating in the secret meeting of Cathars, boasting that the religious sect is "how we keep control. Rule and order." The choice to involve a heretical sect that, by the mid-fifteenth century, was defunct for a hundred years may speak to modern interest in secret societies, but it also considerably muddles the film's depiction of medieval culture. By representing the rule of law in Abbeville as maintained by Cathars, the filmmakers imply that animal trials were all part of a grand conspiracy theory. Moreover, this decision obscures a *more* fascinating reality: medieval lawmakers parsed and debated openly the implications of trying nonhuman animals in both secular and ecclesiastical courts.

The Advocate's filmmakers appear only tangentially interested in considering why medieval lawmakers would have tried a pig for murder. A band of foreign travelers become connected to the pig trial when Samira (Amina Annabi) attempts to offer Courtois sex in exchange for the release of the pig, admitting that the pig is their only source of livelihood. This storyline implies that the pig trial is a veiled attempt to drive the foreigners out of Abbeville. It is unclear which ethnic "others" these foreigners are supposed to represent—they are interchangeably referred to as "Moors" (Muslims of African descent) and "gypsies" (or Romani people)—though it is obvious that the French resent their presence. Courtois's clerk, Mathieu (Jim Carter), remarks upon their arrival in Abbeville that the people from "little Egypt" are "spreading like rats." Courtois never seems genuinely interested in defending the pig, but he becomes invested in freeing *that particular* pig on Samira's behalf when he becomes romantically interested in her.

That the victim is a Jewish boy further complicates the pig trial's racial implications. Courtois begins to suspect that the murders are racially motivated, and thus not the work of a pig, when he discovers the bones of another missing Jewish child. A Jewish apothecary's autopsy supports Courtois's conclusion, but as a Jew, the apothecary is not permitted to testify in court. The murders of multiple Jewish children in the film are reminiscent of medieval blood libel stories in which Jews murder Christian children—the likes of which Chaucer's Prioress relates in *The Canterbury Tales* (*c.* 1387–1400)—however, the victim and perpetrator are inverted.[16] The most coherent interpretation of these plotlines suggests that medieval people, including the better-educated, allowed their prejudices to get in the way of truth and justice. The discovery that the pig did not, in fact, commit the murder prevents the film's narrative and characters from grappling with animal agency in the way that medieval lawmakers did.

CONCLUSION

Although *The Advocate* relies on the most rudimentary stereotypes of medieval peasants and declines to consider the full implications of the practice that inspired the film, it does achieve some nuance in its depiction of the complex relationship between customary law and Roman law in medieval courts. In the original UK version of the film (*The Hour of the Pig*) viewers are left to balance these two dynamics and form their own opinions. The US release of the film, however, explicitly delivers a pejorative message about the backward nature of medieval practice. The opening crawl of text in the US version labels fifteenth-century France as the "Dark Ages" and describes a time when "people were still gripped by ignorance and superstition" and governed by a "confused legal profession." Such accounts do an incredible disservice to the study of history by perpetuating the narrative that the medieval period did nothing to progress human civilization. By genuinely coming to terms with why medieval lawmakers chose to try nonhuman animals for crimes, we can begin to understand more fully the complexities of legal personhood today.

APPENDIX

The Advocate (1993)

PHILIPPE DE BEAUMANOIR (D. 1296), *THE CUSTOMARY LAWS OF BEAUVAIS* (LATE 13TH CENTURY)

On animal trials.

Source: Philippe de Beaumanoir, *Coutumes de Beauvaisis*, ed. A. Salmon, vol. 2, ch. LXIX, no. 1944–45 (Paris: A. Picard et fils, 1899), 481–82. Original in Old French. Translated by Julie K. Chamberlin.

Some people who have governance over their lands indeed try animals when they kill someone: such as if a sow or another animal kills a child, they hang and draw it. But they should not do this, for mute animals (*bestes mues*) do not understand what is right or what is wrong, and because of this judicial procedure is lost on them, for punishment should be vengeance for a crime, and so that the criminal is aware of and understands that for such a crime there is a certain penalty. But dumb animals have no understanding, and because of this they put the dumb animal to death for the crime in vain. But the lord[17] should take it for his own profit because it is his to acquire by right. And it is good in all cases, if it is a young bull or pig or sheep or wild beast, that it should be his, and that he should kill it and use it for his own profit, for then it shall not do the same thing another time. And if it is a horse or mule or an ass, the lord can retain it for his own profit without putting it to death.

Because of this, if my horse, or another animal that belongs to me, kills a person, I cannot be summoned to court for the crime. But if it only injures or does damage, I am obliged to compensate the damage and retain my animal, having paid the fine for the crime. And if it causes death or mutilation, the animal that caused the injury is acquired by the lord by his right and I cannot be summoned to court for the crime. Nevertheless, there is a manner in which my animal could kill or maim someone in which I would be culpable, such as if I made it do what it did. I have made it do it if I am riding on my horse and I spurred the horse at a gallop through the middle of a crowd of people or children and, in its haste to do as directed (*par la radeur de li*),[18] it killed someone: in this case I would be culpable. But if it is clear that my horse charged by its own will or out of insolence, I can defend myself from the crime.

BARTHOLOMEW CHASSENÉE (1480–1541), *CONSILIUM PRIMUM* [FIRST ADVICE] (C. 1531)

On insects and pests that cause harm.

Source: Barthélemy Chasseneuz, "Consilium Primum," *Responsa seu Consilia* (Venice, 1581 reprint; digitized by Bavarian State Library), fol. 1. Original in Latin. Translated by Julie K. Chamberlin and Anthony Perron.

Which can rightly be called a treatise on account of its manifold and hidden teaching, where the question of the excommunication of animals and insects is clearly and carefully treated.

Theme:

The Burgundians have among the other parts of the provinces a certain most fertile one that they call Beaune; it abounds with thick flies commonly called "huberes," which in a strange way harm the grapes and cause the greatest damage. Terrified by these things and wanting a remedy, the region customarily comes to us Aedui[19] urgently requesting that the aforementioned animals should be ordered by the official of the bishop of Autun that they leave the place in which they inflict damage, or that they cease to do harm. If [the insects] do not obey the order, they will be cursed with the bond of anathematization, or with a perpetual curse. When these things are requested, our Aedui are wont to carry them out immediately, but whether it is right and lawful, and how it can be done, remains to be seen.

To analyze the question at hand, I have determined five presuppositions:

First of all, let us decide (so that we do not seem to speak in the common tongue) what these animals of ours should be called in Latin. Secondly, indeed, whether these animals of ours can be summoned. Thirdly, whether they can be summoned by attorneys, and if they personally are summoned, whether they can appear through attorneys appointed by the judge summoning them. Fourthly, who would be a competent judge, whether layman or cleric, and the manner of proceeding in the case and of sentencing? Fifthly, what are anathema and malediction?

And having discussed and analyzed these five, I will come to the main question, whether it is possible for them to be ordered to leave the place in which they cause harm, or to cease causing harm under penalty of anathematization and perpetual curse.

It is true that there was never any doubt about these things in times past, yet I thought it necessary to establish them first, lest I should fall into error (a thing Cicero, in his *De Officiis*, thought should be avoided). That is, that we do not mistake things unknown for things known and rashly agree to them. Many things are unknown until God should come, who illuminates what is hidden and not only "reveals what is deep and hidden," and who "knows what is established in darkness, and the light is with him" (Daniel 2:22), but also by the greatness of His power He gives and strengthens "things which are utterly hopeless," as [Roman Emperor] Justinian [r. 527–65] says in Cod. 1.17.2. On that account, I decided to turn to God himself for the explanation of what had been hidden from me in this difficult matter. And so, according to the saying of the blessed Boethius Severinus [d. 524], we will call upon Him by saying:

> O You, who govern the world with perpetual reason,
> Father, allow (us) to reach the sacred mind of the law.
> Allow (us) to examine the honor of the laws; allow us, with the light revealed,
> to loosen the difficult knots with true understanding.

Reading questions

- *The Advocate* depicts animal trials as the product of ignorance and superstition. How do the two jurists below rationalize trying animals for crimes, and how do their attitudes compare to the film's characterization?
- What kind of legal authorities do these jurists draw upon when discussing animal trials?
- *The Customary Laws of Beauvais* describe a thirteenth-century secular approach to dealing with individual animals that kill or maim humans, while the treatise on legal advice, *Consilium primum*, addresses the sixteenth-century ecclesiastical trials of insects. How do these two different approaches to animal trials compare to the trials shown in the *Advocate*?
- In *The Advocate*, the pig on trial turns out to be innocent. How do medieval lawmakers reconcile with animal criminal culpability in their writing? Whom do they hold responsible in different situations?

NOTES

1. E. P. Evans, *The Criminal Prosecution and Capital Punishment of Animals* (London: Heinemann, 1906).

2. Esther Cohen's account in *The Crossroads of Justice: Law and Culture in Late Medieval France* (Leiden: Brill, 1992) has remained a critical source on the trials. See also Peter Dinzelbacher, "Animal Trials: A Multidisciplinary Approach," *Journal of Interdisciplinary History* 32, no. 3 (2002): 405–21.

3. Philippe de Beaumanoir, *Coutumes de Beauvaisis*, ed. A. Salmon, 3 vols (Paris: A. Picard et fils, 1899). For more on Philippe de Beaumanoir and French customary law in general, see Ada Maria Kuskowski, *Vernacular Law: Writing and the Reinvention of Customary Law in Medieval France* (Cambridge: Cambridge University Press, 2023).

4. Philippe appears to be drawing from Roman civil law (*ius civile*) regarding the culpability of animals, in particular the *lex Aquilia*, which concerned compensation for damages caused to another's property. It is notable that the concept of property applied not only to domestic animals, but also slaves. For further discussion of animal liability in Roman law, see Bernard S. Jackson, "Liability for Animals in Roman Law: An Historical Sketch," *Cambridge Law Journal* 37, no. 1 (1978): 122–43.

5. "Chassenée" is alternatively spelled "Chasseneuz." I used a digitized copy of the 1581 reprint of the *Responsa seu Consilia*, a series of legal tracts on various topics, of which the *Consilium primum* is the first.

6. See, for example, Jody Ender, "Homicidal Pigs and the Anti-Semitic Imagination," *Exemplaria* 14, no. 1 (2002): 201–38.

7. Jessica Grose, "A Death in Yellowstone," *Slate* (April 2, 2012), https://www.slate.com/articles/health_and_science/death_in_yellowstone/2012/04/grizzly_bear_attacks_how_wildlife_investigators_found_a_killer_grizzly_in_yellowstone_.html.

8. Evans, *Criminal Prosecution and Capital Punishment of Animals*, 150.

9. Ibid., 18–21.

10. Ibid., 16. Evidence for this trial is a "curious painting" on the wall of the Holy Trinity Church in Falaise, which "no longer exists," and a reconstruction of that painting by Arthur Mangin in 1872.

11. Evans, *Criminal Prosecution of Animals*, 157, 316–26.

12. For discussion of the "Rats of Autun" trial in scholarship, see Paul Schiff Berman, "An Observation and a Strange but True Tale: What Might the Historical Trials of Animals Tell Us about the Transformative Potential of Law in American Culture," *Hastings Law Journal* 52, no. 1 (2000): 123–80. See also Thomas Fudgé, "Prosecuting Animals as Criminals in Medieval Europe," in *Medieval Religion and Its Anxieties: History and Mystery in the Other Middle Ages* (New York: Palgrave Macmillan, 2016), 15–16; Jen Girgen, "The Historical and Contemporary Prosecution and Punishment of Animals," *Animal Law* 9 (2003): 101–3; and Cohen, *Crossroads of Justice*, 121.

13. The rat story appears to have been first reported in Jean Crispin's *Martyrology of the Protestants* (1570) and then in Jacques-Auguste de Thou's 1604 *Histoire universelle*, in which he describes a conversation between Chassenée and an old friend about the rat trial but does not claim that Chassenée ever wrote about it himself.

14. Evans, *Criminal Prosecution of Animals*, 186.

15. For a useful summary of the state of legal development and codification during this period in France, see Cohen, "The Reality of Late Medieval French Law and its Myths," in *Crossroads of Justice*, 27–53.

16. Filmmakers may also be invoking the life of fifteenth-century French nobleman and convicted serial killer Gilles de Rais (1405–40), who was said to have murdered hundreds of children.

17. The title *sire* generally refers to a feudal lord or nobleman who would have jurisdiction over a set of lands and could adjudicate trials.

18. This phrase means, literally, "in [the horse's] haste to do as directed." I have translated it here to retain a concession of animal agency while showing how the owner could still be responsible for the horse's ardor.

19. "Aedui" refers to the people from Autun. Autun is a commune in the Burgundy region of France near Beaune, where Chasseneé lived in the early sixteenth century, and the purported location of the "Rats of Autun" trial.

WOMEN AND REPRESENTATIONS
OF PREMODERN LAW

CHAPTER ELEVEN
RELIGIOUS WOMEN'S AUTHORITY AND RULES FOR NUNS IN *VISION: FROM THE LIFE OF HILDEGARD VON BINGEN* (2009)

By Lucy C. Barnhouse

The opening scene of *Vision* both draws on and seems to reinforce a range of negative modern ideas about the Middle Ages. Viewers are informed in a caption that it is the eve of the millennium. In the midst of a hostile nighttime landscape sits a church where terrified people are gathered, praying and flagellating themselves. Faint light is provided by votive candles in stands: this is a world lit only by fire.[1] A priest intones solemnly that the people should do penance for their sins, hoping to avoid the wrath of the God who is coming to sit in judgment. When the following day dawns, it is greeted with euphoric astonishment by the first young man to wake. It is greeted by Hildegard von Bingen (1098–1179), still a toddler, as not only a wonder, but a revelation. The film's director collapses a century of time to suggest that this emotionally intense experience was later interpreted by the visionary Hildegard (Barbara Sukowa) as her first experience of "the living light," in which she found divine wisdom. The precise nature of these visions is left deliberately ambiguous and open to multiple interpretations throughout the film. Moreover, the film itself, despite the visual clichés of its opening, is one that presents a multilayered vision of the Middle Ages.

In an interview, *Vision* director Margarethe von Trotta claimed that "faith and knowledge were one and the same in the Middle Ages. . . . Faith was truth." It is true that many people in medieval Europe did accept the claims of Christianity as axiomatic, but von Trotta's framing discounts the complexity of medieval systems of both belief and education. Moreover, the film implies that Hildegard's curiosity and desire for scientific knowledge, which von Trotta acknowledges, were exceptional. Von Trotta also claims that in medieval Europe, "one did not question anything, the way we do in modern life," and even that people believed the world was flat.[2]

Against the background of this imagined Middle Ages, the film's Hildegard appears as an outlier. Analyzing the influence and achievements of powerful medieval women as inherently exceptional, however, is a model that scholars have been criticizing for some years.[3] While Hildegard's achievements and abilities were indeed remarkable, the monastic culture of the twelfth century both facilitated women's learning and created opportunities for them to claim authority. As Penelope D. Johnson has written, "Just by existing in the central Middle Ages [c. 1000–1300], nunneries provided an area in which women could exercise administrative and legal abilities."[4] This chapter examines how *Vision* offers imaginative insights into aspects of medieval society not often explored in film, particularly its portrayal of interior life in a convent governed by church authorities and monastic rules, and of the material culture of law.

HILDEGARD AND THE LAW OF THE CHURCH

As both Hildegard's biography and her own writings demonstrate, she was very ready to use literary tropes and legal realities in her own favor. As the film shows, she wrote to the influential theologian Bernard of Clairvaux (1090–1153, played by Joseph von Westphalen) rhetorically emphasizing her own womanly frailty. When her confessor (Heino Ferch) comments on Bernard's suspicion of women, Hildegard replies with an almost mischievous, "But he loves the Blessed Virgin Mary!" This paradoxical view of women was not uncommon, nor was the readiness of medieval women to exploit it.[5] Hildegard appears acutely aware of how clerical misogyny could work for or against her and of how her visions could be read as a sign of either "heretical folly, or else divine power made perfect in weakness."[6] This stark dichotomy of interpretation could either give women exceptional authority or make them unusually vulnerable to discipline. These tensions are dramatized in a scene in the film where Hildegard is interviewed by Benedictine and Cistercian authorities from nearby abbeys. Such scrutiny of women mystics was characteristic in medieval Europe. The twelfth and thirteenth centuries saw the rise of mysticism among many religious women, particularly in Germany and the Low Countries. While mystics were by definition unusual, it was the norm rather than the exception for religious women to be literate and common for them to have some degree of theological education.[7] As illustrated in the film, religious women could both commission and create works of art and literature. The nature of the medieval cloister as a place of opportunity is typically overlooked by reviews of *Vision*, which tend to characterize medieval Europe as a place of patriarchal oppression and religious superstition.[8]

The readiness of von Trotta's Hildegard to fight male-dominated legal hierarchies for the sake of what she believes to be justice is attested in the historical Hildegard's letters.[9] It is also a characteristic that she shares with the protagonists of several Margarethe von Trotta films. Von Trotta, a feminist activist since the 1970s, has made multiple historical films focusing on influential women, including *Hannah Arendt* (2012), also starring *Vision*'s Sukowa, and *Rosenstraße* (2003), which follows the efforts of women in 1943 Berlin to resist Nazi detention of their Jewish husbands. The twelfth century is chronologically distant from von Trotta's usual subjects, but *Vision*'s focus on women's lives and ambitions and on the uses and abuses of legal and social networks is shared with much of her oeuvre. This commonality has sometimes been overlooked because of *Vision*'s medieval setting. Roger Ebert, for instance, claimed that von Trotta "declines to impose a set of feminist ideas" in the film. Other critics interpreted Hildegard's life as being artificially, anachronistically distorted to fit von Trotta's own vision.[10] The fact that the life of a nun in the twelfth century fit the preoccupations of a lifelong feminist in the early twenty-first appears to have posed an almost insurmountable conceptual challenge for many critics.

Canon law, the law of the church, is thematically and visually significant throughout the film. This large and dynamic body of law governed the property and ceremonies of the church and those individuals who had taken permanent vows. This category included members of the ecclesiastical hierarchy—like bishops, priests, and deacons—and religious persons like Hildegard and her nuns. When Hildegard is first brought to the abbey as an oblate, the interior scene opens on the abbot holding her parents' charter of donation and then placing it alongside other legal documents in a small desk. Hildegard's life and the life of the abbey are thus both visually linked to the law through material evidence. Elsewhere, too, the material culture of law is given visual prominence at key moments in the film. The women's community at Disibodenberg had gradually developed from the enclosure inhabited by Hildegard, her foster mother, and her foster sister, but remained under the abbot's legal authority. Hildegard's attempt to relocate her nuns to a separate cloister, rather than sharing space with the monks of Disibodenberg, legally requires the consent of the archbishop of Mainz (Wolfgang Pregler). Before this consent is reported by Abbot Kuno (Alexander Held), it is symbolized in a charter with the archiepiscopal seal, highlighted in the center of the frame. We later see the archbishop himself issuing a charter of donation to Hildegard in Mainz. The first thing we see after the exterior shot of Mainz's cathedral, captioned as the seat of the archbishopric, is the bishop's assistant appending a seal to the freshly written document. Hildegard herself also appealed to the archbishop to force the abbot of Disibodenberg to provide Rupertsberg with priests. Indeed, Hildegard's legal wrangling with the monks of Disibodenberg, although not depicted in the film, was not infrequent.[11]

The origins of Hildegard's relationship with her confessor, Brother Volmar, are obscure but significant. Hildegard herself characterized this relationship as being one of close collaboration and care. All religious women needed the services of priests to administer penance, the Eucharist, and other sacraments. Additionally, as in the case of Hildegard, female mystics could benefit from the collaboration of their male confessors. While ecclesiastical authorities viewed such close relationships between men and women as potentially suspect, they were also often essential to the communication of women's visions and the establishment of their authority for an audience beyond convent walls.[12] Hildegard herself was accustomed to navigating the daily implications of canon law and the Benedictine Rule within her community. The nuns' status as vowed virgins, she argued, gave them not only spiritual purity, but authority, entitling them not only to their religious habits but to the robes and crowns that, in the film, the sisters wear in their performance of Hildegard's musical drama, to the scandalized astonishment of a more conservative abbess.[13]

Hildegard's own experience of the religious life was also affected by her chronic illness. While the film deliberately leaves the causes of Hildegard's visions ambiguous, the visions themselves appear to cause physical pain as well as affording spiritual insight, bringing both Hildegard's movement and the forward motion of the film's narrative to a temporary halt. Under canon law, physical weakness like Hildegard's exempted monks and nuns from their usual duties within their communities. Experiences of illness, moreover, created rhythms of life apart from those set by the monastic rule.[14] In the scene where Hildegard instructs her sisters in care of the sick, this sense of time and space being set apart is reinforced in several ways. For the man who has whipped himself, patience and time are remedies; Hildegard's work is interrupted by the distressed cries of a woman for whom she provides a remedy that also requires time. By singing one of Hildegard's chants, Sister Sieglinde (Salome Kammer) provides a way of bringing space and time back into order.

A RULE FOR WOMEN? HILDEGARD'S CONVENT AND THE BENEDICTINE RULE

To be a vowed member of a religious order, in the Middle Ages as today, meant to be legally bound by a monastic rule. For Hildegard's community, this was the sixth-century Rule of Saint Benedict, written in Italy by Benedict of Nursia (480–547). The Rule laid out influential guidelines for individual conduct and communal life that were adopted by many monasteries in western Europe during the early medieval period (c. 400–1000). The language of the Rule of Saint Benedict (excerpted in the appendix) reflects that it was originally designed for a male community, but the Rule was applied to men's and women's houses alike in the Middle Ages. Some manuscript copies made for women's houses used female pronouns and modified the vocabulary—for example, putting "sisters" for "brothers." Hildegard herself was an impassioned student of the Rule, as illustrated in her commentary on it.[15] The Rule laid out guidelines for life within monastic houses, including on how daily life should be managed, how monasteries should relate to their neighbors, and how individuals should be admitted into this specially governed way of life, with its particular privileges and obligations.

Vision deliberately treats the practice of child oblation—surprising to modern viewers—as a familiar part of Hildegard's world, as indeed it was. Oblation, the offering of a child to a particular monastery as a gift, was a practice outlined in the Rule of Saint Benedict as a way for families of all social classes to signal their devotion to God. While in theory the practice of oblation signaled a separation of a child from their birth family and acquisition of a new family within the monastery, the reality was often more complicated.[16] As a conspicuous case brought before the archbishop of Mainz in the ninth century illustrates, a parental choice to give a child to a monastery did not necessarily forestall the child's later decision on whether or not to take binding monastic vows and stay with the community permanently. This was not completely clear-cut. While the practice of oblation would gradually peter out from the twelfth century onward, with a growing legal emphasis on adult consent, the ninth-century case caused significant disagreement within the monastery of Fulda. The archbishop, together with an assembly of abbots and monks, ruled that an oblate claiming to have received the tonsure—the haircut marking him as a monk—against his will could legitimately leave the cloister.[17]

For noble families like Hildegard's, it was customary to make decisions about their daughters' futures when girls reached the age of seven or eight. The film's portrayal of Hildegard's entry into the monastic life as a child is based in part on a contemporary *vita*, or saintly biography, devoted to both Hildegard and Jutta von Sponheim (d. 1136, played by Mareile Blendi).[18] The liturgy of reception, which Hildegard would have undergone having attained adulthood, is highlighted in the film using the case of Richildis (Hannah Herzsprung), with Hildegard herself presiding. These rituals accompanying a woman's entry into the religious life provided legitimacy for the life of a nun, her lifelong claustration, and her proximity to God.[19]

As the film illustrates, ties between religious women and their birth families tended to remain closer than those of religiously vowed men, and this could lead to social and legal complications.[20] Richildis' politically powerful mother (Sunnyi Melles) is able to exert her influence as a wealthy patron of Disibodenberg to secure the nuns' move to a new site on the Rupertsberg. But her desire to see Richildis advance politically as an abbess, just as her son has gained political influence through his role as a bishop, leads to conflict within the Rupertsberg monastery. When Richildis is elected as the head of a convent in northern Germany, the film suggests that her family connections were key to this outcome, although the agency of the community electing her—and God in guiding them—is still treated as central. While this kind of unofficial family influence remained within the legal parameters of the Rule of St. Benedict, Hildegard's consent to release Richildis from the community where she had taken her vows was necessary, and was only obtained when the archbishop of Mainz exercised his authority under canon law.

While Hildegard was elected to the position of *magistra* rather than abbess, her role in day-to-day affairs, such as presiding over chapter meetings, was comparable to those of independent monastic superiors; her practical independence was not impeded by her legal subordination to the abbot.[21] That she was elected by her sisters, rather than appointed by the abbot of

Disibodenberg, is reported by her biographer Guibert. Guibert quotes the Rule of Saint Benedict in asserting that Hildegard was chosen for her discretion and moderation. While such praise fulfills tropes of saintly biography, it is also supported by Hildegard's own writings on the Rule and on her own work as leader of her community. The film treats Guibert's account of the election itself, however, as idealizing in its claim of unanimity. "The unanimous decision of the entire community in the fear of God" was the Benedictine ideal. But to have one dissenting voice, implied to be that of Hildegard's foster sister and sometime rival Sister Jutta (Lena Stolze), makes for better drama.[22]

The chapter meeting held shortly after the women's move to the Rupertsberg also highlights both the centrality of the Benedictine Rule and the legal force of collective decision-making. The steps to perfect obedience outlined by St. Benedict are invoked, but the implications for the women's shared life in extraordinary circumstances are much debated. Even in their new location, the women's community remained, legally, under the authority of the abbot of Disibodenberg. But the provost, Hildegard's confessor Volmar, was sympathetic to both her and her vision for leadership. The legal fact of her community's dependence, the film suggests, was less important than the social power of Hildegard's leadership.

CONCLUSION

Both oblation and election were areas where many questions could—and did—arise about how the legal force of the Rule of Saint Benedict should be applied to the lives of individuals and communities. But the governance of the Rule itself was embraced by Hildegard and the women of her community, as it was by many women in the eleventh and twelfth centuries. The religious life provided them with opportunities for freedom from marriage, for education, and in some cases, for writing and preaching. The scope of Hildegard's work is by any measure extraordinary. But the development of her talents and publication of her works were facilitated by the religious life. Though ecclesiastical authorities were divided in their responses to her, the support of the powerful archbishop of Mainz gave her valuable legal support. Unusually among films set in medieval Europe, *Vision* is made more—rather than less—compelling by knowledge of medieval legal and social realities.

APPENDIX

Vision (2009)

ST. BENEDICT OF NURSIA (480–548), *THE RULE OF ST. BENEDICT* (6TH CENTURY)

Chapter 3 and Chapter 64: On seeking counsel and conducting elections in monasteries.

Source: D. Gregorius Arroyo, OSB, ed., *Sancti Benedicti Regula Monasteriorum: Cum Concordantiis Eiusdem* (Burgos: Abbatia S. Dominici de Silos, 1947), 15–16, 87–89. Original in Latin. Translated by Lucy C. Barnhouse.

Chapter 3: On Employing the Brothers in Counsel

Whenever anything important is to be done in the monastery, the abbot should call the whole community together, and tell them what the issue at hand is. And having heard the advice of the brothers, he should consider it for himself and do what he judges to be most useful [for the community]. Indeed, we have said that *all* should be called into this council, because the Lord often reveals to the younger what is best.

Moreover, the brothers should give their advice with all humility and deference, and not presume to obstinately defend whatever their own idea might be, rather letting the decision depend on the abbot's judgment. As he will command whatever he thinks is healthiest for all, let all submit to him. But as it is proper for the disciples to obey their teacher, it is proper for him to make all dispositions both providently and justly.

In all things, therefore, the Rule should be followed as a guide, and no one should rashly turn aside from it. No one in the monastery should be guided by his own desire; nor should anyone presume to shamelessly dispute with his abbot, even outside the monastery. But if anyone should presume to do so, he should submit to the discipline of the Rule. By the same token, the abbot should do everything in the fear of God and observance of the Rule, knowing that he will most assuredly have to answer for all his decisions before God, the most just Judge.

If the business of the monastery is of lesser importance, [the abbot] may use the counsel of only the senior members of the community, as it is written: *Do everything with counsel, and afterwards you will not regret it.*[23]

Chapter 64: On the Appointment of an Abbot

In appointing an abbot, let these guidelines always be followed: that the man should be appointed who has been chosen either by the unanimous decision of the entire community in the fear of God, or else by a part of the community, however small it may be, if its advice is wiser. Moreover, merit in life and wisdom in teaching should distinguish the one who is to be elected, even if he were to be the last in the order of the community.

But if the whole community were to elect a person who would consent to their vicious conduct—which God forbid—then, if these vices become known in some way to the bishop to whose diocese the house belongs, or to neighboring abbots or other Christians, then these people should prevent the triumph of this wicked agreement, instead setting a worthy steward over the house of God, knowing that they will receive a great reward for this action if performed with pure intent and the zeal of the Lord; and that it would be a sin to neglect [this duty of intervention].

Once appointed, let the abbot constantly reflect on the nature of the burden he has taken up, and to whom he shall give an account of his management. Let him also know that his duty is more to make himself useful than to take command. Therefore, he should be learned in divine law, in order that he may know and profit by things both new and old; he should be chaste, sober, and merciful; and he should always prefer mercy to judgment, that he himself may receive mercy [from God]. He should hate vices and love his brothers. In giving correction, he should always act modestly, never going to excess, lest he break the pot in trying to scrape off the rust. He should always be mindful of his own weakness and remember that *a bruised reed ought not to be broken*.[24] We are not saying that he should allow vices to flourish, but rather that he should cut them off while exercising prudence and charity, as may be best in each case, as we have already said. And let him seek to be more loved than feared. He should not be volatile and anxious, nor stubborn and intemperate, nor over-zealous and suspicious; for then he would never be at rest. In his commands, he should be thoughtful and considerate. Whether the task that he enjoins concerns God or the world, he should be discerning and temperate, bearing in mind the wisdom of holy Jacob, saying: *If I cause my sheep to go further, they will all die in one day.*[25] Taking up these and other examples of discretion, the mother of virtues, he should temper all things so that the strong will have something to desire, and the weak will not turn away.

Taking this, then, and other examples of discretion, the mother of virtues, let him so temper all things that the strong may have something to strive after, and the weak may not run away. And above all, let him keep this rule in all things, so that after having ministered well, he may hear from the Lord what the good servant heard, who gave wheat to his fellow-servants in its due season: Verily I say unto you, he will be set over all his goods. And especially let him keep this Rule in all its details, so that after a good ministry he may hear from the Lord what the good servant heard who gave his fellow-servants wheat in due season: *Indeed, I tell you*, said [Jesus], *he will set him over all his goods.*[26]

Reading questions

- How do you see the communal life of the religious women in the film *Vision* as shaped by the Benedictine Rule?
- How do these passages from the Benedictine Rule change, or support, your perception of Abbot Kuno in *Vision*?
- In what ways does *Vision* illuminate the flexibility of the Benedictine Rule?

NOTES

1. William Manchester, *A World Lit Only by Fire: The Medieval Mind and the Renaissance—Portrait of an Age* (Boston: Little, Brown, 1992), a popular history, written by a journalist, that was condemned by historians for its inaccurate and negatively stereotyped view of the Middle Ages.

2. Margarethe von Trotta, *Margarethe von Trotta: Interviews*, ed. Monika Raesch (Jackson: University Press of Mississippi, 2018), quoted at 70 and 67; Winston Black, *The Middle Ages: Facts and Fictions* (Santa Barbara: ABC-CLIO, 2019), 29–48, addresses the flat earth myth.

3. For the evolution of this debate, see Eileen Power, *Medieval Women*, ed. M. M. Postan (Cambridge: Cambridge University Press, 1975); Maryanne Kowaleski and Mary C. Erler, eds., *Women and Power in the Middle Ages* (Athens: University of Georgia Press, 1988); Maryanne Kowaleski and Mary C. Erler, eds., *Gendering the Master Narrative: Women and Power in the Middle Ages* (Ithaca: Cornell University Press, 2003); Heather J. Tanner, ed., *Medieval Elite Women and the Exercise of Power, 1100–1400: Moving beyond the Exceptionalist Debate* (London: Palgrave Macmillan, 2019).

4. Penelope D. Johnson, *Equal in Monastic Profession: Religious Women in Medieval France* (Chicago: University of Chicago Press, 1991), 206. See also Alison I. Beach, "Living and Working in a Twelfth-Century Women's Monastic Community," in *The Cambridge Companion to Hildegard von Bingen*, ed. Jennifer Bain (Cambridge: Cambridge University Press, 2021), 37–51.

5. Johnson, *Equal in Monastic Profession*, 4–5, 243–44. On Hildegard specifically, see Fiona J. Griffiths, *The Garden of Delights: Reform and Renaissance for Women in the Twelfth Century* (Philadelphia: University of Pennsylvania Press, 2007), 222.

6. Barbara Newman, "Divine Power Made Perfect in Weakness: St. Hildegard on the Frail Sex," in *Peace Weavers*, ed. John A. Nichols and Lillian Thomas Shank (Kalamazoo, Mich.: Cistercian Press, 1987), 104–5, quoted at 104.

7. See Griffiths, *Garden of Delights*; Rosalynn Voaden, "Mysticism and the Body," in *The Oxford Handbook of Medieval Christianity*, ed. John H. Arnold (Oxford: Oxford University Press, 2014), 396–412.

8. Stephen Holder, "A Multitasking Nun in Medieval Germany," *New York Times*, October 13, 2010; Roger Ebert, "A Mystic, Herbalist and Politician," *RogerEbert.com*, November 3, 2010, https://www.rogerebert.com/reviews/vision-from-the-life-of-hildegard-von-bingen-2010, last accessed June 8, 2023; Gary Goldstein, "A 'Vision' of Uncommon Reach," *Los Angeles Times*, November 12, 2010. See also Griffiths, *Garden of Delights*, 11–16 et passim.

9. Editions and translations of several of these can be found at "Hildegard von Bingen," *Epistolae: Medieval Women's Latin Letters*, https://epistolae.ctl.columbia.edu/woman/115.html (last accessed June 8, 2023).

10. Ebert, "A Mystic, Herbalist and Politician," https://www.rogerebert.com/reviews/vision-from-the-life-of-hildegard-von-bingen-2010, last accessed June 8, 2023; Evan Torner, "Review of von Trotta, Margarethe, dir., *Vision: From the Life of Hildegard von Bingen*," H-German, H-Net Reviews, February 2011, http://www.h-net.org/reviews/showrev.php?id=32228, last accessed June 10, 2023.

11. Fiona J. Griffiths, *Nuns' Priests' Tales: Men and Salvation in Medieval Women's Monastic Life* (Philadelphia: University of Pennsylvania Press, 2018), 181.

12. Franz J. Felten, "What Do We Know About the Life of Jutta and Hildegard at Disibodenberg and Rupertsberg?," in *A Companion to Hildegard of Bingen*, ed. Beverly Mayne Kienzle, Debra L. Stoudt, and George Ferzoco (Leiden: Brill, 2014), 27–28; Griffiths, *Nuns' Priests' Tales*, 9–38.

13. Griffiths, *Nuns' Priests' Tales*, 181–82.

14. Amelia Kennedy, "Crip Time in the Medieval Monastery: Cistercian Writers on the Time-Scapes of Infirmity, c. 1150–1250," *Journal of Medieval Monastic Studies* 10 (2021): 67–87.

15. Hugh Feiss, "Explanation of the Rule of Benedict by Hildegard of Bingen," *Vox Benedictina* 7, no. 2 (1990): 117–57, includes an English translation; Felten, "What Do We Know About the Life of Jutta and Hildegard," 21, 34.

16. Mayke de Jong, *In Samuel's Image: Child Oblation in the Early Medieval West* (Leiden: Brill, 1996), 216–27; Eva Schlotheuber, "Klostereintritt und Übergangsriten: Die Bedeutung der Jungfräulichkeit für das Selbstverständnis der Nonnen der alten Orden," in *Frauen—Kloster—Kunst: Neue Forschungen zur Kulturgeschichte des Mittelalters. Beiträge zum Internationalen Kolloquium vom 13. bis 16. Mai 2005 anlässlich der Ausstellung 'Krone und Schleier,'"* ed. Jeffrey F. Hamburger, Carola Jäggi, Susan Marti, and Hedwig Röckelein (Turnhout: Brepols, 2007), 46–50.

17. De Jong, *In Samuel's Image*, 71–99.

18. Felten, "What Do We Know About the Life of Jutta and Hildegard," 16–20. See also Sabina Flanagan, "Oblation or Enclosure: Reflections on Hildegard of Bingen's Entry into Religion," in *Wisdom Which Encircles Circles: Papers on Hildegard of Bingen*, ed. Audrey Ekdahl Davidson (Kalamazoo, Mich.: Medieval Institute Publications, 1996), 1–14.

19. For more on the canon law of nuns' claustration, see Spencer Strub's chapter on *The Little Hours* (2017) in this book.

20. Schlotheuber, "Klostereintritt und Übergangsriten," 46, 51–54.

21. Griffiths, *Garden of Delights*, 41.

22. Felten, "What Do We Know About the Life of Jutta and Hildegard," 20–21.

23. Sirach [Ecclesiasticus] 32:24.

24. Isaiah 42:3.

25. Genesis 33:13.

26. Matthew 24:47.

CHAPTER TWELVE

WAR, FAMILY, AND THE LAW OF THE KYIVAN RUS IN *ALEXANDER NEVSKY* (1938)

By Asif A. Siddiqi

The Soviet film *Alexander Nevsky*, directed by Sergei Eisenstein and released on December 1, 1938, remains a film riddled with contradictions. It ostensibly brought to celluloid the heroic life of Prince Alexander (1221–63), the ruler of the medieval principality of Novgorod, an area that had been part of Kyivan Rus. The present-day nations of Russia, Ukraine, and Belarus all, in some fashion or other, trace their origins to Kyivan Rus, a conglomeration of principalities that existed across a large region from roughly from the late ninth to the mid-thirteenth centuries. By the end of this period, Kiyvan Rus fell into decline, as each principality—such as Novgorod—assumed independent status, resulting from both the contraction of the Byzantine Empire and aggressive Mongol activity from the east. The Mongol invasion of these lands, especially the initial incursion from 1237 to 1240 in areas of northern Rus under the rulership of Batu (*c.* 1205–55), the grandson of Genghis Khan, completely disrupted and devastated the existing social order in principalities such as Ryazan, Vladimir, and Kiev.[1]

It was during this period, just after the Mongols extended their influence into the northern and western lands of former Kiyvan Rus, that Prince Alexander came to prominence. Alexander was born to Prince Yaroslav (of the principality of Pereyaslavl just southeast of Kyiv) and his third wife, Fedosya Igorevna. At the age of fifteen, Alexander was appointed by his father to be prince (*knyaz*) of Novgorod, one of the few major cities that were relatively unscathed in the wake of the Mongol invasion.[2] Two years later, in 1238, Alexander assumed sole rulership of Novgorod when his father was called away to Vladimir to deal with Batu. By some accounts, he had a rather contentious relationship with the wealthy merchants and nobles in Novgorod, who exercised power through a town assembly known as the *veche*.[3]

In its finished form, the film *Alexander Nevsky* was largely a work of fiction that owed little to extant historical evidence. And though the film was set in the Middle Ages, the themes presented were unambiguous allegories commenting on the Soviet Union of the 1930s. Because of these contradictions, it represents a perfect opportunity to explore the contentious, contingent, and often contorted relationship between history and art in twentieth-century cinema. In disentangling that relationship, this chapter focuses on how *Alexander Nevsky*, despite its apparent lack of verisimilitude, might tell us something about the social and legal conventions that governed the lives of people—especially women—in the medieval Russia of Prince Alexander's time. Historian John Aberth has noted that the film "has almost nothing to say about the historical Nevsky, whose memory . . . is largely mined from a hagiographical legend composed long after his lifetime."[4] Such claims are nominally true, but, as this chapter demonstrates, the film communicates a *flavor* of the ways in which people's lives interacted with legal regimes prevalent in the principalities of the former Kiyvan Rus.

PRINCE ALEXANDER'S BATTLES IN HISTORY AND MEMORY

Soon after his ascension, the historical Alexander Nevsky found himself entangled in two battles that would later shape his memory.[5] The first of these occurred in 1240 against the Swedes, Norwegians, and Finnish tribes on the northwestern frontier. Having been summoned by the *veche*, Alexander successfully routed the Swedish in the Battle of the Neva, because of which, two centuries later, Alexander was given the title "of Neva" (which, in the Russian genitive case, became "Nevsky"). A year later, the *veche* called upon him again when Novgorod came under threat, this time from the Germanic Livonian Order (allied with Estonians) who had taken the principality of Pskov (close to the border with Estonia) and were now threatening Novgorod. These incursions were part of broader Christian colonization campaigns in the twelfth and thirteenth centuries—later called the "Baltic Crusades"— against pagan, and to a lesser extent Slavic, peoples in the greater Baltic region.[6] Alexander reluctantly returned to Novgorod, retaking Pskov and then pushing further into Estonian-German lands, where his army fought a battle on the ice of Lake Peypus.[7]

Because there were no contemporaneous accounts of these battles, Alexander Nevsky's legacy was carefully forged and reforged in the centuries after his passing. The principal source was a hagiography, *The Tale of the Life and Bravery of the Blessed and Grand Prince Alexander*, produced in the late thirteenth and early fourteenth centuries, and one that may have been in the form of a secular military narrative. This original story was later transformed into a "saint's tale" pitting the Orthodox Church against Catholicism sometime in the second half of the fourteenth century.[8] To Nevsky's lionization as a military genius and a saint was also added a new twist, suggesting that Alexander's inarguable appeasement of the Mongol Golden Horde—he not only submitted fully to them but also violently battled his own people when they refused to pay taxes to the khan—was not so much an act of betrayal as an effort to save his own people from the ravages that might be visited upon them were he to resist.[9]

Perhaps the most influential source for Alexander Nevsky's modern image was Russian historian Nikolai Mikhailovich Karamzin (1766–1826), whose *History of the Russian State* (published 1829–33), having drawn its information from various chronicles, "had a profound influence not only on historians, but also on the famous poets and writers of Russia's literary golden age, such as Aleksandr Pushkin (1799–1837) and Feodor Dostoevsky (1821–81)."[10] By the early twentieth century, influenced by Karamzin, Alexander Nevsky had become an avatar for the defender of the "Russian national idea"—that is, a civilizational concept that presented Russia on a unique and sacred journey with no quarter given to enemies, either political or religious, that threatened its stability. In that sense, he was a natural subject for cinematic treatment and one that caught the eye of director Sergei Mikhailovich Eisenstein (1898–1948).

One of the most influential filmmakers of the early twentieth century, Eisenstein came of age as a director after the Bolshevik Revolution in 1917, which brought the communists to power in the new Soviet Union. He achieved fame early on with what many consider his masterpiece, *Battleship Potemkin* (1925), a silent film that dramatized a mutiny that occurred during the 1905 Revolution under the czars. In introducing his concept of *montage*—a series of differing shots to convey a particular theme—Eisenstein successfully molded high concept with revolutionary theater.

At some point in the mid-1930s, after a lengthy trip abroad (including to the United States), Eisenstein was commissioned by the Soviet government to develop a film based on Alexander Nevsky's life.[11] The choice of a historical figure for a film treatment was not anomalous at the time. In the second half of the 1930s, the Stalinist regime devoted increasing attention to fostering national pride through appeals to older non-socialist traditions dating from before the Bolshevik Revolution.[12] In bringing Nevsky to the big screen, Eisenstein also tapped into the perceived growing threat from fascist Germany ubiquitous in the Soviet media through the 1930s. Enabled by Hitler's own bloodthirsty tirades against the Bolsheviks and the "Slavic race," many in the Soviet Union genuinely believed (correctly, as it turned out), that the Nazis would try to invade the Soviet Union. Simultaneously, the Soviet propaganda apparatus invested enormous resources to feed the cult of Josef Stalin (1878–1953). Eisenstein noted at the time that "we have taken a historical episode from the thirteenth century, when the ancestors of today's Fascists, the Teutonic and Livonian knights, waged a systematic struggle to conquer and invade the East in order to subjugate the Slav and other nationalities in precisely the same spirit that Fascist Germany is trying to do today, with the same frenzied slogans and the same fanaticism."[13]

Eisenstein was also seduced by another aspect of the Nevsky story: he told a colleague that "nobody knows much about him, and so nobody can possibly find fault with me."[14] The final script, written by Eisenstein (and well-known writer Pyotr Pavlenko), was scrutinized by a panel of historians, ostensibly to check for historical accuracy, but in reality, it was to ensure that the themes of the movie were unambiguous and within authorized discourse, describing the heroic, modest, and self-sacrificial nature of a Stalin-like figure protecting the homeland at a time of great peril in the form of Germanic hordes at the border.[15]

WAR AND ITS AFTERMATH

The film itself opens with Alexander Nevsky (Nikolai Cherkasov) just having defeated the Swedes and fishing among his people in his childhood principality of Pereyaslavl. Representatives of the Mongol Horde (obviously standing in for the contemporary Japanese threat from Manchuria) approach and demand the people join up with their cause. While everyone submits, Alexander, standing alone, refuses to acquiesce to them. When the Tatars leave, he tells his people that the fight at hand is not with the Mongols but with "the Germans," who pose a greater threat. After the citizens of Novgorod learn of the German advance, first to Pskov and then toward Novgorod, Alexander is summoned to Novgorod to lead a peasant army against the Germans. His response—"I will stand up for the land of Rus"—seems to elevate him already into exalted status. Throughout the film, there is a tension between the suggestion that Nevsky was a saintly and religious figure (which would have been prohibited under Stalin) and his portrayal as a secular and practical man. This tension is never fully resolved, and at times Nevsky remains elusive, impenetrable, and lacking Earthly concerns, while at other times he is shown to be a man of the people, cavorting and relating with the peasants of Novgorod.

The enemy is obviously a stand-in for Nazi Germany. They are shown, especially in the "Rape of Pskov" scene, as cruel and violent, mobilized by both ethnic and theocratic supremacy. These thirteenth-century Germans wear insignias that seem to suggest swastikas, and their priests are dressed in long-flowing white habits, evoking the treacherous Whites (former Nobles) from the recent Russian Civil War (1918–20). They show no mercy as they throw infants onto huge pyres, while large black crosses loom over the victims. Eisenstein drew from contemporaneous fascist imagery of the late 1930s to inform this eruption of violence, including the fascist terror-bombing of Guernica in Spain in 1937 and the Nazi seizure of the Sudetenland (in Czechoslovakia) in 1938.[16]

A subplot in the movie is designed to provide a sense of peasant folk culture and involves two former warriors, Gavrilo (Andrey Abrikosov) and Buslai (Nikolai Okhlopkov), who had fought with Nevsky against the Swedes but are now jockeying for the affections of a young woman, Olga (Valentina Ivashyova). They each ask for Olga's hand in marriage, but she, unable to decide, avers that she will give her hand to the one who is the bravest. Such scenes effectively underscore the role of the common peasant in securing victory. The final tactical strategy used to defeat the Germans—a pincer strategy to pin the enemy—is, in fact, proposed by a rank-and-file man, the armorer Ignat (Dmitry Orlov).

There are a number of themes taken up in the film as Alexander prepares his army, motifs that would have been obvious to viewers in the late 1930s as the Stalinist Great Purges engulfed entire communities in suspicion and terror. We find, for example, the "enemy within" Novgorod—that is, merchants or clerics who would appease the invaders. Tverdilo Ivanovich (Sergey Blinnikov), the mayor of Pskov, betrays his city and the Orthodox monk, Ananias. There are also clear allusions to the First Five-Year Plan, the Stalinist economic programs that regulated all work in the 1930s. Artisans are shown having quotas to fill (1,000 spears, 500 shields) and some highly motivated workers, such as Ignat, are shown as self-sacrificing; he donates his weapons to others, although this leaves him defenseless.

The central set piece, a thirty-minute battle on the iced-over Lake Peypus, is suitably epic, with bodies, swords, axes, and armor all collectively elevating what must have been gruesome violence to grand spectacle. The battle concludes with Alexander personally defeating the German "grand master" in a duel while fleeing German soldiers run across the iced lake, which collapses under their weight and swallows them up. We return to the sub-plot involving Olga, who comes upon her two suitors, Buslai and Gavrilo, the latter of whom has been badly injured. Buslai and Olga raise Gavrilo to his feet and the three walk off together, having acknowledged their great triumph.

The final act foregrounds the legal world of Prince Alexander in two critical scenes. First, as the citizens of Pskov pay homage to the many Russian dead, Alexander shows mercy to the captured Germans, freeing the rank-and-file soldiers, while the people pounce on the mayor of Pskov, Tverdilo, who had traitorously betrayed the Russians. Here, charity and vengeance are contrasted as polar ends of the domain of justice in Pskov. Second, Olga asks Prince Alexander himself to decide on whom she should marry, Buslai or Gavrilo. Buslai interjects, gamely noting that neither he nor Gavrilo was the bravest—although he concedes that the injured Gavrilo was the second bravest. We find out that the bravest of all was one Vasilisa (Alexandra Danilova), a young woman who had fought fearlessly in the battle. At this point, we see Olga run to console the injured Gavrilo, while Vasilisa succumbs to Buslai's silent appeal for her hand in marriage.

OLGA'S STORY

There are many incongruencies between the movie and what little we know of Alexander Nevsky's actual life. For example, Alexander never resisted Mongol demands but in fact served as their vassal; the army that he put together to defeat the Livonian Order and the Teutonic Knights was not from the peasantry but made up of private retainers; Alexander had a contentious relationship with the *veche* of Novgorod, who had actually run him out of the principality; and medieval Novgorod was, in fact, an agricultural economy and not a mercantile one as depicted in the movie. The famed historian John Fennell has noted that the battle of Lake Peypus, as well as the earlier one against the Swedes, were "relatively minor victories... blown up to epic proportions" in the original *Life of Alexander Nevsky*.[17]

The subplot surrounding Olga, in particular, conveys some sense of the intersection between gender and religion. In making a film suitable for Stalinist times, Eisenstein denuded the movie of any presence of the Orthodox Church in either Novgorod or in neighboring Pskov, but such a strategy inadvertently illustrated the deeply contingent nature of the relationship between church and law in the lands of Kyivan Rus in the thirteenth century. In general, the corpus of Kievan law showed an interest in only very elementary forms of conflict resolution, ones that did not endanger the security of officials or their property and incomes.[18] The most notable legal document governing the lives of the population was the so-called *Russkaya pravda* (Justice of Rus), a composite document originally produced in the eleventh and twelfth centuries. Among its many goals was to support the ownership of private property (including the enslaved), protect commerce, maintain the powers and status of the nobility, including the prince, and "provide the norms in a multi-racial society."[19]

A separate church-based legal system also emerged at the time, manifested in charters such as Vladimir's Church Statute and Yaroslav's Church Statute. Besides ensuring the authority of the church in all matters, these edicts mainly regulated the authority of princely and church power in all areas of social life, including supporting the family, maintaining a social hierarchy, eliminating pagan practices, and most important, ensuring the penetration of Orthodox Christianity into these areas.

Yet, the Yaroslav Church Statute, excerpted in the appendix, was not very successful in its mission, especially in its goal of regulating the family. Historian Daniel H. Kaiser has noted that "one of the most repeated complaints voiced by the clerics was their lack of success in inducing the natives to accept the Christian view of marriage, and to permit the church to conduct the ceremony," especially among ordinary people. Typically, "most marriages were consummated through bride abduction and other pagan consecrations."[20] Because most peasant marriages were not consecrated in the eyes of a Christian God, church authorities tried to sanction those who, at least in their eyes, lived as fornicators, by calling them "heretics" and ordering others not to associate with them. In the church's many edicts condemning fornication, adultery, bigamy, divorce, and so forth, we find a system desperately trying to regulate the moral economy of these principalities in ways that would give them more power over their daily lives.

Which brings us to the tale of Olga in the movie *Alexander Nevsky*. Her story, as presented in the film, has an arc: at the beginning, she is an agent of her own fate, having the privilege of selecting her future husband. Two men vie for that honor in the hope that she will grant them that privilege. By the film's end, the decision has moved to the men surrounding her. The first person she asks to resolve her dilemma is, of course, Alexander Nevsky. Although there is no church to intercede, Nevsky—shown outside the church and drinking from what appears to be a Communion chalice—serves as an obvious Christ-like figure whose assent is absolutely necessary for the marriages to occur. In that sense, the film expertly portrays a kind of transition: in the initial section, we have a woman who is an agent of her own destiny and perhaps her sexual freedom who is then, by the end of the movie, brought firmly into the legal regime that the church sought to often violently impose on the principality. And this representation of "Russian" virtue was paradoxically at odds with the "native" practices of pagan culture in the region.

The Statute of Prince Yaroslav conveys the striking ways in which this reach for church power occurred in the thirteenth century, underscoring the church's mission to regulate every aspect of a woman's sexual identity. The statute, thought to have belonged to Yarsolav the Wise (d. 1054), who also contributed to the *Russkaya pravda*, comes to us only in copies dated to the fifteenth century. A good portion of the statute deals with contact with or participation in "pagan" practices, with many injunctions on not to do so. We also find a great degree of concern about sexual activity, especially if initiated by a woman, and in cases of contact with Muslims or Jews. Finally, there is a cluster of laws designed to control every aspect of marriage, including divorce. All of these stipulations suggest a deep concern with asserting the church's goals of eliminating what they considered the heretical nature of pagan life. Their objective was a social order dominated by patriarchy and a desire to retain control of wealth and property.

CONCLUSION

Olga's journey through Sergei Eisenstein's *Alexander Nevsky* is a minor one, overshadowed by the grandeur of a heavily fictionalized battle between

Nevsky and his personal army and the Livonian Order. The movie served as a powerful allegory for an imagined Nazi invasion of the Soviet Union, thwarted by the stoic and heroic bravery of a Stalin-like figure, overcoming internal enemies and the timidity of some of his allies. The movie seemed to suggest that the "Russian national idea" could not and would not be vanquished so easily. Yet, within that higher heroic and highly stylized fictional narrative, we find the lives of everyday people in the principalities of medieval Rus. From the beginning of the movie, when Olga is a young single woman who would choose her destiny ("Let her choose!," says one of her suitors, Buslai), to the denouement, in which her destiny is chosen for her, we find the entire arc of possibility for a woman in thirteenth-century Novgorod, a society where the world of pagan Kiyvan Rus' came into contact with an increasingly draconian and regulatory world of the Orthodox Church.

APPENDIX

Alexander Nevsky (1938)

THE STATUTE OF PRINCE YAROSLAV ON CHURCH
COURTS (C. 11TH–12TH CENTURIES)

These excerpts from the Statute of Prince Yaroslav are primarily concerned with regulating the behavior of women, both within and beyond the conventions of marriage.

Source: Iaroslav Nikolaevich Shchapov, ed., "Ustav kniazia Iaroslava o tserkovnykh sudakh: Arkheograpficheskii izvod," in *Drevnerusskie kniazheskie ustavy, XI–XV vv.* (Moscow: Nauka, 1976), 93–99. Original in Old Church Slavonic. Translated by Asif A. Siddiqi.

5. If a girl engages in sexual intercourse or becomes pregnant [while still living] with her father or mother, or while she is a widow, after having established [this], put her in a church house [convent].

11. If a wife goes from her husband to another man, or if she has intercourse [with that man] apart from her husband, take that wife into a church house [convent], and the newlywed [couple] is to pay [a marriage fee] to the Metropolitan [bishop].

19. If a man separates from his wife by his own wish, and if there was a church wedding, then [they] shall give the Metropolitan 12 grivnas.[21] And if they were not married in a church [they are to pay] the Metropolitan 6 grivnas.

20. If a Jew or Muslim [takes] a Rus' woman [to wed], or [if] another [non-Orthodox] foreigner [takes a Rus' woman], [he is to pay] the Metropolitan 50 grivnas and take the Rus' woman into a church house [convent].

30. If a girl does not wish to marry, [and] then the father and mother give her [in marriage] by force, if the girl renders [harm] to herself, then the father and mother are guilty before the Metropolitan, and they are to pay [the cost]. Likewise with a young man [who wishes not to marry].

36. If the cheese be cut for a girl [thereby concluding a marriage agreement according to a pagan ritual], [those who participate in this are to pay] one grivna for that cheese, and [pay] her [the girl] 3 grivnas for the dishonor and what is lost, ... and [pay] 6 grivnas to the Metropolitan, and the prince punishes [them].

37. If a wife steals from her husband, and [he] catches her, [she is to pay] 3 grivnas to the Metropolitan, and her husband punishes her, but for this they are not divorced.

40. If a woman be a maker of charms, or a witch, or a pagan sorceress, or a maker of potions, then her husband, having caught her [doing these things], punishes her but does not separate from her, and [pays] the Metropolitan 6 grivnas.

42. If a woman beats her husband, [she is to pay] the Metropolitan 3 grivnas.

46. If a monk, or nun, or priest, or priest's wife, or widow, or the woman who bakes the Eucharist bread, or a person who looks after the church falls into fornication, the Metropolitan is to judge them separately from laymen, and [he is] free to condemn them according to his will.

50. If someone eats pagan food by his own volition, whether it be mare's meat, or bear's meat, or any other forbidden meat, he is guilty before the Metropolitan and [is subject to] punishment.

52. Do not eat or drink with those people who are not baptized or with a foreigner or from our own people if he be not [baptized], until he is [baptized]. And whoever knowingly eats and drinks [with unbaptized persons] will be guilty before the Metropolitan.

54. If someone engages in intercourse with a Muslim or Jewish woman and he does not separate [from her], let them be excommunicated from the Church and from Christians, and [pay] the Metropolitan 12 grivnas.

56. And for these causes divorce a man from his wife:

And this is the first cause. If a wife hears from other people that they plot against the tsar, or against the prince, but she does not tell her husband about this, and later is discovered [to have known about the plot], divorce them.

And this is the second cause. If a man catches his wife with an adulterer or starts a case against her [based on] good witnesses, divorce them.

And this is the third cause. If a woman plots against her own husband with poison or with other people, if she learns that [people] wish to kill or murder her husband, but she says nothing to her husband, and later this comes to light, divorce [them].

And this is the fourth cause. If a wife without her husband's permission goes [around] with other people, or drinks or eats [with them], or sleeps outside his house, and then the husband discovers this, divorce [them].

And this is the fifth cause. If a wife without her husband's permission goes to the pagan dances in the day or at night, and her husband finds out, but she does not obey [his command to stop], divorce her.

And this is the sixth cause. If a wife leads thieves to her husband, orders [them] to rob the house of her husband, or herself robs [him], having stolen [his] goods or from a church, and gives [the stolen property] to others, divorce them.

Reading questions

- The Statute of Prince Yaroslav suggests a number of primary preoccupations of the Orthodox Church in the twelfth and thirteenth centuries. How would you characterize these preoccupations? Do we see any hint of these preoccupations in *Alexander Nevsky*?
- If *Alexander Nevsky* was hoping to depict the status of women more accurately (as reflected in the Statute of Prince Yaroslav), how do you think the depiction of the principal women in the movie would change? (Note: There are at least three women who have important roles.)
- How is moral policing connected to generating revenue, as shown in this Statute? Does *Alexander Nevsky* give a sense of how revenue is generated? Who pays for the armies that fight the invaders? How are merchants in general depicted?

NOTES

1. Janet Martin, *Medieval Russia, 980–1584*, 2nd ed. (Cambridge: Cambridge University Press, 2007), 163–64.

2. Ibid., 162.

3. For the *veche*, see Ferdinand Feldbrugge, *Law in Medieval Russia* (Leiden: Nijhoff, 2009), 147–65.

4. John Aberth, *A Knight at the Movies: Medieval History on Film* (New York: Routledge, 2003), 107.

5. Perhaps the most thorough recounting of the relationship between Nevsky, the historical figure and Nevsky, the memorialized myth, can be found in Eugene Smelyansky, *Medievalisms and Russia: The Contest for Imaginary Pasts* (Leeds: Arc Humanities Press, 2024), 39–66.

6. Anti Selart, *Livonia, Rus' and the Baltic Crusades in the Thirteenth Century* (Leiden: Brill, 2015).

7. John Fennell, *The Crisis of Medieval Russia, 1200–1304* (London: Longman, 1983), 102–5; Artis Aboltins and Erich Anderson, "Controversial Hero," *Medieval Warfare* 4, no. 1 (2014): 6–10; Donald Ostrowski, "Alexander Nevskii's 'Battle on the Ice': The Creation of a Legend," *Russian History* 33 (2006): 289–312.

8. Donald Ostrowski, "Dressing a Wolf in Sheep's Clothing: Toward Understanding the Composition of the Life of Alexander Nevskii," *Russian History* 40, no. 1 (2013): 41–67; Smelyansky, *Medievalisms and Russia*, 42–43.

9. Martin, *Medieval Russia, 980–1584*, 168–69.

10. Mari Isoaho, *The Image of Aleksandr Nevskiy in Medieval Russia: Warrior and Saint* (Leiden: Brill, 2006), 375–76.

11. Leonid Kozlov, "The Artist and the Shadow of Ivan," in *Stalinism and Soviet Cinema*, ed. Derek Spring and Richard Taylor (London: Routledge, 2013), 109–30, esp. 111.

12. Peter Kenez, "Soviet Cinema in the Age of Stalin," in Spring and Taylor, *Stalinism and Soviet Cinema*, 54–68; David Brandenberger, *National Bolshevism: Stalinist Mass Culture and the Formation of Modern Russian National Identity, 1931–1956* (Cambridge, Mass.: Harvard University Press, 2002), 77–94.

13. Eisenstein, quoted in Aberth, *Knight at the Movies*, 108.

14. Ibid., 107.

15. For more on the resonance of the movie in the 1930s, see Smelyansky, *Medievalisms and Russia*, 52–60; Paul A. Cohen, *History and Popular Memory: The Power of Story in Moments of Crisis* (New York: Columbia University Press, 2014), 149–70.

16. Aberth, *Knight at the Movies*, 116.

17. Fennell, *Crisis of Medieval Russia, 1200–1304*, 103–6.

18. Richard Hellie, "Foreword: Russian Law from Oleg to Peter the Great," in *The Laws of Rus'—Tenth to Fifteenth Centuries*, trans., ed. Daniel H. Kaiser (Salt Lake City: Schlacks, 1992), xiii.

19. Hellie, "Foreword," xviii–xix.

20. Daniel H. Kaiser, *The Growth of the Law in Medieval Russia* (Princeton, N.J.: Princeton University Press, 1980), 168.

21. Grivna (plural: Grivnas) was the primary unit of currency in Kiyvan Rus.

CHAPTER THIRTEEN

CHURCH LAW, COMMUNITY PRACTICE, AND THE WITCH TRIAL THAT WASN'T IN *SORCERESS* (1987)

By Rachel Ellen Clark and Lucy C. Barnhouse

If you have watched movies set in the Middle Ages, you might picture an era chock-full of witch beliefs and witch trials. Consider the witchlike Maleficent in *Sleeping Beauty* (1959) or the enchantresses in adaptations of Arthurian legend, from Madam Mim in *The Sword and the Stone* (1963) to Nimue in *Cursed* (2020) or Morgan le Fay in *Camelot* (2011) and *The Green Knight* (2021). Fantasies set in a pseudo-medieval world also invoke witches. Recent examples include Yennefer in *The Witcher* (2019–) and Sofina in *Dungeons & Dragons: Honor among Thieves* (2023). The cinematic medieval loves (to hate) a witch.

The 1987 French film *Le moine et la sorcière* (released in the US as *Sorceress*) similarly features a character, Elda (Christine Boisson), who is tried for witchcraft and sorcery. While the film draws on a medieval text, Étienne de Bourbon's *On the Seven Gifts of the Holy Spirit* (written c. 1250), neither the character nor the trial exists in the source.[1] De Bourbon (d. 1261) belonged to the Dominicans, an order of preaching friars created in the early thirteenth century alongside other new religious orders, such as the Franciscans.[2] Designed as a resource for preachers writing sermons, *On the Seven Gifts of the Holy Spirit* compiled stories taken from eyewitnesses' accounts, the Bible, saints' lives, and de Bourbon's personal experiences as a preacher and inquisitor in France. In one section of this work, "On Superstition," de Bourbon describes the cult of St. Guinefort, a greyhound. (A translation of this account appears in the appendix.) The film, however, makes significant changes to the source material to highlight the limits of the law. This version of Étienne (Tchéky Karyo) and the legal system he represents are both separate from and opposed to the affairs of the village community. In the film, the exercise of secular and ecclesiastical legal power leads to deprivation and cruelty, while the care of local communities centers the power of women to heal and nurture—a power that the film's Étienne can interpret only as witchcraft.

Sorceress correctly emphasizes the distinction between ecclesiastical and secular law, but it often exaggerates and misrepresents medieval understandings of heresy, superstition, and magic. In the movie, Étienne overzealously treats folklore as heresy in a way that reveals much more about 1980s perceptions of the medieval church than it does about the historical de Bourbon. But the narrative has much more to say—and more myths to propagate—about the supposed links among pagan religion, witchcraft, and medicine. This chapter argues that *Sorceress*, especially by introducing a witch trial that never appears in the source, presents a feminist logic of community and justice as an alternative to attempts by secular and canon law to regulate both.

THE MONK

In the second half of the thirteenth century, canonists and communities were scrambling to accommodate the diversification of medieval Christianity. Preceding decades had seen the multiplication of not only religious orders, but also the ways in which laypeople (those who are not clergy) chose to express their religious beliefs. These vibrant, diverse religious expressions sometimes included unorthodox elements that attracted ecclesiastical disapproval.

Canon law, the law of the church, was comprehensive but far from unified. It could be created through councils, synods, and papal letters; its implications were dissected and debated by commentators. From the late twelfth century onward, it expanded alongside ecclesiastical infrastructure. In theory, it regulated many aspects of people's lives. In practice, however, as the film illustrates, people often and cheerfully had illicit sex, made offerings to fairies, and used the Eucharist for magical purposes.[3] By preaching and hearing confessions, Étienne de Bourbon sought to ensure that people adequately understood basic theology and abided by the essential teachings of the church. Defining what this meant could be complicated, and clerical and lay definitions of acceptable Christian practice often diverged.

Infractions of canon law requiring penance did not, in themselves, make someone a criminal. However, the lines between canon and secular law could blur. Secular authorities sometimes upheld and reinforced the power of official church doctrine by imposing legal penalties for heresy, such as burning at the stake—penalties that canon law could not enforce. Even the church's judicial inquiries into heresy, which were commissioned by the pope and called "inquisitions," had to rely on secular authorities to carry out a sentence of death on the rare occasions when it was called for. The film illustrates this process when Étienne accuses Elda of heresy. He claims she is a "sorceress" who "teaches diabolical chants." However, even after the hasty trial he conducts, he cannot impose execution; instead, he must defer to the Count (Féodor Atkine).

The historical de Bourbon would have been shocked by such a turn of events. The process of medieval inquisition bore little resemblance to that of the state-sponsored apparatus of the early modern period (c. 1500–1700), when trials for witchcraft flourished, and even less to today's stereotypes. Instead, it looked more like de Bourbon's self-described duties: preaching and hearing confessions (see text in appendix). But as scholars of both heresy and witchcraft have argued, the process of inquisition itself could help to create categories of unacceptable belief and behavior.[4] Thus, when de Bourbon wrote his treatise for the benefit of other clergy, he used the story of Guinefort—the veneration of an animal as a saint—as one example of beliefs that cross the line of acceptability.

When de Bourbon was dispatched as inquisitor, the Languedoc region of southern France was grappling with the aftermath of the so-called Albigensian Crusade (1209–29), which pitted northern French Catholic nobles against the heretical Cathars. In 1233, Pope Gregory IX (r. 1227–41) put the Dominican Order in charge of a new inquisition there to stamp out the remaining Cathars. As a Dominican friar, de Bourbon traveled through Languedoc to educate the laity and eradicate heretical belief. This process involved both active, responsive listening to the community through the sacrament of confession and public communication with them through preaching.[5] Contrary to modern stereotypes of "the inquisition" (in fact, there were many inquisitions, in different periods and regions), de Bourbon and his fellow inquisitors did not view folk traditions as heresy. In fact, in *Sorceress*, the permissiveness of the curé (Jean Carmet) toward the cult of St. Guinefort illustrates the medieval church's willingness to tolerate or even absorb non-heretical folk beliefs rather than persecuting them. By destroying Guinefort's shrine and persuading the local authorities to impose a fine for visiting the site, de Bourbon attempted to enforce stricter categories of acceptable Christian practice using the power of secular law. Including the story of Guinefort in his treatise allowed him to model possible options for other clergy in similar situations.

By preserving de Bourbon's distinctions between secular and canon law, *Sorceress* gives a veneer of historical accuracy to a major change the film makes to his narrative. Historically, de Bourbon never called the woman who performed rituals in the forest a heretic. After all, he locates the story of Guinefort in the section of his book on "superstition," and not in the later section on "heresy." But the film draws on older scholarship assuming that women were both unusually attracted to and unusually active within heretical movements.[6] According to this outdated narrative, social and religious institutions marked women as deviant and dangerous; therefore, those women found alternate sources of authority and power through forbidden religious and ritual practices.[7]

In contrast, medieval churchmen's concerns about women's spiritual lives did not focus on access to forbidden power; rather, they worried that women's spiritual and physical weakness made them vulnerable to the devil.[8] Étienne, in the film, echoes these paternalistic beliefs, at the same time using them to offer a ready-made excuse: Elda's gendered lack of understanding, he suggests, has led to her innocent but dangerous error. "You can go back to your herbs and potions," he says, as long as she stops performing her customary healing rite in the woods. He changes his mind about her only when he is confronted about the rape he committed as a young man and its living evidence in the form of his daughter Agnes. If Elda's sin derives from her susceptibility to temptation, so does his. He pursued masculine aggression too far, a result of his shame at proving unable to dress a deer at the successful conclusion of a hunt.

Resolution comes when Étienne recognizes that women and illiterate peasants also have valid moral codes and ways of knowledge, even if they differ from the church's. Not all magic is heretical; not all folk practices are magical; the church has room for both the traditional veneration of St. Guinefort, the very good boy, and a statue that will legitimize him as a human saint for any future inquisitors.

THE SORCERESS

Sorceress's handling of women and witchcraft derives directly from the second-wave feminism of the 1970s and '80s.[9] Screenwriter Pamela Berger, an art historian at Boston College, had recently published a book exploring how medieval Christians allegedly appropriated the iconography of grain goddesses to reuse for female saints.[10] Interested in recuperating and imagining the unwritten experiences of medieval women, Berger places Elda at the center of the narrative, even though de Bourbon's Elda figure, an unnamed old woman, remains at the periphery. In an interview with *Cinéaste*, Berger explains that the character of Elda "came from what I imagined she would say as a healer, from the things we know she did, such as tend the sick, and from my own research into women healers"—research that she contributed to the famous second-wave feminist health and sexuality handbook *Our Bodies, Ourselves* (1973).[11] Elda's tranquil, nurturing earth-mother persona aligns her with the New Age, body-oriented feminism that surrounded Berger in the 1980s. As Monica Green has pointed out, such narratives about medieval women's medicine argued for continuities in women's history without undertaking serious analysis of the historical and cultural construction of gender.[12] Instead, women's historical knowledge and networks were imagined as separate from and working counter to those of men.

Throughout *Sorceress*, the care of women stands against the misguided fervor of elite masculine power, including both the Count who mistreats his people and the church that sends Étienne to stamp out heresy. Constance Bouchard has argued that the film treats men as oppressors, and not particularly imaginative ones at that.[13] In contrast, nursing mothers nurture and strengthen the entire community. The film opens with the image of a woman nursing a baby, and an important subplot involves a young mother who breastfeeds her husband to keep him alive while he starves in prison for having destroyed the Count's new carp pond. The nourishment provided by female bodies vividly symbolizes communal ingenuity and compassion.

However, the movie also includes male laborers in the practice of communal care. Knowledge of the land belongs to all. Everyone suffers when the Count ignores the peasant men, who know that only clay soil should be flooded, and turns their arable land into a fishing pond. St. Guinefort also belongs to all, not only to women. The curé supports the rite, and it is a little boy who tells Étienne that Guinefort is a dog. In fact, the movie shows that the common people benefit when they embrace both masculine and feminine ways of being and knowing, and when everyone—men and women, clergy and laypeople—ignores harshly patriarchal legal codes.

WITCHCRAFT AND WITCH TRIALS

Many people think of witch hunts as medieval, and the myth of the "Burning Times" in neopagan circles often includes the Middle Ages.[14] But large-scale witch hunts, whether ecclesiastical or secular, did not become common until the sixteenth century. Before the fifteenth century, witchcraft accusations tended to be isolated occurrences.

Secular and canon law treated magic differently. The secular authorities focused on magic as a crime, a way of harming others, and the associated penalties might consider the type and severity of the harm, as with other crimes. Church authorities focused not only on the harm, but also on the offense against God, and could impose penance or, more rarely, excommunication on practitioners.[15] In the later Middle Ages, the most common legal categories of witchcraft were *maleficium* (plural *maleficia*) and *veneficium* (plural *veneficia*). *Maleficia*—literally "evil deeds"—signified acts of magic that harmed others: attacks on people or their animals or crops, as well as natural disasters. *Veneficia* primarily meant acts of poisoning, perhaps associated with magic via potions.[16] Whether or not the accused witch had committed *maleficia* was a central question that inquisition sought to answer. But the conviction that witchcraft could cause very real damage determined both late medieval and early modern responses to it.

The late fifteenth century saw the development of ideas about witches and witchcraft that would come to underpin early modern witch hunts. These ideas drew on the categories created by Dominican inquisitors like Étienne de Bourbon.[17] Despite the official positions hostile to magic, however, clergy (including bishops, cardinals, and popes) discouraged people from accusing others of witchcraft and in fact dismissed rumors of magic as fictions.[18] So while Europe has a long history of witch persecution, de Bourbon lived and worked in a thirteenth-century environment that remained relatively unbothered about witchcraft.

Berger's screenplay, following a second-wave feminist argument, presents witch trials as a way of persecuting women who threatened the patriarchal status quo. The anthropologist Margaret Murray's "witch-cult hypothesis," which posited that witch trials tried to eliminate an old goddess-focused pagan religion, dominated conversations about the early modern witch trials through the mid-twentieth century; her book was published in 1921, and Norman Cohn's thorough takedown not until 1974. Yet you can see

Murray's influence in Étienne's reactions to the "paganism" of the cult of St. Guinefort: "I have witnessed a midnight rite from the dark ages of human sacrifice." When the village women blame "fauns" (elves, fairies) and "wood spirits," he grows enraged, accusing them of worshiping pagan deities or demons. Given the outright, legitimate threats that the Cathar and Waldensian heresies posed to the church, the fictional Étienne's reaction to a gentle midnight rite—a much gentler rite than the one the historical de Bourbon records—wildly exceeds the medieval evidence.

Étienne's focus on Elda makes sense, however, in the context of Berger's second-wave feminist politics. In the *Cinéaste* interview, Berger praised Barbara Ehrenreich and Deirdre English's 1973 book *Witches, Midwives, and Nurses: A History of Women Healers*.[19] Ehrenreich and English argued that midwives and other female healers suffered disproportionately from witchcraft accusations because men wanted to professionalize and masculinize medicine. As they acknowledged in the 2010 preface to the second edition, this argument stems from the need for the women's health movement "to confront women's ignorance of their own bodies," an ignorance that the overwhelmingly male medical establishment preserved and perpetuated.[20] Frustrated by the past marginalization of women in the academic study of history and the disempowerment of women in medicine, Ehrenreich, English, and Berger all sought a lost tradition of feminine knowledge and healing—and an explanation, albeit a simplistic one, for how that tradition was lost. The university-trained male medical professionals who gained increasing prominence in the later Middle Ages may have disparaged women's medical expertise. In the medieval reality, however, this vital expertise contributed to the essential work of households and communities and was sought out as such.[21]

Moreover, no evidence suggests that female medical practitioners were disproportionately accused of witchcraft. Many midwives and healers did find themselves involved in witch trials, but most women's occupations were not recorded, rendering any calculation of percentages impossible. It seems likely that midwives and healers faced accusations because of their proximity to health crises, rather than because authorities wanted to stamp out unsanctioned medical practitioners. Wolfgang Behringer points out that landladies were accused even more often than midwives,[22] but we have not seen anyone arguing that witch trials represented a systematic attempt to eliminate the profession of landladying.

In many ways, then, Berger's version of de Bourbon's "old woman" represents the conscious choice to prioritize women's stories, women's work, and women's agency as part of a thriving and supportive community. Berger positions Elda and the villagers against the rapacious, destructive behaviors of Étienne and the Count. Magic and ritual are part of the healthcare that Elda practices; good Christians (like the curé) accept these practices and prioritize communal harmony over the letter of the law.

CONCLUSION

The film's ambiguously happy ending presents a syncretism of Christianity, pagan tradition, and magic as the best possible outcome. Étienne pardons Elda, suggests building a chapel where the grove once stood, and promises to provide a statue of a man with a greyhound at his feet, thereby synthesizing the demands of the church (no animal saints) with the flexibility for the people to maintain their age-old traditions. In fact, as the end titles point out, the cult of St. Guinefort persisted into the twentieth century.

Despite a clear and consistent effort to distinguish between the legal authorities of the church and the Count, the movie does muddy the histories of witchcraft and heresy in the thirteenth century. Relying heavily on the arguments of second-wave feminists, Berger's screenplay perpetuates myths about medieval witchcraft that scholars have been debunking since the 1970s. When reckoning with the complexities of the past, we must return, always, to the evidence. Nevertheless, *Sorceress*—like the feminist scholarship it echoes—raises important questions about whose voices are preserved, how we can recuperate alternate perspectives from the historical record, and how complex and nuanced the relationships were among commoners, nobles, laypeople, and clergy.

Even today, popular myths insist that witch trials purposely suppressed certain categories of women (midwives, healers, practitioners of some previous pagan religion). In fact, you may encounter these myths on #WitchTok or in other neopagan spaces, both online and off. They persist for many reasons, not least of which is that many of us desire to find versions of ourselves in historical records.[23] These impulses can lead to exciting new research, as demonstrated by growing bodies of scholarship in the histories of medieval gender, race, sexuality, and disability. And movies like *Sorceress* and the other films analyzed in this volume remind us that the stories we tell about the past work actively to shape how we think about the present and the future.

APPENDIX

Sorceress (1987)

ÉTIENNE DE BOURBON (D. 1261), "OF THE WORSHIP OF GUINEFORT THE DOG" (C. 1250)

Étienne de Bourbon's De septem donis Spiritus Sancti (Of the Seven Gifts of the Holy Spirit) *compiled stories for use in sermons; his personal encounter with Guinefort's cult serves as an exemplum for his fellow preachers.*

Source: Jean-Claude Schmitt, *The Holy Greyhound: Guinefort, Healer of Children since the Thirteenth Century* (Cambridge: Cambridge University Press, 1983), 2–4. Original in Latin. Translated by Rachel Ellen Clark.

Sixth, I must talk about outrageous superstitions, some of which are an affront to God and some of which are an affront to our neighbors. These superstitions that attribute divine honor to demons, or to any other creatures, offend God because they are idolatrous. Wretched fortune-telling[24] women also commit idolatry when they seek salvation by worshipping elder trees[25] or giving offerings to them; by scorning churches or holy relics; and by carrying their children to elder trees or to anthills or to other places in order to restore their health.

This happened recently in the diocese of Lyons, where I preached against fortune-telling. While I was hearing confessions, many women admitted that they had taken their children to Saint Guinefort. I thought that this [Guinefort] was some holy man, so I investigated. Finally, I heard that he was a dog—actually, a greyhound—who was killed in the following way.

In the diocese of Lyons, near the nuns' convent called Neuville, on the lands of the lord of Villars, there was a castle. The knight who lived there and his wife had a baby boy. Now it happened that the lord and lady went out, and so did the baby's nurse. The baby was lying alone in his cradle when an enormous snake entered the house and headed toward the baby's cradle. The greyhound, who had stayed behind, saw the snake. He quickly sprang into hot pursuit and chased it under the cradle, which toppled over. The dog and the snake attacked each other, biting each other viciously. At last, the dog killed the snake and flung it far from the baby's cradle. The cradle, the floor, the dog's mouth and head—everything was gory with the snake's blood. The dog was standing next to the cradle, having been injured by the snake.

Now the nurse came in and saw this scene. She thought the dog had killed and eaten the baby, and she started screaming and wailing. Hearing the wails, the baby's mother also came running. When she saw the blood everywhere, she too believed that the dog had killed her son, and she joined the wailing. The knight likewise rushed in, and he thought the same thing. Thus, drawing his sword, he killed the dog.

Only then did they approach the baby and discover that he was safe and sound, sleeping sweetly. As they investigated further, they found the snake that the dog had ripped apart and killed. Recognizing the truth of the matter, they were distressed and mourned the unjust killing of such a helpful dog. They threw him into a well in front of the castle gates. They then made an enormous pile of stones above him and planted trees around him as a monument to his deeds.

It was the will of God that the castle fell into ruin and the land returned to wilderness, abandoned by its inhabitants. But the peasants heard about the dog's remarkable actions and how he died, innocent, for something that should have won him praise. They visited this grove, and they honored the dog as a martyr. They prayed for his help with sickness and other needs. There the devil seduced and toyed with many people so that he could deceive them and lead them into error.

Most of all, women brought their frail and sick babies to this site. In a certain town about a league away from the grove, they welcomed an old woman who taught them how to perform the rituals to make offerings to demons and to invoke them, and she would lead the women to the memorial. When they arrived, they would make an offering of salt and other things. Then they would use thorns from the surrounding thornbushes to pin their babies' swaddling clothes to the trees that grew above this place. They would put the naked baby into a hole between the trunks of two trees, with the mother holding the baby on one side and tossing it nine times to the old woman standing on the other side. Meanwhile, they would invoke demons and plead with the forest spirits[26] that lived in the Rimite Forest to take away this sick, weak baby—which the women said belonged to the spirits—and to bring back in its place the real child, the one that is big and plump, thriving and healthy.

Having done this, the murderous mother takes the naked baby and places it at the foot of a tree, on top of some straw from its cradle. Using fire they brought with them, they light two candles about the length of a thumb, and they affix those candles to the tree trunk above, on either side of the baby's head. While the candles burn, the women retreat far enough away that they can neither see the baby nor hear it crying. And the candle flames have burned and killed several babies, as we discovered from others in that place.

In addition, one woman told me that when she had invoked the forest spirits and was backing away, she saw a wolf emerge from the woods and move toward her baby. If her motherly love had not prevailed, the wolf—or, as she said, the devil in the form of a wolf—certainly would have devoured her baby.

If mothers returned to their babies and found them still alive, they would then take the baby down to the swift waters of a nearby river, called the Chalaronne. They would immerse the baby nine times in the river. Any infant who survived such intensely harsh treatment without dying right then or soon thereafter must have been made of tough stuff.

So we went to the grove, and we called together all the people of that region, and we preached against this legend. We had the dead dog dug up and the grove cut down, and we burned the wood together with the bones said to be the dog's. We then persuaded the lords of these lands to issue an edict stating that anyone who gathers at this site for any reason related to this practice can have their belongings confiscated and sold off.

Reading questions

- How does de Bourbon define idolatry and superstition? What sets these things apart from orthodox practice and belief?
- What do you make of this version of Étienne compared with his characterization in *Sorceress*?
- De Bourbon speaks of the forest rites as invoking demons; how do the women of the village seem to have understood their actions as part of a coherent belief system? How might they have deliberately used language aligning with de Bourbon's expectations?

NOTES

1. We distinguish between the fictional and historical versions of Étienne de Bourbon by referring to the film character as "Étienne" and the historical figure as "de Bourbon."

2. See Nathan Melson's chapter on *Francesco* (1989) in this book for the origins of the Franciscan Order.

3. Sara McDougall, "Women and Gender in Canon Law," in *The Oxford Handbook of Women and Gender in Medieval Europe*, ed. Judith M. Bennett and Ruth Mazo Karras (Oxford: Oxford University Press, 2013), 163–66.

4. John H. Arnold, "The Cathar Middle Ages as a Methodological and Historiographical Problem," in *Cathars in Question*, ed. Antonio Sennis (Woodbridge: York Medieval Press, 2016), 53–58.

5. On the centrality of this communication both to de Bourbon's mission and to how he understood it, see Catherine Rider, "Elite and Popular Superstitions in the Exempla of Stephen de Bourbon," *Studies in Church History* 42 (2006): 78–88, esp. 78–79.

6. John H. Arnold, "Heresy and Gender in the Middle Ages," in Bennett and Karras, *Oxford Handbook of Women and Gender*, 497–500.

7. For an example of this argument, see Elspeth Whitney, "Witches, Saints, and Other 'Others': Women and Deviance in Medieval Culture," in *Women in Medieval Western European Culture*, ed. Linda E. Mitchell (New York: Garland, 1999), 295–312.

8. Arnold, "Heresy and Gender in the Middle Ages," 498.

9. "Second-wave feminism" focused on women's autonomy: reproductive rights (including not only legal abortion but also the freedom to take contraception without a husband's permission and the implementation of protections against being fired for getting married and/or pregnant), equal pay for equal work, freedom from sexual harassment, and financial independence (i.e., being able to get a credit card without a male co-signer).

10. Pamela C. Berger, *The Goddess Obscured: Transformation of the Grain Protectress from Goddess to Saint* (Boston: Beacon Press, 1985).

11. Lynne Jackson, "Sorceress: An Interview with Pamela Berger," *Cinéaste* 16, no. 4 (1988): 45; Boston Women's Health Book Collective, *Our Bodies, Ourselves: A Book by and for Women*, 2nd ed. (New York: Simon & Schuster, 1973), which was originally distributed as *Our Bodies, Ourselves* in 1970 as a xeroxed pamphlet.

12. Monica H. Green, "Gendering the History of Women's Healthcare," *Gender & History* 20, no. 3 (2008): 487–518.

13. Constance B. Bouchard, "The Sorceress and the Greyhound," in *Medieval Women in Film: An Annotated Handlist and Reference Guide, with Essays on Teaching "The Sorceress,"* ed. Virginia Blanton, Martha M. Johnson-Olin, and Charlene Miller Avrich, Subsidia Series, 2nd ed. (Iowa City, IA: Medieval Feminist Forum, 2000), 1:89–90.

14. The phrase "Burning Times" was coined by Gerald Gardner, the creator of Wicca, and became popular through works by second-wave feminists who sought to trace a throughline from a prehistoric matriarchy to nature religions to twentieth-century neopaganism. See Ronald Hutton, *The Triumph of the Moon:*

A History of Modern Pagan Witchcraft (Oxford: Oxford University Press, 1999), 344–45.

15. Richard Kieckhefer, *Magic in the Middle Ages* (Cambridge and New York: Cambridge University Press, 2000), 234; Felicity Hill, *Excommunication in Thirteenth-Century England* (Oxford: Oxford University Press, 2022), 297–302.

16. Wolfgang Behringer, *Witches and Witch-Hunts* (Cambridge and Malden, Mass.: Polity Press, 2004), 48, 52.

17. Amiri Ayanna, "Witchcraft, Heinrich Kramer's Nuremberg Handbook, and Ecclesiasticus: The Construction of the Fifteenth-Century Civic Sorceress," in *Magic and Magicians in the Middle Ages and the Early Modern Time: The Occult in Pre-Modern Sciences, Medicine, Literature, Religion, and Astrology*, ed. Albrecht Classen (Berlin: De Gruyter, 2017), 565–68; Michael D. Bailey, *Battling Demons: Witchcraft, Heresy, and Reform in the Later Middle Ages* (University Park: Pennsylvania State University Press, 2003), 118–38. See also, foundationally, R. I. Moore, *The Formation of a Persecuting Society: Power and Deviance in Western Europe, 950-1250* (Oxford: Blackwell, 1987), 140–46.

18. Ronald Hutton, *The Witch: A History of Fear, From Ancient Times to the Present* (New Haven: Yale University Press, 2017), 156.

19. Jackson, "Sorceress: An Interview with Pamela Berger," 45.

20. Barbara Ehrenreich and Deirdre English, *Witches, Midwives, and Nurses: A History of Women Healers*, 2nd ed. (New York: Feminist Press at the City University of New York, 2010), 9.

21. Montserrat Cabré, "Women or Healers? Household Practices and the Categories of Health Care in Late Medieval Iberia," *Bulletin of the History of Medicine* 82, no. 1 (2008): 18–51.

22. Behringer, *Witches and Witch-Hunts*, 87.

23. Hilary Rhodes, "Premodern Pedagogies: Queer Medieval Materiality," *Quidditas* 42 (2021): 238–45; Usha Vishnuvajjala, *Feminist Medievalisms: Embodiment and Vulnerability in Literature and Film* (Leeds: Arc Humanities Press, 2024), 2–4.

24. De Bourbon chooses the word *sortilegia* here and in the next paragraph. It refers to a form of fortune-telling based on interpreting the casting of lots. It is associated with magical practices that were condemned by the church.

25. De Bourbon uses *sambucas*, referring to a specific species (rather than "elder" in the sense of "old"). Black elder trees (*Sambucus nigra*) are common in Europe. Elderflowers can be harvested to make elderflower cordial and have traditionally been used to alleviate respiratory symptoms, such as with the flu. (Studies have not shown it to be very effective.) Elderberries can be used to make wine. These associations have often linked elder trees with practices that blur the lines between magic, medicine, and witchcraft.

26. The Latin *faunus* has several meanings; in addition to general spirits of the forest, it can mean classical fauns (hybrid man-goat creatures, like Mr. Tumnus in *The Lion, the Witch, and the Wardrobe*), forest gods, or, in the singular, even the god Pan. *Sorceress* translates this word as "elves." The rest of the sentence links

these creatures with European fairy lore; a common belief about fairies was that they habitually stole human children and replaced them with changelings, who could be identified by their poor health, failure to thrive, continual crying, or emotionless affect. Today, many people view changeling beliefs through a functional lens, interpreting them as a way for premodern parents to try to address diseases and conditions they did not know how to explain or treat.

CHAPTER FOURTEEN

THE MYTH OF *JUS PRIMAE NOCTIS*, OR THE "RIGHT OF THE FIRST NIGHT," IN *BRAVEHEART* (1995)

By Lorraine Kochanske Stock

Cinematic medievalism featuring a culture of rape and sexual abuse provides a distant mirror reflecting issues of sexual misconduct occurring in the present, such as the sexual harassment of subordinate women by famous or powerful men that inspired activist Tarana Burke's 2006 "#MeToo" movement. Twenty-first-century cases of sexual abuse involving an imbalance of power between the accused rapist and victim evoke a similar unequal power dynamic in purported cases of authorized sexual assault during the medieval period. Although there is almost no contemporaneous documentary evidence for its legality, this so-called "right" was referred to variously in post-medieval media as *jus primae noctis* (right of the first night), *droit du seigneur* (right of the feudal lord), or *droit de cuissage* (right of the lord to place a bare leg, or thigh [*cuisse*], upon the marriage bed). The now-debunked phenomenon generally entitled some male social superior (king, feudal overlord, political superior, even a knight) to sexually assault a female social inferior. Specifically, it entitled a feudal social superior (the *seigneur*) to violate the virginity of a vassal's or subordinate's bride on their first night (*primae noctis*) of marriage. The Latin *jus* (right or law) and the French *droit* (right, law, duty) conferred a quasi-legality, and therefore authenticity, to the concept.

Although eighteenth- and nineteenth-century historians believed *jus primae noctis* (hereafter the *jus*) was enforced, subsequent scholars repudiated this view.[1] Contemporary filmmakers continue to encourage audiences, who rely on movies for their knowledge of the European medieval era, to believe the *jus was* a reality, reenforcing the perception of a "Dark Ages" characterized by physical and sexual violence. Exemplifying this trend is director and producer Mel Gibson's 1995 *Braveheart*, in which Gibson also portrayed the film's eponymous protagonist, William Wallace. Alongside other violence, *Braveheart* organizes its plot by incorporating the violent *jus* as a recurring motif.

Although less-well-known films also feature the *jus* in their plots, *Braveheart* was an award-winning blockbuster.[2] Therefore, its promotion of what it calls *prima nocte* as a practice of the English lords over their Scottish subordinates reinforced credence in the mythic medieval "law." This chapter explores why, despite scholars' thorough correction of the record, creators of movie medievalism—even films claiming historical accuracy like *Braveheart*—continue to showcase the *jus* as if real.[3] Counterbalancing *Braveheart's* notorious ultra-violent barbarity (brutal battles, hangings, executions, torture, and a defenestration), the exercises of institutionalized rape through *prima nocte* occur offscreen, with *Braveheart's* tenderest scenes revolving around the Scots' response to the mythical *jus*. This chapter argues that, although it deliberately misrepresents the historicity of the *jus*, *Braveheart's* inclusion of episodes depicting the *jus* nevertheless reflects medieval class-conscious cultural mores about rape, as illustrated by Chaucer's *Wife of Bath's Tale* and Andreas Capellanus's *De Amore*. Thus, the *jus*, which physically facilitates England's colonization of Scotland, is a crucial aspect of *Braveheart*.

MEDIEVAL ANALOGUES OF THE *JUS*

Rape and its legal consequences occur in medieval fictional works and legal records. In 1380, poet Geoffrey Chaucer (d. 1400) was involved in litigation over *raptus*—legally defined as stealing an employee, physical abduction, or enforced sex or rape—for which Chaucer paid the plaintiff Cecily Chaumpaigne monetary compensation, settling the case, sealing the records.[4] Previously, scholars presumed *raptus* signified sexual coercion, but new evidence reframes Chaucer and Chaumpaigne as codefendants in a labor dispute concerning Chaucer's hiring of Chaumpaigne away from her previous employer, Thomas Staundon. Arguably, his experience with the Chaumpaigne *raptus* case, which nearly implicated him in the same capital crime the knight committed in the story, influenced Chaucer's inclusion of the commission of *raptus* in his late-fourteenth-century *Wife of Bath's Tale*.[5]

The *Tale*, excerpted in the appendix, features an unnamed Arthurian knight's violent rape of a lower-class virgin, his subsequent trial at King Arthur's court, his sentence of decapitation, and his eventual rehabilitation by answering the riddle, "What thing do women most desire?" Though abhorrent, the knight's ravishment of the "maid" reflects what twelfth-century author Andreas Capellanus counsels a youth named Walter concerning the varieties of love. In *De Amore*, also excerpted in the appendix, Capellanus advises courtiers like Walter to use flattery and coercion to achieve the sexual assault of female peasants. Both texts operate on the medieval presumption that inclusion in the upper social rank of the nobility entitles the perpetrator to assault someone of the lower order. However, Chaucer's text concludes with the old, poor woman teaching the knight-rapist that true nobility does not derive from wealth or hereditary titles, but from noble deeds.

Why does the belief that the medieval nobility possessed this legal "right" to exploit commoners sexually endure as a widely held misconception about the European Middle Ages? The concept of a powerful male's right to rape a subordinate's bride on the wedding night is ancient, occurring in the Mesopotamian *Epic of Gilgamesh* (2100 BCE), where King Gilgamesh oppresses the young women of Uruk by claiming sex with them on their wedding night.[6] One scholar who supports the authenticity of the European *jus* cites anthropological studies of primitive cultures, where lords, priests, and even nonhuman primates claim this "right" as a display of masculine power and superior genital size, thereby asserting dominance over the group's other males and guaranteeing reproductive (and ultimately evolutionary) success.[7] In popular culture, the association of the Middle Ages with brutality inspired the line, "Ima *get medieval* on your ass" in Quentin Tarantino's 1994 *Pulp Fiction*, where "getting medieval" implies applying extreme violence to wreak vengeance. Further encouraging pervasive belief in its practice, despite connoting medieval misogyny, the *jus* is sexually titillating, causing even feminist scholars to acknowledge "the eroticism of inequality."[8] French historian Alain Boureau notes, "The sexual content of the *droit de cuissage* . . . fascinates for its total otherness; it feeds the fantasy of the institutional, even a juridical consent to violence. The very formality of the 'right' enchants by its radical inversion of our values. Its paired terms combine the gravity of the law with a whiff of the bawdiness in the word *cuisse* [thigh], evoking an entire folklore of sexuality."[9]

Despite scant documentary evidence from the medieval period, postmedieval association of the *jus* with *medieval* Europe persisted.[10] It began as early as the sixteenth century, when Scots chronicler Boece, in his 1527 *Scotorum Historiae* (*History of Scottish People*), claimed the *jus*, instituted by early Scots monarch King Ewen (Evenus) in 16 BCE, was practiced in Scotland until 1061, when King Malcolm Canmore abolished it.[11] Early modern dramatists incorporated the *jus* in their plays, including Shakespeare's *Henry VI, Part 2* (1591) and John Fletcher and Philip Massinger's *The Custom of the Country* (1647). The continued belief in the authenticity of the *jus* as a medieval law or customary right encouraged eighteenth-century playwrights to feature it in drama about life in the medieval period, including plays titled *Le droit du seigneur* by Louis de Boissy (1735), Voltaire (1763), P. B. J Nougaret (1763), and Desfontaines (1784). Beaumarchais's play *The Marriage of Figaro* (1784), the basis for Mozart's 1786 opera, further promoted the bogus myth as "history."

Perhaps reflecting Boece's story about an early Scots king inaugurating the *jus*, in their *Journals* about the Scottish islands, Samuel Johnson (1773) and Robert Boswell (1785) also discussed the practice as *Mercheta Mulierum*, a payment substituting for physical assault of the bride.[12] In the 1797 *Annals of Scotland*, chronicler David Dalrymple dismissed Boece's 1527 identification of the practice with King Evenus as "one of the worst fables in [Boece's] fabulous history."[13] Despite that condemnation, Scots novelist Walter Scott featured the *jus* in *The Fair Maid of Perth* (1828), set in the fifteenth century. Scott also wrote novels set earlier during the Middle Ages, including *The Talisman* (1825), set during the Third Crusade (1189–92), and *Ivanhoe* (1820), featuring Richard I and Robin Hood. *The Talisman* was adapted into the films *King Richard and the Crusaders* (1954) and Ridley Scott's *Kingdom of Heaven* (2005).[14] *Ivanhoe* was adapted in films (1952, 1982) and a television mini-series (1997). Walter Scott's medievalism was so influential, it provided famed historian Jacques Le Goff's entrée into medieval studies, and its film adaptations inspired other cinematic medievalism, including *Braveheart*.[15]

THE *JUS* AS PLOT DEVICE

Braveheart's plot depicts the Scots' thirteenth-century war for independence, led by William Wallace (d. 1305, dubbed "Braveheart") against their English oppressors. Exploiting the political vacuum left when Scots king Alexander III (r. 1249–86) dies heirless, King Edward I "Longshanks" (r. 1272–1307) invades Scotland, killing local nobles, including Wallace's father and brother. Eventually, to exact retribution, Wallace unites various clans to wage war against the English, including major battles at Stirling and Falkirk.

Showcasing the *jus* as a thematic device, *Braveheart* thus cinematically culminates the piecemeal "historical" genealogy of the bogus *jus* that earlier Scots authors entertained. This throughline connects Boece, Boswell and Johnson, Dalrymple, and Scott, all of whom engaged with the issue of the *jus*. Two of Walter Scott's sources for *The Fair Maid of Perth* were John Barbour's 1375 *The Bruce*, about Robert the Bruce, an important figure in the Scots' insurrection and a character in *Braveheart*, and Blind Harry's 1477 romance *The Wallace*, neither of which includes the *jus*. These romances also informed Randall Wallace's screenplay for *Braveheart* and his novel of the same title.[16] Edward I precipitated the war by offering to English noblemen both lands and *prima nocte* over Scottish brides. To avoid submitting to the *jus*, Wallace covertly married his peasant sweetheart, Murron (Catherine McCormack). When English soldiers attempt to rape Wallace's bride, she resists and is executed by having her throat slit. Per *Braveheart*, consequences of the *jus* thus motivate Wallace's revenge against England's attempt to colonize Scotland by exercising the *jus*—raping its women with the goal of replacing Scots bloodlines with English blood.

Structurally, *Braveheart* exploits the medieval myth of the *jus* by setting up parallel weddings, consummations (or non-consummations), and a putative subsequent pregnancy. These episodes are organized in scenes of sexual tension between Longshanks (Patrick McGoohan), his daughter-in-law Princess Isabelle (Sophie Marceau), Scots leader Wallace, and his secret bride, Murron (historically, it is not clear if Wallace ever married). The fulcrum connecting the four figures is the minor but pivotal character, the unnamed (and uncredited) "bride" whose peasant wedding to Morrison (Tommy Flanagan) is interrupted by the arrival of Lord Bottoms (Rupert Vansittart), the English "lord" who intends to claim his "right." This bride's submission to the ordeal of what Longshanks calls "*prima nocte*" provides the catalyst for the war of independence that Wallace inspires his fellow Scotsmen to wage against their English colonizers, who assume cultural superiority over the colonized, constructing them as almost subhuman barbarians.

Preceding (and paralleling) this wedding of ordinary, colonized Scottish country-folk is the metaphoric wedding of England with France, officiated literally at the grand nuptials of French princess Isabelle to Longshanks's son and heir, Edward II (r. 1307–27, played by Peter Hanly). *Braveheart* portrays the groom as a homosexual grudgingly submitting to a universally acknowledged sham marriage. Problematically for Longshanks, if the union of Edward and Isabelle remains unconsummated on their "first (or any) night," Longshanks's Plantagenet royal bloodline will end. Robert the Bruce (r. 1306–27, played by Angus Macfadyen), the voiceover narrator of *Braveheart*, ominously predicts, "As bride for his son, Longshanks had chosen the daughter of his rival, the King of France. It was widely whispered that for the princess to conceive, Longshanks would have to do the honors himself. That may have been what he had in mind all along." Bruce's quip bodes ill for the union. Longshanks's inappropriate, incestuous lust for his daughter-in-law and his purported intent to substitute for his son on the "*prima nocte*," possibly fathering the royal heir, anticipates a later scene wherein Longshanks proposes "*prima nocte*" as official policy in English-Scots relations. It also adumbrates a crucial scene at the film's end when Isabelle taunts the dying king by boasting that her lover, Wallace, has fathered the next heir to the throne.

Plotting to gain political control of Scotland, Longshanks convenes his advisors, including Isabelle, substituting for the immature prince, who prefers being with his lover Phillip to state business. Longshanks proclaims, "Nobles are the key to the door of Scotland. Grant our nobles lands in the north." Throughout his speech, Longshanks trains his male gaze lasciviously over Isabelle as he asserts:

> The trouble with Scotland is that it's full of Scots. Perhaps the time has come to reinstitute an old custom. Grant them *prima nocte*. First night, when any common girl inhabiting their lands is married, our nobles shall have *sexual* rights to her on the night of her wedding. If we can't get them out, we breed them out. That should fetch just the kind of lords we want to Scotland.[17]

With lurid emphasis, McGoohan extends his pronunciation of all three syllables of "sex-u-al." His lingering carnal gaze on Isabelle during a speech about legalizing sexual assault reinforces Bruce's assessment of Longshanks's intent about Isabelle. Thus, Longshanks grants what *Braveheart* calls *prima nocte* (first night) to English lords, "legally" conferring the right to rape any Scottish bride under their purview on her wedding night. Edward calculates that this crude "privilege" will induce the "right kind" of English lords to relocate to Scotland, thus ensuring England's dominion over the Scots.

Longshanks's new "law" is exercised at the aforementioned wedding in the village of Falkirk, tonally the opposite of the pretentious (and portentous) royal wedding of Isabelle and Edward in a castle's chapel. This raucous outdoor wedding is attended by Wallace, newly returned from European travels, and his future wife, Murron, the now-grown-up girl who comforted young Wallace by handing him a thistle at his father's funeral. Wallace and Murron, destined to be married themselves in the future, exchange flirtatious glances, heightening the romance in a scene that quickly turns ugly. The unnamed bride, identified by the floral garland encircling her head, mixes with the crowd of celebrating guests playing games of strength and dancing to Celtic music. The jubilant mood is shattered by the arrival of a troop of English soldiers, accompanying Lord Bottoms, the local English nobleman attracted to overseeing Lanark by the promised sexual "right," which he now claims, demanding, "I have come to claim the right of *prima nocte*. As lord of these lands, I will bless this marriage by taking the bride into my bed on the first night of her union," repeating, "It is my noble right." When Morrison, the groom, resists Lord Bottoms, a dagger is poised at his throat. The bride silently defuses the imminent violence, removing the dagger, circling Morrison, and murmuring into his ear while gently kissing and caressing his face. The dramatic scene takes a full minute of screen time to unfold in slow motion, with no dialogue, only the ethereal soundtrack providing ironic counterpoint to the eventual offscreen assault when the peasant bride humbly sacrifices herself to the English lord's rape, thus preventing her husband's and father's deaths. Later, Morrison encounters Bottoms during Wallace's attack on the English garrison. Invoking Bottoms's claim of his lord's "right," Morrison declares his grievance before bludgeoning Bottoms's head with a flail, "I am here to claim the right of a husband." Wallace demands, "Go back to England and tell them there that Scotland's daughters and her sons are yours no more. Tell them Scotland is free," before ordering the garrison burned.

Lord Bottom's claim of *prima nocte* prompts William and Murron to marry hurriedly in a covert ceremony to prevent Bottoms from claiming his "right" to her. Their earlier courting on horseback was accompanied by James Horner's ethereal symphonic soundtrack featuring Uilleann pipes. The same evocative aural backdrop heightens the idealization of their nighttime wedding—before a Celtic crucifix, officiated by a druidical-looking priest—combining Christian and Celtic symbolism. Like the daytime outdoor peasant wedding, it provides another stark contrast with Edward and Isabelle's formal church nuptials.

The camera cuts abruptly from this idyllic scene to the routine reality of Lanark's market day and then intercuts between shots of Murron and William exchanging knowing glances as she wanders through the wares, carrying a basket of items she obtained, and furtively arranging their next nocturnal meeting. Some English soldiers, including the old lecher Smythe, who have been ogling the beautiful Murron, intuit the couple's intimacy from their coy interactions at the market. They follow Murron, offering to help her carry the basket. Paralleling Longshanks's leering at his daughter-in-law while planning the *prima nocte* edict, Smythe blocks her, saying "O, you remind me of my daughter back home." Smythe relentlessly pursues Murron until she is trapped, surrounded by Smythe and other inebriated English soldiers who seem ready to take their "right" in a gang rape. Murron defends herself, punching Smythe, who overpowers her. The old man passes his long tongue over her face repeatedly, licking her features with lecherous gusto, kissing her, attempting to obtain her compliance. The drunken soldiers' warning to him to "keep it quiet, Smythe" demonstrates their collective acknowledgment that their behavior is morally, if not "legally," wrong and they must exercise discretion. The acts of these "knights" reflect the knight casually committing the rape in Chaucer's *Wife of Bath's Tale*. Like the English soldiers, he assaults the vulnerable lower-class "maiden" whom he presumes he is entitled to violate simply by "seeing" her. Smythe also follows the playbook of Capellanus's *De Amore*—about first seeking compliance through flattery, then, without it, enforcing sex on a peasant female—when he attempts to ingratiate himself with his victim, saying she resembles his daughter, and manipulatively offers to help carry her basket, before pursuing Murron with intent to rape.

After their secret marriage ceremony, the *prima nocte* of William and Murron could not differ more from the humiliating non-consummation of Isabelle and Edward or the offscreen subjection of the unnamed bride to Bottoms's assault. But *Braveheart* later posits an invented and chronologically impossible collaboration and sexual liaison between Wallace and Isabelle, the wife of Longshanks's son, whose royal marriage (per the novel and film) was unconsummated because of Edward's homosexuality. Just as Isabelle reminds Wallace of Murron, the consensual sex between Wallace and Isabelle resembles Wallace and Murron's gently erotic *prima nocte*. Isabelle's purported virginity is a key aspect of *Braveheart*'s treatment of their affair as a reversal of the *jus*. Instead of an English lord raping a Scottish peasant girl, a Scots warrior enjoys consensual sex with an equally aroused

French-English princess. And, as suggested in *Braveheart*, Isabelle's *prima nocte* with Wallace produced the usually hoped-for result of consummation, a pregnancy, though not what Longshanks anticipated. Thus, inadvertently, the invented affair with Isabelle is also Wallace's exercise of reverse *prima nocte*, for instead of English colonizers breeding English genes into the Scots, Wallace bred Scottish blood into the Plantagenet royal line.

In one of *Braveheart*'s last scenes, her usually indifferent husband taunts Isabelle about her affinity for Wallace, for whom she has begged mercy before his brutal execution for treason. Framed in extreme close-up shots, with tears streaming from her eyes, Isabelle whispers her revenge into the dying Longshanks's ear: "You see, death comes to us all. But before it comes to you, know this. Your plot dies with you. A child who is not of your line grows in my belly. Your son will not sit long on the throne, I swear it." Although, historically, this child fathered by Wallace is utterly fictional, in the arc of the film's plot, wherein the English king opens by boasting of breeding out the Scots through *prima nocte*, there could be no better dramatic irony. Isabelle (and Wallace) did get revenge on both Edwards by way of a child who, per the film's rewriting of history, will eventually occupy the English throne, fathered by a Scottish rebel.

CONCLUSION

Using three female characters—two invented (Morrison's unnamed bride and Wallace's wife, Murron) and one nonhistorical (Edward II's wife, Isabelle)—*Braveheart* employs *jus primae noctis* as a sustained motif shaping the plot. Early in *Braveheart*, an occurrence of *jus* at the peasant wedding and the execution of his secret wife, Murron, for avoiding submission to the *jus* motivate Wallace to lead the Scots' insurrection against the English. The later invented sexual liaison between Wallace and Isabelle provides a reversal of the *jus*.[18] Countering chroniclers and writers' inclusion of episodes featuring the *jus primae noctis* as established practice, late nineteenth- through twenty-first-century scholars Schmidt, Boureau, Bullough, Howarth, Jordan, and Classen firmly repudiated the historical validity of this medieval "right." Notwithstanding the *jus*'s debunked historicity, by featuring three episodes representing the *jus* as plausible and emotionally engaging plot devices, Gibson's 1995 *Braveheart* reinvigorated the myth for audiences of cinematic medievalism.

APPENDIX

Braveheart (1995)

GEOFFREY CHAUCER (D. 1400), *WIFE OF BATH'S TALE* (LATE 14TH CENTURY)

The Wife of Bath recounts an Arthurian romance that begins, not with the expected chivalrous saving of a damsel from distress, but with a violent rape perpetrated by a knight of Arthur's court upon a vulnerable peasant virgin while she walks alone in the forest.

Source: *The Wife of Bath's Prologue and Tale* (https://chaucer.fas.harvard.edu/pages/wife-baths-prologue-and-tale-0). Original in Middle English. Modernized by Lorraine Kochanske Stock.

882 And so it happened that this King Arthur
883 Had in his house a lusty bachelor,
884 That one day came riding back from hawking,
885 And it happened that, alone as he was at birth,
886 He saw a maiden walking before him;
887 From that maiden, straightaway, despite all she could do,
888 By extreme force, he despoiled her maidenhead;
889 For that act of oppression there was such clamor
890 And such demand to King Arthur for justice
891 That this knight was condemned to death,
892 By course of law, and should have lost his head—
893 Perhaps such was the statute then—
894 Except that the queen as well as other ladies
895 Beseeched the king for grace for so long
896 Until he granted the knight his life right there,
897 And gave him to the queen, to be completely at her will,
898 For her to choose whether she would save him or execute him.
899 The queen thanked the king with all her might,
900 And after this she spoke thus to the knight,
901 When she saw her time, upon a day:
902 "You stand yet," she said, "in such a condition,
903 That you have no assurance yet of your life.

904 I grant you life, if you can tell me
905 What thing do women most desire?
906 Beware, and keep your neck-bone from the axe! ...

Here, an old, poor woman supplies the life-saving answer to the queen's riddle in exchange for the knight marrying her. On their "first night," he is reluctant to consummate the marriage. Refuting his contempt of her low status, she argues that true "nobility" reflects virtuous behavior:

1083 Extreme was the woe the knight felt in his mind,
1084 When he was brought to the marriage bed to be with his bride;
1085 He wallowed and tossed and turned.
1086 His old wife lay smiling at all times,
1087 And said, "O dear husband, blessed be!
1088 Does every knight behave with his wife as you do?
1089 Is this the law of King Arthur's court?
1090 Is every knight of his so reluctant?
1091 I am your own love and your wife;
1092 I am she who has saved your life,
1093 And, certainly, I have never yet done you any wrong;
1094 Why do you treat me this way on this first night?
1095 You behave like a man who had lost his wits.
1096 What am I guilty of? For the love of God, say it,
1097 And it will be amended, if I may do so."
1098 "Amended?" said the knight, "Alas, no, no!
1099 It will never again be amended.
1100 You are so loathly, and so old,
1101 And you come from such an inferior class,
1102 That it is little wonder that I wallow and squirm.
1103 Would that God make my heart explode!"
1104 "Is this," she said, "the cause of your disquiet?"
1105 "Yes, certainly," he said, "and it is no wonder why."
1106 "Now, sir" she said, "I could amend all this,
1107 If I wanted to do so, before three days time,
1108 If only you might behave well towards me.
1109 But, since you bring up nobility
1110 That is passed down from old money,
1111 That therefore proves that you must be noble people,

1112 Such arrogance is not worth a hen.
1113 Look, if you will, at he who is most virtuous always,
1114 Both secretly and openly, and who most intends, always,
1115 To perform whatever noble deeds he is capable of;
1116 Consider him to be the greatest noble person.
1117 We derive our nobility from Christ,
1118 Not from our ancestors because of their old money.
1119 For, though they bequeath to us all their inheritance,
1120 For which we claim to be of noble rank,
1121 Yet they cannot, in any way, transfer
1122 To any of us their virtuous lifestyle,
1123 For which they were called noble men,
1124 And advised us to follow them in that kind of virtuous pedigree."

ANDREAS CAPELLANUS, "ON THE LOVE OF PEASANTS," FROM *DE AMORE* (C. 1184–1186)

Chapter 11 of this twelfth-century treatise on the varieties of love, addressed to a young courtier named Walter, demonstrates medieval class-consciousness in determining acceptable and inappropriate choices of love-objects.

Source: E. Trojel, ed., *De amore libri tres* (Copenhagen: In Lib. Gadiana, 1892), 235–36. Original in Latin. Translated by Anthony Perron.

[1] But lest you should believe that what we considered above regarding the love of commoners should also apply to farmhands, we are adding for your benefit a little bit about their love. For we say that it scarcely could happen that farmers might be found to serve as knights in the court of love, but by nature, just like a horse and a mule, they are prompted to acts of Venus just as the force of nature shows them. [2] Therefore, for the farmhand, constant toil and the never-ending and ceaseless comforts of the plow and hoe are enough. But while sometimes (albeit rarely) it happens that they are aroused by the sting of love beyond their nature, nonetheless it is not beneficial to instruct them in the teaching of love, lest when [the peasants] strive after acts by nature alien to them, we should see the estates upon which mankind depends, which are accustomed to bear fruit by their labor, made sterile for us owing to the lack of a cultivator. [3] However, if the love of those women should by chance attract you, remember to seduce them with many praises, and if you find a suitable opportunity, you should not hesitate

to take what you are after and obtain it with a forceful embrace. For scarcely will you be able to soften their stiff exterior to the point where they say they will grant you quiet embraces or allow you to have the comforts you want, unless the remedy of at least modest compulsion catches their shyness off guard. [4] Moreover, we say these things not as if wishing to make the love of peasant women appealing to you, but so that, if you should be unwisely drawn to fall in love with them, you might be able to know in a short lesson how you should go about it.

Reading questions

- The aristocratic knight presumes that his social position entitles him to rape the female peasant he encounters. How does this situation reflect the unequal power dynamic that underpins the mythic "right" of *jus primae nocte*?
- How does the knight's attitude reflect the advice Andreas Capellanus gives to Walter about sexual relations with female peasants in *De Amore*?
- How is the sentencing of capital punishment for the knight's crime of rape reflected in *Braveheart*'s depiction of Morrison's response to Lord Bottoms to avenge the lord's exercise of his "right" upon Morrison's bride?
- How does the moral of the old woman's "first night" lecture about what constitutes real "nobility" argue against the class-driven presumptions of *jus primae noctis*: that aristocrats have the "right" to deflower the brides of their feudal subordinates?
- How does Andreas's pronouncements about the value of farmworkers reflect the attitudes of Longshanks and the other English lords toward the Scots, who are mostly farmers?
- How is Andreas's advice about what Walter should do if he is attracted to a female peasant reflected in the behavior of Smythe and the other English soldiers who stalk Murron in *Braveheart*?
- How does Andreas acknowledge the general need for the labor peasants perform and yet contemptuously exclude them from the kind of courtly love permitted to what Longshanks refers to as his "nobles" in *Braveheart*?

NOTES

1. Scholarship about the historicity of the *jus* that informs this chapter includes Karl Schmidt, *Jus Primae Noctis: Eine Geschichtliche Untersuchung* (Freiburg: Herder, 1881); Alain Boureau, *The Lord's First Night: The Myth of the Droit de Cuissage*, trans., Lydia G. Cochrane (Chicago: University of Chicago Press, 1998); Vern L. Bullough, "Jus Primae Noctis or Droit Du Seigneur," *Philosophos: Journal of Sex Research* 28, no. 1 (1991): 163–66; W. D. Howarth, "'Droit du Seigneur': Fact of Fantasy?," *Journal of European Studies* 1 (1971): 291–312; William Chester Jordan, "Droit du Seigneur," *Dictionary of the Middle Ages: Supplement 1* (New York: Charles Scribner's Sons, 2004), 167–68; and Albrecht Classen, "Another Myth: The *Jus Primae Noctis*, or *The Droit du Cuissage* (Droit du Seigneur)," in *The Medieval Chastity Belt: A Myth-Making Process* (New York: Palgrave Macmillan, 2008), 147–54.

2. *The Warlord* (1965) and Disney-produced television film *A Knight in Camelot* (1998) feature the *jus*.

3. In the director's commentary on the *Braveheart* DVD, Gibson admits the unhistorical *prima nocte* was included to create a "more compelling" plot.

4. Gwen Seabourne, "Rape and Law in Medieval Western Europe," in *A Companion to Crime and Deviance in the Middle Ages*, ed. Hannah Skoda (York: Arc Humanities Press, 2023), 343–44.

5. On Chaucer's *raptus* case, see Christopher Cannon, "*Raptus* in the Chaumpaigne Release and a Newly Discovered Document Concerning the Life of Geoffrey Chaucer," *Speculum* 68, no. 1 (1993): 74–94; Susanna Fein and David Raybin, "The Case of Geoffrey Chaucer and Cecily Chaumpaigne: New Evidence," *Chaucer Review* 57, no. 4 (2022): 403–6; Jennifer Schuessler, "Chaucer the Rapist?: Newly Discovered Documents Suggest Not," *New York Times* (October 14, 2022), https://www.nytimes.com/2022/10/13/books/geoffrey-chaucer-rape-charge.html.

6. Jörg Wettlaufer, "The *jus primae noctis* as a Male Power Display: A Review of Historic Sources with Evolutionary Interpretation," *Evolution and Human Behavior* 21 (2000): 112.

7. Ibid., 118–19.

8. Sandra Gilbert and Susan Gubar, *The Madwoman in the Attic: The Woman Writer and the Nineteenth-Century Literary Imagination* (New Haven: Yale University Press, 1979), 506.

9. Boureau, *The Lord's First Night*, 4–5.

10. Allusions to anything resembling the practice are severely limited geographically and do not use the postmedieval terms *jus* or *droit*.

11. Howarth, "'Droit du Seigneur': Fact of Fantasy?," 298.

12. Ibid., 299.

13. Ibid., 305.

14. See Esther Liberman Cuenca's chapter on *Kingdom of Heaven* in this book for more on this film.

15. Richard Utz, "'Mes souvenirs sont peut-être reconstruits': Medieval Studies, Medievalism, and the Scholarly and Popular Memories of the 'Right of the Lord's First Night,'" *PhiN* 31 (2005): 49–59; James Watt, "Sir Walter Scott and the Medievalist Novel," in *The Oxford Handbook of Victorian Medievalism*, ed. Joanne Parker and Corinna Wagner (Oxford: Oxford University Press, 2020), 162–74.

16. Randall Wallace, *Braveheart* (New York: Pocket Books, 1995).

17. In his director's commentary on the DVD, Gibson likens Longshanks's plan to "ethnic cleansing."

18. Longshanks tortured and executed Wallace in 1305. The marriage between Edward II and twelve-year-old Isabelle of France did not occur until 1308, after Longshanks's death in 1307, thus rendering *Braveheart*'s suggestion of an affair between Isabelle and Wallace chronologically impossible.

CHAPTER FIFTEEN

MEDIEVAL SATIRE AND THE CANON LAW OF CLAUSTRATION IN *THE LITTLE HOURS* (2017)

By Spencer Strub

The Little Hours is probably the only twenty-first-century American sex comedy that hinges on an episcopal visitation. A loose adaptation of the first two *novelle* told on the Third Day of Giovanni Boccaccio's *Decameron* (c. 1348–52, rev. 1370–71), writer-director Jeff Baena's 2017 film depicts the worldly hijinks of a community of nuns in mid-fourteenth-century Garfagnana, Tuscany.[1] The film's humor depends largely on the disjunction between its medieval monastic setting and its raunchy contemporary dialogue, mostly improvised by an ensemble of American comic actors. In the film's opening minutes, beatific scenes of nuns at work are interrupted when Sister Fernanda (Aubrey Plaza) bombards the convent's lay gardener with turnips and abuse. The replacement gardener, Masetto (Dave Franco), confessing to the hapless nuns' priest Father Tommaso (John C. Reilly), recounts in vivid detail the sexual escapades that drove him from his previous lord's service. When Bishop Bartolomeo (Fred Armisen), conducting a tribunal in the wake of the midnight revelation of the convent's various scandals, enumerates the sins committed by Sister Ginevra (Kate Micucci), including "ingesting drugs, lying with a woman, not being baptized . . . envy, fornication, homosexuality," he adds after the last, by way of explanation, "That's the same as lying with a woman, but we separate those."

The film's playful anachronism sparked controversy in the Catholic press. The director of the Catholic League, Bill Donohue, denounced the film in a press release: "It is trash, pure trash."[2] (The film's trailer quotes that endorsement.) In contrast, the Jesuit magazine *America* ran both a generally appreciative review and a vigorous defense of the film's approach to the faith, citing it as a valuable riposte to "the impulse to assume that all religion or depictions of religious people must be pure, clean and undefiled."[3] While these divergent responses reflect tensions between the conservative and liberal wings of modern American Catholicism, the film also offers insight into the institutional tensions that defined the medieval church. Baena, who minored in Medieval Studies, leavens anachronism with real historical insight.[4] The film acknowledges the importance of prayer and physical labor. It depicts lay patronage's role in supporting comparatively impoverished women's houses. The bishop's visitation exposes the convent's various foibles: witchcraft, financial mismanagement, and a lot of sex.

For all its comic hyperbole, the film illustrates genuine disputes that arose between the masculine church hierarchy and women's religious communities that sought the right to govern themselves. This chapter focuses on the anxiety over religious women's sexuality that defined these struggles. That anxiety led Pope Boniface VIII (r. 1294–1303) to issue the watershed 1298 decretal *Periculoso*, which for the first time made nuns' claustration the universal law of the church (excerpted in the appendix). Claustration is the practice of remaining strictly within the cloister, without traveling or hosting guests, which scholars also refer to as "enclosure" or simply "cloister." Prohibitions on guests entering the convent are known as "passive cloister," while prohibitions on nuns leaving it are called "active cloister."

The abuses *Periculoso* laments, the stringent governance it establishes, and the sexual practices it seeks to prevent—between women, most importantly, but also between nuns and their priests—are all subjects in the film. But nuns' sexuality is also a recurrent subject of satires like Boccaccio's, part of a literary tradition that both mocked monastic hypocrisies and celebrated its subjects' transgressions. This chapter traces these roots of *The Little Hours* by turn: first, the practices of chastity and claustration as articulated in monastic rules and underlined by thirteenth-century legislation; and second, the satirical tradition that provided the medieval template for *The Little Hours*.

CHASTITY, CLAUSTRATION, AND THE HISTORY OF MONASTICISM

Early in *The Little Hours*, Sister Fernanda misses Lauds. The convent's donkey broke loose and needed to be recovered, she claims afterward, an excuse Mother Marea (Molly Shannon) grudgingly accepts. As the film goes on, it becomes clear that the wandering donkey is mere pretext: Sister Fernanda leaves its paddock unlocked so she might sneak away under cover of darkness, meeting her friend Marta (Jemima Kirke) to get drunk in her cell and conduct nude rites in the woods. It is a canonist's nightmare.

In Latin Christianity, chastity and claustration were linked and were fundamental to monastic vows, regardless of gender. Histories of Christian cenobitic ("common-life") monasticism, the communal form of religious life that came to predominate in both the Eastern (Greek) and Western (Latin) churches, usually begin in fourth-century Egypt. The traditional narrative skews male. Pious men withdrew into the desert away from the temptations of society; their ascetic practices aimed to snuff out sexual desire, and they vigorously eschewed women's company. Pachomius (d. 348) pioneered the organization of solitary hermits into communities. Basil of Caesarea (d. 379) made Pachomian monasticism the norm of the Eastern Church, while John Cassian (d. 435) did the same for the Western. In the West, the Rule of Saint Benedict (*c.* 530) consolidated Cassian's early rules into a form still used today, defined by a structured life of prayer and labor, governed by vows that mandate chastity, poverty, obedience to an abbot and stability within the more-or-less sealed space of the monastery.[5]

But religious women played a more central role in the development of Western monasticism than that traditional narrative might suggest. The male ascetic in the desert was inspired in part by the consecrated virgins (*sanctimoniales*) of urban society, who carved a new vocation out of Roman patriarchy in the second and third centuries.[6] Moreover, women retreated into the desert, too.[7] Early men's monasteries were often paired with "sister houses" of nuns; there were two women's communities among Pachomius's foundations. The earliest nuns' formal organization may even have preceded male cenobitic monasticism.[8] The oldest surviving copy of the Benedictine Rule is a seventh-century adaptation for women religious, the *Regula Donati*.[9] The *Regula ad virgines* by Caesarius of Arles (d. 542), the first monastic rule explicitly intended for women's communities, was composed at the same time as the Benedictine Rule.[10]

Nuns helped set the terms for Western monasticism, but they were consistently subject to restrictions their brothers did not face. The Benedictine rule insists on stability but allows exceptions. By contrast, Caesarius's rule begins by prescribing strict claustration: "If a girl, leaving her parents, desires to renounce the world and enter the holy fold to escape the jaws of the spiritual wolves by the help of God, she must never, up to the time of her death, go out of the monastery."[11] This mandate—and parallel rules forbidding guests, both men and laywomen—would be revived repeatedly in the centuries to come.[12] In periods of reform, monasteries would be more stringently disciplined according to their founding rules or even subjected to direct control by bishops or the leadership of their order. Although such reforms could be invigorating for men's foundations, for women's houses, they were often disastrous. Because nuns could not perform masses, restrictions on travel and hospitality limited convent incomes. Moreover, strict claustration diminished the autonomy of women's communities. As Jane Schulenberg explains, fully enclosed nuns depended on the male church officials responsible for their temporal needs.[13] In *The Little Hours*, Tommaso is thus charged with traveling to market to sell textiles made by Garfagnana's nuns—a task he badly fumbles.

CLOISTER AND CANON LAW

The decretal *Periculoso* was the culmination of repeated cycles of reform and restriction. The thirteenth century saw a proliferation of new modes of religious life. The mendicant orders emerged in Italy in the early decades of the century, initially as all-male affairs but soon accommodating nuns (strictly cloistered, unlike their male brethren) and affiliated laypeople, called tertiaries, of all genders. In the Low Countries, the Beguines developed a new kind of women's religious community, pious and withdrawn but uncloistered and unvowed. Across Europe, laypeople increasingly pursued what Kaspar Elm terms the *vita semireligiosa* (semi-religious life), which emulated monastic discipline without abandoning secular life.[14] These impulses attest to broadening interest in formal religion, but also the perception that the existing institutions of the church—nuns included—were exhausted, corrupt, and in need of transformation.

Periculoso responds to these developments in two ways. First, its stringency clearly distinguishes vowed nuns in formal orders from the semireligious and unvowed. As the decretal avers in its opening lines, it seeks to restore "monastic modesty" to the former. It is unambiguously concerned with threats to the perceived chastity of nuns. Strict cloister serves the dual aim of protecting nuns from "public and worldly eyes" and denying them any "opportunities for wantonness" à la Sister Fernanda.[15] Second, it borrows directly from earlier reforming legislation specific to certain orders or places. But, as Elizabeth Makowski notes, *Periculoso* was unprecedented in its universality.[16] Unlike previous legislation, it does not apply to a particular region or order, but to *all* nuns under the pope's authority. *Periculoso* was first promulgated in Boniface's 1298 *Liber Sextus*, the "sixth book" that supplemented the existing corpus of canon law—the legal system that still governs the Latin Church—with as-yet uncodified thirteenth-century legislation. The *Liber Sextus*, binding as soon as it was issued, was circulated to law faculties across Europe, while *Periculoso* was also sent directly to bishops and monastic superiors charged with overseeing women's houses.[17]

Its terms are uncompromising. It mandates that all nuns should remain enclosed under all circumstances and admit no guests. Few exceptions are allowed: when absolutely necessary, church authorities can grant guests license to enter a monastery; abbesses can only travel to pay homage to a lord, and they must return to their convent promptly. Though the decretal ends by saying that convents will preserve their autonomy in other matters, they have no discretion over the terms of enclosure. This "law of papal cloister" continues to govern Catholic women's monasticism today.[18]

As with other watershed legislation in the medieval church, the actual implementation of *Periculoso* was more scattershot than its legal universality might suggest. Some orders and dioceses imposed it immediately. Church councils held in fourteenth-century northern Italian dioceses down the road from *The Little Hours*' Garfagnana even strengthened it with penalties as severe as excommunication.[19] Elsewhere, enclosure was practiced more loosely.[20] The responses to strict enclosure among women's communities themselves likewise varied. The sisters of St. Catherine's convent in fifteenth-century Augsburg, as Marie-Luise Ehrenschwendtner discusses, used "spits and poles as weapons" against the workmen charged with immuring them.[21] Other women's communities actively sought claustration, however, for reasons both pragmatic and spiritual. Strict cloister could preserve nuns' autonomy and hold off meddling secular authorities while it made manifest a nun's repudiation of the world and facilitated her prayers. As Ehrenschwendtner puts it, "Enclosure generally is the environment where the religious prepares to transcend the limitations of his or her existence."[22] Regardless of canon law or local practice, however, a popular image of dissolute, "bad" nuns persisted. For that, the nuns had the satirists to thank.

SATIRE AND SEX IN THE CONVENT

The narrator Filostrato begins his tale of Masetto in the *Decameron*, excerpted in the appendix, by declaring that "there are a great many men and women who are so dense" as to believe that a monastic vow makes a woman chaste, "as though the very act of making her a nun had caused her to turn into stone."[23] Judging by the surviving textual record, Filostrato overstates the case: nuns' peccadilloes were celebrated and attacked in poetry and prose, in Latin and vernacular languages, from the early Middle Ages on.[24] By the time Boccaccio put those words in Filostrato's mouth, the sinful sister was a well-worn trope.

Convent satires sit at the intersection of two distinct literary modes, both pioneered by religious men: anti-monastic satire and the so-called "misogynist tradition." The former may originate among monks picking on rival orders or even the moral laxity of their own brothers. Though much of it pokes comparatively gentle fun at monks dining and dressing luxuriously, it could also be much harsher, attacking the entire monastic profession for corruption, hypocrisy, and greed.[25] The latter descends from religious men writing against marriage, in favor of men's religious chastity, advancing vicious stereotypes about women's unfaithfulness, seductiveness, and vanity. As Jill Mann points out, "The failings attributed to nuns are identical with those assigned to women in general."[26] Though medieval misogyny appeared in many textual genres, nun-satire offered a unique cross-pollination of broad misogynist sentiments with critiques of vowed religion common in anti-monastic satire.

Like monks, nuns were accordingly mocked as gluttons and clotheshorses. Like laywomen, they were depicted as gossips and quarrelers. In the English poem *Piers Plowman* (c. 1375), the personified sin Wrath goes to work in a convent; the gossiping nuns fall to brawling, and even Wrath is taken aback by their violence: "Had they had knives, by Christ! one would have killed the other."[27] But what the satirists returned to most consistently was sex. What sets Wrath's nuns to fisticuffs is, among other things, a rumor that one was a priest's mistress with an illegitimate child. Geoffrey Chaucer's Prioress wears a brooch inscribed with the message, "Love conquers all"—maybe it means Christian love, maybe not.[28] Some writers were straightforwardly moralizing: the French Benedictine abbot Gilles le Muisit (d. 1352), addressing nuns, complains that when they engage in foolish love-affairs, "the assignations very often hinder all devotions."²⁹ Others emphasize humor instead. At the bottom of a folio in a manuscript of the poem *Le Roman de la Rose*, the Parisian illuminator couple Jeanne and Richart de Montbaston (fl. 1325–55) made the marginal illumination perhaps best-known today: a nun plucks penises from a penis-tree, gathering them in a penis-filled basket.³⁰ The image appears less than ten minutes into *The Little Hours*.

Boccaccio's tale of Masetto is more like the Montbastons's penis-tree than le Muisit's denunciations. The convent gardener Nuto, dissatisfied with his pay and frustrated by the nuns, quits and returns to his home village of Lamporecchio. Complaining to his fellow villagers that the nuns "are all young and seem to me to have the devil inside them," Nuto disavows his promise to find a replacement.³¹ But his complaints inspire the handsome young Masetto. Pretending to be deaf and mute, he convinces the convent steward to hire him. Two nuns soon decide to shirk their vows and have their way with him. The other nuns notice and decide to follow suit. In short order, even the abbess is sleeping with Masetto. At last, exhausted, he breaks his silence: he is being overworked, and the nuns must make a sustainable arrangement or bid him farewell. They work things out, Masetto stays on, the nuns are happy, and "although he fathered quite a number of nunlets and monklets," everything is kept discreet, and Masetto retires on a pension.³² In contrast to some of his sources, Boccaccio's story does not deal out any brutal moral correction.³³ If there is any moralizing, it is delivered with a wink. The tale ends with Masetto reflecting on his happy life among the brides of Christ, concluding "that this . . . was the way Christ treated anyone who set a pair of horns on His crown"—that is, cuckolded Him.³⁴

CONCLUSION

In his accounting of nuns' sins, le Muisit exclaims, "The Pope would do well if he enclosed them quickly."³⁵ For moralizing satirists, *Periculoso* was an unfinished project. For writers like Boccaccio, on the other hand, claustration provided an opportunity for writerly invention, ribald and comic. His tale of Masetto has a long afterlife. Pier Paolo Pasolini's *Decameron* (1971) faithfully put it to film, spawning a semipornographic genre, the "Decamerotico," following Pasolini's example to less exacting artistic standards. Like its medieval and modern antecedents, the latter-day Decamerotico *The Little Hours* takes the terms of *Periculoso* as pretext for comic juxtaposition:

bodily desires persist despite ascetic discipline; profanity breaks monastic silence; vows of chastity occasion lurid imaginings.

Still, the film's transgressions show the decretal's force as much as its failings. In the film's final act, Masetto, handed over by the bishop to a lord bent on punishing him, is rescued by the nuns. To return, he must don the habit: the gardener becomes a nun, at least temporarily. At the same time, Mother Marea and Father Tommaso (exiled to a monastery) briefly reunite for their own illicit tryst. Returning to the convent, Masetto and his rescuers spy the wayward donkey. The subtext is clear. As Boniface insisted, even the abbess needs a good reason to leave the cloister.

APPENDIX

The Little Hours (2017)

POPE BONIFACE VIII (R. 1294–1303), *PERICULOSO* (1298)

In Liber Sextus, 3.16: *On the claustration of nuns.*
Source: Emil Ludwig Richter and Emil Friedberg, eds., *Corpus Iuris Canonici*, vol. 2 (Leipzig, 1881; repr. Graz: Akademische Druck- u. Verlagsanstalt, 1959): *Sexti Decretalium*, 3.16, 2:1053. Original in Latin. Translated by Spencer Strub.

Desiring to healthily improve the dangerous and detestable condition of some nuns—who, loosening the reins of respectability and shamelessly throwing away monastic modesty and the bashfulness of their sex, sometimes wander outside their monasteries through the homes of secular people and frequently admit suspicious people into said monasteries, to the grave offense of Him to whom they voluntarily vowed their chastity, to the disgrace of the religious life, and the scandalizing of many—we ordain, by the present constitution that will remain in force perpetually and irrefutably, that nuns collectively and individually, present and future, of whatever religious community or order they might be, existing in any part of the world, should henceforth remain perpetually enclosed in their monasteries. None of them, whether tacitly or expressly professed in religion, shall hereafter have the ability to leave these monasteries for any cause or reason (unless by chance a nun is found to obviously suffer from such an illness that she cannot stay with the others without serious danger or scandal). And no person in any way disreputable, or even reputable, shall be allowed to enter or leave the same monastery unless a clear and reasonable cause exists, and with special permission from the relevant authorities. Thus, the nuns can serve God more freely, entirely hidden from public and worldly eyes. With opportunities for wantonness taken away, they might more faithfully guard their hearts and bodies in total chastity.

§1. Indeed, so that this healthy statute might be observed more easily, we most strictly forbid any sisters from being received henceforth in any monastery not of the mendicant orders, unless the said monasteries can support them with their goods or income without penury. Any action to the contrary will be found invalid.

§2. But when an abbess or prioress of any monastery needs to pay homage or swear fealty for a fief that the said monastery holds from any prince or temporal lord, she may leave the monastery (unless a procurator standing in for her could accomplish the task instead), in this case licitly, with reputable and decent company. Having paid homage or sworn fealty, let her retrace her footsteps back to the said monastery as soon as possible, so that no deceit in residence or delay of claustration can occur....

§4. And since it would be insufficient to establish laws unless someone were entrusted with duly enforcing them, we strictly order (in virtue of holy obedience, under the prospect of divine judgment and the threat of eternal damnation) that patriarchs, primates, archbishops, and all bishops diligently impose enclosure where it is absent in the monasteries of nuns within their city or diocese and under their jurisdiction, and indeed also in those directly governed by the Roman Church under the authority of the Holy See. And also, abbots and others—exempt as well as non-exempt prelates of the church, of whatever monastery and order—shall do likewise in the monasteries subject to them. If they wish to avoid our bitterness and divine indignation, they will try to provide for the expenses of the said monasteries and the said nuns out of the alms that they will procure from the faithful. Those who object or rebel will be curbed by ecclesiastical censure without appeal. If necessary, the aid of the secular arm will be invoked.

GIOVANNI BOCCACCIO (1313–1375), *DECAMERON* (1348–1352, REV. 1370–1371)

Day 3, Tale 1: The story of Masetto of Lamporecchio.

Source: Giovanni Boccaccio, *Decameron*, ed. Vittore Branca (Turin: Einaudi, 1980), 332–33. Original in Italian. Translated by Spencer Strub.

Now it so happened that, after a hard day's work, Masetto was resting. Two young nuns who were walking through the garden approached where he lay and began to look at him. He seemed to be sleeping. The bolder of the two said to the other: "If I thought you could keep a secret, I'd tell you a thought that's sometimes occurred to me, which might be good for you too."

The other replied: "Say it, of course! I definitely won't tell anyone."

Then the bold one began: "I don't know if you've noticed how strictly we're kept here, and that no man ever dares to enter here, except the steward, who's old, and this mute. And I've heard again and again from many ladies who have come to us that all the other sweetnesses of the world are a joke compared to the pleasure a woman has when she does it with a man. So, it's crossed my mind more than once that, because no one else is available, I should try it with this mute to see if it's really so great. And, in fact, he's the best man in the world to try it with, because even if he wanted to blab about it, he couldn't: you see that he's a stupid kid, too big for his brains. I'd like to hear what you think."

"My goodness!" said the other. "What are you saying? Don't you know that we've promised our virginity to God?"

"Oh," she said, "so many things are promised to him, and not a single one is kept. So, if we've made a promise, let Him find someone else to keep it."

Reading questions

- What motivations does Boniface provide for his decretal? What moral values and attitudes toward female religious, implicit or explicit, are expressed in his statement?
- What do the exceptions to strict cloister reveal about the relationship between women's communities and the broader world? What does the mechanism of enforcement reveal about their place in the ecclesiastical hierarchy?
- How does the portrait of monastic life in *The Little Hours* compare to both the idealized and negative images of nuns in this decretal?
- How would you compare the film to its source material, *Decameron*, and particularly the Masetto story?

NOTES

1. The film also borrows the image of an abbess mistakenly donning her priest-lover's breeches as her veil from a third *novella*, *Tale Two of the Ninth Day*.

2. Bill Donohue, "Sundance Film Festival Trashes Nuns" (January 24, 2017), https://www.catholicleague.org/sundance-film-festival-trashes-nuns.

3. For the review, see John Anderson, "Laughing at Flawed Nuns and Priests in 'The Little Hours,'" *America* (June 15, 2017), https://www.americamagazine.org/arts-culture/2017/06/15/laughing-flawed-nuns-and-priests-little-hours. I quote from Eric Sundrup, SJ, "A Defense of 'The Little Hours': Finding Grace in Vulgarity," *America* (June 29, 2017), https://www.americamagazine.org/arts-culture/2017/06/29/defense-little-hours-finding-grace-vulgarity.

4. Jessica Roy, "Q&A: Alison Brie, Aubrey Plaza and Molly Shannon Talk F-Bombs and Faith in 'The Little Hours,'" *Los Angeles Times* (July 4, 2017), https://www.latimes.com/entertainment/movies/la-et-mn-the-little-hours-aubrey-plaza-alison-brie-molly-shannon-20170703-htmlstory.html.

5. I draw here on Marilyn Dunn, *The Emergence of Monasticism: From the Desert Fathers to the Early Middle Ages* (Oxford and Malden, Mass.: Blackwell, 2000).

6. See, e.g., Peter Brown, *The Body and Society: Men, Women and Sexual Renunciation in Early Christianity* (New York: Columbia University Press, 1988), 259–84, and Susannah Elm, *Virgins of God: The Making of Asceticism in Late Antiquity* (Oxford: Oxford University Press, 1994).

7. See Maria Chiara Giorda, "Egyptian Nuns in Late Antiquity as Exemplars," trans. Alessia Berardi, in *The Cambridge History of Medieval Monasticism in the Latin West*, ed. Alison I. Beach and Isabelle Cochelin (Cambridge: Cambridge University Press, 2020), 1:97–111.

8. Albrecht Diem, "The Gender of the Religious: Wo/Men and the Invention of Monasticism," in *The Oxford Handbook of Women and Gender in Medieval Europe*, ed. Judith Bennett and Ruth Mazo Karras (Oxford: Oxford University Press, 2013), 432–46.

9. Albrecht Diem, "New Ideas Expressed in Old Words: The *Regula Donati* on Female Monastic Life and Monastic Spirituality," *Viator* 43 (2012): 1–38.

10. Albrecht Diem and Philip Rousseau, "Monastic Rules (Fourth to Ninth Century)," in Beach and Cochelin, *Cambridge History of Medieval Monasticism*, 176.

11. Caesarius of Arles, "The Rule for Nuns," in *Western Monastic Spirituality*, ed. Roger Haight, SJ, Alfred Pach, and Amanda Avila Kaminski (New York: Fordham University Press, 2019), 48 (cf. 78).

12. On guests, see Caesarius, "Rule for Nuns," 59–61.

13. Jane Tibbetts Schulenburg, "Strict Active Enclosure and Its Effects on the Female Monastic Experience (ca. 500–1100)," in *Medieval Religious Women*, vol. 1, *Distant Echoes*, ed. John A. Nichols and Lillian T. Shank (Kalamazoo: Cistercian, 1984), 51–86, 73.

14. Kaspar Elm, "*Vita regularis sine regula*: The Meaning, Legal Status and Self-Understanding of Late-Medieval and Early-Modern Semi-Religious Life," in *Religious Life Between Jerusalem, the Desert, and the World: Selected Essays by Kaspar Elm*, ed. and trans. James D. Mixson (Leiden: Brill, 2016), 277–316.

15. *Corpus Iuris Canonici*, 2 vols., ed. Emil Friedberg (Graz: Akademische Druck- u. Verlagsanstalt, 1959), Sexti Decretalium 3.16, 2:1053. Translations my own.

16. Elizabeth Makowski, *Canon Law and Cloistered Women: "Periculoso" and Its Commentators, 1298–1545* (Washington, D.C.: The Catholic University of America Press, 1997), 42.

17. Makowski, *Canon Law and Cloistered Women*, 43–48.

18. See, e.g., Congregation for Institutes of Consecrated Life and Societies of Apostolic Life, Instruction *"Cor orans"* (April 1, 2018), https://www.vatican.va/roman_curia/congregations/ccscrlife/documents/rc_con_ccscrlife_doc_20180401_cor-orans_en.html, cap. 3.

19. Makowski, *Canon Law and Cloistered Women*, 46–47.

20. See, e.g., Elizabeth Makowski, *English Nuns and the Law in the Middle Ages: Cloistered Nuns and their Lawyers, 1293–1540* (Woodbridge: Boydell Press, 2011), 17–20.

21. Marie-Luise Ehrenschwendtner, "Creating the Sacred Space Within: Enclosure as a Defining Feature in the Convent Life of Medieval Dominican Sisters (13th–15th C.)," *Viator* 41 (2010): 301.

22. Ehrenschwendtner, "Creating," 309. See also Anne Winston-Allen, *Convent Chronicles: Women Writing About Women and Reform in the Late Middle Ages* (University Park: Pennsylvania State University Press, 2004), 129–67.

23. Giovanni Boccaccio, *Decameron*, ed. Vittore Branca (Turin: Einaudi, 1980), 328; Giovanni Boccaccio, *The Decameron*, 2nd ed., trans. G. H. McWilliam (1972; repr. London: Penguin, 1995), 192.

24. Graciela S. Daichman, *Wayward Nuns in Medieval Literature* (Syracuse: Syracuse University Press, 1986), 31–64.

25. Sita Steckel, "Satirical Depictions of Monastic Life," in Beach and Cochelin, *Cambridge History of Medieval Monasticism*, 1154–70.

26. Jill Mann, *Chaucer and Medieval Estates Satire* (Cambridge: Cambridge University Press, 1973), 129.

27. *Piers Plowman: The B Version*, ed. George Kane and E. Talbot Donaldson (London: Athlone, 1975), 5:165. Translation my own.

28. Geoffrey Chaucer, *General Prologue*, in *The Riverside Chaucer*, 3rd ed., gen. ed. Larry D. Benson (Boston: Houghton Mifflin, 1987), I:162.

29. "Nonnains," in Émilie Goudeau, ed., "Gilles le Muisit, *Registre*" (unpublished Ph.D. diss., Université Clermont-Ferrand II–Blaise Pascal, 2009), l:201. On this poem, see Daichman, *Wayward Nuns*, 36–39.

30. Paris, Bibliothèque Nationale de France MS Fr. 25526, f. 106v. On Jeanne and Richart de Montbaston, see Michael Camille, *Image on the Edge: The Margins of Medieval Art* (Cambridge, Mass.: Harvard University Press, 1992), 147–49; Camille suggests Jeanne may have painted the manuscript's penises solo after Richart's 1353 death.

31. Boccaccio, *Decameron*, ed. Branca, 330; trans. McWilliam, 193.

32. Boccaccio, *Decameron*, ed. Branca, 336; trans. McWilliam, 199.

33. On the sources and critical tradition, see Massimo Ciavolella, "The Tale of Masetto da Lamporecchio (III.1)," in *The "Decameron" Third Day in Perspective*, ed. Francesco Ciabattoni and Pier Massimo Forni (Toronto: University of Toronto Press, 2014), 9–21.

34. Boccaccio, *Decameron*, ed. Branca, 337; trans. McWilliam, 199.

35. Le Muisit, "Nonnains," l.245.

RELIGIOUS CONFLICT AND FORGING COMMUNITIES THROUGH LAW

CHAPTER SIXTEEN

LATE ROMAN LAW, WOMEN'S STATUS, AND
CLASSICAL EDUCATION IN *AGORA* (2009)

By Christopher Bonura

Agora, directed and cowritten by Alejandro Amenábar, stars Rachel Weisz as the philosopher Hypatia of Alexandria (d. 415), a historical figure caught up in religious conflict in Alexandria, Egypt. In the fourth century, when the movie takes place, the Roman Empire was still going strong; Alexandria was a major city and center of learning, and it, along with the rest of Egypt, would remain part of the Eastern Roman Empire (or Byzantine Empire) until the 640s, when Egypt was conquered by the Muslim Arabs. The film takes place during the Christianization of the Roman Empire and centers on two acts of Christian violence: the attack upon the temple complex called the Serapeum in the year 391, and the events that culminated in 415 with the murder of Hypatia, instigated by Cyril, the bishop of Alexandria.

The film follows a media tradition that has used Hypatia as a symbol among scientists, critics of religion, and feminists. These can be traced back to a 1720 book by the Irish philosopher John Toland, who portrayed Hypatia as a symbol of Enlightenment values persecuted by Christianity.[1] But the film deploys this narrative in a new historical context. It was written and filmed not long after the September 11, 2001, attacks in the United States, as well as other attacks by Islamic terrorists, including the 2004 train bombings in Madrid, where Amenábar grew up. The "War on Terrorism" and the so-called "clash of civilizations" with the Islamic world was often depicted as a struggle between Western rationalism and Middle Eastern religious fundamentalism.[2] *Agora* speaks to this charged moment. The movie implies that Hypatia discovered evidence of the heliocentric model of the solar system but was murdered by religious fanatics before she could publicize her breakthrough, with the result that science was set back for over a millennium. This is completely fictional, but it serves the film's implied message that religion and scientific rationality are opposed to one another, and symbolic of the clash between Islam and the West. Indeed, Weisz, the star of the film, explicitly related the film's themes to modern Islamic fundamentalism.[3] The film takes place centuries before the rise of Islam, but in a land (Egypt) that would eventually become central to the Muslim world; the radical Christians in the film are implied precursors to Muslim extremists. As scholar Edward Watts puts it, "*Agora*'s monks and clergy look more like the Taliban than the Christian ascetics we imagine today."[4] Indeed, this message is visually coded with the film's cast: English actress Weisz and Anglo-French actor Michael Lonsdale play Hypatia and her father, Theon, the enlightened pagans, while the Christian leaders (Theophilus, Cyril, Ammonius) are played by native Middle Eastern and Maltese actors. The racial coding in *Agora* relies on modern expectations about West and East that would have made little sense to the people of the Roman Mediterranean.

Although *Agora* is certainly a product of its own time, this chapter explores how it can lend insight into late Roman law, as well as another topic central to the legal system: education. Still, as argued here, the film consistently draws a stark contrast between pagans and Christians, portraying the former as more rational, scientific, and enlightened than they probably were, and the latter as more extremist, anti-intellectual, and repressive than in reality; in doing so, *Agora* paints a picture of religious confrontation that overlooks the religious fusion and coexistence of late antiquity (the period from the third to the ninth centuries CE).

LATE ROMAN EDUCATION

Agora includes scenes of Hypatia teaching her students, providing a window into education in the late Roman world. This system of education, rooted in classical antiquity, bonded together young Roman elites from cities across the vast empire, building a shared class identity. Members of this social class competed for careers in government service, which conferred aristocratic status. Other prestigious careers included law and leadership in the church. In preparation, the central goal of Roman education was perfection of public speaking and, to a lesser extent, writing. The film accurately depicts Hypatia's students as young men from noble families who would become, for example, civil administrators (i.e., Orestes, played by Oscar Isaac) and bishops (i.e., Synesius, played by Rupert Evans).

As the film depicts, Roman education did not take place in centralized schools with administrators, staffs, faculties, and large student bodies like modern universities. Roman schools generally consisted of a few dozen students learning from a single teacher (who sometimes employed assistants). Teaching often would take place in public spaces—like the Serapeum of Alexandria (though there is no evidence Hypatia taught there). Roman children would progress through different stages of education. Education was almost entirely private, and each stage became progressively more expensive, so fewer and fewer would have access. Elite children might be tutored by slaves in the household, but education outside the home would begin around age seven under a *litterator* ("schoolmaster"), who taught basic reading and writing. Children of the wealthy, around age twelve, came under the tutelage of a *grammaticus*, who taught grammar, literature, and formal writing. Young men from especially wealthy families would continue to study under a *rhetor* ("teacher of rhetoric") to learn how to deliver effective public speeches. The few students who completed this training were theoretically ready for the most prestigious careers and government assignments.

Rhetorical education was useful for elite careers, but students from the very pinnacle of wealthy elite might delay their careers to spend a few years studying mathematics, astronomy, and philosophy, the sort of rarefied education shown in the film. Philosophical education could only be pursued by a select fortunate few because it was not useful for getting a job. But it was valued because it was believed to mold the character of students and give them insight into the working of the universe and of the divine. Philosophy teachers could only be found in a few major cities, such as Alexandria. Hypatia was one such teacher of mathematics, astronomy, and philosophy in Alexandria.

The film depicts Hypatia lecturing on scientific concepts like gravity, but in reality, a philosophical education of the sort Hypatia offered would have focused on more metaphysical ideas. Hypatia wrote commentaries on earlier mathematical and astronomical treatises, but for philosophers like her, understanding numbers and the heavens served a larger aim of helping students understand and achieve unity with God, as most educated pagans by the fourth century believed in a single supreme God, even if they also believed in multiple lesser gods.

Hypatia was a teacher of Neoplatonism and would have spent a lot of time discussing the writings of the philosopher Plato. She taught in the tradition of the most famous Neoplatonist, Plotinus, a third-century pagan philosopher who believed there was a single supreme God with three emanations—a major influence on the Christian doctrine of the Trinity.[5] While the film implies that Hypatia was an atheist and depicts her as a forerunner to Copernicus or Galileo, she probably had much more in common with Christian theologians of her time.

Philosophy professors tended to be pagans, but they often took on Christian students. Most of the great Christian theologians of the fourth century studied under pagan teachers in places like Athens and Alexandria. Hypatia's murder seems, in the short term, to have had a stifling effect on pagan teachers in Alexandria, but soon the sort of philosophical training she offered thrived again in the city. Pagan philosophy teachers were still active through the sixth century. Tensions remained, and sometimes violence flared up with Christians, but the willingness of pagan teachers to take on Christian students meant that elite Christians were invested in the Alexandrian philosophical schools.[6] Gradually, the great teachers of Alexandria all adopted Christianity, but their teachings did not change much.

The biggest threat to the traditional educational curriculum in the fourth century was not Christianity but the rise of law schools. Earlier, a rhetorical education was considered adequate preparation for a career in law or the imperial government—rhetoric students learned to plead cases by writing speeches condemning or defending mythological or literary characters. By the late Roman period, however, the law had become very complex, and what lawyers really needed was a grasp of legal principles and the great mass of legislation that had accumulated over the empire's long history. As a result, specialized law schools developed in Rome, Constantinople, and Beirut. Legal training lasted five years. Law students attended three or four years of public lectures, after which they hired a private teacher or studied on their own.[7] Rhetoric professors in late antiquity complained that they were losing students to law schools, and that even men of humble background were training as law clerks and rising to positions of power. Teachers also griped that legal training was overly technical and unliterary.[8] But as the Roman Empire became more bureaucratized and centralized, many jobs in the government opened up for men with legal training, and so knowledge of the law became a common path to success.

ELITE WOMEN'S STATUS IN THE LATE ROMAN WORLD

Hypatia had much in common with other teachers in Alexandria, but she stood out for being a woman. In the film, Hypatia is depicted coming and going as she pleases and teaching in the patriarchal world of Alexandria, which reflects the evidence found in her biographical accounts (see the source by Socrates Scholasticus in the appendix). The film has the future prefect Orestes fall in love with Hypatia and propose marriage, only for Hypatia to reject the married life. The film accurately shows that the ultimate decision, however, rests with Hypatia's father, who decides that marriage would distract his daughter from her important work.

The film, in emphasizing Christian intolerance, portrays Christians as generally more repressive toward women than pagans, but this was often not the case. Women of all religions and social classes were generally forced to marry at a young age and bear children; at age twelve, girls were deemed ready for marriage and childbearing (though some families married off daughters at around sixteen to eighteen).[9] Women were supposed to consent to their husbands but in practice had little power over whom they married. By the late imperial period women had gained the right to divorce their husbands, but after divorce they would have been expected to marry again quickly.[10] Childbirth was very dangerous in the premodern world. Women were expected to produce many heirs, but every pregnancy brought a risk of death. Part of Christianity's appeal for women was that it gave them an escape hatch from marriage and procreation: they could adopt asceticism and become nuns. Some married Christian women convinced their husbands to cease sexual activity and live as "brother and sister," dedicating themselves to God. Christianity hardly offered sexual freedom—by modern standards, women's choices were extremely limited, but virginity offered an alternative to marriage and childbirth.[11] Hypatia would have been one of the few non-Christian women who could pursue asceticism because pagans deemed such a lifestyle appropriate for a philosopher.

How common was it for women to reach Hypatia's level of education? Girls tended not to be educated to the same extent as their brothers, mostly because education was very expensive. Parents paid handsomely to prepare their sons for their careers, but women could not practice law or hold public office. Women also married at younger ages than men and would have had to cut short their education to focus on running a household and producing children. Only the daughters of the extremely wealthy might gain an education in grammar or rhetoric, mostly to ensure that they would fit into high society and could pick the right teachers for their sons. The daughters of teachers could also get a thorough education because their fathers could provide it themselves without having to pay.[12]

Hypatia was unusual, but there were other well-educated daughters of great teachers in this period. One was a woman named Athenais. Born around the time that Hypatia died, she was the daughter of a Neoplatonic teacher in Athens. She had a very different fate from Hypatia's. When her father died her brothers received all the inheritance and took over the school, so Athenais moved to Constantinople (present-day Istanbul, Turkey) to live with an aunt. She became acquainted with the imperial family, and soon married the emperor, converted to Christianity, and changed her name to Aelia Eudocia. Her work combined classical pagan and Christian traditions. A poet, the empress remixed lines from Homer's *Iliad* and *Odyssey* to tell the story of Christ's life and crucifixion. Despite *Agora*'s black-and-white depiction of religious life in the late Roman Empire, Hypatia's revered status among Christian students and Aelia Eudocia's synthesis of pagan and Christian thought reveal that late antiquity was not just a time of religious conflict, but a fruitful period of fusion that made possible the continuation of both the classical and Christian traditions into the Middle Ages.

LATE ROMAN LAW AND RELIGION

The standoff that led to the destruction of the Serapeum, depicted in *Agora*, was widely regarded as a watershed moment in the Christianization of the Roman world. We know about it because many Christian church historians of the fifth century mention the incident. We also have an account from a pagan teacher of rhetoric named Eunapius. These sources give often contradictory accounts, and the film does a reasonable job in piecing together a mostly plausible version of what could have happened—though one false note is that our sources indicate that the Christians focused on destroying the statue of Serapis, not books (see the source by Rufinus in the appendix).

Notably, the film shows the Roman legal apparatus in action. The pagans, after losing a bloody street brawl with the Christians, barricade themselves within the Serapeum temple complex. The film depicts an imperial official reading a ruling by Emperor Theodosius I (r. 379–95), which decrees that the pagans in the Serapeum may go free, but the Christians can demolish the Serapeum. Emperor Theodosius had issued a rescript, a "response" to a petition. Our sources indicate that this really happened after the prefect (the civilian governor of Egypt) and count (commander of military forces in Egypt) petitioned the emperor in Constantinople for legal clarification on how they should deal with the situation at the Serapeum.

Such a direct appeal to the emperor was not unusual. By the late Roman period, an emperor's time was taken up with legal responsibilities. The emperor was the highest legal authority in the late Roman Empire and became the source of most of the law. Emperors could issue edicts, also called constitutions, addressed to the empire at large that added to existing law. Rescripts, in contrast, often clarified what should be done in light of existing law.[13] One of the major legal privileges of Roman citizens was their right to petition the emperor. Even freed slaves and women could petition the emperor. A petition had to be delivered in person to the imperial court, by the petitioner or someone representing them.[14] Cities might send representatives to the emperor to plead for tax relief after a natural disaster or for clemency after a riot. The men sent to plead such cases commanded respect because they were the highly educated, and their rhetorical training enabled them to sway those in power.[15]

Getting a favorable response often depended on having friends and influence at the imperial court. Sometimes friends could be bought. A list of the bribes Bishop Cyril (the antagonist of *Agora*, played by Sami Samir) doled out to the imperial officials in Constantinople has survived: he sent them furniture, rugs and tapestries, exotic pets, and various sums of money totaling 1,400 pounds of gold.[16] As bishop of one of the empire's richest cities, Cyril clearly recognized that it was important to spend a lot to maintain influence in the imperial court.

Most petitions were actually answered not by the emperor himself but by officials trained at law schools and employed by the imperial palace: these men drafted replies and sent them to the emperor to be signed. But emperors might step in to decide an issue if a petition involved issues or people of interest to them. The fates of the Serapeum and the insurgents barricaded inside were likely important enough that the emperor decided to address the issue himself. In such cases, emperors often relied on a council staffed by men with distinguished legal educations, chief among these the Quaestor of the Sacred Palace, the emperor's main legal advisor.[17]

Once the answer to a petition was made and the emperor signed, a copy would be made and kept in the imperial archives. Records of rescripts were also copied out in vast books for use in the major law schools of the empire, since rescripts might establish future precedent. The details of these processes are uncertain, but we know that they were overseen by the legally trained officials at court. Either the original or a copy would be sent back to the petitioner. The emperor's reply—the rescript—might be displayed in public, and its recipients might have it read aloud publicly.[18]

Theodosius's rescript about the Serapeum does not survive, but a contemporary account can be found in historian Rufinus's *Ecclesiastical History* (excerpted in appendix). This rescript was not the end of the legal question concerning pagan temples in Alexandria. A few months later, Theodosius issued another rescript, preserved in a later collection of Roman law known as the Theodosian Code, to the same civilian and military officials ordering the temples of Alexandria closed.[19] Something approximating this rescript is read aloud publicly in the movie in the scene where the former slave Davus (Max Minghella) leaves Hypatia's household.

It should be emphasized that Christian emperors also tried to use law to maintain order and protect non-Christians. In 423, several years after Hypatia's murder, the emperor issued a law emphasizing that pagans and Jews, along with their property, were protected (preserved in the Theodosian Code; see appendix). Several imperial edicts protected Jewish synagogues.[20] Certainly religious violence took place, but in making its point about religious intolerance, *Agora* downplays the level of coexistence that was fostered by imperial law.

CONCLUSION

Education and law were intimately linked in the late Roman Empire. The growing complexity of Roman law meant that formal legal education became increasingly necessary for those who would serve in the imperial government. *Agora* depicts a different sort of education—namely, the rarified philosophical education offered by Hypatia in Alexandria—but the role of Roman law lies behind many of the events in the film. *Agora* also takes place at a crucial moment when the fates of the Western and Eastern halves of the Roman Empire were beginning to diverge. The system of education changed after Western Roman imperial authority collapsed. In the early medieval West, elite education became simpler, and aristocrats focused more on military skills. But Christian clergy still studied and taught the texts central to the Latin educational curriculum, which were preserved by monasteries. In the eastern Mediterranean, the old system of education persisted. Alexandrian philosophers relocated to Constantinople, and a rigorous system of education for the elite persisted here well into the Middle Ages. Roman law also continued in Constantinople and all places subject to it, though eventually the language of law would change from Latin to Greek. In the West, Roman law provided a model for canon law. Priests and bishops would go to Rome to petition the popes, who, in place of emperors, would issue rescripts. Hypatia's death hardly inaugurated some sort of dark age. Education and Roman law would live on in the Middle Ages.

APPENDIX

Agora (2009)

RUFINUS (C. 345–411), *ECCLESIASTICAL HISTORY* (C. 402)

Book 11, Chapter 22: *A Christian's account of the siege of the Serapeum and the rescript ordering the destruction of the cult statue.*

Source: Theodore Mommsen, ed., *Eusebius Werke: Die Kirchengeschichte*, vol. 2.2 (Leipzig: J. C. Hinrichs, 1908), 1025–28. Original in Latin. Translated by Christopher Bonura.

In the meantime, in Alexandria new tumults, contrary to the faith of the times, were also stirred up against the church; the cause was as follows. There was a certain basilica [i.e., a courthouse or meeting hall] built for public use that was old and very neglected. . . . Seeing this, the bishop in charge of the church at that time asked the emperor for it, so that the houses of prayer might increase to accommodate the increase in the number of Christians [lit. "faithful people"]. When he received it and began to renovate it, certain secret caverns and underground chambers more suited to villainy and crimes than to religious ceremonies were discovered there.

The pagans, when they saw the lairs of their iniquities and caves of disgraces being uncovered, could not bear to have revealed this evil which so many centuries and darkness had concealed. All of them became violent and began to rage openly, as if they had drunk from the cup of serpents. Nor was it their usual noise and protests anymore, but they pressed forward to wage battle with weapons and swords, and each side made close combat in the streets and came together in open battle with one another. Our side's number and strength were much greater but less ferocious due to the mild nature of our religion. As a result, having repeatedly wounded many from our side and having even killed some, they [the pagans] took refuge in the temple [i.e., the Serapeum] as if it were some stronghold. Carrying away with them several Christians whom they captured, they forced them to make burnt sacrifices upon fiery altars. Those who refused they killed with new and elaborate tortures. . . .

But when those charged with the care of keeping the laws of Rome and with declaring judgement learned what happened, they rushed to the temple, disturbed and fearful, to investigate the cause of the insolence and ask the reason for the disturbance in which the blood of citizens was spilled with such wickedness before the altars. Having barricaded the entrance, they [the pagans] replied with shouts in confused and discordant voices rather than an explanation for what they had done. Nevertheless, messages were sent to them to remind them of the power of Roman authority, of the legal punishments, and what sort of things were accustomed to follow these.

However, since the place was so fortified that nothing could be done against those attempting such madness without greater force, the matter was reported to the emperor. He, who with an innate clemency of mind prefers to improve rather than to destroy those who go astray, wrote back [*rescribit*] that vengeance would not be sought for those who had been made martyrs by the spilling of blood before the altars and in whom the glory of rewards had overcome the pain of death. But otherwise, the cause of the evil events and roots of the discords, which originated in the defense of the idols, should be eliminated, since when these were gone the cause of the fighting might also cease.

When this document arrived and the people assembled before the temple after a kind of short-term truce, as soon as the first page of the letter was disclosed, the beginning of which blamed the vain superstition of the pagans, our side raised up an enormous cheer, while shock and fear fell upon the pagans. Every single one of them sought a hiding place, to find alleys through which to flee, or to stealthily blend in among our people. . . .

When the rescript had been read out, our people were prepared to overthrow the author of error [i.e., the cult statue of Serapis], but a story had been spread by the pagans that if a human hand touched that idol, the earth would immediately split open and dissolve into chaos, and the sky would suddenly come crashing down. This gave the people a short pause, until—behold! One of the soldiers, fortified with faith rather than weapons, grabbed a two-headed axe and, raising himself up, struck the false idol's jaw with all his might. A cry was raised up by both sides, but the sky did not fall, nor the earth sink. Then, with blow after blow, he felled the smoke-dried deity of rotten wood, which, upon being cast down, burned as easily as dried wood when fire was put to it.

SOCRATES SCHOLASTICUS (C. 380–AFTER 439), *ECCLESIASTICAL HISTORY* (5TH CENTURY)

Book 7, Chapter 15: A Christian's account of Hypatia's life and death.

Source: Philip Schaff and Henry Wace, eds., trans., *A Select Library of Nicene and Post-Nicene Fathers* (New York: Christian Literature, 1890), 160. Original in Greek. Revised by Christopher Bonura.

There was a woman at Alexandria named Hypatia, daughter of the philosopher Theon, who made such attainments in literature and science, as to far surpass all the philosophers of her own time. Having succeeded to the school of Plato and Plotinus, she explained the principles of philosophy to her listeners, many of whom came from a distance to receive her teachings.

On account of the self-possession and ease of manner which she had acquired from the cultivation of her mind, she not infrequently appeared in public in presence of the magistrates. Nor did she feel embarrassed in coming to an assembly of men. For all men on account of her extraordinary dignity and virtue admired her the more. Yet even she fell victim to the political jealousy which at that time prevailed. For, as she had frequent meetings with Orestes, it was maliciously reported among the Christian populace that it was she who prevented Orestes from being reconciled to the bishop. Some of them therefore, carried away by a fierce and bigoted zeal, whose ringleader was a reader named Peter, waylaid her returning home, and dragging her from her carriage, they took her to the church called Caesareum, where they completely stripped her, and then murdered her with tiles. After tearing her body to pieces, they took her mangled limbs to a place called Cinaron, and there burnt them. This affair brought not the least opprobrium, not only upon Cyril, but also upon the whole Alexandrian church. And surely nothing can be further from the spirit of Christianity than the allowance of massacres, fights, and things of that sort. This happened in the month of March during Lent, in the fourth year of Cyril's episcopate, under the tenth consulate of Honorius, and the sixth of Theodosius.

THE THEODOSIAN CODE (438)

A law fostering coexistence between Christians, Jews, and pagans.

Source: Theodore Mommsen, ed., *Theodosiani Libri XVI* (Berlin: Weidmann, 1905), 904–905 (bk. 16, tit. 10, const. 24.1). Original in Latin. Translated by Christopher Bonura.

But this we especially demand of those who truly are, or are said to be, Christians: that they should not abuse the authority of religion and dare lay hand upon Jews and pagans who are living quietly and not attempting anything unruly or against the law. For if they should act violently against those living quietly or if they should steal their goods, they shall be compelled by the court to repay not only what they took, but three or even four times what they have stolen. Furthermore, the provincial governors and their officers [i.e., staff] and the citizens of the provinces shall know that if they allow such things to happen, they who have done so will be punished. Dated the sixth day before the Ides of June, in Constantinople, in the consulship of Asclepiodotus and Marinianus (June 8, 423).

Reading questions

- Our surviving evidence about Hypatia is very limited. What details about Hypatia does *Agora* invent to fill in the blanks? In what sense (plot, characterization, etc.) do you think the film adapt details from Christian sources like Socrates and Rufinus?
- The word "agora" means public square or marketplace in Greek. Why you think this film, dramatizing this time in history, is called *Agora* and not *Hypatia*? How does the agora (or public spaces) appear in either of the histories, written by Socrates or Rufinus?
- How do the Christian primary sources differ in their perception of the attack on the Serapeum? How does *Agora*'s depiction of the attack on the Serapeum and Hypatia's murder differ from the primary source accounts?
- How would you describe the legal status of Jews and pagans under the Christian Roman Empire? What aspects of pagan life were Christian rulers determined to eliminate, and what did they tolerate? In what ways is this reflected in *Agora*?
- All of the primary sources here were written by Christian hands and thus show a Christian perspective of history and the law. How would you characterize the perspective shown in *Agora*?

NOTES

1. John Toland, *Hypatia: Or, The History of a Most Beautiful, Most Vertuous, Most Learned, and Every Way Accomplish'd Lady, etc.* (London: M. Cooper, 1720).

2. See, for example, Sam Harris, *The End of Faith: Religion, Terror, and the Future of Reason* (New York: Norton, 2004).

3. Larry Rohter, "Science vs. Zealots, 1,500 Years Ago," *New York Times* (May 23, 2010), https://www.nytimes.com/2010/05/23/movies/23agora.html.

4. Edward Watts, *Hypatia: The Life and Legend of an Ancient Philosopher* (Oxford: Oxford University Press, 2017), 146.

5. Watts, *Hypatia*, 31–50.

6. Edward Watts, *Riot in Alexandria: Tradition and Group Dynamics in Late Antique Pagan and Christian Communities* (Berkeley: University of California Press, 2017); Watts, *City and School in Late Antique Athens and Alexandria* (Berkeley: University of California Press, 2006), 216–25, 260–61.

7. Anton-Hermann Chroust, "Legal Education in Ancient Rome," *Journal of Legal Education* 7, no. 4 (1955): 520–28.

8. Raffaella Cribiore, *The School of Libanius in Late Antique Antioch* (Princeton: Princeton University Press, 2007), 205–13; Robert Kastor, *Guardians of Language: The Grammarian and Society in Late Antiquity* (Berkeley: University of California Press, 1988), 47–48.

9. Aline Rousselle, *Porneia: On Desire and the Body in Antiquity*, trans. Felicia Pheasant (Cambridge, Mass: Blackwell, 1988), 24–46.

10. Gillian Clark, *Women in Late Antiquity* (Oxford: Clarendon Press, 1993); Eve D'Ambra, *Roman Women* (Cambridge: Cambridge University Press, 2007).

11. Peter Brown, *The Body and Society: Men, Women, and Sexual Renunciation in Early Christianity* (New York: Columbia University Press, 1988).

12. Watts, *Hypatia*, 23–26, 93–106; Raffaella Cribiore, *Gymnastics of the Mind* (Princeton: Princeton University Press), 74–101.

13. John Matthews, *Laying Down the Law: A Study of the Theodosian Code* (New Haven: Yale University Press, 2000), 13–14.

14. Tony Honoré, *Emperors and Lawyers*, 2nd ed. (Oxford: Clarendon Press, 1994), 34–36.

15. Watts, *City and School*, 7.

16. *St. Cyril of Alexandria: Letters 51–110*, trans. John I. McEnerney (*The Fathers of the Church* 77) (Washington, D.C.: The Catholic University of America Press, 1987), 151–53.

17. A. H. M. Jones, *The Later Roman Empire, 284-602: A Social, Economic, and Administrative Survey* (Oxford: Blackwell, 1964), 504–7; Jill Harries, *Law and Empire in Late Antiquity* (Cambridge: Cambridge University Press, 1999), 38–47; Honoré, *Emperors and Lawyers*, 43–48.

18. Matthews, *Laying Down the Law*, 13.

19. Theodosian Code 16.10.11

20. Theodosian Code 16.8.9, 16.8.12, 16.8.20, 16.8.21, 16.8.25.

CHAPTER SEVENTEEN
DEPICTING THE PROPHET, SOCIAL JUSTICE, AND THE PILLARS OF ISLAM IN *THE MESSAGE* (1976)

By Maria Americo

In bringing to life the vision for the English-language version of his 1976 film *The Message*, Syrian American director Moustapha Akkad, who also shot the film in Arabic with different actors, faced significant creative challenges. He wanted a cinematic depiction of the prophet Muhammad and the origins of the religion Islam that was palatable for Western and especially American audiences, but he also wanted, as the intertitle from the beginning of the film proclaims, to "honour the Islamic tradition which holds that the impersonation of the prophet offends against the spirituality of his message." Akkad improvised an innovative way to satisfy both of these goals, which was, as that intertitle goes on to explain, never to show "the person of Mohammad" on screen, a decision he followed in both the English and Arabic versions of the film.[1]

Another intertitle explains that Akkad consulted with Islamic leaders of jurisprudence in directing the film: "The scholars and historians of Islam—the university of Al-Azhar in Cairo and the high Islamic congress of the *shiat* in Lebanon—have approved the accuracy and fidelity of this film." With this artistic choice, Akkad and his religious consultants judged that his aim had been met: he could create a full sensory experience of sixth-century Mecca that was lavishly filmed, seemingly with traditional music, period costuming, camels, dramatic battle sequences, scenes shot in the desert, caravans and bustling marketplaces, and Islamic calls to prayer, while still focusing on the spirituality of the prophet's message rather than the actual presence of his person.[2]

The Message centers on Muhammad's rise to prophethood and tells the story of the earliest days of Islam, from the first prophecy that Muhammad received (the message) about the oneness of God (Allah) to the conquest of Mecca and the conversion of many Arabs to the new religion. Because of the restrictions on depicting the prophet, Akkad used minor historical figures, such as Hamza (Anthony Quinn), the prophet's uncle, and the antagonist Hind (Irene Papas), to anchor the plot of the film.[3] As with many films depicting the premodern world, *The Message* also deals with questions of law and justice that would have resonated with contemporary viewers of the film. As such, this chapter examines how the film's depiction of the prophet and his family, racial and women's equality, and the practice of the core tenets (or pillars) of Islam represented Akkad's attempt to balance modern sensibilities with the medieval evidence for early Islamic history. The film's narrative paid special attention to law and custom, as these were not only important in early Islamic society, but also crucial to the didactic nature of this film, which sought to introduce modern, non-Islamic audiences to Islam.

MODERN AND PREMODERN CUSTOMS ON DEPICTING THE PROPHET

When anyone speaks to Muhammad during the course of the film, the speaker breaks the fourth wall and looks directly at the camera, creating an interesting, if somewhat odd, cinematic experience for the viewer, because it seems that Muhammad himself is in fact holding the camera. His companions, then, speak directly to the audience, who now stand in for the prophet. A light bulb was mounted on the camera during the scenes when other characters were present with Muhammad, a cinematic manifestation of the holiness of his figure. A few times throughout the film, a voice speaks the words of Muhammad—most notably at the end of the film, when Muhammad's Farewell Sermon is delivered during the *hajj* (pilgrimage) on Mount Arafat outside of Mecca—still without ever showing the person of Muhammad on screen.

It is important to note, however, that, in medieval contexts, attitudes toward physical representations of the prophet in art were not as clear-cut as the intertitles of Akkad's film make it seem. It would ignore the nuances of premodern Islamic art history to suggest that there was a simple injunction against the depiction of Muhammad, his family, and companions or even of human and animal subjects in general. In the surviving body of Islamic art from the Middle Ages, especially in the realm of Islamic illuminated manuscripts, in which stories of Islamic history were accompanied by illustrations occupying the same manuscript folia, artists in fact seem to have had a variety of choices available to them when deciding how they would depict the prophet Muhammad and other holy figures. Some artists chose to depict Muhammad and others close to him (such as, for example, his wives) with their faces completely veiled in white and with a halo of flame surrounding their heads to indicate their holiness, but their bodies visible to the viewers of the art. In the film, we never see Muhammad's first wife, Khadijah, who dies offscreen, but she is spoken of reverently by the other characters—a type of artistic veiling in its own right. Some premodern Islamic artists, however, chose to depict the face and full embodied person of Muhammad—this was especially customary in the art of medieval Persia (Iran). Art is not and has never been monolithic, not in any era, and it would be ahistorical to suggest that it was.[4]

Instead, we may see Moustapha Akkad as being one in a long line of Muslim artists deciding how to address the sensitive question of the depiction of the prophet Muhammad in the context of his art. We can imagine that Akkad made the choice that seemed right based on his personal faith; the goals, capabilities, and limitations of his art form; what he believed would satisfy his audience; the recommendations of the specific leaders of Islamic jurisprudence that he consulted; and the historical context of his own time (the twentieth century) and place (Syria, Lebanon, and the United States).

MODERN AND PREMODERN SOCIAL JUSTICE

Two aspects of Muhammad's message on which Akkad's film focuses are racial equality and women's rights, which were important social justice movements in the 1970s. In *The Message*'s imagining of sixth-century Arabia, the struggle for racial equality was embodied primarily in the person of Bilal, an enslaved Meccan man who gains his freedom by accepting Muhammad's message and becoming a member of the Muslim community, according to historical sources known as the *hadith* (more on this source in the following section), and who was played in the film by Senegalese actor Johnny Sekka. Many of the film's scenes emphasize Islam's message of racial equality, that all peoples of all colors are considered equal within Islam, as well as the discomfort and anger of Muhammad's Meccan opposition at the notion that a free, wealthy Meccan could be considered equal to an enslaved black person. For example, in the film, Bilal is chosen as Islam's first *muezzin*, who delivers the call to prayer from a rooftop in Medina, both literally and figuratively elevating the person and voice of a formerly enslaved person as one with religious and social authority. In Islamic religious tradition, Bilal, who is reported to have been a former slave from Abyssinia, was indeed the first *muezzin*, chosen by Muhammad himself to deliver the call to prayer, as recorded in the Islamic hadith tradition. During the scenes of the building of the first mosque in Medina, men of visibly different social classes, ages, and skin colors all work together toward a common religious goal that benefits the entire community of believers—this collective in Islam is known as the *ummah*. Meanwhile, a Meccan spy who is present in Medina, pretending to have accepted Muhammad's message, expresses that he is "tired of the politics of kissing slaves," showing the reluctance of those in power to accept the overturning of the status quo.

In the vein of women's rights, *The Message* also devotes a lot of time to a question of great legal and social import in sixth-century Arabia: female infanticide, a practice later denounced in the *Qur'an*, the holy book of Islam. Perhaps one of the film's most moving scenes on this topic is between Ammar (Garrick Hagon), one of the earliest followers of Muhammad's message, and his parents, Sumayyah (Rosalie Crutchley) and Yasir (Ewen Solon), at their home in Mecca. When challenged by his parents and faced with their fear that he is following dangerous people and ideas, Ammar elaborates some of the social aspects of Muhammad's message, including socioeconomic equality and women's rights, particularly a woman's right to choose her own marriage and the forbidding of female infanticide, believed to be common in sixth-century Mecca.[5] Sumayyah, Ammar's mother, then tells a story from her childhood: that her father buried two older sisters of hers when the girls were infants. At the burial of her second sister, Sumayyah recounts, the baby took hold of her father's finger and, for a long moment, did not let go. The horror of undertaking this action disturbed Sumayyah's father so deeply that he was unable to repeat it a third time at Sumayyah's birth; otherwise, Sumayyah says, she too would have died, she and Yasir never would have met, and their son Ammar would never have been born. She then expresses her belief that the custom of female infanticide is wrong and that Muhammad's message is good. This scene is the seed of Sumayyah's eventual acceptance of the message of Islam. Though the issue of female infanticide would have been more relevant to the sixth century than the 1970s, the women's liberation movement of the 1970s very well might have been on viewers' minds; indeed, it might continue to be on the minds of today's viewers.

THE FIVE PILLARS OF ISLAM

Aside from the *Qur'an*, believed by Muslims to be the word of God given to the prophet through the angel Gabriel, the most important document for guidance on how to live the proper Muslim life is known as the *hadith*. The *hadith* is the collected sayings, actions, and approvals of the prophet Muhammad, as he was, and still is, considered the finest example of a person leading the most morally upright Muslim life. Because there is evidence in the historical sources that Muhammad could neither read nor write (which characters in *The Message* frequently emphasize), the *Qur'an* and *hadith* were not written physically by him. His companions wrote down the revelations he received from God (which became the text of the *Qur'an*), as well as the details of his life (which became the collection of the *hadith*), and both were later codified into the forms we know today.

The *hadith* reports that there are five pillars upon which Islam is built—actions and states of being that the faithful must fulfill to be considered Muslims. These pillars encompass dogma, or the aspects of belief within a religion, as well as praxis, or the set of actions required of the participants in a religion. The most respected *hadith* collection is by Muhammad al-Bukhari (810–70), who lived some two hundred years after the life of Muhammad (570–632). He was Persian, from the city of Bukhara in present-day Uzbekistan, and from a family of scholars; his father, Ismail ibn Ibrahim, was also a scholar of *hadith*. Al-Bukhari was highly educated in the Islamic traditions, and, as his legend goes, after he made the pilgrimage to Mecca with his family at the age of sixteen, he became inspired to record a collection of the doings and sayings of the prophet Muhammad. The project is said to have taken sixteen years, during which al-Bukhari traveled all around the Islamic world, speaking with hundreds of people and eventually recording 7,397 *hadith* traditions, a collection known as *al-Jami' al-Sahih*, or *The Authentic Collection* (excerpted in the appendix).

The establishment of four of the five pillars of Islam is depicted in the film *The Message*, and these are, according to Al-Bukhari's collection, (1) to profess that there is no god but God and that Muhammad is the messenger of God; (2) to perform the five daily obligatory prayers; (3) to give charity to those less fortunate; (4) to make the holy pilgrimage, known as the *hajj*, to Mecca, the birthplace of Islam and its most sacred site; and (5) to fast daily from sunup until sundown during the month of Ramadan, which commemorates the revelation of the *Qur'an* to Muhammad. Ramadan is the only pillar not dramatized in the film because the narrative spans only a little over a decade. The custom of fasting required some time to become fully established.

The first pillar, *shahada* ("testimony" or "bearing witness"), involves taking an oath, shown in *The Message* as the moment when someone becomes a Muslim. It is a transformative act of speaking that shifts a person's state from non-Muslim to Muslim. In *The Message*, for example, the Meccan aristocrat Khalid ibn Walid (Michael Forest), who had once led battles against Muhammad, comes to the Muslim community in Medina and takes the oath of the *shahada* in front of Muhammad and his companions, saying, "I witness that there is only one God, and that Muhammad is His messenger." But even before the characters in the film take the oath on screen, the importance of the *shahada* as a life-changing profession of faith has already been established. Near the beginning of the film, before open hostilities between Muhammad and the Meccans have begun, the city leaders offer Muhammad money and power if he will renounce his message, as his mission is tearing families apart. But it is reported in the film that Muhammad says that he would not renounce his message even if the Meccans were able to offer him the sun in one hand and the moon in another.

There are numerous mentions of the second pillar, the five obligatory daily prayers, in *The Message*. The Muslim method of prayer requires purification of the body with water and cycles of rising and prostration. A communal act, these prayers are often undertaken at a mosque with other Muslims. *The Message* depicts the building of the first Islamic prayer house and mosque by the entire community in Medina, stressing its importance as a place that welcomes all those who are Muslim, regardless of their social class, race, age, and other secular markers of identity. The physical acts of prayer—namely, the kneeling and prostration—are also emphasized in the film. For example, Hind, the wife of the Meccan leader Abu Sufyan (Michael Ansara) and (at first) one of the fiercest opponents of Muhammad and his new religion, ridicules the Muslims by describing the ritual as "wiping [one's] face on the floor five times a day, praying." She indicates that such an act is considered unworthy and unbecoming of a wealthy, aristocratic person. By willingly undertaking this act, the film suggests that Muslims eschew the markers of status and wealth and choose submission to God instead.

The third pillar, charity, is one of the most frequently and meaningfully depicted of the pillars in *The Message*. For example, after Khalid ibn Walid takes the *shahada* in Medina, marking his conversion to Islam with the transformative act of speaking, he immediately solidifies his commitment to the Muslim community and its ethos of charity by removing all his jewels. When Khalid first enters the gathering, the contrast between his person, clad in ornaments and colorful clothing, and the Muslims, seated outside on the ground in plain white garments, is visually striking. He then slides off his jeweled rings and tears his necklace from his throat, saying, "Here are my jewels. What they are worth, I give to the poor." Khalid thus supports the Islamic economic doctrine of the redistribution of wealth. Charity is also shown as codified in Islam when Muhammad's followers begin preaching his message beyond the communities of Mecca and Medina, sharing God's revelation to Muhammad (which would one day become the text of the *Qur'an*) and stories from Muhammad's life (which would one day become part of the *hadith*) with others. In one of these scenes, one of Muhammad's followers tells the gathering of people who have come to hear the prophet preach, "Unless you desire for your neighbor what you desire for yourself, you don't have faith. A man who goes to bed with his belly full while his neighbor is hungry—he isn't a Muslim." In other words, it is not possible to be a Muslim without a commitment to charity. This deep commitment to charity, codified within the tenets of Islam, also reinforces the religion's overall message of social justice, echoed in its attitude toward the rights of women in sixth-century Arabia, as explored previously.

Some of the final scenes in *The Message* depict the fourth pillar, the *hajj* to Mecca, though there were other minor pilgrimages shown of early Muslim refugees, such as their arrival at the court of the Abyssinian king, suggesting to viewers how Islam spread to Africa in one particular way. But before Muhammad and his followers make the pilgrimage to Mecca, some of the characters in the film express worry that it will be dangerous for the Muslims to reenter the city, that they might face violence from the Meccans. But the Muslims are instructed not to storm doors or walls of people's homes or to take anything that does not belong to them, and the scenes of the *hajj* are mostly joyful ones, as the Muslims are reunited with their hometown and their loved ones after many years of exile. Muhammad enters the *ka'ba*, the inner sanctum or shrine of Mecca that until then was the center of pagan worship in the city, and smashes the figurines of the idols, a powerful visual moment for which there is also evidence in the *hadith*. This was the first *hajj* by the Muslims to Mecca, and it would later become an obligation for all Muslims to undertake at least once during their life.

CONCLUSION

Akkad's *The Message* provides many depictions of medieval Islamic law, justice, customs, and social ideals. One of the film's major themes is how Islam disrupted the socioeconomic status quo and challenged the inequities of race, social status, and gender. Muhammad's message in this film and the vision of the Muslim world that his message sought to usher in were those of charity, the rights of girls and women to live and choose their husbands, and equality among the races. *The Message* also provides viewers with a notion of a clean slate. As Bilal puts it, in the scene when Khalid ibn Walid converts to Islam and gives away his jewels with an air of regret and shame, "Islam does away with all that went before it." Ultimately, the message here is that Islam is a religion of compassion, mercy, and forgiveness.

Some of these notions of justice are more relevant to the sixth- and seventh-century historical context the film portrays; for example, the outlawing of female infanticide and the institution of a woman's right to accept or refuse a marriage proposal.[6] Others likely emerged from the modern-day context in which the film was made, particularly the issue of racial equality. In one scene, one of Muhammad's followers, using racialized language more common to 1976, says, "Nor [is] a white man superior to a black." Other notions of justice, perhaps, have been more universal as an ideal then and now; for example, the idea of the redistribution of wealth through charity. But as we continue to live in a world with deep socioeconomic inequality and systemic and intersectional oppression, the religious and social ideals of *The Message* are as relevant today as they were in the 600s. In these ways, Moustapha Akkad's film has a lot to teach us as students of history, not only about the social and legal world of early Islam, but about our contemporary world, as well.

APPENDIX

The Message (1976)

AL-BUKHARI (810–870), *AL-JAMI' AL-SAHIH* (9TH CENTURY)

On matters of faith and the observance of Islam (hadith).
Source: *Ṣaḥīḥ al-Bukhārī*: The Authentic Collection [of Hadith] of *al-Bukhārī* (https://sunnah.com/bukhari). Original in Classical Arabic. Translated by Maria Americo.

Ibn 'Umar reported that God's prophet—may peace and blessings be upon him—said that Islam is built upon 5 [pillars]: testifying that there is no god but God and that Muhammad is His prophet; performing prayer; giving charity; making the pilgrimage; and fasting during Ramadan (Volume 1, Book 2, Hadith 7).

Abu Huraira reported that on a particular day, the prophet—may peace and blessings be upon him—was in the company of some people, and Gabriel came to him and said, "What is faith?" He said, "Faith is to believe in God, His angels, the meeting with Him, and His prophets; and to believe in resurrection." [Gabriel] asked, "What is Islam?" He said, "Islam is to worship God and not to hold any other gods above Him, to perform prayer, to give the compulsory charity, and to fast during Ramadan." [Gabriel] asked, "What is perfection?" He said, "To worship God as though you can see Him; but if you cannot see Him, then as though He can see you." [Gabriel] asked, "When will the hour [of judgment] be?" He said, "The one being asked has no more knowledge than the one asking. But I will tell you about its portents: when a slave gives birth to her master and when the shepherds of black camels compete with each other about buildings [i.e., something that is oxymoronic]. But it is one among five things which no one knows except God." Then the prophet—may peace and blessings be upon him—recited the [Qur'anic] verse, "God alone has knowledge of the hour [of judgment]." Then [Gabriel] left. [Muhammad] said [to his companions], "Call him back." But they could not see anything. So he said, "That was Gabriel who came to teach the people about their religion." Abu Abdallah said, "He [Muhammad] considered all of that a part of faith." (Volume 1, Book 2, Hadith 43).

Abdallah said that when the prophet—may peace and blessings be upon him—entered Mecca on the day of its conquest, there were 360 idols around the *ka'ba*. He began stabbing them with a stick in his hand and he said, "The truth has come and falsehood has vanished. Falsehood will not begin again, and it will not return." (Volume 3, Book 43, Hadith 658).

Abu Huraira reported that the prophet—peace and blessings be upon him—said, "A matron should not be married until she has been consulted, and a maiden should not be married until she has given permission." And they said, "O prophet, how will she give her permission?" He said, "By being silent." (Volume 7, Book 62, Hadith 67).

Aisha reported that she said, "O prophet! But a maiden feels shy." He said, "Her silence is her consent." (Volume 7, Book 62, Hadith 68)

Ubada bin As-Samit—may God's blessing be upon him—reported: I gave the pledge of allegiance to the prophet—may peace and blessings be upon him—amongst a group of people, and he said, "I accept your pledge that you will not worship anything except God, that you will not steal, that you will not commit infanticide, that you will not fabricate slander about others and spread it, and that you will not disobey me in anything good. Whoever among you fulfills [these obligations], his reward is with God. And whoever commits any of these crimes and receives punishment in this world, that is his atonement and purification. But if God judges his crime, then it will be up to God, if He wishes to punish him or to forgive him." (Volume 8, Book 81, Hadith 793).

Ibn 'Umar reported that, when the Muslims came to Medina, they would assemble and guess the time for the prayer; the call to prayer had not yet been introduced. So in those days they discussed this matter. Some said that they should use a bell, like the Christians. Others suggested a trumpet like the horn used by the Jews. 'Umar was the first to suggest that a man should make the call to prayer. So the prophet—may peace and blessings be upon him—said, "Bilal, rise up and perform the call to prayer." (Volume 1, Book 10, Hadith 604)

THE QUR'AN, SELECTIONS (C. 635)

On female infanticide.

Source: *The Holy Qur'an* (https://quran.com/). Original in Classical Arabic. Translated by Maria Americo.

When the female infant is questioned for what crime, she was killed (Surat al-Takwir, 81:8–9).

They attribute daughters to God—glory be to Him—and so they get what they are asking for. And when one of them is told of [the birth of] a female, his face grows dark, and he suppresses grief. He hides from the people because of the evil of which he has been informed. Should he keep it in humiliation or bury it in the dirt? No matter what, evil is what they decide (Surat al-Nahl, 16:57-59).

Say, "Come! Let me tell you what your Lord has forbidden for you. Do not worship anything except for Him. Honor your parents. Do not kill your children out of fear of poverty. We provide for you and for them. Do not approach abominations, whether openly or secretly. Do not kill a soul, made sacred by God, except in the name of what is right. This is what He has commanded you, so that you may understand" (Surat Al-Anam, 6:151).

Reading questions

- Compare the depiction and practice of the pillars of Islam in *The Message* and in the collection compiled by Bukhari. Which of the five pillars do you think is the most vividly depicted in the film?
- According to Islamic tradition, the prophet Muhammad could neither read nor write. How, based on your reading of Bukhari's sources, was this information written down and transmitted?
- Compare the treatment of women in *The Message* and the description of how women are meant to be treated according to these sources.

NOTES

1. For the making of the film, see Freek L. Bakker, "The Image of Muhammad in *The Message*, the First and Only Feature Film about the Prophet of Islam," *Islam and Christian–Muslim Relations* 17, no. 1 (2006): 77–92.

2. Despite Akkad's preemptive attempts to ensure that his film met with the approval of at least some leaders of Islamic jurisprudence, both its filming and release were marred by controversy. See R. H. Greene, "40 Years On, a Controversial Film on Islam's Origins Is Now a Classic," *NPR* (August 7, 2016), https://www.npr.org/sections/parallels/2016/08/07/485234999/40-years-on-a-controversial-film-on-islams-origins-is-now-a-classic; Axel Madsen, "Arab Oil Dollars Pay for Anthony Quinn Epic," *Kansas City Star* (January 26, 1975), https://www.newspapers.com/article/114139073/the-kansas-city-star/; and Amir Hussain, "Images of Muhammad in Literature, Art, and Music," in *The Cambridge Companion to Muhammad*, ed. Jonathan E. Brockopp (Cambridge: Cambridge University Press, 2010), 287.

3. One of the main medieval narrative sources for these figures was composed by Ibn Isḥāq (c. 704–67). See Alfred Guillaume, trans., ed., *The Life of Muhammad: A Translation of Isḥāq's Sīrat rasūl Allāh* (Oxford: Oxford University Press, 1955).

4. For more on Muhammad in medieval art, see Thomas W. Arnold, *Painting in Islam: A Study of the Place of Pictorial Art in Muslim Culture* (Oxford: Clarendon Press, 1928); Oleg Grabar, "The Story of Portraits of the Prophet Muhammad," *Studia Islamica* 96 (2003): 19–38 and VI–IX; and Christiane Gruber and Avinoam Shalem, eds., *The Image of the Prophet Between Ideal and Ideology: A Scholarly Investigation* (Berlin: De Gruyter, 2014). Also relevant to the discussion of the depiction of the prophet Muhammad in art and reception of such depictions in academia today is the 2022 controversy at Hamline University in Saint Paul, Minnesota. For a scholarly view on this controversy and an introduction to the various choices made by premodern artists who depicted Muhammad in the manuscript art of the medieval world, see Christiane Gruber, "An Academic Is Fired Over a Medieval Painting of the Prophet Muhammad," *New Lines Magazine* (December 22, 2022), https://newlinesmag.com/argument/academic-is-fired-over-a-medieval-painting-of-the-prophet-muhammad/.

5. For more on this practice in the sources, see Avner Giladi, "Some Observations on Infanticide in Medieval Muslim Society," *International Journal of Middle East Studies* 22 (1990): 185–200.

6. For more on marriage and married women's rights in premodern Arabia, see Robert Hoyland, *Arabia and the Arabs: From the Bronze Age to the Coming of Islam* (London: Routledge, 2001), 128–34.

CHAPTER EIGHTEEN
LAWFUL LANGUAGE AND GLOBAL NORTH ENCOUNTERS IN *THE 13TH WARRIOR* (1999)

By Daniel Armenti and Nahir I. Otaño Gracia

The 13th Warrior reimagines Michael Crichton's 1976 novel *Eaters of the Dead*, itself a fictionalized intersection of two medieval sources: Ahmad ibn Fadlān's tenth-century account of his travels, the *Risāla* ("account" or "message"), and the Old English epic *Beowulf*. Released in 1999, pre-9/11 America, the film is extraordinary for viewers after the Iraq War, given that our perspective character, Ahmed ibn Fahdlan (Antonio Banderas), is a fictionalized version of the tenth-century Arab ambassador and traveler from the court of Baghdad.[1] Throughout the film, Ahmed acts as the "civilized" perspective, out of his depth in a land of barbarians, "Northmen," under attack themselves by a more savage and monstrous threat, the Wendol. Ahmed's role in the film draws his Arab character and the modern viewer closer together, utilizing the trope that casts medieval Muslims in the position of both exotic and civilized.

The medieval material adapted for *The 13th Warrior* demonstrates the complexities of cultural encounter during the Middle Ages, highlighted by access to language. This is certainly the case in its treatment of the character Ibn Fadlān's observations of the Northmen's social practices and rituals, which must be initially translated for him; notably, the funeral he observes closely follows the historical Ibn Fadlān's actual account of a Rūs funeral.[2] However, the movie portrays many other points of cultural encounter, perhaps none so memorable or impactful as Ahmed listening to and learning the Northmen's language over the course of their travels and his sudden and surprising access to their community. Nevertheless, the antagonists of the film, the Wendol, a people more "barbaric" than the Northmen, are excluded from this kind of access and understanding. Demonstrating an emphasis on body language rather than spoken language, there can be no point of contact between the Northmen and the Wendol except one of violence.

This chapter offers a close reading of the *The 13th Warrior* as an adaption of *Beowulf* and the *Risāla* to show how language and multicultural encounters in the Global North Atlantic World could play out, both within the imaginary world of the film and within the literary world of these medieval texts. As this chapter shows, it is language and its codification of social norms—either in ritualistic or written form—that not only legitimize violence but also identity in the Global North. Violence can be found in the Northmen's political and religious lives, from funeral rites to succession and duels. Violence itself was a kind of language. For the film's Wendol, who stand in for indigenous people, there is an exclusion from language and, with this, an exclusion from legitimacy or justice.

LANGUAGE, ENCOUNTER, AND TRANSLATION IN THE GLOBAL NORTH ATLANTIC

The first scenes of *The 13th Warrior* focus on encounters of cultures in the Global North Atlantic and the problem of language at first contact. One of the tenets of Global North Atlantic studies is to understand how North Atlantic cultures—broadly defined as coming from the areas of the British Isles, Iceland, Scandinavia, the English Channel, and the Low Countries—participated in and were changed by interactions with the rest of the globe during the Middle Ages. The film exemplifies these relations through the interactions of Ahmed's character with the Northmen and its representation through the English language.

From its initial scenes, the protagonist Ahmed narrates the film in modern English. This English is exoticized by Antonio Banderas's Spanish accent, which functions to alert the viewer that although they *hear* English, it stands for Ahmed's tenth-century Arabic, then, later, the Northmen's language. This creates a double consciousness for the audience: the base language of the film assumes an English-speaking audience, but the narration engulfs the viewer in a medieval Muslim, Arab perspective. By the end of the film, however, a third understanding arises; the narrative presented in the film becomes the basis for the Old English *Beowulf*, transmitted to and adapted by a Christian English poet sometime between the seventh and eleventh centuries. The fiction depicted by the film is that a pagan Scandinavia was represented in Arabic by a tenth-century Muslim Arab, then conveyed to Britain, where it was rewritten in Old English by a Christian author. The story then mimics its own thematic content of cultural contact through a Global North Atlantic framework.

From its initial scenes, the perspective shared by an American audience with a medieval Arab is normalized through Baghdad's urban and "civilized" management of conflict. Ahmed is sent on an embassy that only signifies exile; he is not killed or harmed for his sexual indiscretion. Moreover, the character's adherence to Islam is reinforced throughout the film, and, notwithstanding modern conflicts between the largely Christianate West against an Islamicate Middle East, his statement "There is only one God" allows for an easier entry point for an American perspective. These elements stand in contrast to Ahmed's initial encounters with the Northmen, in which they demonstrate a willingness to commit violence, a shocking disregard for cleanliness, and a religion that does not exclude human sacrifice. These differences, witnessed by the paired American-Arab observer, highlight certain cultural commonalities held by the audience and the protagonist.

Ahmed's perspective on the Northmen, their dual barbarity and allure, models the historical accounts of Ibn Fadlān's journeys through central Asia and eventual encounter with the Rūs. The Rūs were possibly Scandinavian, purportedly a tribe of Swedes recorded to have gone viking and trading as far west as the Spanish Peninsula and as far east as the Volga River and the Caspian Sea.[3] Ibn Fadlān writes of them in both awed and disgusted tones, describing initially, "I have never seen bodies as nearly perfect as theirs. As tall as palm trees, fair and reddish. . . ."[4] But soon after, he writes, "They are the filthiest of all God's creatures. They have no modesty when it comes to defecating or urinating and do not wash themselves when intercourse puts them in a state of ritual impurity. They do not even wash their hands after eating. Indeed, they are like roaming asses."[5] These initial observations shift to descriptions of cultural practice and communication.

The film constructs cultural encounters through attention to language and the need for interpretation. In their initial encounter, it is unclear whether the Northmen will be peaceable with the Arab embassy. In frustration, Ahmed exclaims, "I'm an ambassador, damnit, I'm supposed to talk to people!" It is Melchisidek (Omar Sharif) who becomes the primary point of communication in the Northmen's tent, attempting several languages (English, Arabic, and Greek) before arriving at Latin (the closed captions continue to label it as Greek) as a shared tongue with the Northman Herger

(Dennis Sterhøi). During this scene, the Northmen's language is also heard, spoken by Buliwyf (Vladimir Kulich), the new leader of the Northmen whose name is meant to be a variation of Beowulf, and several others. Although the closed captioning labels it "native language," the language used in the film is Norwegian. It is only through an interpreter, the character of Melchisidek, that Ahmed and the audience have access to the events that unfold, until Ahmed learns the language of Northmen.

Once the film establishes the languages of communication—Norse/Norwegian, Latin/Greek, Arabic/English—the film relies on translation and interpretation to present the plot of the film. Buliwyf, the new heir apparent of the Northmen, receives news of an evil presence in a far North kingdom. A seer, the "Angel of Death," reads the bones and determines that thirteen warriors must go to save the kingdom. Buliwyf immediately volunteers and is followed by eleven other Northmen to raucous applause. Then the seer interrupts and declares that the thirteenth warrior "must be no Northman." In the stunned silence of this declaration, all turn to look at Ahmed, who, with the question, "What the hell are you saying?" comes to understand with the audience that he is the final warrior to join the group and creates the conditions of multiculturalism that underlie the exchanges in the film.[6]

Although the film begins with English signaling Arabic, the film switches its linguistic equivalency in an extraordinary scene set around multiple campfires on the warriors' way up North. The audience sees Ahmed in intense concentration listening to the "native language" of the Northmen. Through the use of repetition, the audience sees and hears as the words shift from the "incomprehensible" native language of the Northmen to English, signaling Ahmed's immersion into the language. The scene ends with Ahmed shocking the Northmen by suddenly responding to their taunting in their own language. As his alarmed companions confront him with the question, "Where did you learn our language?" Ahmed responds, "I listened." The scene demonstrates the masculine multiculturalism of the film: the Northmen are impressed with Ahmed's ability not just to speak their language, but to be able to use it to retort to their taunting and to taunt back, effectively winning the verbal fight ("And I at least know who my father is, you pig-eating son of a whore") and proving his right to equal consideration and manhood, if not religious superiority, through that exchange.[7]

LANGUAGE, WRITING, AND RELIGION

The role of language in *The 13th Warrior* as connective tissue between cultures and the recognition of cultural difference are fundamental to the narrative of the film. Language plays an important role in the constructed identities of Ahmed and Buliwyf. Ahmed's role, entwined with language usage, is first as a poet and then ambassador. In contrast, Buliwyf, a leader and a warrior, is laconic, neither silent nor frivolous with his words. The suspicion of frivolity or even the unmanliness of language is confirmed at the conclusion of the film, with Ahmed's final words, which prioritize bloodshed over writing: "May [Allah's] blessing be upon pagan men who loved other gods, who shared their food and shed their blood that his servant, Ahmed Ibn Fahdlan, might become a man and a useful servant of God."[8] In retrospect, we understand that the character we observed at the beginning of the movie had not yet become a man or useful to God. However, this is not a one-sided realization: Buliwyf's request that Ahmed write down his story acknowledges the limitations of his own powers just as it approves a manly and divine practice for Ahmed's skills.

From his initial scenes in the film, Buliwyf demonstrates an interest in song and poetry in his request to Ahmed that he sing a "song of glory." Buliwyf's interest in language and storytelling continues after the scene in the campfire. Impressed with Ahmed's ability to learn language, he asks, "You can draw sounds?" "Yes, I can draw sounds, and I can speak them back." "Show me." Ahmed writes in Arabic and says in the Norsemen's language (now represented by English in the film), "There is only one God, and Mohammed is his prophet." Buliwyf learns this and is able to reproduce the written Arabic with some help from Ahmed. Given what we know of the historical Ibn Fadlān's role as ambassador and his multiple accounts of assisting in the conversion of the peoples he met, we might understand this scene as a nod to that evangelical activity. It also establishes a fundamentally religious character for the act of writing.

Indeed, we see acts of writing only twice in the film: once here in this scene and then, finally, at the end of the film, as Ahmed writes the whole story down at Buliwyf's implied request. The progression from storytelling to written language is tied to both men's narrative arc, and the results are twofold: Ahmed, a masculinized ideal of a poet, no longer concerned with love songs or politics but with God, heroism, and reputation; and Buliwyf, his immortality ensured through the lasting power of a written language, closely tied to the divine approval of a single God (Allah).

In this way, the film associates written language to Ahmed's monotheism and Buliwyf's laconic masculinity. The latter is a departure from the medieval epic *Beowulf*: unlike the terse, largely silent Buliwyf, Beowulf engages in several lengthy and frankly fantastical boasts about his past exploits.[9] This discrepancy between them is key to understanding the masculine bonds the film tries to establish through written language and its connection to religion: Buliwyf does not need to boast to be immortalized, and the boastful Beowulf does not fit within the confines of a film that seeks to ground itself in supposedly realistic fiction. For Ahmed's character, language in the service of a greater purpose is worthy of being written down, and recording the struggle against the Wendol becomes an extension of that struggle, one with the mark of divine approval. In this sense, the product of Ahmed's pen will adhere more closely to the eventual product of the *Beowulf* poem, a work that is explicitly Christian.

There is a divine approval in the violence against the Wendols, and it is written text that affirms that divinity. In contrast to this formulation of written, divinely approved language, there are several other scenes of pagan religious ceremony, generally accompanied by spoken language. When the prayer for Valhalla is spoken later in the film, for example, it is done so directly in English rather than in a "native" language, and just after Ahmed's personal prayer to God. Herger watches Ahmed closely as he speaks this prayer, and there is a compatibility reached between Muslim and pagans that was not present at the beginning of the film, allowing for multicultural acceptance in the characters' farewells:

HERGER: "We will make prayers for your safe passage."

AHMED: "Prayers to who?"

HERGER: "In your land perhaps one god is enough, but here we are in need of many! I will pray to all of them for you, do not be offended."

AHMED: "I'll be in your debt!"

The religious rituals and prayers of the pagan Norsemen and the Muslim Arabs become compatible, especially with the understanding that the more distasteful aspects of pagan religion will be relegated to the past.

LANGUAGE AND INDIGENEITY

If *The 13th Warrior* proposes a multicultural intersection of medieval Islamic and pagan cultures, it does so at the expense of an indigenous-coded enemy, the Wendol. Substituting for *Beowulf*'s Grendelkin, the Wendol in both *Eaters of the Dead* and *The 13th Warrior* are presented as the earliest living inhabitants of the lands in question and thus an indigenous population.[10] Recent research on *Beowulf* has caught up to reading the Grendelkin as indigenous, and by relying on postcolonial, critical race, and indigenous studies, these scholars have begun to question Hrothgar and Beowulf's settler colonial and imperial aggression.[11] We can analyze the representation of the Wendol similarly, as it becomes clear that the Northmen and Ahmed reject any reconciliation with the Wendols' religious and cultural practices.

Perhaps two aspects of Wendol religion, so far as it is revealed to us, might upset the pagan Northmen who confront it: the presence of women in hierarchical positions of power, symbolized through the goddess figurine and embodied in the position of "Mother,"[12] and the usage of human bodies as an aspect of religious ritual, specifically the collection of heads and display of skulls. But in these two practices, there might be some common ground. After all, "the old ways" of the Northmen incorporate both human sacrifice and direction by a female figure, the Angel of Death. The viewer will remember that the thirteen warriors sent to contend with the Wendol threat were directed to do so by a woman, but part of their own community. What is distinctly lacking for these opposed cultures, however, is a translator, like Melchisidek, or the will to listen and learn, as demonstrated by Ahmed. Neither the Northmen nor the Wendol seem inclined to attempt this bridge of linguistic understanding, which might create mutual customs and cultures.

The impasse between the Northmen and the Wendol replicates the impasse between the Danes and the Grendelkin in *Beowulf*, a selection from which can be found in the appendix. From the point of view of the Northmen/Danes, the Wendols'/Grendelkin's chaotic, uncivilized "nature" threatens the order established by the Northmen/Danes. And yet, the film reminds us, especially when King Hrothgar explains, "We are hunted now in our own land. It wasn't always such. At first we thought to build, to leave something, farms as far as the eye could see," that it is the Northmen that settle, construct, and expand into the lands of the Wendol. The Northmen threaten the order of the Wendol and impose their own order on the land.[13] Similarly, while the Northmen, especially Buliwyf, understand the power of storytelling and the written word as a form of communication, by contrast, the Wendol seem to communicate through body language. Adam Miyashiro points out that, in *Beowulf*, "the language describing Grendel and the Grendelkin clearly illustrates the relationship between writing and sovereignty, through poetic dismemberments that link the 'mark' of the Grendelkin's banishment with writing."[14] The connection between the Northmen and Ahmed through language, especially written language, grants the Northmen sovereignty over the Northlands in order to justify aggression against the Wendol, which leads to their genocide. At the end of the film, it is only the Wendol that encounter annihilation and the Wendol that lead Ahmed to state that he was wrong to describe the Wendol as men. Lest we forget, the film begins by Buliwyf killing his own kin to keep the kingship. Acts of violence performed by the Wendol are unacceptable, and the acts of violence of the Northmen are justified through both oral and written language, resulting in the Wendols' sovereignty over the land being erased and transferred over to the Northmen.

CONCLUSION

During the Middle Ages, multicultural encounters were a frequent and necessary aspect of economic, ideological, and literary exchange. Such encounters highlight the interconnectedness of the global medieval world, from the North Atlantic to the Middle East and beyond. *The 13th Warrior*, in its portrayal of an Arab-Scandinavian intersection, features multicultural encounters of many kinds: Islam and paganism; speech and violence; fundamental differences in the definition of "civilization." The film's narrative arc allows us to understand how peoples from disparate places during the Middle Ages might still find points of commonality. But there are limits to these multicultural encounters, such as those that exclude the Wendol from participating in these exchanges. The Arab and Northman characters of the film recognize the Wendol, ultimately, as humans—"They are men!"—but only to the extent that they are mortal and therefore defeatable.

For both medieval European and Middle Eastern writers, the dehumanization of other peoples was common practice.[15] The way in which the Wendol are excluded from human society in *The 13th Warrior* is indicated, first and foremost, by their lack of comprehensible speech and the fundamental belief of the other "civilized" characters, perhaps shared by the audience, that efforts to communicate with them would be futile. These prejudices are reflected in the historical Ibn Fadlān's descriptions of other peoples he met during his travels—no people more so than the Turks.[16] *The 13th Warrior* relies on language and its forms to create human connections or sever them. As an adaptation of a Michael Crichton novel, itself a rewriting of two medieval texts, as well as its use of translation and language immersion to bridge the gap between Ahmed and the Northmen and its representation of the Wendol as incomprehensible and subhuman, the film's representation of language as lawful becomes a defining measure of humanity.

APPENDIX

The 13th Warrior (1999)

AHMAD IBN FADLĀN (FL. 921), RISĀLA (10TH CENTURY)

In these two excerpts, Ibn Fadlān describes the prayer and vision of an enslaved girl, as well as the lighting of the pyre that reveals the religious and cultural differences between Arabs like himself and the other Northmen.

Source: Albert Stanburrough Cook, trans., "Ibn Fadlān's Account of Scandinavian Merchants on the Volga in 922," *Journal of English and Germanic Philology* 22, no. 1 (1923): 54–63. Original in Arabic.

When it was now Friday afternoon, they led the girl to an object which they had constructed, and which looked like the framework of a door. She then placed her feet on the extended hands of the men, was raised up above the framework, and uttered something in her language, whereupon they let her down. Then again they raised her, and she did as at first. Once more they let her down, and then lifted her a third time, while she did as at the previous times. They then handed her a hen, whose head she cut off and threw away; but the hen itself they cast into the ship. I inquired of the interpreter what it was she had done. He replied: "The first time she said, 'Lo, I see here my father and mother'; the second time, 'Lo, now I see all my deceased relatives sitting'; the third time, 'Lo, there is my master, who is sitting in Paradise. Paradise is so beautiful, so green. With him are his men and boys. He calls me, so bring me to him.'" Then they led her away to the ship. Here she took off her two bracelets and gave them to the old woman who was called the angel of death, and who was to murder her....

The pile was soon aflame, and everything else in the ship. A terrible storm began to blow up, and thus intensified the flames, and gave wings to the blaze. At my side stood one of the Northmen, and I heard him talking with the interpreter, who stood near him. I asked the interpreter what the Northman had said, and received this answer: "'You Arabs,' he said, 'must be a stupid [lot]! You take him who is to you the most revered and beloved of men, and cast him into the ground, to be devoured by creeping things and worms. We, on the other hand, burn him in a twinkling, so that he instantly, without a moment's delay, enters into Paradise.' At this he burst out into uncontrollable laughter, and then continued: 'It is the love of the Master [God] that causes the wind to blow and snatch him away in an instant.'" And, in very truth, before an hour had passed, ship, wood, and girl had, with the man, turned to ashes.

ANONYMOUS, *BEOWULF* (C. 7TH–11TH CENTURIES)

The first passage, from lines 86–95, describes Grendel and the Scop (poet), and, in the second, taken from lines 710–27, Grendel's entrance to the hall of the Danes.

Source: Jean Abbott, eds., *Beowulf by All: Community Translation and Workbook* (Leeds: Arc Humanities Press, 2021). Original in Old English. Translated by Murray McGillivray, Heidi Estes, and David Johnson.

[1]

Then the powerful spirit miserably
Endured the time, he who lived in the shadows,
When he each day heard merriment
Loud in the hall. There was the music of the harp,
The clear song of the *scop*. He spoke, who knew how
To narrate from afar the origin of men,
Said that the Almighty created the earth,
The bright beauteous land, as the water surrounds it,
Established victorious the sun and moon,
The luminaries as light for land-dwellers . . .

[2]

Then Grendel came, scrambling from the moors under misty cliffs: he bore God's fury. The evil killer meant to capture some human in the hall, the high one. He advanced under cloud-cover until he was sure he knew the gilded wine-hall, golden gathering-place of men. Not that it was the first time that he had sought out Hrothgar's home. Never in the days of his life, before or after, did he find a harder fate among heroes. Then the striding warrior came to the hall, despoiled of joys. The door sprang quickly open,

> made fast with fire-forged bands, as he touched it with his hands.
> Then with baleful intent, angered as he was, he ripped open
> the mouth of the hall. Immediately then
> the enemy trod forth on that patterned floor,

angry of mood he advanced. From his eyes there shone
a horrible light like that of fire.

Reading questions

- In this funeral ritual, what is the importance of the enslaved girl's prayer, for herself and for the other mourners? In what ways is the prayer of the enslaved girl changed and expanded on in *The 13th Warrior*? How does it affect our understanding of the role played by Ahmed and his companions when they speak it themselves?
- *The 13th Warrior* adapts two medieval sources (*Risāla* and *Beowulf*) that stemmed from different cultures and blended them together to tell a new story. Do you think the film reflects more of the Arabic (Ibn Fadlān's) perspective or the Old English tradition represented by *Beowulf*?
- Do you think Ibn Fadlān displays a particular attitude or opinion toward the rites of the Northmen in *Risāla*? How do the Northmen perceive Arab custom? Are these attitudes carried over into the film?
- In the first passage from *Beowulf*, Grendel attacks the Danes. How does our view of Grendel's attack in *Beowulf* and the Wendol in *The 13th Warrior* shift when we read Grendel's attack as a response to both the Danes taking over his lands and his pain from listening to the merriment of the conquering Danes? In what respect could these narratives, in both the text and film, be reframed with Grendel and the Wendol as the protagonists and/or heroes?
- Taking into account the role of the *Scop*, the poet and oral storyteller of Old English poetry, and the role of storytelling and language in *The 13th Warrior*, how can we interpret this second passage from *Beowulf* in light of the role Ahmed, as a poet and warrior, plays in *The 13th Warrior*?

NOTES

1. To differentiate between the historical and film versions of Ahmad ibn Fadlān, this chapter refers to the historical version as Ibn Fadlān and the film version as Ahmed.

2. Michael Crichton, *Eaters of the Dead* (New York: Vintage Books, 2012), 35–41; compare to Ibn Fadlān's account of the Rūs funeral (sections 80–88), ed.

and trans. James E. Montgomery as "Mission to the Volga," in Philip F. Kennedy and Shawkat M. Toorawa, *Two Arabic Travel Books* (New York: New York University Press, 2014), 163–297 (hereafter cited as Montgomery, followed by page and section numbers). For more on medieval Rūs, see Asif Siddiqi's chapter in this book on *Alexander Nevsky* (1938).

3. Paul Lunde and Caroline Stone, eds., trans., "Appendix 2: The Rūs," in *Ibn Fadlān and the Land of Darkness: Arab Travellers in the Far North* (London: Penguin Classics, 2012), 204–6.

4. Montgomery, 241: section 74.

5. Montgomery, 243: section 76.

6. For a discussion of how multiculturalism reinforces the status quo, see Ali Rattansi, *Multiculturalism: A Very Short Introduction* (Oxford: Oxford University Press, 2013).

7. Elizabeth Sklar, "Call of the Wild: Culture Shock and Viking Masculinities in *The 13th Warrior*," in *The Vikings on Film*, ed. Kevin J. Harty (Jefferson, N.C.: McFarland, 2011), 127–29.

8. Ibid., 121.

9. For the verbal match between Unferth and Beowulf in the mead-hall, see *Beowulf by All* (Leeds: Arc Humanities Press, 2021), lines 528–609.

10. Although in the Appendix of *The Eaters of the Dead*, "The Mist Monsters," Michael Crichton-as-narrator tentatively raises the possibility that the Wendol might have been a remnant community of Neanderthal man, the "Factual Note" added to the second edition in 1992 explicitly states that the Wendol were conceived as Neanderthals. This Appendix is part of Crichton's pseudo-academic apparatus; the note was added after curious readers (according to Sklar, "Call of the Wild," 122–23) sought one of his fictional manuscripts at the University of Oslo Library.

11. Adam Miyashiro, "Homeland Insecurity: Biopolitics and Sovereign Violence in Beowulf," *postmedieval* 11, no. 4 (2020): 384–95; Christopher Abram, "At Home in the Fens with the Grendelkin," in *Dating Beowulf*, ed. Daniel C. Remein and Erica Weaver (Manchester: Manchester University Press, 2019), 120–44; and Catalin Taranu, "Men into Monsters: Troubling Race, Ethnicity, and Masculinity in Beowulf," in *Dating Beowulf*, 189–209. Several film adaptations of *Beowulf* (*Beowulf*, 1999; *Beowulf and Grendel*, 2005; *Beowulf*, 2007) play on fears of miscegenation, the 1999 and 2007 versions depicting Grendel's mother as a deviously seductive character and the 2005 version introducing a child of Grendel conceived in rape.

12. This figurine is clearly modeled on the Venus of Willendorf, a paleolithic-era figurine (*c*. 29,500 years old), whose significance is debated but ultimately unknown. See Natural History Museum of Vienna, https://www.nhm-wien.ac.at/presse/top10/venus_of_willendorf (accessed June 8, 2023).

13. Abram, "At Home in the Fens," 138.

14. Miyashiro, "Homeland Insecurity," 392.

15. See Suzanne Conklin Akbari, *Idols in the East: European Representations of Islam and the Orient 1100–1450* (Ithaca: Cornell University Press, 2009), esp. "The Saracen Body," 155–99; and Nahir I. Otaño Gracia and Daniel Armenti, "Constructing Prejudice in the Middle Ages and the Repercussions of Racism Today," *Medieval Feminist Forum* 53, no. 1 (2017): 176–201.

16. On the Bāshghird, see Montgomery, 215: section 37: "We were on high alert, for they are the wickedest, filthiest, and most ferocious of the Turks. When they attack, they take no prisoners. In single combat they slice open your head and make off with it."

CHAPTER NINETEEN

JEWISH ASSIMILATION AND THE ABSENT "SARACENS" AND AFRICANS OF *IVANHOE* (1952)

By Celia Chazelle

The film *Ivanhoe* (1952), directed by Richard Thorpe and produced by Pandro S. Berman, is an adaptation of the novel of this title published by Sir Walter Scott in 1820. The story unfolds during the reign of Richard I "the Lionheart" (1189–99), the sixth monarch of England since the Norman Conquest (1066), who was partly of Norman lineage. Scott inaccurately represented Richard's England as still riven by antagonism between Normans and the conquered Saxons or Anglo-Saxons. The years "had not sufficed to blend the hostile blood" of these two "races," Scott asserted.[1] His vision of Saxon-Norman enmity—and, as examined later, his portrayal of other groups in medieval England—reflected the influence on his thinking of newly emergent theories about race as a fixed category of human differentiation.[2] Scott considered the eventual mixture of Saxon with Norman blood to have brought certain benefits, yet the English remained, in his belief, Saxon at their core.

The popularity of Scott's *Ivanhoe* has been credited with inspiring the growth in nineteenth-century Britain and the United States of the vibrant movement known as medievalism: a system of ideas and values grounded in nostalgia for the Middle Ages expressed through art, architecture, popular culture, and scholarly pursuits.[3] In the twentieth century, films with medieval themes helped keep this nostalgia alive. With exciting scenes of knightly combat and romance and a celebrity cast including Elizabeth Taylor, the Thorpe-Berman *Ivanhoe* was exemplary in this respect. The film earned three Oscar nominations and was the second-highest grossing film of 1952.[4]

The movie's streamlined version of the novel effaces, however, both the latter's moral complexity and key aspects of its historical background. The first concern of this chapter, an issue often discussed in studies of the film, is its departure from Scott's ambivalent depiction of medieval English Jews and from historical evidence regarding their persecuted status. The second concern has largely escaped scholarly attention: missing from the film are groups besides Jews, Saxons, and Normans that Scott represents as also part of medieval England's social fabric. Of particular interest is the absence of the enslaved "Saracens" (Scott's term for Muslims) and Africans who play minor but striking roles in his novel. A 1913 American silent film of *Ivanhoe*, directed by Herbert Brenon, left out the Africans but included the Muslims.[5] Why were both groups excised from the 1952 film, and why have studies not commented on their erasure? The omission of Scott's Muslims and Africans enabled the makers of *Ivanhoe* (1952) to foreground—falsely—imagery of "white" assimilation in England encompassing its Jews. Such imagery was at odds with Jews' situation in Britain and the United States following World War II and with later medieval English royal and legal objectives, but also with the presence in medieval Britain of somatically dark populations from Africa and the Middle East.

MEDIEVAL JEWS AND SCOTT'S JEWS

Scott clearly perceived the treatment of Jews in Richard's England as unjust. "Upon the slightest and most unreasonable pretenses, as well as upon accusations the most absurd and groundless," he stated in *Ivanhoe*, "their persons and property were exposed to every turn of popular fury."[6] Implicitly, his novel also condemns prejudices against Jews in contemporary Britain, where they did not gain full civil rights until the later nineteenth century. Despite his sympathy, though, his narrative has significant anti-Semitic elements. An important character, the Jew Isaac of York, loves his daughter Rebecca and willingly assists the Saxon hero Ivanhoe; but Isaac is a miserly, avaricious usurer—a moneylender charging unreasonable interest rates. Rebecca is devoted to her father; brave and intelligent, she heals Ivanhoe's wounds. Yet her dark hair and dress recall nineteenth-century orientalist fantasies about Middle Eastern women's dangerous foreign allure.

Scenes in the 1952 film suggest analogous stereotypes. The supposed Jewish preoccupation with wealth is on display in the jewels, coins, and exchange certificates (precursors of banknotes) that Isaac collects to ransom Richard from captivity. Jews and Christians in twelfth-century England did not necessarily dress differently, but in the film Rebecca's dresses are more form-fitting, with an exotic flair, than those of the Christian Rowena, and

Rebecca and Isaac anachronistically wear the Star of David.[7] Unlike the novel, however, the film only attributes overt anti-Semitism to the wicked Norman usurper John and his circle; the Saxons and Richard treat Jews with tolerance. And whereas at the novel's close, Rebecca and Isaac move to Granada to escape persecution, the movie implies they remain in England.

The plan for a new movie of *Ivanhoe* arose in the 1930s but was delayed by World War II. A 1946–47 series of screenplay drafts radically altered Scott's story by having Ivanhoe marry Rebecca; Rowena, Ivanhoe's true love in the novel, was to be his half-sister. This planned version of the film was shelved, probably in part because of worries about audience reaction to a Christian-Jewish marriage. There was also perhaps fear of the House Un-American Activities Committee, which after the war associated pro-Jewish messages in Hollywood cinema with communism. But while Ivanhoe remains with Rowena in the 1952 film, it too celebrates assimilation. The final scene depicts Jews, Saxons, and Normans cheering Richard's command to live together peacefully. Interviews with Berman, who was Jewish, indicate that by thus departing from Scott's narrative, he and Thorpe sought indirectly to challenge modern anti-Jewish sentiment.[8]

Such a depiction of medieval English Judaism deviates not only from Scott's *Ivanhoe* but also from the historical record. Norman rulers of England offered Jews protection for the sake of their financial skills. By Richard's reign, Jews provided a major part of royal revenue through moneylending and, increasingly, taxes (tallages).[9] But their wealth, distinctive customs, and ties to secular elites, along with the indebtedness of Christian borrowers, exacerbated resentment. William de Montibus expressed a widely held view when he described Jews as "blood-suckers of Christian purses."[10] This attitude and allegations that Jews practiced "ritual murder" of Christian children encouraged attacks.[11] So did the Crusades: the belief that God blessed the extermination of Muslims was easily transferred to Jews. As described in the *Annals* of Roger of Hoveden (d. c. 1202), excerpted in the appendix, an effort by Jewish leaders to gain entrance to Richard's coronation (1189) led to massacres in multiple cities. Confronted with a choice between forced baptism or death, in March 1190, many of York's Jews took their own lives.[12]

Over the next decades, the English crown developed new strategies to protect Jews, yet at the same time to control them through legal coercion.[13] An 1190 charter confirmed previously granted liberties, but Jews were subsequently forced to contribute to Richard's ransom; the donation was not voluntary, as the 1952 film pretends. The 1194 ordinances of the Jews, which are described and quoted by Roger in the appended excerpt from his *Annals*, established the *archa* system requiring that records of Jewish financial transactions be kept in chests (*archae*) in designated towns. Each transaction was taxed. Further legislation restricted where Jews lived. The Fourth Lateran Council (1215) mandated that they wear an identifying badge representing not the Star of David, but the tablets of the Ten Commandments; Henry III (d. 1272) ordered the enforcement of this decree in 1218.[14] Legal restrictions and financial pressures continued to accumulate thereafter, until all Jews were expelled from England in 1290.

SCOTT'S "SARACENS" AND AFRICANS

Like Rebecca, the enslaved Muslims of Scott's *Ivanhoe* conform to nineteenth-century orientalist conventions. Chapter 2 directs attention to the pair's "dark visages," "swarthy arms and legs," silver slave collars, and garments marking them as "natives of some distant eastern country." They ride Arabian horses and carry curved swords along with "Turkish daggers."[15] "Saracen" was a generic name for "Muslim" and sometimes other non-Christians from Africa or the Middle East. A note in Scott's *Magnum Opus* edition (1829–33) identifies the "Saracens" of *Ivanhoe* as "negroes," implying sub-Saharan ancestry.[16] The portrayal of the African slaves introduced in Chapter 43, though, as Rebecca's would-be executioners, is more emphatically negative. In line with physiognomic theories that human external attributes corresponded to internal qualities and the traditional belief that the devil was black, Scott presented a derisory account of the Africans' appearance as indicative of evil. Their black features, he wrote, "appalled the multitude, who gazed on them as on demons employed about their own diabolical exercises." He then augmented his racist rhetoric:

> And when, in speech with each other, they expanded their blabber lips, and shewed their white fangs, as if they grinned at the thoughts of the expected tragedy, the startled commons could scarcely help believing that they were actually the familiar spirits with whom the witch [the falsely accused Rebecca] had convened, and who now, her time being out, stood ready to assist in her dreadful punishment.[17]

Scott drew for this passage on racist caricatures of Black people circulating in Britain at the time. Contemporary defenders of colonial slavery argued that its practice saved Africans from themselves, since they were vilified as innately savage and Africa as a place of depravity, bestiality, and devil worship. Parliament ended Britain's transatlantic slave trade in 1807, some thirteen years before Scott published *Ivanhoe*, but the Slavery Abolition Act providing for emancipation of the slaves already in Britain's colonies—about 665,000—was not passed until 1833, the year after Scott's death.[18] Meanwhile, both slavery's supporters and abolitionists accepted the principle of African inferiority while debating the causes and whether Blacks were capable of social or intellectual advancement.[19] Increasingly rigid race theories emerged mid-century, prompted by—among other factors—the declining influence of the anti-slavery movement; pseudo-scientific studies "proving" that a biological hierarchy existed with Africans at the bottom; and growing concerns, provoked, for example, by the Indian Rebellion of 1857, about the British Empire's ability to control its dark-skinned subjects.[20]

Scott's attitude toward Britain's colonial slavery is uncertain, even as his acceptance of racist ideologies current in his day is clear. He was exposed to the slave trade growing up in Edinburgh, where his neighbors included investors. He signed anti-slavery petitions in 1790 but refused, possibly out of shame, to attend the funeral of his brother Daniel, who died in 1806 after returning in disgrace from Jamaica because he failed to suppress a slave rebellion.[21] In 1822, Scott gained the right to depict a "Moor proper" (meaning in this case an African) holding a lowered torch as a "supporter" of his heraldic crest. African figures had been European heraldic motifs since the thirteenth century, with no necessary connection to slavery, yet it is telling that Scott's figure wears only a loincloth and a headband, apparently signifying submission to the white conqueror.[22] Another partial analogue to the racist description of Africans in *Ivanhoe* occurs in Scott's narrative poem *Rokeby*, where the white Bertram Risingham returns from the Caribbean transformed by its sun into a dark, menacing alien.[23]

While, however, the portrayal of *Ivanhoe*'s Africans reflected prevailing stereotypes of Scott's era, the fact that he represented them and Muslims living in medieval England had historical foundation. The *Magnum Opus* note mentioned earlier refers to a fourteenth-century romance, *Fouke le Fitz Waryn*, in which one noble, Johan de Rampaygne, frees another from Shrewsbury Castle. To gain access, Johan disguises himself as an

Ethiopian minstrel, dyeing his hair and body "entirely black like jet."[24] As Scott pointed out in his note, the author of *Fouke* presumed this disguise was plausible. "Negroes," Scott observed, "must have been known in England in the dark ages."[25]

Recent studies support this hypothesis. Archaeological and textual sources show that individuals of African and Middle Eastern descent came to Britain during the Roman occupation between the first and fifth centuries CE. It has been estimated that 10–25 percent of Rome's soldiers in Britain had African ancestry.[26] More significant as background to Scott's *Ivanhoe* is the travel between Britain, Africa, the Middle East, and Muslim-ruled Iberia that took place during the Crusades. Sub-Saharan Africans counted among enslaved populations in the Islamic Mediterranean; the Crusades opened new channels for them as well as for North Africans and Muslims to reach England.[27] The 1192 *Chronicle of Richard of Devizes* warns readers to beware London's *Garamantes*, an ancient term for a Libyan people.[28] A skeleton excavated at an Ipswich friary was identified, in 2010, as a thirteenth-century North African male.[29] A sub-Saharan African man is depicted in a thirteenth-century abbreviation of the *Domesday Book* (1086).[30] A fourteenth-century chronicle from St. Albans records the transport of "Saracen" captives to England in 1272.[31] A writ of Henry III notes the escape of a "Saracen" and "Ethiopian" slave named Bartholomew from a Sicilian knight in England.[32]

Late medieval literature is filled with anti-Black rhetoric, but some romances about the legendary King Arthur's circle contain positive representations: the "Saracen" Palamedes in the *Prose Tristan* (an excerpt is also a reading appended to this chapter), whose love for Yseult (Iseult or Isolde) was unrequited even as his valor earned esteem; the "Saracen" Priamus in Malory's *Le morte Darthur*; Feirefiz in *Parzival*, son of the white Gahmuret and the Moorish Queen Belakane, whose people were "dark as night"; the Moorish hero of *Morien*, who was "all black, even as I tell ye: his head, his body, and his hands ... saving only his teeth." Like the reported Ethiopian disguise in *Fouke*, these stories must have seemed credible to intended audiences.[33]

CONCLUSION

The filmmakers of the 1952 *Ivanhoe* may have been unfamiliar with the evidence that, historically, medieval England's population encompassed Muslims and Africans. Still, the absence of Scott's enslaved Muslims and

Africans from the movie deserves consideration. Its only clearly unfree person is the Saxon jester Wamba. As he removes Wamba's collar, Ivanhoe promises that all English will feel free once Richard returns from captivity. One reason for leaving the Muslims and Africans out of the film was undoubtedly Scott's racist portrayal of the Africans, especially, while another likely factor was that both enslaved groups jarred with Ivanhoe's avowal of English freedom. Yet given how the filmmakers reshaped Scott's portraits of Isaac and Rebecca to convey the decidedly unhistorical notion of Jewish assimilation in medieval England, one needs to ask why the novel's Muslim and African characters were not reworked in a comparably sympathetic manner. They could, for instance, have been represented as free men, even perhaps as knights like Palamedes or Morien. The emergent US civil rights movement as the film was planned might have justified this approach.[34] Several US court decisions of the 1940s and early 1950s, among them the 1954 ruling "Brown v. Board of Education," forbade discrimination against Blacks in the political system, education, and other areas. Efforts were also made in these and following years to reduce Hollywood stereotyping of Blacks. Berman doubtless supported those initiatives; he was a producer of the important film *A Patch of Blue* (1965), which explored the possibility of color-blind love.

Whereas early twentieth-century Jews in Britain and the US were generally considered a distinct race, World War II led to their recognition as racially white.[35] By excising the Muslims and Africans from the 1952 film of *Ivanhoe*, therefore, its makers assured that no character disrupted their depiction of an England inhabited solely by white people: Jews, Saxons, and Normans promising Richard to live in harmony. This imagery diverged from the historical reality while conforming, instead, to the enduring fictitious belief in medieval England's exclusive whiteness, a concept that gained strength in the nineteenth century alongside pseudo-scientific theories of race and white supremacy. A corollary was growing usage of the term "Anglo-Saxon" to designate the modern heirs of this allegedly superior racial legacy.[36]

Twentieth-century Hollywood helped sustain the fiction of a white medieval England through films like *Ivanhoe* as well as *The Knights of the Round Table* (1953), another Thorpe-Berman production set in England with an all-white cast. The "Saracen" and "Moorish" knights of Arthur's circle are nowhere to be seen in *Knights*. That recent critical studies do not mention the erasure of dark figures found in sources on which such movies are based is testimony to the force of the Anglo-Saxon myth still today.

APPENDIX

Ivanhoe (1952)

ROGER OF HOVEDEN (OR HOWDEN, D. C. 1202), *ANNALS* (LATE 12TH CENTURY)

The persecution and ordinances of the Jews during the reign of Richard I.

Source: Henry T. Riley, ed., trans., *The Annals of Roger de Hoveden: A.D. 1181 to A.D. 1201* (London: H.G. Bohn, 1853), 2:119–20, 338–39. Original in Latin.

While the king [Richard] was seated at table, the chief men of the Jews came to offer presents to him, but as they had been forbidden the day before to come to the king's court on the day of the coronation, the common people, with scornful eye and insatiable heart, rushed upon the Jews and stripped them, and then scourging them, cast them forth out of the king's hall. Among these was Benedict, a Jew of York, who, after having been so maltreated and wounded by the Christians that his life was despaired of, was baptized by William, prior of the church of Saint Mary at York, in the church of the Innocents, and was named William, and thus escaped the peril of death and the hands of the persecutors.

The citizens of London, on hearing of this, attacked the Jews in the city and burned their houses; but by the kindness of their Christian friends, some few made their escape. On the day after the coronation, the king sent his servants, and caused those offenders to be arrested who had set fire to the city; not for the sake of the Jews, but on account of the houses and property of the Christians which they had burnt and plundered, and he ordered some of them to be hanged.

On the same day, the king ordered the before-named William, who from a Jew had become a Christian, to be presented to him, on which he said to him, "What person are you," to which he made answer, "I am Benedict of York, one of your Jews." On this the king turned to the archbishop of Canterbury, and the others who had told him that the said Benedict had become a Christian, and said to them, "Did you not tell me that he is a Christian?," to which they made answer, "Yes, my lord." Whereupon he said to them, "What are we to do with him?" to which the archbishop of Canterbury, less circumspectly than he might, in the spirit of his anger, made answer, "If he does not choose to be a Christian, let him be a man of the Devil"; whereas he ought to have made answer, "We demand that he shall be brought to a Christian trial, as he has become a Christian, and now contradicts that fact." But, inasmuch as there was no person to offer any opposition thereto, the before-named William relapsed into the Jewish errors, and after a short time died at Northampton; on which he was refused both the usual sepulture of the Jews, as also that of the Christians, both because he had been a Christian, and because, he had, "like a dog, returned to his vomit."

■

All the debts, pledges, mortgages, lands, houses, rents, and possessions of the Jews shall be registered. The Jew who shall conceal any of these shall forfeit to the King his body and the thing concealed, and likewise all his possessions and chattels, neither shall it be lawful to the Jew to recover the thing concealed.

Likewise, six or seven places[37] shall be provided in which they shall make all their contracts, and there shall be appointed two lawyers that are Christians and two lawyers that are Jews, and two legal registrars, and before them and the clerks of William of the Church of St. Mary's and William of Chimelli, shall their contracts be made.

And charters shall be made of their contracts by way of indenture. And one part of the indenture shall remain with the Jew, sealed with the seal of him, to whom the money is lent, and the other part shall remain in the common chest: wherein there shall be three locks and keys, whereof the two Christians shall keep one key, and the two Jews another, and the clerks of William of the Church of St. Mary and of William of Chimelli shall keep the third. And moreover, there shall be three seals to it, and those who keep the seals shall put the seals thereto.

Moreover, the clerks of the said William and William shall keep a roll of the transcripts of all the charters, and as the charters shall be altered so let the roll be likewise. For every charter there shall be threepence paid, one moiety thereof by the Jews and the other moiety by him to whom the money is lent; whereof the two writers shall have twopence and the keeper of the roll the third.

And from henceforth no contract shall be made with, nor payment made to, the Jews, nor any alteration made in the charters, except before the said persons or the greater part of them, if all of them cannot be present. And the aforesaid two Christians shall have one roll of the debts or receipts of the payments which from henceforth are to be made to the Jews, and the two Jews one and the keeper of the roll one.

Moreover, every Jew shall swear on his Roll, that all his debts and pledges and rents, and all his goods and his possessions, he shall cause to be enrolled, and that he shall conceal nothing as is aforesaid. And if he shall know that anyone shall conceal anything he shall secretly reveal it to the justices sent to them, and that they shall detect, and shew unto them all falsifiers or forgers of the charters and clippers of money, where or when they shall know them, and likewise all false charters.

ANONYMOUS, *PROSE TRISTAN* (LATE 12TH CENTURY)

The "Saracen" prince, Palamedes, accomplishes feats of chivalry and gets involved in a love triangle.

Source: Lewis Porney, ed., trans., *A New and Complete Collection of Interesting Romances and Novels* (London, 1780), 208, 287–88. Original in Old French.

Several companions of the Round-table and other Knights, held at that time a tournament. A Saracen Prince by name Palamedes, had all the advantage the first day, and was brought to court where a splendid entertainment was prepared for him, at which Tristan, who was much recovered, begged to be present. Yseult appeared, and Palamedes was struck with wonder, and without recollecting where he was, ventured at this very first visit to declare his passion; but fate had marked him out for the victim of ill-requited love. Tristan took notice of the presumption of Palamedes, and the jealousy which he felt at the discovery convinced him that Yseult reigned sovereign over his conquered heart.

The tournament was to be renewed the next day. Tristan, during the preceding night, put on his armour, and, leaving the palace, concealed himself in a forest. As soon as the Knights had entered the list, he made his appearance, overcame every opponent, and unhorsed Palamedes; then, falling on him sword in hand, forced him to sue for his life. But so violent an exercise, opened his wound afresh, and he was carried off to the palace, where Yseult attended him with a concern which daily grew more serious. The Princess discovered that a subtle and corrosive poison prevented the wound from being healed, and having made a poltice of several antivenemous plants effected a perfect cure. Tristan made an open avowal of his love to his fair physician, without acquainting her with his real name and quality, and Yseult thought that he spoke better and more feelingly than Palamedes....

... The Saracen Prince [Palamedes] spent a few days at the castle, but the trial was too hard, and he could not bear to be a daily witness of their [Tristan and Yseult's] happiness, nor think of disturbing of it, after he had sworn everlasting friendship to Tristan. "Happy man, said he to him one day, you justly deserve the brilliant destiny you enjoy: May I soon end my wretched life, and may you and the fair Yseult honour my memory with the tears of friendship": having thus said he took leave, and went in quest of the most perilous adventures. Yet though he courted death with wishful eagerness, he lived long and ever constant to his first amours.

Reading questions

- What option was available to the Jews to avoid massacre, according to Roger of Hoveden? To what extent does the 1952 film *Ivanhoe* reflect the ordinances described by Roger of Hoveden that governed the contracts forged between Christians and Jews? Do you think these ordinances were fair to both parties? Why or why not?
- How does Roger's representation of Benedict of York and Christian-Jewish relations in King Richard's England compare (or contrast) with the representation of Isaac of York and his Jewish community in the 1952 film of *Ivanhoe*?
- What comparison can be drawn between the attitudes toward Benedict expressed in Roger's narrative and Walter Scott's representation of the African slaves?
- What differences can be noted between the representation of Palamedes in the *Prose Tristan* and of the "Saracens" in Walter Scott's *Ivanhoe*? How do the film and the *Prose Tristan* compare or contrast in their representation of "race"?
- How does the love triangle set out in the *Prose Tristan* compare with that between Ivanhoe, Rowena, and Rebecca in the 1952 film of *Ivanhoe*? How are the people involved comparable?

NOTES

1. Sir Walter Scott, *Ivanhoe: A Romance* (Edinburgh, 1820), 1:16.
2. Esther Liberman Cuenca, "'Normans' vs 'Saxons': Cinematic Imaginaries of Race and Nation in Angevin England, 1938–1964," *Open Library of Humanities* 9, no. 1 (2023): 5–7.

3. Alice Chandler, "Sir Walter Scott and the Medieval Revival," *Nineteenth-Century Fiction* 19, no. 4 (1965): 315–32.

4. AFI Catalogue of Feature Films, *Ivanhoe*, https://catalog.afi.com/Film/50525-IVANHOE?sid=4a5ce785-4111-4777-bf43-cf77ba522c9b&sr=11.445145&cp=1&pos=0 (accessed August 7, 2023).

5. Eye Filmmuseum, *Ivanhoe* (1913), https://www.youtube.com/watch?v=-oha89NyNo4 (accessed August 7, 2023). On the problematic nature of the term "Saracen," see Shokoofeh Rajabzadeh, "The Depoliticized Saracen and Muslim Erasure," *Literature Compass* 16 (2019): 1–8.

6. Scott, *Ivanhoe*, 1:61.

7. Sara Lipton, *Dark Mirror: The Medieval Origins of Anti-Jewish Iconography* (New York: Metropolitan Books / Henry Holt, 2014), 158–59.

8. Jonathan Stubbs, "Hollywood's Middle Ages: The Development of *Knights of the Round Table* and *Ivanhoe*, 1935–53," *Exemplaria* 21, no. 4 (2009): 405–10; Felice Lifshitz, "'A Piece of Cachou Called *Ivanhoe*': Elizabeth Taylor, Medievalist Historical Film and American Interfaith Marriage," *Journal of Jewish Studies* 70, no. 2 (2019): 375–97, esp. 380–81.

9. R. R. Mundill, *The King's Jews: Money, Massacre and Exodus in Medieval England* (London: Continuum, 2010), 23–42.

10. "Harley Charter 43 A 60B Transactions with Jewish Moneylenders, 13th Century": https://www.bridgemanimages.com/en-US/english-school/harley-charter-43-a-60b-transactions-with-jewish-moneylenders-13th-century/nomedium/asset/3296429 (accessed Dec. 1, 2024).

11. The first known case is that of William of Norwich, who died in 1144: see now Heather Blurton, *Inventing William of Norwich: Thomas of Monmouth, Antisemitism, and Literary Culture, 1150–1200* (Philadelphia: University of Pennsylvania Press, 2022).

12. *Medieval Sourcebook*, "Roger of Hoveden: The Persecution of the Jews, 1189," Fordham University, https://sourcebooks.fordham.edu/source/hoveden1189b.asp (accessed August 7, 2023).

13. Mundill, *King's Jews*, 1–20.

14. Robert Stacey, "The Massacres of 1189–90 and the Origins of the Jewish Exchequer 1186–1226," in *Christians and Jews in Angevin England*, ed. Sarah Rees Jones and Sethina Watson (Woodbridge and Rochester, N.Y.: Boydell Press, 2013), 106–24; John Tolan, "The First Imposition of a Badge on European Jews: The English Royal Mandate of 1218," in *The Character of Christian-Muslim Encounter*, ed. Douglas Pratt et al. (Leiden: Brill, 2015), 145–66.

15. Scott, *Ivanhoe*, 1:25.

16. J. H. Alexander et al., eds., *Edinburgh Edition of the Waverly Novels*, vol. 25B (Edinburgh: Edinburgh University Press, 2012), 19–20.

17. Scott, *Ivanhoe*, 3:383.

18. B. W. Higman, "Population and Labor in the British Caribbean in the Early Nineteenth Century," in *Long-Term Factors in American Economic Growth*, ed.

Stanley L. Engerman and Robert E. Gallman (Chicago: University of Chicago Press, 1986), 605.

19. Peter Kitson, "'Candid Reflections': The Idea of Race in the Debate over the Slave Trade and Slavery in the Late Eighteenth and Early Nineteenth Century," in *Discourses of Slavery and Abolition*, ed. Brycchan Carey, Markman Ellis, and Sara Salih (New York: Palgrave Macmillan, 2004), 11–25.

20. Christine Bolt, "Race and the Victorians," in *British Imperialism in the Nineteenth Century*, ed. C. C. Eldridge (New York: St. Martin's Press, 1984), 126–47.

21. Carla Sassi, "Sir Walter Scott and the Caribbean: Unravelling the Silences," *Yearbook of English Studies* 47 (2017): 224–40; Tessa Rodrigues, "Scott, Globalisation and Race: Father of 'Imperial Romance' or Silent Supporter of Abolitionism?," *University of Edinburgh Library & University Collections* (July 30, 2021), https://libraryblogs.is.ed.ac.uk/blog/2021/07/30/scott-globalisation-and-race-father-of-imperial-romance-or-silent-supporter-of-abolitionism/ (accessed February 8, 2025).

22. Crispin Agnew, "Sir Walter Scott of Abbotsford and the Enigma of his 'Moor Proper' Heraldic Supporter," *History Scotland* 122 (2021), https://www.research.ed.ac.uk/en/publications/sir-walter-scott-of-abbotsford-and-the-enigma-of-his-moor-proper- (accessed February 8, 2025)

23. Susan Oliver, "Crossing 'Dark Barriers': Intertextuality and Dialogue between Lord Byron and Sir Walter Scott," *Studies in Romanticism* 47 (2008): 15–35, esp. 24–26.

24. "Entierement auxi neyr come geet," in Keith Busby, "Performance, Trahison, Espionnage," *Le Moyen Âge* 121, no. 3–4 (2015): 668. My thanks to Renate Blumenfeld-Kosinski for the translation of "geet."

25. Alexander, *Edinburgh Edition*, vol. 25B, 20.

26. Maghan Keita, "Race: What the Bookstore Hid," in *Why the Middle Ages Matter: Medieval Light on Modern Injustice*, ed. Celia Chazelle et al. (New York: Routledge, 2012), 131.

27. John Hunwick, *West Africa, Islam, and the Arab World* (Princeton: Markus Wiener, 2006), 75–90.

28. John T. Appleby, ed., trans., *Chronicle of Richard of Devizes* (London: T. Nelson, 1963), 65–66.

29. Hollie-Rae Merrick, "Historic Ipswich Skeleton Finally Identified," *East Anglian Daily Times* (May 5, 2010), https://www.eadt.co.uk/news/21789890.historic-ipswich-skeleton-finally-identified/ (accessed February 8, 2025).

30. *National Archives*, E 36/284, https://discovery.nationalarchives.gov.uk/browse/r/h/C4248218 (accessed February 8, 2025).

31. Henry Richards Luard, ed., *Flores Historiarum* (London, 1890), 3:24.

32. Michael Ray, "A Black Slave on the Run in Thirteenth-Century England," *Nottingham Medieval Studies* 51 (2007): 111–19.

33. Maghan Keita, "Saracens and Black Knights," *Arthuriana* 16, no. 4 (2006): 65–77; Keita, "Race," 134–38.

34. James N. Gregory, *The Southern Diaspora: How the Great Migrations of Black and White Southerners Transformed America* (Chapel Hill: University of North Carolina Press, 2005), 260–82.

35. Karen Brodkin Sacks, "How Did Jews Become White Folks?," in *Race*, ed. Steven Gregory and Roger Sanjek (New Brunswick, N.J.: Rutgers University Press, 1994), 78–102.

36. David Wilton, "What Do We Mean by *Anglo-Saxon*? Pre-Conquest to the Present," *Journal of English and Germanic Philology* 119, no. 4 (2020): 425–56, esp. 442–54.

37. Might refer to London, Lincoln, Norwich, Winchester, Canterbury, Oxford, Cambridge, Nottingham, Hereford, or Bristol.

CHAPTER TWENTY

MEDIEVAL SCIENCE, THE SPANISH INQUISITION, AND RELIGIOUS VIOLENCE IN *1492: CONQUEST OF PARADISE* (1992)

By Eugene Smelyansky

In 1992, the five hundredth anniversary of Christopher Columbus's first voyage produced a wave of commemoration. Among several films released for the occasion, *1492: Conquest of Paradise*, directed by Ridley Scott, stands out for its artistic ambition, a rousing New Age soundtrack by Greek composer Vangelis, and the desire to recast Columbus as an unquestionably heroic and somewhat relatable protagonist. In the process, Scott produced nothing less than an epic retelling of the circumstances that placed Columbus (1451–1506)—depicted as a charming but straight-talking outsider—at the helm of his voyage across the Atlantic, only to be villainized at the hands of the jealous and backward-thinking Spanish nobility and the all-powerful church. As the audience, we are expected to see Columbus as a harbinger of modernity: a man daring to rebel against the "Dark Ages" of late medieval Spain and condemned to suffer for it.

The film's portrayal of Columbus (Gérard Depardieu) as a fallible but generally positive character was not accidental. The screenwriter, Roselyne (Rose) Bosch, desired to save Columbus from being associated with the "cliché of genocide."[1] Scott, likewise, dismissed the negative portrayal of the explorer, seeking to humanize his protagonist throughout the film and defend him from any revisionism. To accomplish this, the film needed a foil: the period of the Middle Ages itself. To sustain its apologetic depiction of Columbus, the film draws on well-established tropes about the Middle Ages, presenting the period as defined by its religious intolerance, grotesque public executions, and control by the church over any pursuit of knowledge.[2] In doing so, *1492* perpetuates the "Black Legend," an outdated but influential discourse that paints Spain as uniquely mired in violence and oppression. The "Black Legend" became a popular trope among Protestant authors during the Reformation, contrasting "medieval" Catholic

Spain with its more "modern" Protestant competitors in Europe and the New World.[3] In the movie, Columbus becomes an outsider leading Spain over the threshold of modernity.

A closer look at the actual events represented in the film, however, demonstrates how enmeshed Columbus and his voyages were in the late medieval world. As such, this chapter analyzes the film's medieval setting by exploring two interrelated themes. First, it shows that Columbus was just as shaped by traditions of medieval learning, and science in particular, as his contemporaries, which in turn influenced his own understanding of the lands and people he "discovered." Second, the film's depiction of religious violence in late medieval Spain, and especially of the Inquisition, is shown first and foremost as a threat for pioneering thinkers like Columbus, and the film downplays the actual violence committed by the Spanish crown and the church during this period. Likewise, *1492* exonerates Columbus's participation in carrying out colonial violence, enslavement, and genocide in the name of the Spanish crown across the ocean. The film, instead, contrasts his conquest of "paradise"—represented by indigenous people and their lands seemingly untouched by "medieval" corruption—with the religious violence of the Spanish Inquisition that was exemplary of the "Black Legend."

THE DISCOVERY OF MODERNITY?

The movie *1492* does everything to present Columbus as a man ahead of his time, ready to usher in a "New World" at any cost. Indeed, the opening scroll explains that, 500 years ago,

> Spain was a nation gripped by fear and superstition, ruled by the crown and a ruthless inquisition that persecuted men for daring to dream. One man challenged this power. Driven by his sense of destiny, he crossed the sea of darkness in search of honor, gold, and the greater glory of God.

The image of Spain mired in the "dark ages," requiring Columbus to step into the light, deserves closer examination. The movie *1492* received generous funding from Spain's Ministry of Culture as part of the festivities celebrating the anniversary of Columbus's first voyage, which included the Summer Olympics in Barcelona and a Universal Exposition in Seville.[4] In short, in 1992 Spain celebrated not only Columbus's "discovery" but also its present-day embrace of modernity and globalization—less than two decades after the end of the dictatorship (1939–75) of Francisco Franco (1892–1975).

From this perspective, describing late medieval Spain as repressive can easily be seen as a criticism of the country's more recent past. Just as modern Spain dared to leave authoritarianism behind, so did Scott's Columbus lead the Spain of his time "out of darkness into light towards the renaissance."[5] As Noelia V. Saenz has argued, films like *1492* exhibit "imperialist nostalgia" reminiscent of the "heritage film" genre—popular during Franco's dictatorship for perpetuating nationalist myths—in painting Columbus's voyages as progressive enterprises.[6] By praising Columbus, *1492* channels modern Spain's longing for the power status it once had globally and ignores how this status was first acquired—through violent colonialism.

The film's depiction of Columbus as a daring visionary is, of course, not new. It largely follows the biography written by Columbus's son Ferdinand (1488–1539), later popularized by other authors. In fact, *1492* opens and ends with Ferdinand (Loren Dean), our principal witness to his father's heroic life. In the first scene, we see Columbus teaching his son about Earth's curvature, a clear reference to the regretfully popular idea that, before Columbus, medieval people believed Earth to be flat. While the film avoids using this cliché directly, the audience is nevertheless led to believe that Columbus's ideas were revolutionary for his time and therefore rejected by the church, eager to suppress all original thought.

MEDIEVAL SCIENCE AND GEOGRAPHY

What drove Columbus to embark on his voyage? Studies of late medieval science demonstrate that Columbus's geographical and navigational knowledge were products of centuries of learning developed in the ancient and Islamicate worlds, as well as in medieval Europe.[7] Many of the surviving descriptions of Columbus's plans appear to have been written after his "discovery," making it highly possible that he adjusted his original ideas to create the impression that he was correct all along. An ambitious man, he spared no ink celebrating his vindication.

The film includes very little explanation of the geographical knowledge that inspired Columbus to seek a route to India. Early on, *1492* eagerly depicts Columbus's confrontation with a scholarly panel convened by King Fernando II of Aragon (r. 1479–1516, played by Fernando García Rimada) and Queen Isabel I of Castile (r. 1471–1504, played by Sigourney Weaver) to evaluate his ideas at the University of Salamanca. The film portrays the argument between a passionate Columbus and reactionary clerics who gathered to humiliate him. Although neither Columbus's original proposal nor the panel's response have survived, the arguments at Salamanca were certainly more complex and likely dealt with the accuracy of Columbus's calculations. He believed, inaccurately, that the circumference of the Earth was significantly smaller than accepted during his time. The imagined location and size of Japan, southeast of China, likewise made his proposed voyage across the open ocean shorter and thus achievable.[8] The movie *1492* even includes a scene of Columbus confessing to knowingly misrepresenting the distance in his proposal, as if to protect him from accusations of error. The historic Columbus most likely believed his numbers were accurate; he would not have been reckless enough to sail the ocean without any hope of crossing it.

Aside from the accuracy of Columbus's calculations, his proposal would have stirred up another controversy: namely, why seek a route to India in the first place? Columbus planned to sail not westward but southwest, seeking the riches of Asia in the tropics. The dominant school of thought held that the lands further south from the Mediterranean had excessively hot climates unsuitable for trade or colonization. Even if Columbus's voyage was possible, there was little reason for it. Columbus—or, rather, the authorities he marshaled in his support—argued otherwise, believing that the riches of Asia were to be found within the tropical zone by anyone who could access them. One position held that the heat of the sun rendered all tropical lands arid and barren, populated with monstrous beings; the other that the torrid climate stimulated an abundance of crops, game, and wealth. Both positions were equally tenable at the time in medieval thought, with such accepted authorities as Ibn Sīnā (980–1037) and Albert the Great (d. 1280) supporting the latter side.[9] Far from rebelling against medieval science, Columbus was its proud son.

Having made landfall in the Caribbean, Columbus emphasized that the land he found bore the signs of bountiful tropics. Already in his pre-voyage annotations on works by medieval geographers, Columbus emphasized that earthly paradise must be located in the tropics. Now, he could record its natural abundance firsthand. In letters to various patrons, he stressed "thousands" of species of trees, birds, and fruits, with similar superlatives used to describe the fertile fields, rich mines, convenient harbors, and other related bounties.[10] These descriptions likely inspired the creators of *1492* to depict the New World as an otherworldly, unspoiled natural paradise. While Columbus undoubtedly exaggerated the wealth of these lands, he did so in accordance with pre-established beliefs about India and to stress the natural abundance that Spain's new tropical possessions could offer.

While Columbus emphasized the tropical advantages of San Salvador and Hispaniola (Santo Domingo), in his descriptions of the people inhabiting those islands he drew on older Aristotelian theories combining geography, climate, and physiology. As Aristotle argued in *Politics*, with a long line of later ancient and medieval authors following in his stead, climate defined the physiological and personal traits of the people living in it by affecting their humors (the four fluids that shaped one's physical and mental disposition). Thus, colder climes of northern Europe gave its inhabitants thicker blood, manifesting itself in their slower wit, excessive bravery, and freedom-loving spirit. Conversely, a hot climate made the people near the tropics produce thinner blood, resulting in smarter but craven and easily subjugated populations.[11] Columbus's description of the indigenous people he encountered during his first voyage in his journal (excerpted in the appendix) demonstrates that he saw them through an Aristotelian lens. In his records, Columbus stressed the striking timidity of the Taíno, who used no weapons and preferred to evade the Spaniards. Contrary to the whitewashed depiction of Columbus in *1492*, the real man found this perceived timidity an invitation to enslave. The Taíno were yet another "natural" bounty to exploit.

Columbus was no stranger to the practice of enslavement, an institution prevalent in the medieval Mediterranean, including in his native Genoa.[12] He also certainly encountered enslaved people during his stay in Portugal and voyages along the western coast of Africa, all the way to São Jorge da Mina (Elmina in present-day Ghana), which was a major hub of the Atlantic slave trade even in the late fifteenth century. But perhaps most instructive was his fleet's stopover in the Canary Islands. The invasion of the archipelago took several decades and was still ongoing during Columbus's visit, with Castilians enslaving many of the surviving islanders and even shipping some back to Iberia.[13] The colonization of the Canaries, located in the same tropical zone where Columbus "discovered" the Taíno, became the blueprint for his actions. Indeed, in a letter to his royal patrons, Columbus included the Taíno in a list of trade goods Spain's new possessions could provide in abundance, promising to deliver the crown as many enslaved "idolaters" as needed.[14]

Arguing against some ancient and medieval authorities while using the works of others, Columbus thus relied on medieval science, geography, and ethnographies to promote his voyages and make sense of the lands and people he encountered. These writings cast a long shadow and informed the legal framework that underpinned Spanish claims to the New World. In the decades after Columbus's first voyage, Spanish jurists and theologians debated the place of the indigenous people in accordance with natural law. Some authorities argued that the indigenous inhabitants of the New World lacked even those institutions of authority possessed by the "Old World infidels," putting their very humanity into question. Columbus's descriptions of the Taíno as childlike and uncivilized provided justification for Spanish domination.[15] Others, Bartolomé de las Casas (1484–1566) among them, claimed that natural law applied to all humankind, including Spain's colonial subjects. Columbus's understanding of indigenous people, however, and justifications for his actions in the Caribbean had long-term impact on the development of international law.

THE SPANISH INQUISITION

The movie *1492* depicts Columbus as a "modern" man who is constrained by the superstitions of his time and horrified by its "medieval" excess. These superstitions are exemplified by an anti-science church and the Spanish Inquisition in the movie. But far from rebelling against medieval society, the historical Columbus shared its religious outlook. For example, besides trade, his voyage to Asia sought to forge a new transcontinental alliance between Europe and the powerful rulers of the East in hopes of launching a new Crusade and conquering Jerusalem.[16]

To raise the stakes for its protagonist at the beginning of the film, *1492* implies that Columbus's ideas about crossing the Atlantic were dangerous or even heretical. The discussion of his proposal at the University of Salamanca is preceded by a gruesome scene of a public execution. The scene—clearly included for shock value—features a group of women and men burned at the stake in a city square. Numerous spectators, brutal punishments meted out by the church, and even macabre closeups of the contorted faces of the victims all illustrate the "barbarity" of the Middle Ages, implying that Columbus risked being sent to the stake himself. After all, as Columbus's mentor warns him immediately before the execution scene, "they are burning people for less."

As with all depictions of medieval Spain in *1492*, the film uses the Inquisition as a dramatic backdrop and striking example of the backward customs Columbus had to overcome. In doing so, the filmmakers distorted the Inquisition's own violent history and misled the audience about its actual victims: Iberian Jews and *conversos* (converts from Judaism to Christianity). As a rule, *1492* avoids the topic of anti-Judaism altogether. For example, the expulsion of Jews from Spain is absent from the narrative, despite taking place shortly before Columbus's first voyage. The Alhambra Decree, issued in March 1492, ordered all Jews either to convert to Christianity or leave Spain by July 31, just four days before the explorer set sail. By shocking the audience during the execution scene and then never mentioning the Inquisition again, the film also creates the impression that this institution belonged in the medieval past. The truth was far from it. Founded in 1478, the Spanish Inquisition was in fact poised to intensify its operations and expand by 1492. Significantly, the Spanish crown also later installed the Inquisition in Latin America as part of its judicial apparatus, allowing colonial authorities to enact sanctioned violence against indigenous people and enslaved Africans.[17]

Despite its treatment in the film, the history of the Spanish Inquisition is important for understanding Spain's de facto unification and transformation in the years before and after Columbus's voyages. The intensification of religious intolerance that followed Spain's conquest of Granada in January 1492 was integral to political consolidation—a parallel and necessary process for Spain's transformation into an empire—during the reign of Fernando and Isabel. Although scholars disagree on the precise reasons for the Inquisition's founding, its roots lie in the need to ensure political stability in Castile after the civil war that preceded Queen Isabel's reign. Rumors about plots hatched against Isabel by powerful Castilian *converso* families undoubtedly turned the Inquisition into an instrument of royal power, staffed by the clergy but controlled by the monarchy.[18] As the Inquisition became established, however, the enforcement of religious purity and uniformity became a goal of its own.

The founding of the Inquisition in 1478 was preceded by close to a century of intensifying anti-Judaism (and sporadic religious violence before that). Since the wave of anti-Jewish violence in the spring and summer of 1391, Jews living in the kingdoms of Aragon and Castile faced increasing religious scrutiny and pressure to convert to Christianity. This situation prompted many Iberian Jews to convert, often for pragmatic reasons. The existence of wealthy and influential *conversos*—including Columbus's backers Luis de Santángel (Frank Langella) and Gabriel Sánchez (Armand Assante), who are characters in the film—suggested that a timely conversion could provide a boost to one's financial and political prospects. Many others converted as means of survival.

The rising number of *conversos* post-1391 created anxiety among Iberian authorities: were these "New Christians" sincere in their faith? From the perspective of church officials, practicing any elements of Judaism after conversion (so-called judaizing) constituted heresy—a crime against established Christian norms and dogma—and merited serious punishment.[19] The final expulsion of Jews from both Aragon and Castile in 1492 pressured those unwilling to leave to become Christian, exacerbating fears of judaizing and providing the Inquisition with an ever-growing list of suspects.

To detect judaizing *conversos*, the new Inquisition relied on the methods of its medieval predecessors to investigate heretics since the thirteenth century. Medieval inquisitors relied on confessions and compiled vast amounts of information about their targets, using it to guide further inquests.[20] In the Spanish context, inquisitors looked to interpret certain actions as evidence of judaizing. As a result, the inquisitors criminalized mundane behavior, such as eating certain foods or lacking knowledge of Christian prayers (understandable for recent converts). Each inquisitorial campaign ended with an *auto-da-fé*, a public ritual punishing the convicted *conversos*. These punishments performed a crucial, didactic purpose: they communicated forbidden beliefs and behaviors to spectators and demonstrated the fate of the errant. Surviving inquisitorial records—some included in the appendix—provide brief but insightful examples of these prohibited actions.

At least in its early years, the Inquisition's actions prompted resistance; occasionally, violence bred more violence. In 1485, the murder of inquisitor Pedro Arubés inside the Saragossa cathedral was likely a desperate attempt at derailing an investigation; tragically, the inquisitorial scrutiny only increased in response.[21] Many other *conversos* resisted quietly and in private, creating syncretic rituals that combined elements of Judaism and Christianity to avoid detection.[22] The coercive nature of the Inquisition makes it difficult to distinguish between *conversos*' genuine resistance and their false confessions, which were prompted by torture or intimidation.[23]

CONCLUSION

Although the film's brief-but-memorable depiction of the Inquisition casts it as an attribute of the "dark" Middle Ages, the Spanish Inquisition's scope, centralization, and subordination to royal authority ensured its survival until the nineteenth century. Moreover, the voyages of exploration—and the ensuing Spanish colonization of the Americas—brought the Inquisition to the New World. Just as Columbus's observant eyes made a note of the opportunities to exploit the indigenous people he encountered, the Inquisition's knack for criminalizing behavior made it into an effective tool of colonial control and cultural genocide.

The movie *1492: Conquest of Paradise* represents a sincere belief in progressive, linear historical development, inspired not only by Spain's democratization in the late twentieth century but also by the recent end to the Cold War (1947–91). The idea of Columbus ushering Spain (and, by extension, Europe) from the "Dark Ages" to an enlightened age of Renaissance, though ahistorical, can seem compelling. It builds on the audience's preconceived notions about the backwardness of the Middle Ages and Spain's "Black Legend" in particular. But a closer look at the medieval Spain of Columbus's time reveals a more complex picture. Yes, the voyages of exploration transformed European perspectives, but medieval understandings of science and geography fueled these voyages and helped categorize the people and places Columbus encountered. Likewise, Spain's colonization across the Atlantic coincided with late medieval campaigns of religious coercion that became paradigmatic for its later colonial policies. Both science and colonization thrived on creating rigid categories that held certain people and places as inferior. These are also useful to our understanding of how forms of medieval intolerance thrived long after the Middle Ages.

APPENDIX

1492: Conquest of Paradise (1992)

CHRISTOPHER COLUMBUS (1451–1506), *JOURNAL OF THE FIRST VOYAGE* (1492)

Columbus recounts to the Spanish monarchs what he has seen during his voyages.

Source: Christopher Columbus, *Journal of Christopher Columbus (During His First Voyage, 1492–93), and Documents Relating the Voyages of John Cabot and Gaspar Corte Real,* ed. and trans. Clements R. Markham (London: Hakluyt Society, 1893), 41–42, 114. Original in Castilian. Revised and modernized by Eugene Smelyansky.

[October 14, 1492]: I saw a piece of land which appeared like an island, although it is not one, and on it there were six houses. It might be converted into an island [fort] in two days, though I do not see that it would be necessary, for [the indigenous] people are very simple with regards to the use of weapons, as your Highnesses will see from the seven that I ordered to be taken, to bring home and learn our language and return; unless your Highnesses should order them all to be brought to Castille, or to be kept as captives on the same island; for with fifty men they can all be subjugated and made to do what is required of them. Close to the above peninsula there are gardens of the most beautiful trees I ever saw, and with leaves as green as those of Castille in the months of April and May, and much water.

[December 16, 1492]: Your Highnesses may believe that these lands are so good and fertile, especially these of the island of Hispaniola, that there is no one who would know how to describe them, and no one who could believe if he had not seen them. And your Highnesses may believe that this island, and all the others, are as much yours as Castille, only wanting a settlement and the order to the people to do what is required. For I, with the force I have under me, which is not large, could march over all these islands without opposition. I have seen only three sailors land, without wishing to do harm, and a multitude of Indians fled before them. They have no weapons and are without warlike instincts; they all go naked and are so timid that a thousand would not stand before three of our men. So that they are good to be ordered about, to work and sow, and do all that may be necessary, and to build towns, and they should be taught to go about clothed and to adopt our customs.

SPANISH INQUISITIONS (1484–1486)

Conversos *Sentenced and Executed in Saragossa.*
   Source: Henry Charles Lea, ed., *A History of the Inquisition of Spain* (New York: Macmillan, 1906), 1:593–97. Original in Castilian. Translated by Esther Liberman Cuenca.
   Auto-da-fés [*public rituals punishing lapsed conversos*] of the year 1484.
   Felipe Salvador, alias Santicos, a grocer, for judaizing rituals, eating meat on Friday and during Lent; he was the first cousin of Pedro de la Cabra, a Jew.
   Leonor Catorce Valenciana, wife of the said Santicos, for judaizing rituals, eating *amin* [a Jewish broth] and meat on Friday and Saturday and having fasted on the fast of *Quipur* [Yom Kippur].
   Isavel Muñoz Castellana, for the same crimes, and for when she recited the Creed and came to the words *et in Jesum Christum* [and in Jesus Christ], she would say, *Here the donkey fell.*
   All were given penance for heresies and their property confiscated.
   On 20 of December [1485], Friday, in the back of the Hospital of our Lady of Portillo, the Dominicans' Prior preached, and the following were burned:
   Alvaro de Segovia for judaizing rituals, eating *amin* and slaughtered meats during his rites, including in the time of Lent, and for fasting during *Quipur*, reading the Bible in Hebrew under a canopy, and afterward compelling his children to worship the in same manner—he was burned.
   Joana Sinfa because as a Jewish convert to Christianity she returned to judaizing rites and continued to live as a Jew—she was burned.
   Friday, 28 of April [1486], in the same place. Master Crespo preached. The following were punished:
   Pedro de Orrea, merchant, for judaizing rituals, and for having himself circumcised, and when kissing the cross or the Blessed Sacrament he would hide himself so as to avoid venerating them—he was burned.
   Anton de Pomar, grocer, for judaizing rituals, and being a Christian he neither knew the Pater Noster [the Lord's Prayer] nor the Creed—he was burned.

Master Pedro Monfort, Vicar General of Zaragoza, for having gone against the Inquisition of Mallorca and Zaragoza. [He] said that a good Jew could save himself like a good Christian, and among the Jews he swore by the law of Moses and Ten Commandments, telling the Jews that they had a good and holy law—he was burned as a statue [in effigy].

Manuel de Almazan, merchant, for judaizing rituals, for eating *amin* and *arrequequer* [a food associated with Jews, most likely a type of bread], giving alms and paying a Rabbi for reading him the Law of Moses—he was burned.

On 25 June, Friday [1486]. Master Martin Garcia preached; penances were given to the following heretics:

Felipe de Moros, an innkeeper from Almunia, because he married two women still living, for judaizing rituals, and for having taken a Christian woman.

Clara Mateo, wife of Alvaro de Segovia, for judaizing rituals and saying that our Savior was not present in the Eucharist, and for not giving a true confession because she believes, without the Law of Moses, it is all a mockery.

On the 28 of July, Friday [1486], Master Crespo preached, and the following were condemned to the fire:

Caspar de Santa Cruz as a Christian ate, fasted, and performed rituals like a Jew, and he and [John] de Perosanchez offered Juan de Labadia their favor and 500 florins if he killed the Holy Inquisitor. And for conspiring and plotting this assassination . . . , and for fleeing to Toulouse [France], where he died, they burned him as a statue.

Martin de Santangel, because he was a Christian and practiced judaizing rituals, and was complicit in the death of the Holy Inquisitor, having given money for his assassination, and for carrying four orations in Hebrew in his Book of Hours and using them for prayer—he was burned as a statue.

Violante Salvador, wife of Caspar de Santa Cruz, for judaizing rituals and not observing the Sunday. For which reason her servants said that her house looked more like that of Jews than Christians, and before going to mass she ate, and put bacon in the young men's pot but not in her own because she kept the law of Moses. They burned her as a statue.

Reading questions

- What features of the islands and their inhabitants does Columbus emphasize in his journal entries? What factors might have influenced his description of them? Does *1492*'s Columbus view indigenous people the same way Columbus does in this source?
- Do you think *1492* was effective in bringing to life these sources? Why or why not?
- What behaviors did the Inquisition consider to be evidence of practicing Judaism in secret? How do you think the inquisitors were able to acquire information about the lives of the *conversos*?
- What can this document tell us about the lives of *conversos* in the late fifteenth-century Saragossa?
- What roles do the church and the Spanish Inquisition play in *1492*'s narrative? How does the film portray Jews and Muslims ("Moors")? Do you think the punishments (or penances) described here are more shocking than how they are portrayed in *1492*? Why or why not?

NOTES

1. Silvio Torres-Saillant, "1492 and the Ethics of Remembering," in *The Culture and Philosophy of Ridley Scott*, ed. Adam Barkman, Ashley Barkman, and Nancy Kang (Lanham, Md.: Lexington Books, 2013), 107.

2. Amy S. Kaufman and Paul B. Sturtevant, *The Devil's Historians: How Modern Extremists Abuse the Medieval Past* (Toronto: University of Toronto Press, 2020), 12–18.

3. Margaret R. Greer, Walter D. Mignolo, and Maureen Quilligan, *Rereading the Black Legend: The Discourses of Religious and Racial Difference in the Renaissance Empires* (Chicago: University of Chicago Press, 2008).

4. Torres-Saillant, "1492 and the Ethics of Remembering," 108. For a discussion of Spain's lavish celebration, see Stephen J. Summerhill and John Alexander Williams, *Sinking Columbus: Contested History, Cultural Politics, and Mythmaking during the Quincentenary* (Gainesville: University Press of Florida, 2000), esp. Chapter 5.

5. Ibid., 103.

6. Noelia V. Saenz, "Reframing Empire: Mediating Encounters and Resistance in Spanish Transatlantic Cinema since 1992," in *Global Genres, Local Films: The Transnational Dimension of Spanish Cinema*, ed. Elena Oliete-Aldea, Beatriz Oria, and Juan A. Tarancón (New York: Bloomsbury Academic, 2015), 127–28.

7. Valerie I. J. Flint, *The Imaginative Landscape of Christopher Columbus* (Princeton: Princeton University Press, 1992); Evelyn Edson, *The World Map, 1300–1492:*

The Persistence of Tradition and Transformation (Baltimore: Johns Hopkins University Press, 2007); Hyunhee Park, "The Transfer of Geographic Knowledge of Afro-Eurasia in the 'Bright' Middle Ages: Cases of Late Medieval European Maps of the World," in *The Bright Dark Ages*, ed. Arun Bala and Prasenjit Duara (Leiden: Brill, 2016), 143–60.

8. Edson, *World Map*, 205.

9. Nicolás Wey Gómez, *The Tropics of Empire: Why Columbus Sailed South to the Indies* (Cambridge, Mass: MIT Press, 2008).

10. Ibid., 227.

11. Aristotle, *The Politics*, ed. Stephen Everson (New York: Cambridge University Press, 1988), Book 7, Chapter 7.

12. On slavery in the Mediterranean and Iberia, see Hannah Barker, *That Most Precious Merchandise: The Mediterranean Trade in Black Sea Slaves, 1260–1500* (Philadelphia: University of Pennsylvania Press, 2019); William D. Phillips, *Slavery in Medieval and Early Modern Iberia* (Philadelphia: University of Pennsylvania Press, 2014).

13. Henry Kamen, *Empire: How Spain Became a World Power, 1492–1763* (New York: Harper Collins, 2004), 12–13.

14. Christopher Columbus, *Journals and Other Documents on the Life and Voyages of Christopher Columbus*, trans. Samuel Eliot Morison (New York: Limited Editions Club, 1963), 186.

15. L. C. Green and Olive P. Dickason, *The Law of Nations and the New World* (Edmonton: University of Alberta Press, 1989), 183–84. See also Rolena Adorno, *Polemics of Possession in Spanish American Narrative* (New Haven: Yale University Press, 2007).

16. Alan Mikhail, *God's Shadow: The Ottoman Sultan Who Shaped the Modern World* (New York: Liveright, 2020), esp. Chapter 7.

17. On the Inquisition's activity outside of Spain, see Robin Vose, "Beyond Spain: Inquisition History in a Global Context," *History Compass* 11, no. 4 (2013): 316–29. See also Edward Peters, *Inquisition* (Berkeley: University of California Press, 1988), esp. Chapter 3.

18. Henry Kamen, *The Spanish Inquisition: A Historical Revision*, 4th ed. (New Haven: Yale University Press, 2014), esp. Chapters 3 and 4.

19. David Nirenberg, *Anti-Judaism: The Western Tradition* (New York: W. W. Norton, 2013), 218–19, 227–28.

20. For more on inquisition, see M. Christina Bruno's chapter on *The Name of the Rose* (1986) and Henry Ansgar Kelly's on *The Passion of Joan of Arc* (1928) in this book.

21. Helen Rawlings, *The Spanish Inquisition* (Malden, Mass.: Blackwell, 2008), 59.

22. Joseph Pérez, *The Spanish Inquisition: A History* (New Haven: Yale University Press, 2005), 36–37.

23. See, for example, Renée Levine Melammed, *Heretics or Daughters of Israel?: The Crypto-Jewish Women of Castile* (Oxford: Oxford University Press, 2002). For a discussion of this approach, see Kamen, *Spanish Inquisition*, 44–45.

ACKNOWLEDGMENTS

We, the editors, would like to thank Will Cerbone, Andrew B. R. Elliott, John Garza, Nicholas Paul, Luke Sunderland, and Usha Vishnuvajjala for their assistance prior to the publication of this book.

Additionally, we would like to thank Robbin Crabtree, dean of the Bellarmine College of Liberal Arts at Loyola Marymount University, for contributing funds toward the publication of this book.

This book benefited enormously from the work conducted at the Institute for Advanced Study in Princeton, which provided the necessary time and resources for editing this book, as well as connections to authors who ended up contributing chapters.

We also extend our gratitude to Fordham University's Center for Medieval Studies.

This book is dedicated to our students.

CONTRIBUTORS

MARIA AMERICO is Assistant Professor of History at Saint Peter's University in New Jersey.

DANIEL ARMENTI is Assistant Professor of Italian at High Point University in North Carolina.

LUCY C. BARNHOUSE is Assistant Professor of History at Arkansas State University, Jonesboro.

CHRISTOPHER BONURA is Assistant Professor of History at Mount Saint Mary's University in Maryland.

M. CHRISTINA BRUNO is Associate Director of the Center for Medieval Studies at Fordham University in New York.

JULIE K. CHAMBERLIN is Advanced Lecturer in English at Loyola University Chicago in Illinois.

CELIA CHAZELLE is Professor of History at The College of New Jersey.

RACHEL ELLEN CLARK is Associate Professor of English at Wartburg College in Iowa.

ESTHER LIBERMAN CUENCA is Assistant Professor of History at the University of Houston-Victoria in Texas.

CASEY IRELAND is Visiting Assistant Professor of English at the University of Richmond in Virginia.

HENRY ANSGAR KELLY is Distinguished Research Professor in the English Department at the University of California, Los Angeles.

SARAH C. LUGINBILL is Visiting Assistant Professor of History and Humanities at Trinity University in Texas.

CORAL LUMBLEY is Assistant Professor of English at Macalester College in Minnesota.

SARA MCDOUGALL is Professor of History at John Jay College of Criminal Justice and the CUNY Graduate Center in New York.

NATHAN MELSON is a History Lecturer at Hunter College in New York.

NAHIR I. OTAÑO GRACIA is Assistant Professor of English at the University of New Mexico.

ANTHONY PERRON is Associate Professor of History at Loyola Marymount University in California.

DAVID M. PERRY is Senior Academic Advisor in the History Department at the University of Minnesota.

ASIF A. SIDDIQI is Professor of History at Fordham University in New York.

EUGENE SMELYANSKY is Assistant Professor of History at Washington State University, Pullman.

LORRAINE KOCHANSKE STOCK is Professor of English at the University of Houston in Texas.

SPENCER STRUB is Associate Research Scholar in the Humanities Council at Princeton University in New Jersey.

INDEX

13th Warrior, The (film), 237–45
1492: Conquest of Paradise (film), 265–69, 270–71, 273

Aberth, John, 154
Abiron (biblical character), 32, 35n18
Abraham, F. Murray, 50
Abrikosov, Andrey, 157
absolute poverty, 37, 41, 43, 53
Abu Sufyan, 230
Academy Awards (Oscars), 10, 89, 251
Adorf, Mario, 39
Adventures of Robin Hood, The (film), 101–8
Advocate, The (*The Hour of the Pig,* film), 126, 127, 128–33
Africans in England, 252, 254–57
Agora (film), 211–13, 215, 216–17, 218
Akkad, Moustapha, 227, 235n2; *The Message* (film), 225–32, 235n2
Al-Bukhari, Muhammad, 229; *al-Jami' al-Sahih,* 229, 233–34
Albert the Great (saint), 268
Albigensian Crusade, 168
Alexander III (pope), 11, 12, 17
Alexander III (Scotland), 183
Alexander Nevsky (film), 153, 154, 155–61
Alexander Nevsky (prince, Novgorod), 153, 154–61
Alexandria, Egypt, 211, 214, 215, 222. *See also* Serapeum, Alexandria
Alexios I Komnenos (Byzantium), 92–93
Alfred de Solny, 105, 107
Alhambra Decree, 271
Al-Kamil (sultan of Egypt), 38
Amenábar, Alejandro: *Agora* (film), 211–13, 215, 216–17, 218
America (magazine), 195
Ammar (early follower of Islam), 228
anathema, 23, 28–29, 31–33, 128, 135

Andreas Capellanus: *De Amore,* 79, 181, 182, 187, 191–92; "On the Love of Peasants," 191–92
Angelo (follower of Francis of Assisi), 39, 40
Angevin Empire, 24–25, 34n3, 101, 108
Anglo-Normans, 24–25
Anglo-Saxons, 251, 257
Anhalt, Edward, 10
animal trials, 127–34, 137n4
animals: 127–36, 137n4, 168, 174. *See also* Guinefort (animal saint)
Annabi, Amina, 132
Annals of Hildesheim, 29
Annaud, Jean-Jacques: *The Name of the Rose* (film), 49–51, 53–54, 55–56, 59n2
Anonymous of Perugia, The, 40
Anouilh, Jean: *Becket, ou l'honneur de Dieu* (*Becket, or the Honor of God,* play), 10, 12–13
Ansara, Michael, 230
anti-Judaism, 271–72. *See also* anti-Semitism
anti-monastic satire, 200
anti-Semitism, 252, 253. *See also* anti-Judaism
apostolic poverty, 50, 51, 57
appointment of religious leaders, 146–47, 149–50
Arabia, 227, 228, 231
Aristotle: *Politics,* 269
Armisen, Fred, 195
Armitage, Richard, 22
Arnold, John, 54, 55
art, Islamic, 226–27, 236n4
Artaud, Antonin, 66
Arubés, Pedro, 272–73
asceticism, 40, 197, 202, 215
Assante, Armand, 272
assertory oaths, 91
assimilation, Jewish, 252, 253

284　INDEX

Assisi Compilation, The, 40
Assize of the Forest (Henry II), 105–6, 109–10
Athenais (Aelia Eudocia), 216
Atkine, Féodor, 168
auto-da-fé, 272, 275–76
Autun, France, 129, 135, 138n13, 138n19

Baena, Jeff: *The Little Hours* (film), 195–97, 198, 201–2, 205n1
Balian of Ibelin, 89, 94, 95, 97, 98–99
Baltic Crusades, 154
Banderas, Antonio, 237, 238
Barbour, John: *The Bruce*, 184
Bardou, Camille, 66
Basil of Caesarea, 197
Baskin, Elya, 51
Battle of Hattin, 89, 95
Battle of Lake Peypus, 154, 158, 159
Battle of the Neva, 154
battle, trials by, 114–17, 121, 122
Batu (Mongol ruler), 153
Beaune, France, 128, 135
Beaupère, Jean, 64, 66, 67, 68
Becket (film), 9, 10, 13–14, 15, 16
Becket, ou l'honneur de Dieu [*Becket, or the Honor of God*] (play, Anouilh), 10, 12–13
Becket, Thomas, 9–19
Beguines, 198
Beguins, 56, 57–58
Behringer, Wolfgang, 172
belongings, 45–46
Benedict of Nursia, 41. *See also* Benedictine Order; Benedictine Rule
Benedictine Order, 25–26
Benedictine Rule, 41, 42, 145, 147, 148–50, 197
Beowulf, 91, 237, 238, 242, 243, 244, 247–48
Berger, Pamela: *Sorceress* (*Le moine et la sorcière*, film), 166–70, 171–73, 178n26
Bergman, Ingrid, 61
Berley, André, 67
Berman, Pandro S., 251, 253; *A Patch of Blue* (film), 257; *The Knights of the Round Table* (film), 257. *See also Ivanhoe* (film, dir. Thorpe)
Bernard Gui, 50, 53–54, 55–56; *Manual on the Inquisition of Heretical Depravity*, 56, 57–59
Bernard of Clairvaux, 26, 119, 142
Bernardo da Quintavalle, 39
Bernthal, Jon, 22
Berthold of Reichenau, 29
Bilal (companion of Muhammad), 227–28, 232, 234
"Black Legend," 265–66, 273
Black people in England, 254–57
Blakelock, Alban, 12
Blendi, Mareile, 146
Blind Harry: *The Wallace*, 184
Blinnikov, Sergey, 157
Bloom, Orlando, 94
Boccaccio, Giovanni: *Decameron*, 195, 196, 200, 201, 204–5, 205n1
Boece, Scotorum *Historiae*, 182–83, 184
Boethius Severinus, 136
Boisson, Christine, 166
Bonaventure of Bagnoregio, 40
Bonham-Carter, Helena, 39
Boniface VIII (pope): *Liber Sextus*, 199; *Periculoso*, 196, 198–99, 201–4
Bosch, Roselyne (Rose), 265
Boswell, Robert, 183, 184
Bouchard, Constance, 170
Boureau, Alain, 182
Bradshaw, Peter, 76
Braveheart (film), 180–81, 183–88, 193n3, 194n17
Braveheart (historical figure). *See* Wallace, William "Braveheart"
Brenon, Herbert: *Ivanhoe* (film), 252
Britain. *See* England
bulls, papal, 43, 52, 93
Burke, Tarana, 180
Burnham, Louisa, 53
"Burning Times," 171, 177n14
Burr, David, 52
Burton, Richard, 10
Bush, George W., 89
Bussotti, Fabio, 39

INDEX 285

Caesarius of Arles: *Regula ad virgines*, 197
Canary Islands, 269
canon law, 142–45; appeals, 15, 16, 18–19, 21n17, 62, 63; differences between letter and practice of, 167–69, 173, 199; secular law and, 9–19, 131, 167–69, 171, 219
canonization, 12, 39, 40, 61
Canterbury, archbishop of, 11–12
Canterbury Tales, The (Chaucer), 132, 200
Caribbean, 268–70
Carmet, Jean, 168
Carrouges, Jean de, 114, 116, 117, 118, 120, 122–23, 125n12
Carter, Jim, 132
Cassian, John, 197
Catani, Pietro, 38
Cathars, 131, 168
Catherine (saint), 70, 71
Cauchon, Pierre, 63–69, 70
Cavani, Liliana: *Francesco* (film, 1989), 36–39, 40, 41, 43, 48n16; *Francesco* (film, 2014), 36; *Francesco d'Assisi* (film, 1966), 36
cenobitic monasticism, 40, 197
charity, 229–30, 231, 232, 233
Charles VI (France), 116
Chassenée, Bartholomew: *Consilium primum*, 127–28, 129, 131, 135–36, 138n13, 138n19
chastity, 51, 197, 198, 200, 202, 203
Chaucer, Geoffrey: *The Canterbury Tales*, 132, 200; *raptus* litigation, 181; *Wife of Bath's Tale*, 181–82, 187, 189–91
Chaumpaigne, Cecily, 181
Cherkasov, Nikolai, 156
Chiara (Clare) of Assisi (saint), 39, 43, 48n16
chivalric code, 77. See also chivalry; honor
chivalry, 76–81, 260–61
Choudhury, Sarita, 81
Christ. See Jesus Christ
Christianity: appeal to women, 215; ascetic practice, 40, 197, 202, 215; conflict with Muslims, 27, 90, 94, 97–98; diversification of, 167; in England, 252–53; Jews and, 218, 222–23, 253–54, 258–59, 272; pagans and, 212, 214, 222–23 (*see also* Hypatia of Alexandria; Serapeum, Alexandria); sainthood, 39–40
Christianity, Eastern (Greek), 197
Christianity, Orthodox, 159, 161
Christianity, Western (Latin), 197, 199
Christianization of Roman Empire, 211, 214, 216, 218
Christians. *See* Christianity
Chronicle of Ernoul and of Bernard the Treasurer, The, 95–96, 97–99
Chronicle of Richard of Devizes, 256
chronicles, medieval. *See* medieval chronicles
Chronique d'Ernoul et de Bernard le Trésorier, 95–96, 97–99
church thieves, 23, 28–29, 31–33
Cinéaste, 170, 172
cinematic hagiography, 43
cinematic medievalism, 3. *See also* medieval cinema
Cistercian Order, 25–26
civil law, 14, 16, 127, 131, 137n4
civil rights, 252, 257
Clare (Chiara) of Assisi (saint), 39, 43, 48n16
Clarendon, Constitutions of, 11, 12, 13, 14, 17
class consciousness, 181, 182, 187, 191–92
claustration, 196, 197–99, 201–4
clerical immunity, 13–15, 17
climate, 269
cloister (claustration), 196, 197–99, 201–4
clothing, 44–45, 65, 66–67
cniht, 77
coexistence, religious, 212, 213–14, 216, 218, 222–23
Cohn, Norman, 171
colonialism, 94–96
colonization, 269–70, 271, 273
Columbus, Christopher, 265, 266, 267–71, 273; *Journal of the First Voyage*, 274–75

Columbus, Ferdinand, 267
combat, trials by, 114–17, 121, 122
Comer, Jodie, 114, 119
"Comment on the Trial by Combat of Jacques Le Gris" (Le Coq), 122–24, 125n18
Common Law (English), 9–17
community practice, 166–67, 170, 172–73
Connery, Sean, 49
Consilium primum (Chassenée), 127–28, 129, 131, 135–36, 138n13, 138n19
Constantinople, 30, 219
Constitutions of Clarendon, 11, 12, 13, 14, 17
convent satire, 195–96, 199–202, 204–5
conversos, 271–73, 275–76
coronations, 12
Corsini, Matteo, 39
Council of Nicaea, 25
Council of Northampton, 11, 14
Courcelles, Thomas, 64, 70
courtly behavior, 77, 79
courtly love, 79–80, 182, 187, 191–92
coutumes, 127, 130, 132, 134, 137n4
Coutumes de Beauvaisis (Philippe de Beaumanoir), 127, 134, 137n4
Crichton, Michael: *Eaters of the Dead*, 237, 243, 245, 249n10
Criminal Prosecution and Capital Punishment of Animals, The (Evans), 126, 128–29
crusades, 23, 30, 92–99, 117, 253, 256. See also names of specific crusades
crusading oaths, 92
Crutchley, Rosalie, 228
Csokas, Marton, 94
Culhwch and Olwen, 77
cultural encounters, 237, 238–40, 244, 246–47, 251–61
Curtiz, Michael: *The Adventures of Robin Hood* (film), 101–8
customary laws, 127, 130, 132, 134, 137n4
Customary Laws of Beauvais, The (Philippe de Beaumanoir), 127, 134, 137n4
customs, folk, 168–69, 173, 174–76
Cyril (bishop of Alexandria), 211, 217, 222

Dalleu, Gilbert, 66
Dalrymple, David: *Annals of Scotland*, 183, 184
Damon, Matt, 114
Danilova, Alexandra, 158
Dathan (biblical character), 32, 35n18
De Amore (Andreas Capellanus), 181, 182, 187, 191–92
de Bourbon, Étienne. See Étienne de Bourbon
De ecclesiasticis disciplinis (Regino of Prüm), 28–29
de Havilland, Olivia, 101
De Ortu Waluuanii, 77
de Vere, Aubrey, 9
Dean, Loren, 267
Decameron (Boccaccio), 195, 196, 200, 201, 204–5, 205n1
Decretum Gratiani, 14
dehumanization, 244–45
deleo, 29
Depardieu, Gérard, 265
depiction of Muhammad, 225–27, 236n4
Disibodenberg monastery, 143–44, 146, 147
Dolcinites (Dulcinians), 56
Dolcino (leader of Dolcinites), 56
Dominic de Guzmán (saint), 54
Dominican Order, 54, 166, 171
Donohue, Bill, 195
Dreyer, Carl Theodor: *The Passion of Joan of Arc* (*La Passion de Jeanne d'Arc*, film), 61–62, 66–69
Driver, Adam, 114
droit de cuissage. See *jus primae noctis*
droit du seigneur. See *jus primae noctis*
duels, 115, 116, 121. See also combat, trials by
Dulcinians (Dolcinites), 56
d'Yd, Jean, 67

Eastern (Greek) Christianity, 197
Eaters of the Dead (Crichton), 237, 243, 245, 249n10
Ebert, Roger, 49, 75–76, 143
Ecclesiastical History (Rufinus), 218, 220–21

INDEX   287

Ecclesiastical History (Socrates Scholasticus), 221–22
ecclesiastical jurisdiction, 13–15, 17
ecclesiastical processions, 26–28
Eco, Umberto, 49, 59n2; *The Name of the Rose* (novel), 49, 56
Edgerton, Joel, 80
education, late Roman Empire, 212–14, 215–16, 218–19
Edward I "Longshanks" (England), 110, 111, 183–85, 186, 188, 194nn17–18
Edward II (England), 184–85, 186, 187, 194n18
Edward III (England), 110, 111
Egypt, 211. *See also* Alexandria, Egypt; Serapeum, Alexandria
Ehrenreich, Barbara: *Witches, Midwives, and Nurses*, 172
Ehrenschwendtner, Marie-Luise, 199
Eisenstein, Sergei Mikhailovich, 155; *Alexander Nevsky* (film), 153, 154, 155–61; *Battleship Potemkin* (film), 155
election of religious leaders, 146–47, 149–50
Elias of Cortona, 41
Eliot, T. S.: *Murder in the Cathedral* (play), 9–10, 12
Elm, Kaspar, 198
elves, 172, 179n26
emperors, Roman, 217–18, 221
enclosure (claustration), 196, 197–99, 201–4
England: canon law and royal law, 9–19; forest law, 101–11; multiple cultures in, 251–61
English, Deirdre: *Witches, Midwives, and Nurses*, 172
enslavement, 137n4, 213, 227–28, 246–47, 252, 255, 256–57, 269–70
Epic of Gilgamesh, 182
equality, racial, 227–28, 232
Estivet, Jean, 63, 64, 65, 67
Étienne de Bourbon, 166–67, 168, 171, 172, 173; *On the Seven Gifts of the Holy Spirit*, 166, 168–69, 170, 172, 174–76, 178nn24–25; "Of the Worship of Guinefort the Dog," 174–76

Eudocia, Aelia (Athenais), 216
Eugenius III (pope), 93; *Quantum praedecessores*, 93
Eunapius, 216
Evans, E. P.: *The Criminal Prosecution and Capital Punishment of Animals*, 126, 128–29
Evans, Rupert, 212
Ewen (Evenus), king of Scotland), 183
excommunication, 15–16; of animals and insects, 127–28, 135–36; by Becket, 11, 12, 14, 15–16, 17–19, 20n6; formula for, 31–33; for movement of relics and reliquaries, 23, 27, 28–29, 30
executions, 117, 168, 270–71, 275–76
Exiit qui seminat (Nicholas III), 52, 53

Fair Maid of Perth, The (W. Scott), 115, 183, 184
fairies, 172, 179n26
faith, 141, 231, 233. *See also* Christianity; Islam
faith, errors of, 65
faith, trials of, 61–66
Falconetti, Renée, 61–62
false accusations, 117
faunus, 172, 178n26
Fedosya Igorevna, 153
female infanticide, 228, 234–35
feminism, 143, 167, 169–70, 171–72, 173, 177n9, 177n14
Fennell, John, 159
Ferch, Heino, 142
Fernando II (Aragon), 267, 271
feuds, 27–28. *See also* combat, trials by
Finch, Jon, 96
First Crusade, 26, 27, 92–93
Firth, Colin, 126
Fitzstephen, William, 14
five pillars of Islam, 226, 229–32, 233
Flanagan, Tommy, 184
Fleming, Victor: *Joan of Arc* (film), 61
Flynn, Errol, 101
Foliot, Gilbert, 11, 12, 13, 15–19
folk traditions, 168–69, 173, 174–76
forest eyre justices, 107, 110
forest eyres, 106–7, 110–11

forest law, 101–11
Forest, Michael, 230
Fouke le Fitz Waryn, 255–56
1492: Conquest of Paradise (film), 265–69, 270–71, 273
Fourth Crusade, 22, 30
Fourth Lateran Council, 62, 254
France: animal trials, 126–36; inquisitions, 61–72; trials by combat, 114–24; witchcraft and witch trials, 166–76
Francesco (film, 1989), 36–39, 40, 41, 43, 48n16
Francis of Assisi (Francesco di Pietro di Bernardone) (saint), 36–43, 51; Primitive Rule (*Regula primitiva*), 41, 43; *Regula non bullata*, 41; Testament, 38, 42–43. *See also* Franciscan Order; Franciscan Rule
Franciscan Order, 36, 37, 38, 41, 43, 50–57. *See also* Franciscan Rule
Franciscan Rule, 36–46, 50–53, 56, 57; Primitive Rule, 41, 43
Franco, Dave, 195
fraticelli, 56
Frederick II (Sicily), 116
Froissart, Jean, 117
Fulda monastery, 146
fundamentalism, religious, 89–90, 211–12

Gallus, Johannes. *See* Le Coq, Jean (Johannes Gallus)
Game of Thrones (television series), 115
Gardner, Gerald, 177n14
Gauge, Alexander, 12
Gawain (fictional character), 75, 77–80, 81–86
Geoffroi de Charny: *Book of Chivalry*, 80–81
geographical knowledge, 267–70, 273
Germany, Nazi, 156, 157, 161
Gest of Robyn Hode, A, 104, 105
Gibson, Mel: *Braveheart* (film), 180–81, 183–88, 193n3, 194n17; *The Passion of the Christ* (film), 61
Gilbert of Clare, 13–14, 15
Gilles de Rais, 138n16
Glaber, Rodolfus: *Histories*, 27, 31

Gleeson, Brendan, 94
Glenville, Peter: *Becket* (film), 9, 10, 13–14, 15, 16
Global North Atlantic, 238–40
Gospels, 61–62
Greek (Eastern) Christianity, 197
Green, Judith, 106
Green Knight, The (film), 75–76, 78–80, 81–83
Green, Monica, 170
Greene, Graham, 72n1
Gregory IX (pope), 39, 43, 52, 168; *Quo elongati*, 43
Groser, John, 10
Guardian, 76
Guinefort (animal saint), 166, 168–70, 172–76
Guinness, Alec, 37
Guy of Lusignan, 94, 97–98

hadith, 227, 228, 229, 231, 232, 233–34
hagiography, 39–40
hagiography, cinematic, 43
Hagon, Garrick, 228
hairstyles, 118–19
hajj, 226, 230, 231, 233
Hamza (Muhammad's uncle), 226
Hanawalt, Barbara, 104
Hanly, Peter, 185
Hatot, Georges, 6n2
healthcare, 172–73, 174, 178n25
Held, Alexander, 144
Henri d'Avranches, 39
Henry I (England), 106, 109
Henry II (England), 24, 34n3; Assize of the Forest, 105–6, 109–10; Becket and, 9–18; forest use, 107
Henry II (Germany), 29; pontifical sponsored by, 31–33
Henry III (England), 254, 256
Henry VI (England), 64
Henry VIII (England), 24
Henry the Young King (England), 12
heresy: judaizing, 272, 275, 276; regarding poverty, 50–59; women and, 169

heresy trials (trials of faith), 61–66. *See also* inquisitions
Herzsprung, Hannah, 146
Hickey, William, 53
Hildegard von Bingen, 141–46
Hind (wife of Abu Sufyan), 226, 230
Hispaniola, 269, 274–75
History of the Kings of Britain (Geoffrey of Monmouth), 77
Hoellering, G. M.: *Murder in the Cathedral* (film), 9–10
Holland, Tom, 22
Holm, Ian, 131
Holzapfel, Heribert, 41
honor, 75, 76, 78, 80–82, 83
Honorius III (pope), 41, 51
Horner, James, 186
Houppeville, Nicolas, 67
Hour of the Pig, The (*The Advocate*, film), 126, 127, 128–33
Hundred Years' War, 61, 77, 130
Hunter, Ian, 101
hunting, 101–3, 105
Hypatia of Alexandria, 211, 213–16, 218, 219, 221–22

Iberian Jews, 271–73
Ibn Fadlān, Ahmad, 239, 241, 245; *Risāla*, 237, 238, 246–47
Ibn Ibrahim, Ismail, 229
Ibn Sīnā, 268
Ibn Walid, Khalid, 230, 231, 232
illness, 144–45
imitation of Jesus Christ, 36, 38, 41, 42, 51–53
immunity, clerical, 13–15, 17
indigenous peoples: Columbus and, 269–70, 274–75; language and, 237, 238, 243–45
indigenous religion, 243–44
infallibility, papal, 53
infanticide, female, 228, 234–35
Innocent III (pope): Francis of Assisi and, 37, 38, 41, 43, 51; *Qualiter et Quando*, 62; on relics, 23, 30
inquisitions, 50, 53–59, 61–69, 168, 272. *See also* Spanish Inquisition

investigation, 50; of heresy, 53–56 (*see also* inquisitions)
Ireland, 23–28, 30
Isaac, Oscar, 212
Isabel I (Castile), 268, 271
Isabelle (princess, France), 184–85, 186, 187–88, 194n18
Islam, 94, 225–35, 237, 239. *See also* Muslims
Islamic art, 226–27, 236n4
Islamic fundamentalism, 89–90, 211–12
Italy, 55, 198, 199
Ivanhoe (film, dir. Thorpe), 251–53, 254, 256–57
Ivanhoe (novel, W. Scott), 115, 183, 251–57
Ivashyova, Valentina, 157

Jackson, Peter: *Lord of the Rings* trilogy (films), 89
Jager, Eric: *The Last Duel* (book), 114, 117
Jerusalem, 23, 89, 90, 93–99
Jesus Christ: imitation of life of, 36, 38, 41, 42, 51–53; passion of, 61–62; poverty, 50, 53, 56, 57
Jews, 132, 218, 222–23, 251–54, 257–60; Iberian, 271–73
Joan of Arc (saint), 61–69
John (king of England), 24, 107
John XXII (pope), 49, 53, 58
John, Gospel of, 61
Johnson, Penelope D., 142
Johnson, Samuel, 183, 184
judaizing, 272, 275, 276
Judas Iscariot, 32
judicial combats, 114–17, 121, 122
Julian of Speyer, 39
jurisdiction, ecclesiastical, 13–15, 17
jus primae noctis, 180–88, 193n3
Jutta (Hildegard von Bingen's foster sister), 147
Jutta von Sponheim, 146

ka'ba, 232, 233
Kaeuper, Richard, 76
Kaiser, Daniel H., 159
Kammer, Salome, 145

Karamzin, Nikolai Mikhailovich: *History of the Russian State*, 155
Karyo, Tchéky, 166
Keighley, William: *The Adventures of Robin Hood* (film), 101–8
Kellyman, Erin, 79
Keoghan, Barry, 79
Khadijah (wife of Muhammad), 227
kingdom of heaven, 93–96
Kingdom of Heaven (film), 89–90, 93–96, 183
Kirke, Jemima, 197
Kleinberg, Aviad, 40
Knight, Stephen, 106
knighthood, 77, 78–79, 80–82
Komnene, Anna: *The Alexiad*, 93
Komnene, Maria, 95
Kulich, Vladimir, 240
Kurosawa, Akira: *Rashomon* (film), 114
Kyivan Rus, 153–64

La Passion de Jeanne d'Arc (film), 61–62, 66–69
labor, 45
Ladvenu, Martin, 67
Langella, Frank, 272
Langland, William: *Piers Plowman*, 104, 200
language, 24–25, 49, 50, 55–56, 58–59, 237–45; lawful, 238, 244, 245
Languedoc, France, 168
Lapierre, Isambart, 67
las Casas, Bartolomé de, 270
Last Duel, The (film), 114, 115, 117, 118–21
Latin (Western) Christianity, 197, 199
Latin America, 271, 273
Latin Record (Joan of Arc's trial), 64, 66, 70–72
law: cinematic perspectives of, 130–33; in medieval society, 2–3; as narrative, 9, 12–16, 183–88. *See also* canon law; civil law; Common Law (English); customary laws; forest law; Roman law
law enforcement, 106–8
law schools, 214

Le Coq, Jean (Johannes Gallus), 115; "Comment on the Trial by Combat of Jacques Le Gris," 122–24, 125n18
Le Goff, Jacques, 183
Le Gris, Jacques, 114, 116, 117, 118–19, 122–23, 125n14
Le moine et la sorcière (film), 166–70, 171–73, 178n26
Le Muisit, Gilles, 200–1
leaders, religious, 146–47, 149–50
legal appeals, 21n17
legal education, 214, 218
legal medievalism, 2–3
Legend of the Three Companions, The, 40
Lemaistre, Jean, 63, 64, 65, 66, 67, 70
Leone (follower of Francis of Assisi), 39, 43
lex Aquilia, 137n4
Libellus de expugnatione Terrae Sanctae per Saladinum, 95
Little Hours, The (film), 195–97, 198, 201–2, 205n1
Livonian Order, 154
Lobbes, Belgium, 27
Lohier, Jean, 64–65
Loiseleur (l'Oiseleur), Nicolas, 66, 67, 68, 69
Longshanks. *See* Edward I "Longshanks" (England)
Lonsdale, Michael, 51, 212
Louis VII (France), 11, 93
Louis IX (France), 116
Louis of Bavaria, 53
love, courtly, 79–80, 182, 187, 191–92
Lowery, David: *The Green Knight* (film), 75–76, 78–80, 81–83
Luke, Gospel of, 61

Macfadyen, Angus, 185
Madden, Thomas, 90
magic, 169, 171, 173, 178nn24–25
Magna Carta, 62, 101, 107
Magnum Opus (W. Scott), 254, 255–56
Mainz, archbishop of, 144, 145–46, 147
Makowski, Elizabeth, 199

Malcolm Canmore (king of Scotland), 183
male violence, 114–15. *See also jus primae noctis*; rape
maleficium, 171
Mann, Jill, 200
Manual on the Inquisition of Heretical Depravity (BernardGui), 56, 57–59
Marceau, Sophie, 184
Margaret (saint), 70, 71
Marguerite de Carrouges (Marguerite de Thibouville), 114, 116, 117, 119–21, 123
Mark, Gospel of, 61, 62
marriage: Islam, 228, 232, 234; Kyivan Rus, 159–60, 162–64; late Roman Empire, 215–16. *See also jus primae noctis*
martyrdom, 25, 39; Joan of Arc, 61, 62, 68
masculinity, 118–19, 121, 241–42
Massieu, Jean, 64, 65, 66, 67, 68
Massoud, Ghassan, 94
Matthew, Gospel of, 61, 62
Matthias the Apostle, 22–23
Mazzoni, Roberta, 37, 39
McCormack, Catherine, 184
McGoohan, Patrick, 184, 185
Me Too, 114, 180
Mecca, 225, 230, 231–32, 233–34
medical care, 172–73, 174, 178n25
medieval chronicles, 28–29, 31, 95–96, 97–99, 103, 106, 117, 182–83, 256
medieval cinema, 1–3, 6n2; cultural and linguistic differences in, 24–25; rape in, 114, 117, 120, 180, 187
medievalism, 1–3, 251; cinematic, 3; gendered, 114, 118–21, 170; legal, 2–3
Medina, 228, 230, 234
Méliès, Georges: *Jeanne d'Arc* (film), 1
Melles, Sunnyi, 146
mendicant, 36, 42, 44, 46, 51, 54, 198. *See also* Dominican Order; Franciscan Order
Message, The (film), 225–32, 235n2
metanarratives, 49
Michael (saint), 66, 71
Michael of Cesena, 50, 53
Micucci, Kate, 195
Middle East, 89–90, 211, 252, 254, 256. *See also* crusades; Islam

Midi, Nicholas, 65
Minghella, Max, 218
misogynist tradition, 200
Miyashiro, Adam, 244
modernity, 265, 266–67, 270–71, 273
Molnar, Stanko, 41
Monahan, William, 89
monastic orders, traditional, 51
monastic rules, 40–41, 42, 145, 197–98. *See also* Benedictine Rule
monasticism, 25–28, 141–47, 197–98. *See also* mendicant; *names of specific monastic orders*
money, 41–42, 45
Mongols, 143, 158
Montbaston (illuminators), Jeanne de and Richart de, 201
Moore, R. I., 54
Moses (biblical character), 35n18
movement of relics and reliquaries, 23, 25–33
Muhammad (prophet), 225–34, 236n4
Muldowney, Brendan: *Pilgrimage* (film), 22–26, 28, 29, 30
Murder in the Cathedral (film), 9–10
Murder in the Cathedral (play, Eliot), 9–10, 12
Murray, Margaret, 171–72
Muslims, 27, 90, 97–98, 237, 241–42, 252–57, 260–61. *See also* Islam
mystics, 142, 144

Name of the Rose, The (film), 49–51, 53–54, 55–56, 59n2
Name of the Rose, The (novel, Eco), 49, 56
narrative, law as, 9, 12–16, 183–88
National Review, 90
Nazi Germany, 156, 157, 161
Neeson, Liam, 95
neocolonialism, 94
Neoplatonism, 213–14
New World, 266, 269–70, 273
New York Times, 76
Nicholas III (pope): *Exiit qui seminat*, 52, 53
nobility, true, 182, 190–91

Normans, 101–3, 106, 251, 253
North Atlantic cultures, 238. *See also* Global North Atlantic
Novgorod, Russia, 153, 154, 158, 161
nuns. *See* religious women

oaths, 90–93, 95–98
oaths, assertory, 91
oaths, crusading, 92
oaths, promissory, 91
obedience, 51
oblation, 145–46, 147
"Of the Worship of Guinefort the Dog" (Étienne de Bourbon), 174–76
Ohlgren, Thomas H., 106
Okhlopkov, Nikolai, 157
Old French Continuation (William of Tyre), 95, 96
Olivi, Peter of John, 52, 53
On the Seven Gifts of the Holy Spirit (Étienne de Bourbon), 166, 168–69, 170, 172, 174–76, 178nn24–25
ordeal, trials by, 116
Orderic Vitalis: *Ecclesiastical History*, 118
orientalism, 94, 252, 254
Orlov, Dmitry, 157
Orthodox Christianity, 159, 161
orthodoxy, 54, 56
Oscars (Academy Awards), 10, 89, 251
O'Toole, Peter, 10
Otto of Brescia, 21n16
Our Bodies, Ourselves, 170

Pachomius, 197
Padelford, F. M., 104
pagans, 212–18, 222–23
palimpsests, 49
papal bulls, 43, 52, 93
papal infallibility, 53
Papas, Irene, 226
Paramount Pictures, 10
Paris, University of, 63, 64, 65, 69
Pasolini, Pier Paolo: *The Decameron* (film), 201
Passion of Joan of Arc, The (film), 61–62, 66–69

Patel, Dev, 75, 78
paternalism, 117, 169
patriarchy, 114, 117, 121, 142–43, 160, 171–72
Pavlenko, Pyotr, 156
Peace of God movement, 26–28, 31
peasants, 127, 132–33
penance, 33, 46, 55, 92, 275, 276
Periculoso (Boniface VIII), 196, 198–99, 201–4
Perlman, Ron, 54
pest animals, 127–28, 135–36
Peter (saint), 29, 32, 33
Peterborough Chronicle, 103
petitions to Roman emperors, 217–18
Peypus, Lake, 154, 158, 159
Philippe de Beaumanoir: *Coutumes de Beauvaisis* (*The Customary Laws of Beauvais*), 127, 134, 137n4
philosophical education, 213–14, 218
physical weakness, 144–45
physiognomy theories, 254
physiology theories, 269
Piers Plowman (Langland), 104, 200
Pilgrimage (film), 22–26, 28, 29, 30
pilgrimages, 24–25, 30, 92
pillars of Islam, 226, 229–32, 233
Plato, 213, 222
Plaza, Aubrey, 195
Pleas of the Forest for Nottinghamshire, 110–11
Pleasence, Donald, 130
Plotinus, 214, 222
poaching, 102, 105–6, 107. *See also* forest law
pontificals, 29, 31–33
Portiuncula chapel, 43
poverty, 36–37, 38, 41–43, 45–46, 50–59
prayers, 229, 230–31, 233, 234, 242
Pregler, Wolfgang, 144
Preminger, Otto: *Saint Joan* (film), 72n1
prima nocte. *See jus primae noctis*
Primitive Rule (Francis of Assisi), 41, 43
privilegium fori, 13–15, 17
processions, ecclesiastical, 26–28
promissory oaths, 91
property, 42–43, 51–52
Prose Tristan, 256, 260–61

INDEX 293

Qualtinger, Helmut, 55
Quinn, Anthony, 226
Qur'an, 228, 229, 230, 231, 234–35

race theories, 251, 255
racial equality, 227–28, 232
racist rhetoric, 254–55, 257
Rains, Claude, 101
Ramadan, 230, 233
rape, 114, 115–17, 120–24. *See also jus primae noctis*
Rathbone, Basil, 101
Rats of Autun trial, 129, 138n13, 138n19
Ravet, Louis, 66
Raynald of Châtillon, 94, 96, 97–98
reception, religious, 146
Reconti, Paco, 39
Regino of Prüm: *De ecclesiasticis disciplinis*, 28–29
Regula Donati, 197
Regula primitiva (Francis of Assisi), 41, 43
Reilly, John C., 195
relics, 22–33; contact, 25; corporeal, 25; cult of relics, 25–28
religion: indigenous, 243–44; law and, 216–18, 220–23; writing and, 241–42. *See also* Christianity; Islam
religious coexistence, 212, 213–14, 216, 218, 222–23
religious fundamentalism, 89–90, 211–12
religious leaders, 146–47, 149–50
religious violence, 27, 94–95, 211–12, 218, 222–23, 237–44, 265–66, 272
religious women, 141–47, 195–205
reliquaries, 22, 23, 25, 26–30, 31
rescripts, 217, 218, 221
rhetorical education, 213, 214
Ribon, Diego, 39
Richard I "Lionheart" (England), 251, 253, 254, 258
right of the first night. *See jus primae noctis*
rights, civil, 257
rights, women's, 228–29, 232, 234
Riley-Smith, Jonathan, 90
Rimada, Fernando García, 267

Rime of King William, 103
Risāla (Ibn Fadlān), 237, 238, 246–47
Robert the Bruce, 184, 185
Robin Hood (legend), 101, 102, 103–5, 106, 108
Robin Hood and the Monk, 104
Roger (archbishop of York), 11, 12
Roger of Hoveden: *Annals*, 253, 254, 258–60
RogerEbert.com, 75–76
Roman emperors, 217–18, 221
Roman Empire, 39, 211–23
Roman law, 214, 216–19, 222–23: animals, 127, 128, 137n4; appeals, 21n17; customary laws and, 130, 132
RottenTomatoes.com, 76
Rourke, Mickey, 36
Rowberry, Ryan, 107
royal law, 11–19. *See also* canon law: secular law and
Rufino (follower of Francis of Assisi), 39, 40
Rufinus: *Ecclesiastical History*, 218, 220–21Rupertsberg monastery, 144, 146, 147
Rūs, 237, 239
Russian national idea, 155, 161
Russkaya pravda, 159, 160

Saenz, Noelia V., 267
St. Catherine's convent, Augsburg, 199
Saint Joan (play, Shaw), 61, 69, 72n1
sainthood, 39–40
Saladin (sultan), 89, 94, 95, 96, 97–98
Salian Franks, 91, 93
Samir, Sami, 217
San Damiano chapel, 39, 43
Sánchez, Gabriel, 272
Santángel, Luis de, 272
satire, 195–96, 199–202, 204–5
Saxons, 101, 102, 105, 106, 108, 251, 252, 253
Schlimm, Matthew, 94
Schulenberg, Jane, 198
Schutz, Maurice, 66
scientific knowledge, 267–70, 273
Scotium Historiae (Boece), 182–83, 184
Scotland, 182–88

Scott, A. O., 76
Scott, Daniel, 255
Scott, Ridley: *1492: Conquest of Paradise* (film), 265–69, 270–71, 273; *Black Hawk Down* (film), 89; *Gladiator* (film), 89; *Kingdom of Heaven* (film), 89–90, 93–96, 183; *The Last Duel* (film), 114, 115, 117, 118–21
Scott, Walter, 115, 255: *The Fair Maid of Perth*, 115, 183, 184; *Ivanhoe*, 115, 183, 251–57; *Magnum Opus*, 254, 255–56; *Rokeby*, 255; *The Talisman*, 183
scutage, 12–13
Seberg, Jean, 72n1
Second Crusade, 93
second-wave feminism, 169–70, 171–72, 173, 177n9, 177n14
secular law. *See* canon law: secular law and
Sekka, Johnny, 227
Serapeum, Alexandria, 211, 216–18, 220–21
sexual violence. *See jus primae noctis*; rape
shahada, 229, 230, 233
Shannon, Molly, 196
Sharif, Omar, 239
Shaw, George Bernard: *Saint Joan* (play), 61, 69, 72n1
sheriffs, 107
Sherwood Forest, 102–3, 110–11
Silvain, Eugène, 66
Sir Gawain and the Green Knight, 75, 77–78, 82–83, 84–86
Slate, 115
Slater, Christian, 49
slavery, 137n4, 213, 227–28, 246–47, 252, 255, 256–57, 269–70
social justice, 227–29, 232
Socrates Scholasticus: *Ecclesiastical History*, 221–22
Solon, Ewen, 228
Sorceress (*Le moine et la sorcière*, film), 166–70, 171–73, 178n26
Soviet Union, 154, 156, 161
Spain, 265–67, 270–73, 275–76

Spanish Inquisition, 266, 270–73, 275–76. *See also* inquisitions
Staffordshire Forest court, 105, 107
Stalin, Josef, 156, 157–58
Statute of Prince Yaroslav on Church Courts, The, 159, 160, 162–64
Staundon, Thomas, 181
Sterhøi, Dennis, 240
stigmata, 38
Stolze, Lena, 147
Stubbs, Jonathan, 1
Sukowa, Barbara, 141, 143
Sumayyah (early follower of Islam), 228
superstition, 166, 169, 174

Taíno people, 269–70
Tale of the Life and Bravery of the Blessed and Grand Prince Alexander, The, 155
Tallerico, Brian, 75–76
Tarantino, Quentin: *Pulp Fiction* (film), 182
teachers, pagan, 213–14
temples, pagan, 218. *See also* Serapeum, Alexandria
Tennyson, Alfred, Lord, 9
Testament (Francis of Assisi), 38, 42–43
theft from churches, 23, 28–29, 31–33
Theodosian Code, 218, 222–23
Theodosius I (Roman emperor), 216–18, 222–23
Thietmar of Merseburg, 28
thieves, church, 23, 28–29, 31–33
Third Crusade, 94
13th Warrior, The (film), 237–45
Thomas of Celano, 39; *Vita Secunda*, 40
Thorpe, Richard: *Ivanhoe* (film), 251–53, 254, 256–57; *The Knights of the Round Table* (film), 257
Toland, John, 211
tonsure, 24
Tony Awards, 10
traditions, folk, 168–69, 173, 174–76
translation of relics and reliquaries, 23, 25, 26–30, 31–33
trials by battle, 114–17, 121, 122
trials by combat. *See* trials by battle

trials by ordeal, 116
trials of faith (heresy trials), 61–66
Trieste, Leopoldo, 50
Twentieth Century Fox Studios, 89

Ubertino of Casale, 53
University of Paris, 63, 64, 65, 69
Urban II (pope), 27, 92–93
Ursmer (saint), 27
usus pauper, 52–53, 57

Vangelis, 37, 265
Vansittart, Rupert, 184
Vargas, Valentina, 54
veneficium, 171
Venus of Willendorf, 249n12
Vikander, Alicia, 79, 80
violence: sanctioned, 76, 115, 266, 270–72. See also *jus primae noctis*; rape; religious violence
Vision: From the Life of Hildegard von Bingen (film), 141–47
visions: Hildegard von Bingen, 141, 142, 144; Joan of Arc, 65, 66–68, 70–72
vita apostolica, 38. See also Francis of Assisi (Francesco di Pietro di Bernardone)
vita semireligiosa, 198
Vladimir's Church Statute, 159
Volmar (Hildegard von Bingen's confessor), 144, 147
von Trotta, Margarethe, 141–42, 143; *Hannah Arendt* (film), 143; *Rosenstraße* (film), 143; *Vision: From the Life of Hildegard von Bingen* (film), 141–47

Wallace, Randall, 184
Wallace, William "Braveheart", 180, 183–84, 185, 186–88, 194n18
Wallis, Hal, 10
War on Terrorism, 89, 90, 211

Warwick, Earl of, 66, 67
Watts, Edward, 212
Weaver, Sigourney, 268
Weber, Stanley, 23
Weisz, Rachel, 211, 212
Western (Latin) Christianity, 197, 199
Westphalen, Joseph von, 142
Wife of Bath's Tale (Chaucer), 181–82, 187, 189–91
William I (England), 101, 103
William de Montibus, 253
William of Aynsford, 13, 14, 20n6
William of Norwich, 262n11
William of Pavia, 21n16
William of Tyre: *Old French Continuation*, 95, 96
Williamson, Nicol, 131
witch trials, 166, 167, 168, 171–73
witchcraft, 166, 167, 168, 171–73, 178n25
Witches, Midwives, and Nurses (Ehrenreich and English), 172
Wolfi, Donald, 13
women: aristocratic, 119–21; and authority, 142–44; education, 215–16; and heresy, 169; as medical practitioners, 172; sex and sexuality, 195–96, 200–5; stereotypes, 120, 127. See also marriage; patriarchy; religious women; witchcraft
women's rights, 228–29, 232, 234
work, 45
writing, 241–42, 244
Writings of Leo, Rufino and Angelo, Companions of St. Francis, The, 40

Yaroslav (prince, Pereyaslavl), 153
Yarsolav the Wise, 160
Yasir (early follower of Islam), 228
yeomanry, 104, 106, 113n12

Zeffirelli, Franco: *Brother Sun, Sister Moon* (film), 37

FORDHAM SERIES IN MEDIEVAL STUDIES

Alessandro Vettori, *Poets of Divine Love: The Rhetoric of Franciscan Spiritual Poetry*

Ronald B. Begley and Joseph W. Koterski, S.J. (eds.), *Medieval Education*

Teodolinda Barolini and H. Wayne Storey (eds.), *Dante for the New Millennium*

Richard F. Gyug (ed.), *Medieval Cultures in Contact*

Seeta Chaganti (ed.), *Medieval Poetics and Social Practice: Responding to the Work of Penn R. Szittya*

Devorah Schoenfeld, *Isaac on Jewish and Christian Altars: Polemic and Exegesis in Rashi and the "Glossa Ordinaria"*

Martin Chase, S.J. (ed.), *Eddic, Skaldic, and Beyond: Poetic Variety in Medieval Iceland and Norway*

Felice Lifshitz, *Religious Women in Early Carolingian Francia: A Study of Manuscript Transmission and Monastic Culture*

Sam Zeno Conedera, S.J., *Ecclesiastical Knights: The Military Orders in Castile, 1150–1330*

J. Patrick Hornbeck II and Michael van Dussen (eds.), *Europe After Wyclif*

Laura K. Morreale and Nicholas L. Paul (eds.), *The French of Outremer: Communities and Communications in the Crusading Mediterranean*

Ayelet Even-Ezra, *Ecstasy in the Classroom: Trance, Self, and the Academic Profession in Medieval Paris*

Miguel Gómez, Kyle C. Lincoln, and Damian Smith (eds.), *King Alfonso VIII of Castile: Government, Family, and War*

Andrew Albin, Mary C. Erler, Thomas O'Donnell, Nicholas L. Paul, and Nina Rowe (eds.), *Whose Middle Ages? Teachable Moments for an Ill-Used Past*

Jordan Kirk, *Medieval Nonsense: Signifying Nothing in Fourteenth-Century England*

Kate Heslop, *Viking Mediologies: A New History of Skaldic Poetics*

Catherine Brown, *Remember the Hand: Manuscript in Early Medieval Iberia*

Ian Christopher Levy, *With a Pure Conscience: Christian Liberty before the Reformation*

Esther Liberman Cuenca, M. Christina Bruno, and Anthony Perron (eds.), *Law, Justice, and Society in the Medieval World: An Introduction through Film*

www.ingramcontent.com/pod-product-compliance
Lightning Source LLC
Chambersburg PA
CBHW020356080526
44584CB00014B/1044